Engaging and real, Margaret Jensen has developed a whole fan club of "Prime Time America" listeners from around the country. She has endeared herself to them through real-life stories of her own family—stories that help us smile, laugh, cry, and regain *new focus,* so that even during the "dark days" we recall God's goodness and understand His love.

"Prime Time America" listeners have discovered that a few minutes of upbeat warmth and sparkle with Margaret Jensen deliver a boost to one's spirit to grab new hope for today!

Jim Warren
Host of "Prime Time America"

From the heart and life of Margaret Jensen come stories of faith and hope. Having known her for thirty-four years, I know that her insights, warmth, and humor come from her deep relationships with God, her family, and her friends. What you read in these pages mirrors life with both its joys and disappointments. At age seventy-seven, Margaret's wisdom is matched only by her youthful spirit of anticipation and joy.

R. Judson Carlberg
President, Gordon College
Wenham, Massachusetts

Margaret's love of life, family, and humor shine radiantly through the pages of this book. She is a dynamic sparkler and these stories shower us with hope and illumination. Thanks for giving me (us) the chance to read and reread some of the best—from one of His best!

Patsy Clairmont
Author of *God Uses Cracked Pots* and *Normal Is Just a Setting on Your Dryer*

Margaret is a delight to meet, to listen to, and to read. She writes with charm and humor while teaching deep truths. Once you meet her, in word or in person, she will be your friend for life.

Florence Littauer
President, C.L.A.S.S. Speakers, Inc.
Persononality Plus, Silver Boxes,
and *Dare to Dream*

Margaret Jensen's colorful, moving writings, taken from life's experiences, convey the simplicity of the gospel through story form.

Horace H. Hilton, Jr.
Pastor Emeritus
Myrtle Grove Presbyterian Church
Wilmington, North Carolina

Margaret Jensen's stories come from the stuff of life. They ring true to the values Norwegian immigrants brought to America with them, but those values have gained relevance as experienced by a woman open to new experiences. Her stories entertain, but in the process they make people laugh, cry, and apply insights gained to their own life situations.

You're never the same after reading one of Margaret Jensen's stories! That's why she is one of America's most beloved storytellers.

Leslie H. Stobbe
Editorial Services Manager
Curriculum Division
Scripture Press

The Sun Is Shining On The Other Side

Margaret Jensen

THOMAS NELSON PUBLISHERS
Nashville • Atlanta • London • Vancouver

Dedicated with love to my four sisters:
Grace Tweten
Doris Tweten Hammer
Joyce Solveig Tweten Jensen
Jeanelle Tweten Stam

From our earliest memories of childhood we were always there for each other.

You will find their names throughout the stories. They not only went through personal storms, but each one also took the hand of a sister and we traveled through the storms together. And together we discovered the sun does shine on the other side.

We were born sisters, but we chose each other for friends.

Published in Nashville, Tennessee, by Thomas Nelson, Inc., Publishers, and distributed in Canada by Word Communications, Ltd., Richmond, British Columbia, and in the United Kingdom by Word (UK), Ltd., Milton Keynes, England.

Unless otherwise noted, Scripture quotations are from The Holy Bible, KING JAMES VERSION.

Scripture quotations noted NASB are from THE NEW AMERICAN STANDARD BIBLE, Copyright © 1960, 1962, 1963, 1968, 1971, 1972, 1973, 1975, 1977 by The Lockman Foundation and are used by permission.

Library of Congress Cataloging-in-Publication Data

Jensen, Margaret T. (Margaret Tweten), 1916-
   The sun is shining on the other side / Margaret Tweten Jensen.
      p.   cm.
   Selections from the author's works compiled as a single narrative.
   ISBN 0-8407-6356-5
   1. Jensen, Margaret T. (Margaret Tweten), 1916- . 2. Christian biography—United States. I. Title.
BR1725.J43A3   1994
209'.2—dc20   94-6206
[B]   CIP

Printed in the United States of America

1 2 3 4 5 6 7 - 99 98 97 96 95 94

CONTENTS

Ralph

Harold

Acknowledgments

A special thank you to Harold, my husband of fifty-three years (who went Home October 31, 1991), for patiently typing eight books. His love and encouragement even enabled me to write two books without him.

Linda Britton took over the computer. Thank you, Linda.

A special thank you to Jean Bryant, who has edited all ten of my books.

Across the miles my precious family and friends have taught me that joy and sorrow, storms and sunshine, tears and laughter, are all a part of living—and the sun does shine on the other side.

1

The Sun Is Shining on the Other Side

We stood with our coffee mugs in hand watching the rain against the bay window of the breakfast room.

"Chris, be careful! That rain could turn to sleet."

Our son Ralph was heading for his shop but waited to see us off to Greensboro, North Carolina, where I was speaking the next morning at the annual Christmas breakfast of Trinity Church.

Chris, Ralph's wife, had checked the books, suitcases, and car, and all systems were go. Harold, my husband of fifty years, looked into the sky and reminded us again to drive carefully—then added, "Have a good time."

Believe me, we planned to do just that. Chris and I were like kids going off to camp. Each trip was an adventure to be enjoyed. We were planning to meet my sisters Grace and Doris for lunch at K & W Cafeteria. Chris and her best friend, Peggy, had plans for Christmas shopping. This was an annual event that we looked forward to—meeting old friends in a familiar setting.

Harold prayed for us before we pulled out of the driveway, and we were on our way.

Almost at once, the rain seemed to come faster; then came the sound of sleet. Before long, a rare blizzard of snow hit, swirling across the highway. Faster and faster it came.

We had never driven in a snowstorm. When snow flurries come to Wilmington, North Carolina, everything shuts down—school, church, even the mall.

We were halfway to Greensboro when we saw the trucks pulling into a small gas station. It looked like a good idea, so we pulled over and joined the parade.

A burly truck driver got out of his pickup truck. "You womenfolk orter to be home—no fittin' place fer women in this storm." We agreed. "Just come from down yonder and I mean to tell you it is worser down there. Orter to turn round and head fer home."

We turned around, terrified of what might be "down yonder."

With great relief we pulled into our driveway, shook off the snow, and soon felt safe in a warm kitchen.

"Whew! Am I glad to see you!" Harold was listening to the news on the radio. "Was the meeting called off? How bad is the storm in Greensboro?"

We looked at each other. "We don't know; we just panicked and turned around for home."

"You didn't call from the gas station?"

Chris grabbed the phone. I just looked sheepish.

"Auntie Do, how bad is the storm? I guess everything has been cancelled. . . . What? No Storm? No Cancellations? Big attendance expected?"

Chris looked at me. "Auntie Do just said, 'Get through the storm. The sun is shining on the other side!'"

And so it came to pass that, with a donut and coffee, and much prayer, we backed out of the driveway again. Auntie Do said, "Get through the storm. The sun is shining here."

We passed the truck stop but kept going this time. We had been halfway to Greensboro (a 200-mile trip from Wilmington).

Sure enough, about a mile "out yonder," it was "worser," but about a mile beyond that point the sky was clear and the sun was shining. Chris put on her sunglasses. *We had turned around too soon.*

2

Later we were told that a freak storm had swept across a small portion of North Carolina. Then it was gone.

We rode in silence for a long time. Then I finally murmured, "Well, he did say it was worse down the road. He really didn't lie to us; it was worse down the road. But he turned around too soon, too."

"I have a feeling a story will come out of this."

Chris was right! She usually is!

I had been struggling with what to say at the annual Christmas breakfast, usually a happy holiday time. But this year it was different. The beloved pastor, Roy Putnam, had been ushered into the presence of the Lord.

For thirty years Roy Putnam had been a light in the community as a great Bible teacher. Now his beloved voice was stilled. The church had fasted and prayed, keeping vigil with the family, believing God would spare their loved one. A sense of despair engulfed the faithful congregation, and questions that had no answers seemed to bounce back from the silent heavens. My sister's message echoed into my heart: "Go through the storm; the sun is shining on the other side."

We missed our family luncheon, but we made it to the Christmas breakfast. The story of the storm brought chuckles, but then God's Spirit spoke to us all. "In the storms of life we often listen to our peers who are in the storm. For a few moments, let us check with some of those who have gone through life's storms.

"We need to go through the storm of our grief, our unanswered questions, even the doubts that creep in like unwelcome guests. What would Roy Putnam say to us? He would say, 'Trinity Church, go through the storm. The sun is shining here. It is here that we see the end from the beginning—God's eternal purpose.'

"I can almost hear the apostle Peter say, 'You are kept by the power of God, and don't forget that the trial of your faith is more precious than gold.'

"Just think of your loved ones who have gone home; you can almost hear them saying, 'Rejoice! One of these days you will

3

see the Son—the light of the world. Go through the storms and cast your cares on Him because He really cares for you.'"

Somehow, during that Christmas breakfast, I could feel the grief slipping out the door, the doubts slinking away. The unanswered questions didn't seem so urgent because the settled Word of God came with the Christmas message: "I bring you tidings of great joy."

It is so easy to ask advice from our peers who are in the storm; but we must go beyond and learn from the generations before us that the sun comes after the storm.

The apostle Paul reminds us that he had a glimpse into the glories of heaven; words were not adequate to paint the picture of what God has prepared for those who love Him.

When Jesus was asleep in the boat, the disciples, in terror, cried for help. Jesus reminded them that their faith was on thin ice. Besides, didn't He say, "We are going over to the other side"? He just didn't clue them in that there could be a storm on the way to the "other side."

Our culture, increasingly hostile to our Christian faith, wants us to believe that there are many roads to the "other side."

But Jesus said, "I am the Way, the Truth, and the Life. No one comes to the Father but by Me."

On a dark night, while shepherds watched their sheep they heard the glorious message that has come through the corridors of time. "God burst into history with a baby's cry" (Roy Putnam).

The shepherds heard, "I bring you tidings of great joy."

Hope came quietly into the hearts of God's people. Tears were wiped away and faith came from a seemingly far-off place. God was there all the time.

The Christmas breakfast turned into a joyful celebration.

"Joy to the world. Let earth receive her King."

Mama

2

The Call

Sunday, January 16, 1977, 2:00 P.M. Bracing against the wind, the young and old quietly entered the First Baptist Church of Stoneville, North Carolina. Five sisters and their families sat in a front row. I, Margaret, the eldest, felt comfort in the presence of Mama's other daughters: Grace, Doris, Joyce, and the "baby," Jeanelle.

The quiet service defied the blizzard raging on the other side of the church walls. The Reverend Mr. J. Ward Burch assured us of God's presence. "Let not your heart be troubled," he read, then continued with old familiar hymns and other favorite Scripture passages.

A settled faith lingered in our hearts as we silently followed the gray casket into the icy wind. *I'm glad Mama is warm*, I thought, *and can't feel this wind, so reminiscent of the Saskatchewan winters.*

Within a few minutes the cars slid slowly over the frozen road toward the family cemetery, to the graveside where the canopy whipped in the wind. I found myself remembering Canada and Mama's long hand-knit ski pants carefully tucked under her flowing dress. I thought I felt her hand as I trudged across the snow to her final place of rest. Had the Canadian wind come to North Carolina to say farewell?

The small cemetery held two older graves covered with snow.

Huddled in coats and scarves, we braced each other around the open grave and remembered our two loved ones whom Mother was joining—our father and their only son, Gordon.

Nearby, the big house, home of my sister Doris and her husband David Hammer, stood like a sentinel against the sky. Its chimney sent smoke signals to the snow-covered wooded hills. Across the road Mama's yellow house slept empty and silent, the coffee pot cold.

The defiant wind could not sweep away the majestic words; they returned again and again, echoing through the valley. "LORD, Thou hast been our dwelling place in all generations. Surely goodness and mercy shall follow me all the days of my life: and I will dwell in the house of the LORD for ever."

Slowly we walked to the big house where logs blazed and coffee perked. As old stories and familiar hymns filled the air, the warmth of friendship and loving memories filled our hearts.

With coffee cup in hand I moved close to the fire to watch the flaming logs. An amber glow of love and warmth engulfed me and I knew that Mama lived on somewhere beyond the storm, safely in the house of the Lord forever.

I also knew that I had to write the story of Mama and her Norwegian coffee, poured with that same amber glow of love.

Being the eldest, I remembered much. The story began for me when I found Mama's Norwegian diary carefully hidden in the right-hand corner of an old chest. But before we start, first we have coffee.

It seems like yesterday. I held the black book in my hand and whispered to my sister Grace, "Close the door."

In front of me sat an enraptured audience of sisters and girlfriends. All promised never to tell and I unfolded the script of a secret drama. In the 1930s we created our own theatrical productions.

Out of Mama's diary, I rendered a not-too-literal translation from Norwegian to English, and wove a story of romance and intrigue. This production should have received a Tony Award.

From the pages of the black book emerged my mother, Elvine

Johannessen, as a fifteen-year-old girl, standing on the deck of the majestic ocean liner, the *United States*.

Her tears said good-bye to Norway's town of Lista, and in the back fields of her mind, she planted happy memories of the midnight sun, fjords, and fishing boats; perhaps the ocean would roll away the painful memories of childhood.

She set her sights on the future. In America she would see her beautiful, mysterious mother and her beloved brother, Joe, who had preceded her across the ocean.

As the sun swept across the water and the moon made a silvery highway over the waves, there was time to think. Someday she would learn why her mother had fled to America and left Joe and her when she was only five years old. Deep in Elvine's heart lay the poignant memory of crying out, "*Mor, Mor* (Mother, Mother)." But her cries had gone unheeded. Her sobbing mother had continued walking away from her, never to return, and her austere aunt had severely scolded, "Do not call her *Mor*. Call her Tilda."

With a toss of her head, Elvine had defiantly declared her ownership, "*Min mor* (My mother)!"

With trembling hands Elvine clutched her knit shawl around her shoulders. The majestic ocean liner was easing into the mouth of the New York harbor. Ahead of her stood the lovely lady, the Statue of Liberty. Ahead of her lay the land of hope and glory.

The next day Elvine felt small and alone in the notorious clamor of Ellis Island's endless inspections and army of officials. But it was all erased from her mind when she saw her beautiful, rebellious mother, who had earlier defied tradition and sailed to America. Someday she would learn the rest of the story. Today it was enough to hear, "*Min kjare Elvine* (My dear Elvine)."

Elvine began her new life in America as a servant girl in a lovely Jewish home on Park Avenue, New York City. While working there she changed her name to Ella. From her wise mistress she learned to love the world of books, music, and poetry. She worked with her hands as she learned with her heart.

Dressed in a deep-blue dress, Bible in hand, Miss Ella

walked to the Baptist Mission to hear the new pastor, the Reverend Mr. Elius N. Tweten. *What blue eyes,* she thought. His blond hair was swept back from a handsome high forehead. The young Norwegian pastor, himself an orphan and in America just a few years, looked over his first congregation. His gaze, falling on Miss Ella, met the most beautiful eyes he had ever seen. In that moment he determined, "She will be my wife."

What began with conversation over a cup of hot chocolate after church blossomed into marriage just three months later.

"Margaret, I didn't know you read Norwegian so well. It's time you started attending the Norwegian services as well as the English."

Mama stood in the doorway, determined to end our fun. She took the book from me and, with misty eyes, softly added, "Someday, I will tell you the rest."

I never saw the diary again.

"Sir." The librarian stood over Papa's shoulder, interrupting his reading. "It is closing time. You'll have to leave now."

"Oh!" Papa looked up, not wanting to believe the librarian. As usual, time had gotten away from him, but today, he knew, it shouldn't have. "I got married yesterday, and I forgot. . . ."

Papa caught the last subway to Brooklyn. When he walked through the door of their honeymoon flat, Mama was reminded of the advice her mother had given her earlier in the day: "Take him as he is and you will be happy. He loves God, the library, and you—in that order. Always keep dinner warm in the oven."

Keep dinner warm, she did.

She loved him, this boy preacher from Norway who had "the call." He had been sent by the ministers of Oslo to study at Morgan Park Seminary in Chicago. He had been hard-working—tending furnaces and waiting on tables to help pay for his tuition, his beloved books, and his degree.

I don't know if Mama, on her wedding day, had any idea what "the call" meant, but she learned early. It was more than a call to preach the gospel and serve God's people. It involved a call to pack and move to community after community. It involved leaving the familiar and seeking new ground that

9

needed planting. It meant following her charming minister husband, who was *so* spiritually minded, but not at all encumbered with working out the practical details of life. It wasn't long before Papa felt the tug of "the call." God's work in Wisconsin needed Elius Tweten.

The train pulled into the station at Woodville, Wisconsin. Mama, dressed in her wide hat, long coat, and high button shoes caught a glimpse of her new surroundings. Papa's call was to preach. Her call was to make her family a home in this wilderness. The battle for survival had made the welcoming congregation of immigrants strong like oaks, trees of righteousness withstanding the storms of spring and blizzards of winter. They had weathered hardships of such magnitude that they didn't notice the hidden needs of a lonely young wife who had come to realize her husband lived in another world—the world of his call, his Bible, his libraries, and his favorite second-hand bookstores. His scholarly mind thirsted for books like a desert thirsts for water. Taking Mama by the hand, walking and talking to her about the beauty around them, never occurred to him. He silently loved Mama. She understood.

She propped poems on the windowsills and pinned them to curtains. She filled her heart with music and poetry. As her hands worked endlessly to sew, scrub, bake, and touch the sick and lonely, she blended love and compassion with Papa's theology.

It was here I was born, Margaret Louise, on Bestemör (Grandmother) Bertilda's birthday, April 18, 1916. Mama poured all the love she had missed into me by singing me songs and telling me endless stories. She sang the Norwegian *"So Ro Til Fiske Shar"* right alongside the American "Rock-a-bye Baby." We rode the country lanes together; strapped to her waist, I held her close as she sat upright in the buggy and snapped the reins of the horse.

Papa, a circuit rider, preached to the forest and hills as he traveled among his scattered, hearty congregation for several years until "the call" came again, bringing us back to Brooklyn. (Bestemör must have sent an S.O.S. to heaven.)

3

The Bowl of Cherries

One of my daughter Jan's thoughtful gifts stands on a shelf in the den, a figurine of a pigtailed country girl sitting on a bench, holding a bowl of cherries.

Jan enjoys browsing through craft fairs and often comes up with gifts that depict the stories I tell. Beside the "cherry girl" stands a country girl with an old-fashioned ironing board. It reminds us of when Mama said, "*Ja, ja,* Margaret. While you're dying, iron." Or how she said through the years, "Do something. Iron. It is a good cure for depression."

Again I looked at the little girl with her bowl of cherries. I touched it gently as my thoughts went back to a women's retreat in 1988.

I love these retreats and the women I meet. In each retreat I see the same expressions on the faces of beautiful women waiting to hear something that will uplift their spirits. I am overwhelmed, and I always remember, "Not by might . . . but by my spirit" (Zechariah 4:6).

As I looked out over this group of women, their expressions spoke of a hunger for God, a longing to know Him. They wanted His grace and strength for their time of need—and we are all needy people. These words came into my spirit: The Lord "is a rewarder of them that diligently seek him" (Hebrews 11:6). I knew God would meet their needs.

I shared the simplicity of Mama's faith and how she taught us the valuable lessons from everyday living. Then I told them about the lesson of the bowl of cherries.

I took the women back to the long winter past, with its snowdrifts and blizzard winds. We sped from season to season until across the blue sky the white clouds floated lazily while the summer breeze blew over the Canadian prairie. It was that wonderful time of the year, I told them, the time of school and baseball.

I was ten and my friends were coming to play ball. I slipped quietly into the kitchen, in case Mama hadn't finished her talk with God. She had, and she had taken the younger children in the buggy to visit a neighbor.

Then I saw it—a bowl of cherries! I had never before seen cherries. I had seen apples with brown spots and oranges divided into six pieces. At Christmas we each had a whole apple and orange—only at Christmas. But now, here was a whole bowl of cherries!

When my friends arrived, I proudly passed around the bowl of cherries. My friends were also children of immigrants and they had never seen cherries before, either. This was my private "show and tell"!

Suddenly I was holding the empty bowl, and I heard Mama coming home, singing, "'Tis so sweet to trust in Jesus." She got out the flour and shortening, ready to make the first cherry pie our oven had ever baked. Then she saw the empty bowl. With stark unbelief she picked it up and, without saying a word, looked at me. I glanced at the pantry door.

Mama kept a small red strap on the pantry door. She also had a jar of red pepper for a sassy tongue. When Mama put the red pepper on our tongue, we had to memorize a Scripture verse before we could get a drink of water. We didn't get by with "Jesus wept." Oh, no. Mama saw to that. We quickly learned to guard our tongues.

The red strap was for the other end. Sometimes we didn't wait—we just went to fetch the strap because Mama had eyes in front, back, and sideways. She always knew when we had done wrong. Punishment was swift and sure! She just had to look at the strap!

Now, Mama held the empty bowl. But she didn't look at the strap—she looked at me. If only she had looked at the strap . . . when she looked at me I knew I had committed the unpardonable sin. Tears welled up in Mama's eyes. Papa had told us that God gave us His best angel to be our Mama and never must we make her cry. I was the eldest, and I was supposed to be a good example. And now I had made my Mama cry!

Mama looked at me long and hard, and then she sank down in the rocking chair and threw her apron over her head, silently weeping.

I couldn't watch Mama cry so I ran! There was only one place to run to and hide, and that was the outhouse. I knew life was over. Never again would we Twetens laugh or sing or tell stories.

Mama sat in the rocking chair, holding the empty bowl. I have an idea she said something like this, "How is it Lord that I am holding the empty bowl when I didn't eat the cherries? I only wanted to do something for my family. Life is like oatmeal most of the time, and then someone gave me cherries. I wanted to surprise the family. I didn't ask for anything for myself."

I also have an idea that line of reasoning lasted only about a minute because I knew Mama. She probably lifted up the empty bowl and said, "Fill my bowl, Lord, with Your love and forgiveness. Don't let the enemies—confusion, self-pity, resentment, and unforgiveness—overtake me. Teach me Your way, Lord, and help me to teach Margaret."

I just know she threw that apron down and got out of that rocking chair of self-pity.

But I was in the outhouse. I realized I couldn't stay in the outhouse forever. Sooner or later I'd have to come out. I hurt so much inside that I couldn't live with the pain. I had to go back to the kitchen, to the empty bowl of cherries. Nothing ever gets solved in the outhouse.

Nothing hurts like a broken relationship. Whatever the cost, the way back begins at the fork of the road where the relationship was broken.

Slowly I left the outhouse. The door seemed heavy on its hinges. It was so easy to run out there, but the road back was so long and so very slow. In my heart I sang my song:

> *Oh, Mama, Mama, won't you hold me?*
> *Hold me like you always do!*
> *Mama, Mama, please forgive me;*
> *Please, forgive and make it all new.*

When she saw me, she didn't reach for the red strap on the pantry door. Mama reached for me.

Throwing my arms around her waist, I sobbed, "Oh, Mama, please forgive me. I know you said pride goes before a fall, but I didn't know bragging and showing off could hurt so bad. If I live to be a hundred, I'll never brag or show off again. Never, never, never!"

"*Ja,* Margaret, it is good to come back to ask forgiveness. *Ja,* I forgive you, and now we ask God to forgive you." Her prayer was quick, simple. "Now, we make an apple pie. You cut out the brown spots and I'll roll out the crust. You see, all things work together for good. This could be one of life's valuable lessons."

I used to hate to cut out the brown spots, but this day I was happy to do it. Mama was singing again. The pie was in the oven and someone was coming for coffee. Through the years I have discovered that life has more apples with brown spots than cherries.

I looked at the dear women in front of me. Then I concluded with a plea to come out of the outhouse of unforgiveness, resentment, hurt, or guilt. I reminded them, "Nothing gets solved in the outhouse. God won't reach for the strap on the pantry door. He will reach for you, for He says in His Word that He has loved us with an everlasting love. The fork of the road is the cross. Come on home!"

The retreat closed. Suitcases and farewells filled the reception hall. Ironically, the dessert was apple pie and someone

14

called out, "We stayed up all night to cut out the brown spots. Someone took the cherries."

P.S. I look at my cherry-girl figurine on the shelf. I know I will be telling the story again in this new year. Once again I will pack my suitcase, and then see the upturned faces of people waiting—not for me, but waiting for God to meet them.

4

Norwegian Holidays in Canada

At the New York City station we said good-bye to Bestemör and boarded a train—to answer "the call" to the First Norwegian Baptist Church in Winnipeg, Manitoba.

At the far end of our trip Mr. Meyer, of the Ellen Street Hotel, met us with a hearty *"Velkommen, velkommen* (Welcome, welcome)" and swooped me up into his big arms with a Norwegian kiss. His mustache, wet with coffee, brushed my face. His warm welcome was a foretaste of things to come. Every Sunday morning I braced myself for the damp, coffee kiss.

The grey parsonage loomed like a castle against the blue Canadian sky. After getting my bearings inside the house, I set out to explore the larger new world. By the end of the day I sat in the lost-and-found department of the Winnipeg police station.

While the policeman's wife fried fish in a black skillet, her husband soaked his feet in a tub of hot water. It had been a long day for all of us. Happily, I crawled up in his lap to answer his probing questions.

"Today is my birthday," I proudly announced, "and I'm five years old. No, my daddy doesn't work, he just reads books.

16

Mama sings and tells stories. I live in a big castle. Mr. Meyer has a coffee kiss. Bestemör lives in Brooklyn, New York. I came on a train. Papa had a call. Don't you have a little girl? I'm hungry."

The policeman seemed to choke on his words as he told me that his five-year-old daughter had died. By the time the fish dinner was ready, I had helped the policeman dry his feet and put on soft woolen socks and slippers. At the table I promptly asked a Norwegian blessing and launched into Papa's theology. "Your little girl is not dead. She is at home in heaven with my sister Bernice. God is taking care of her until you come. Papa says we have to be ready. The greatest verse in the Bible is John 3:16: 'For God so loved the world, that He gave his only begotten Son, that whosoever believeth in Him should not perish, but have everlasting life.' I'll sing a Norwegian song for you, 'Himmel og jord kan brenner.' Mama sings it all the time, and it means that everything can pass away, but God never fails."

Mama had taught me well, but she had never served me a fish dinner like this one.

Suddenly, "Vell, vell," boomed the voice of Mr. Meyer. "Here ve have the little vun."

There, in the doorway, stood Papa—and another coffee kiss.

Reluctantly I kissed my new friends good-bye and left with a polite "Thank you for my birthday party." I did not want to disgrace Papa's ministry.

Lured by the lumber companies' recruiting programs, Scandinavian youth headed to the big woods in search of wealth and adventure. Room and board, pay after six months work—it sounded like the pot of gold at the end of a rainbow. But many staggered back, unable to endure the rigors of the demanding life and the intolerable housing conditions. In bitter despair, with no pay, many knocked at the door of the parsonage on Ellen Street.

Mama took them in. She was always ready to sleep another heartbroken wayfarer.

A Jewish salesman saved his woolen samples of cloth for Mama's quilts, which became pallets spread across the floor on which we children slept. Mama filled the beds with homeless immigrants and missionaries. I was convinced that heaven was a place where we would have our own beds.

For a Norwegian, all hardships are forgotten on two days a year: the seventeenth of May, Norway's Independence Day, and Christmas Eve.

Every seventeenth of May, we marched in Norwegian national dress: red, white, and blue embroidered caps and dresses. The boys wore dark trousers and embroidered shirts and caps. Bands played. Free concerts in the park were followed by Norwegian statesmen pouring forth golden oratory about the glories of the old country, always adding a stern admonition to bring honor to the new land.

Everyone shared the hardships, and thus the burdens dwindled. Everyone shared the triumphs, and thus the joys multiplied. Singing the Norwegian national anthem, *"Ja vi elsker dette landet* (Yes, we love this land)" filled the crowd with memories of the Land of the Midnight Sun and caused them to dedicate themselves afresh to honorable service in the new land. At the end of the festivities the immigrants returned to their labors with renewed hope for another year.

And Christmas Eve. It also brought life to the driest bones. One such night I will never forget.

On the corner, next to the parsonage, stood the old church. Her spire touched the stars. The warm lights that streamed from the many windows sprinkled the snow with millions of diamonds. The relentless winds of a Canadian winter (just forty degrees below zero) whipped fantastic patterns on the frost-covered windows. Inside the creaking walls, a large parlor floor supported a huge spruce tree. The star on the top touched the ceiling and every imaginable homemade decoration trimmed the boughs. Small candles in make-shift candle holders were placed evenly around the huge tree which stood in the center of the room. Tonight was the greatest night of all the year.

My sister Grace, brother Gordon, new baby sister Doris and I had been scrubbed shiny pink and poured into new white, long flannel underwear, an annual gift. The scrubbings were a weekly event. We had that down pat. Papa scrubbed. Mama dried. I, the big sister, "poured."

This afternoon we were all promptly put to bed for an afternoon nap. How could anyone nap with so much excitement in the air? But nap we did, with persuasion. Papa, the persuader, stood by the door.

How could anyone explain the complete joy and expectancy when our naps were over and the thrill of getting dressed for this night of nights filled our young hearts! Mama had, of course, made all the long underwear. We topped that with starched petticoats and ruffled bloomers. Then finally, we donned her masterpieces, our Christmas dresses. The long white stockings, properly fastened with store-bought garters, and the big, colorful, stiff hairbows that matched the dresses provided the perfect finishing touches.

Mama, the angel of Christmas, had treadled the old machine through the quiet night hours to prepare our clothes and small gifts. Papa had helped out by walking with the croupy little ones, preaching endless sermons into their ears.

But tonight their work was over. We all were well and every need had been miraculously supplied through another year. Mama had prepared large platters of lutefisk, part of the traditional Norwegian Christmas dinner. We children begged for meatballs instead of the special fish, but one scornful glance from Mama and we ate lutefisk, a slippery, tasteless fish. Beautiful casseroles of rice pudding baked in the oven of the old cookstove. Dozens of loaves of Mama's bread and *Jule Kakke* (Yule cake) cooled on the kitchen table. Vegetables and fruits added color to the festivities, as did the decorated cookies.

"Here they come," Papa shouted as he heard the steps crunching in the snow. Very dignified in his black suit and starched collar, he stood at the door and welcomed the guests. Who were they?

No, not relatives coming home for Christmas. Having followed "the call," we were far away from loved ones, in a lonely land of strangers. These guests were the lonely Scandinavian immigrants who sat at the railroad station on Christmas Eve day. They were the forgotten ones who congregated at the station, keeping one another company while watching for incoming trains.

That day, as was his routine, Papa visited the railroad station to offer his assistance to the strangers. When he realized that these men (about fifteen of them) had no place to go, he gave an open invitation to come to the parsonage for the traditional Christmas Eve celebration.

They were disillusioned strangers—hungry—and so alone. Filled with dreams, they had come to a land of promise and they were ashamed to return home without their pot of gold. Sweethearts, wives, and mothers waited for them in the faraway Land of the Midnight Sun.

But tonight, this night of nights, the look of despair changed to hope with Papa's hearty *"Velkommen, velkommen* (Welcome, welcome)."

Snow-flaked fur caps, coats, and overshoes were placed near the stove to dry. The musical instruments brought by the guests (at Papa's request) were opened to tune up for the impromptu concert after dinner.

My memory of the immigrants is that they were blonde, rosy-cheeked, blue-eyed, and wore navy-blue serge suits. Under their arms they usually had a guitar, mandolin, or flute. That Christmas was no exception.

Mama, as always, was prepared for the unexpected, and with her compassionate heart made each stranger feel a part of the family. "Ven you have heart room you have house room," she reminded us often.

Just as the guests were seated around the table there was the sound of stomping feet on the porch. From out of the cold emerged two half-frozen men, Barney and John, who had fled the big woods. They had defied the Canadian winter and made it back to Winnipeg for Christmas Eve. Trekking over eighty miles of ice and snow, they were sustained by a burning desire to reach the only home they knew in the new land for Christmas Eve. Rescue stations along the way had served hot tea and biscuits to the desperate travelers. But now they were home, and it was Christmas.

Around that evening's festive table old hurts were forgotten and hope, faith, and courage for tomorrow were rekindled.

Mama always looked like an angel with shining eyes—even if she didn't have a new dress for Christmas. "I'll get one later," she whispered to me. Barney recounted his adventures with a flourish, while John basked in the warmth of fireside and food. The other guests now were no longer strangers—we all seemed like one big family.

As Papa read the Christmas story, we envisioned angels and shepherds and the dear little Babe in the manger. Strange how little we knew of holiday rush, Santa Claus, and expensive gifts. After dinner we gathered in the parlor to join hands, march around the Christmas tree, and sing old Norwegian songs and carols. We opened the gifts. No one had been left out. We welcomed handkerchiefs, aprons, new hairbows, apples, one orange each, and some candy. Any small toy was a rare delight beyond words. Mama made sure that each guest received a small gift.

While the men tuned their instruments, Papa struck the chords of the piano with a flourish. Violins, mandolins, and guitars blended with the piano against the lonely sound of a plaintive flute. Voices raised in joyful song blended in harmony like a great choir. Standing tall and straight I sang with them in the grand finale— "*Den Himmelske Lovsang* (The Heavenly Song of Praise)." I can still remember that sound. I was nine years old. Papa closed in prayer. He lifted up to the throne of God each one of us in the room, and then he left each of us safe and secure in His keeping. Christmas Eve was the night of nights, the prelude to tomorrow, Christmas Day, when church bells would ring out across the sparkling snow, calling the people to worship. Mama would sit straight with her little ones in a row. Papa, in his Prince Albert coat, would announce the opening hymn.

Joy to the world; the Lord has come.
Let earth receive her King.

5

All Through the Week

Mama and Papa, like God, never slumbered nor slept. What a comfort—waking in the night to the sound of the treadle sewing machine and Papa preaching sermons to the dark or practicing his English. How he wanted to remove the Scandinavian accent from his speech. He would shout, "I got it, I got it, Mama. I don't say 'ven' anymore, I say 'ven'! Mama, we must speak good English ven we are in America."

Monday mornings, Papa emerged, in white shirt and tie, to take his place by the washing machine. He held a book in one hand and powered the agitator with the other. While Mama sliced Naptha soap into the hot water, she sang "What can wash away my sin?" Paying her no mind, Papa continued reading aloud, practicing English diction.

One look at the clothesline told the neighbors how often we changed underwear or how many overnight guests Mama had taken in. In the winter the frozen long underwear looked like ghosts hovering in the sky.

Not only was Monday wash day, it was also soup day. The scraps dropped into the kettle of homemade soup and the loaves of Mama's rye bread seemed to multiply like the loaves and fishes in the New Testament story. Regardless of the number of unexpected guests, there was always enough. God and Mama could do anything!

Tuesday was ironing day. A basket of clothes which had been sprinkled and rolled and left to stand overnight was now ready for the all-day ordeal. As the irons heated on the stove, Mama washed the dishes and made the beds. Every sheet was ironed. When Mama finished with them, the ruffles on starched petticoats, dresses, and aprons stood out like rows of fences. As Mama ironed, she taught. Her methods were simple: endless songs and stories and Bible verses for us to memorize. I sat enthralled, listening, watching, and waiting for the day I could iron the dishtowels, then the starched pillowcases, and then graduate to Papa's white handkerchiefs, which had to be perfectly folded. No one but Mama ever ironed Papa's white Sunday shirt or the treasured Sunday-dinner linen tablecloth!

At noon, Mama always stopped for lunch and nap-time. No one—on any day—escaped the nap. Papa went quietly to his study. The house grew still. The children slept. Mama rested thirty minutes (surely she didn't sleep), then rose quietly. She brushed out her long brown hair and put on a crisp starched dress and apron. To complete her preparations for the second half of her day, she sat down and opened her Bible. After reading, she quietly slipped to her knees for her afternoon talk with God. Mama's prayer time was as sure as the sun coming up in the morning. Even the youngest child knew to be quiet until Mama finished.

The Bible closed, Mama, smelling fresh like Palmolive soap and starch, put on the coffee pot. That was the sign that made the sleepy house bound with life. Papa emerged from the study. The children, dressed in starched, afternoon clothing, came to the table for "coffee." For the children, hot water with milk and sugar accompanied the rye bread and jam and the coveted treat—a lump of sugar dipped in Papa's coffee. Papa then left to visit the widows and orphans, but not without a word of caution from Mama about the widows.

Ironing days were full of talk. Childish problems and questions were discussed in the classroom disguised as Mama's kitchen. Papa was unreachable. Within him spanned the stretch of the mountains, the depth of the valley, the pounding of the surf, and the lonely cry of the sea gull. He could place a compassionate arm around a man stumbling in the gutter and lead him to God, but he couldn't hear his children say, "Talk to us, Father!" He couldn't reach us, but he gave us the best that he had—Mama. To him she was a ruby without price, the woman above all women who would show his children how to obey his commands and daily live out the "why" of them. Slowly, but well, we learned—by word, by example, and sometimes "by strap."

In the pantry corner hung a red strap, which held a high place of dignity and honor in the eyes of us four children. One parental glance in that general direction was usually enough to call the troops to attention. No other humiliation could match that of the bending, drawers down, and bare "rumpa" exposed to the world, over Mama's knee. The pain inflicted by the strap was minimal in comparison to the shame of the hanging drawers and the knowledge that you had somehow "disgraced the ministry."

"Children obey your parents," was one of the first Bible verses I ever learned.

One day in a moment of anger, I stuck out my tongue at our neighbor (albeit behind his back). Not only did I encounter the strap, but also red pepper on my tongue. And I suffered through a face-to-face apology. The verse for the day was, "Be ye kind one to another." Discipline was swift and sure! In fact it was so sure that often we reached for the strap and red pepper and pulled down our drawers—the sooner done, the better. There was no escape. Just as sure as the punishment, however, was the sense of cleansing and forgiveness. Our slate was clean. The touch of love was a soft, warm glow.

Wednesday was mending day. Mama slipped the wooden egg into the stockings and her fingers flew, in and out, until a hole was no more. I sat beside her busy at work with a piece of cloth, a needle, and a thread. Patiently she loosened my endless knots, and we started again, until I eventually learned her tricks.

Thursday was visiting day. Hand in hand, we took home-made bread and jars of soup to the lonely and sick. In the afternoon a clean, starched tablecloth covered the table, and china cups were set for afternoon coffee. As we had visited others, so guests were sure to visit us.

Friday was baking day. The dough had been kneaded the night before—to the music of our friend Barney's mandolin. Papa sometimes turned the heavy dough until it was ready for rising. Thursday nights we fell asleep to the smell of yeast and the sound of the mandolin. Friday's reward was the end crust, covered with melted butter. By late Friday afternoon, Mama would have a warm line-up of ten loaves of bread, a sponge cake for Sunday dinner, and, we hoped, some soft cookies plump with raisins.

Saturday—cleaning day. In case there was a shortage of godliness, Mama made up for it with cleanliness. By the time I was seven, she had taught me to do the dishes (properly): wash, rinse, dry, put away, scour the sink, sweep the floor, and put out the garbage. No one, but *no one*, ever left unwashed dishes in the sink. That would be a blot on the ministry that not even God could overlook. When I visited in other homes and saw unwashed dishes, I promptly pulled up a chair to the sink and started washing. I wouldn't allow anyone else to disgrace their ministry, either.

Discipline and order went together, just as coffee and sugar lumps went together.

Our wall motto about the unseen guest in our home, the listener to every conversation, was a reality. God lived in our house. It had to be clean in every way.

Saturday morning involved a literal "rise and shine." Every child had a task. The stove was polished a shiny black. Every chair was scrubbed or polished. Every floor—nook and cranny—felt the power of Fels Naptha soap and a scrub brush. No dallying, every task was accomplished by nap time, or else! Afternoon coffee was a celebration of cleanliness. Sunday would produce the godliness. For now, it was enough that the parsonage be clean.

After an early supper, the Saturday-night-bath special rolled into high gear. Our hair was shampooed with Raleigh's. We were scrubbed clean and robed in fresh flannel nightgowns. All the shoes waited in a row for Papa's polish and buff. Mama laid out clean Sunday clothes, ready for an orderly Lord's Day.

Mama peeled potatoes for Sunday dinner, made meatballs

and gravy, and cooked the carrots to cream with the peas later. A bowl of applesauce cooled. The table was stretched and a linen cloth spread, ready to cover the feet of any who needed a Sunday-noon home.

Sunday school lessons, Bibles, pennies for collection, clean handkerchiefs—all were ready for morning.

Every detail of school and play came up on the bedtime screen. Nothing was hidden from Mama. As she tucked me in, she always said, "Look at me, Margaret. Is there anything you need to tell me before we talk to God?" Knowing her secret line to God, the confessions poured out, and forgiveness flowed. Sleep was sweet.

Papa sat in his study late into the night. Mama looked over the work of the day, saw that it was good, and turned out the light. If she ever did sleep, it was on Saturday night.

Sunday woke like a burst of sunshine. Papa, dressed in striped trousers, swallow-tail coat, and high starched collar, marched off to church with his Bible and songbook in hand. Mama, dressed in her made-over clothes, gathered her children, scrubbed and numbered, unto her. We all would take our places in the house of God. Going to church was *never* a matter of choice, but a matter of obedience. Once there, no one moved. This was a sacred front-row seat over which God and Papa kept a watchful eye. As hard as I tried to concentrate my mind always wandered ahead a few hours. I wondered how many we would have for Sunday dinner and hoped Uncle Barney would come.

The benediction was over. I braced myself for Mr. Meyer's Sunday morning coffee kiss. Barney was coming for dinner. It would be a good day, a day of rest from work but not from what Mama had taught us while working through the week. And sometimes she taught us while laughing.

Days of grief and sorrow pass and are followed by peace and joy; in the same way the weeks of winter would pass and spring would send forth her buds of promise. In her wisdom, Mother would comment, "And summer will surely follow."

This spring, excitement stirred in the parsonage; Mama was to be the guest speaker at the Norwegian Baptist Women's Convention.

The sewing machine treadled through the night as Mama made a new creation out of an old missionary-barrel relic. The made-over dress would be navy-blue, but Mama was not color blind; her only pair of shoes was a contrasting brown. Mama had long ago learned how to manage on a preacher's income. She solicited the help of the shoemaker, who dyed the shoes to match the dress. At a rummage sale she found a large brimmed hat. It was worn and frayed, but the price was right: ten cents. She bought blue dye to cover the hat's light color. After boiling and dipping she sewed ribbons over frayed edges. Mama was dressed in a manner befitting the ministry: navy-blue dress with a soft lace collar, wide straw hat with ribbons, and matching navy-blue shoes, old but shining like new. Gloves and a lace handkerchief added the final touches.

The Baptist women gathered for this meeting under the open blue sky on a lovely, sunny day. String bands played, and choirs sang. The women grew eager for the highlight of the program, a reading by Ella Tweten.

Under the hot sun she stood with dignity, slender, young, and beautiful. Papa would be proud. She began to speak clearly and forthrightly. But the sun refused to keep her cover-up secrets. Slowly the heat melted the hat's dye and beautiful blue streaks ran into her hair and down her forehead. The shoes reeked with the potent shoe dye, not quite dry. Mama finished her presentation with a flourish and quietly sat down, not outwardly flustered. No one would forget the women's conference—and Mama's hat.

"A merry heart doeth good like a medicine." When the conference was over the women joined Mama in peals of laughter. Her hat became a topic for conversation for years to come.

Mama's abounding joy of living carried our family and congregation through many such crises. We learned that the joy of the Lord was our strength. Proverbs 15:15 belonged to Mama: "He that is of a merry heart hath a continual feast." The immigrants shared their sense of humor as well as their joys and sorrows.

Years later, Mama was given a gift of money (for her trip to Norway), and the accompanying note read, "To buy a hat."

6

Angel Unaware

After a while, the time came when the fire dwindled for the Tweten immigrants in Winnipeg, and then it died. The coffee pot grew cold, but Papa and Mama left behind them a warm and mellow glow of love when Papa again felt "the call."

The Norwegian Baptist Conference asked Papa to be a missionary to the Scandinavian settlers throughout the Province of Saskatchewan.

Mama wondered how Papa would manage to travel endless miles alone, care for his clothes, and eat proper meals. However, she rested in one thing: Papa was God's servant. God never failed to care for His children.

After a painful farewell to the First Norwegian Baptist Church, the needy friends who had descended from the immigration trains, and the towering gray parsonage, Papa ushered Mama and her four children into the newly acquired Model-T Ford. Mama had packed a basket of bread and sugared waffles to sustain us on the long journey.

Papa's Model-T, provided by the Baptist Conference, was the only car he ever owned, and it never received due recognition for its service beyond the call of duty. In the days to come, this "soldier of the cross" would travel trackless space. As long as it kept wheels moving in the same direction and patiently listened to endless sermons, it was deemed worthy. Mama wondered how Papa's theological mind would remember the car needed more than words; it also needed gas.

When we arrived at 510 Avenue J, Saskatoon, Saskatchewan, Mama's joy was boundless. The small yellow house boasted white trim and a perfect yard. "Our very own home!" she cried.

Buckets, brushes, and Fels Naptha flew into action. By the time we were finished we could have eaten off the floors. The windows shone with Canadian sunshine, and starched lace curtains framed the view.

Mama added a crowning touch to her "very own" kitchen: red linoleum (slightly damaged), purchased for one dollar. Again life flowed through Mama's kitchen.

In the corner stood the rocking chair, my place of refuge in the time of storm. When Mama needed a refuge, she just threw her apron over her head. Years later we realized her screen hid tears, but this was her world, and no one asked questions.

In another corner stood the water barrel, filled by the town water wagon, which was pulled by two horses. I loved to join the parade of skipping children who followed along and fed sugar lumps to the horses.

Behind the outhouse was an open field, a perfect garden spot. Mama's sharp eye quickly envisioned rows of bright flowers and vegetables.

The adjoining field was to become the neighborhood playground, where balls and kites could sail in the Canadian sky.

Papa unpacked his beloved books and placed them, his dearest companions, around his desk. He would soon have to travel, but now it was time for coffee. We were snugly settled into our cozy house.

The black stove glistened with polish. The coffee pot perked a welcome. Mama placed on the tablecloth set with coffee cups a bowl of violets she had picked. Papa left his books. The children gathered for afternoon coffee and a lump of sugar, dipped in Papa's full cup.

"Mama, you have it good," he added with a bow.

Just a few days later the new neighbors came to watch Papa

crank up the Model-T to begin his first missionary journey. "God Will Take Care of You" became our farewell song.

Papa received only part of his salary from the Baptist Conference; he was expected to raise the rest through offerings gathered on his journeys. If the Conference had only known what Mama suspected—that the offering Papa collected at one place was given to the needy along the way to the next! But everyone was needy—including his family back home. Oatmeal became the staff of life. Mama and God had to manage. They did!

Mr. Olsen, a redhead with a faraway look in his eyes, often wandered into Mama's kitchen for some good soup and rye bread. He spoke seldom, but stared into space—and drank coffee. Mama said he was very sick on the inside. He had left the big woods to work in a factory, trying to save money to bring his wife from Norway.

I had only one complaint of his frequent visits. "But, Mama, his feet smell so bad! Can't you do something?"

Do something, she did.

One cold day she suggested that Mr. Olsen warm his feet in a tub of warm water, to which Mama had added a few drops of Lysol. While he soaked his feet, she washed his stiff socks and dried them over the cookstove. She suggested that he bring them over again with his soiled clothes for washing day.

Mama started a ritual. Every week Mr. Olsen came to soak his feet and pick up a clean bundle of clothes in exchange for the dirty batch he left with Mama. Gradually the dazed look of shock disappeared. As he drank coffee, Mama's guitar music seemed to seep into his thoughts and replace some of his pain. One day he burst into the kitchen, exploding with joy! "My Hilda comes! My Hilda comes!" That ended the foot-washing ceremony in Mama's kitchen. Who would ever have thought the way to a man's heart was through his feet? Mama understood!

Returning from one of his journeys, Papa brought home a young man, Lars.

"I found him in a barn, Mama. I think he has tuberculosis. He was working on a farm, but the farmer refused to pay him when he got sick. They'd agreed he would work six months before he'd be paid. He lived on oatmeal and salt pork but was too sick to travel. I told him you could make him well." We stared open-eyed until Papa's command came, "Say hello to Lars, children."

I moved my pet rabbit off the small enclosed porch and Mama made a bed for the stranger.

Mama said he was dying from homesickness. If she cured that, God would cure the tuberculosis. We boiled his dishes and kept the little ones away from him. She fed him vegetable soup and rye bread; the songs and stories did the rest.

In the meantime she contacted his parents in Norway. They were overjoyed at the prospect of welcoming home their proud, young son, who later became a prosperous citizen of Oslo. Lars had God to thank, and an angel unaware, Mama.

7

The High Button Shoes

I needed shoes! I always needed shoes! Our bank account consisted of "My God shall supply all your need." He did, but not my way!

The coming of the missionary barrel was an annual event. Every outdated relic from the gay nineties seemed to find its way into that barrel: moth-eaten furs, threadbare silks and satins, and shoes of all sizes.

I ran! I had lived through enough missionary barrel debuts! How Mama made dresses out of those costumes I never understood. She cut apart old coats and suits and sewed beautiful coats, lined with silk. She cut off buttons and salvaged trim, and saved them for the right project. Much of the cloth she saved for quilts. We had no shortage of quilts!

"Margaret," Papa called. "We have shoes!"

That was the last thing I wanted to hear. "I'm sure they don't fit." I kept running.

"Margaret!"

I stopped. And I returned to stare in horror at two pairs of high button shoes. One pair was brown and the other black.

"Try them on." Papa left no tone for discussion, and at times his temper moved ahead of reason.

I complained they didn't fit. I tried losing the buttonhook. I said they were too big. "Good," said Papa. "We'll put cotton in the toes." No one was ever sick, so it was no use even to play sick. I had to wear the shoes. No one argued with Papa.

Mama sensed my distress. Tenderly she placed her arms around me and quietly, but firmly, reminded me that we had prayed for shoes. God answered, not the way we think is best, but God heard and answered. Mama never allowed sympathy to obscure a deeper lesson.

Mama continued, "Pride is a terrible thing, Margaret. It is not so important what we put on our feet, but it *is* important where your feet go. Sometimes we have to put on hard things—like the shoes—so God can keep our feet on the right path. If you worry more about how you look than about what you are, you will have many lessons to learn. Someday you will look back and say that this was an important lesson to learn. Remember this: God always answers prayer, but not always your way. Wear your shoes with a thankful, humble heart. Shall I tell you the secret to happiness?"

"Oh yes, Mama."

As she gathered me in her arms and stroked my hair, she whispered softly, "A thankful heart, Margaret. A thankful heart."

I thought about what Mama said, but I also remembered how Papa preached that God can move mountains if we pray, believing.

In desperation I prayed! "Dear God, the Bible says if we have faith we can move mountains. I don't need any mountains moved; I just need two pairs of shoes moved. Thank you."

I lined up the shoes, and the buttonhook, near the bedroom door—making the disappearance as easy as possible—and promptly fell asleep.

Morning came. The shoes had not gone!

"Margaret, you'll be late for Sunday school," Mama called from the kitchen.

Pulling my overshoes over my button shoes, I reluctantly left for Sunday school. Carefully wiping my feet, I started for my classroom. But despite my efforts my classmates called, "Margaret, you're dripping. You have to take off your overshoes."

Slowly, I pulled off my overshoes. There, for all the world to see, were my high button shoes. I was surrounded by silent pity.

Just then my friend Dorothy Faber walked in, carefully wiping her overshoes at the doorway. A cheerful voice called out, "Dorothy, you're dripping. Take off your overshoes."

Slowly Dorothy removed them and there, for all the world to see, were two sock-covered feet. My red-haired, freckle-faced friend had no shoes!

"Good morning, girls," came the crisp English accent of our beloved Sunday school teacher, Mr. Avery. A frail, elderly, blue-eyed gentleman with white hair and goatee, he quietly assessed the situation.

"Dorothy, you sit here on one side of me and Margaret, you sit here on the other." Each Sunday, as we formed a large circle in our class, Mr. Avery chose two to sit beside him. It was almost like sitting near God. He had a way of making God real. No one ever wanted to be promoted to another class.

I remembered very little of what he said that morning. I only remembered what he was—a godly man. I also remembered a Sunday afternoon, long before, in the Winnipeg auditorium, when I had walked down the aisle to give my heart to Jesus. Dr. R. A. Torrey had been conducting a children's crusade. I was six years old, but I knew I belonged to God.

Today I also knew I had a lesson to learn. Mama was right. Pride was a terrible thing.

Mr. Avery was saying, "With Jesus in your heart, you can do anything." I remembered that. And I still remember his love, warm and tender, as he had one arm around me and one around Dorothy.

Dorothy and I left the classroom together. Our boots in the crunching snow created their own special echo.

We never mentioned to each other the high button shoes or the woolen socks. We each learned what Mama would call a lesson.

The day I gave my heart to Jesus, God gave His gift of salvation to me. The day I put on my high button shoes with humility and not rebellion, I gave my gift to God—an obedient and thankful heart. I didn't understand it then. I do now.

8

A Canadian Blizzard

It was getting close to Christmas in Saskatoon and we had not heard from Papa in quite some time. In the four-room house, with an outhouse at the end of the path, we faced the stark reality of another threadbare Christmas. A lonely tree, brought in from the woods, with handmade decorations, stood in the corner. But there were no gifts—not only no gifts, but also no Papa.

The cupboards held little food, and Mama's purse held no money—and worse, the soap dish was empty.

Mama, desperate at such a lack, asked her Icelandic friend, Mrs. Johnson, for some soap. Having only one half-bar herself, she cut it in two. Mama had soap!

"I have only a soup bone left," added Mrs. Johnson.

"That's good," said Mama. "I have a few vegetables from the grocer. There are some brown spots in them, but they will be good for soup. And I have some bread. We will have a feast."

The air of festivity, songs, and guitars filled the little house on Avenue J. The soup and bread seemed to multiply. Mr. Johnson led us in giving thanks to God and our joy continued late into the evening. Since the Johnsons had no children they enjoyed the four of us.

"Like Hannah of old, I have prayed for a child," Mrs. Johnson confided in Mama, "but still nothing."

"Come, we pray together," answered Mama. "God will give you the desires of your heart."

(Mrs. Johnson and Mama soon became close friends, laughing and talking over their afternoon coffee, and one year later Mr. and Mrs. Johnson dedicated their beautiful new baby to God. Papa was right! God and Mama could do anything.)

But Christmas Eve came and still no Papa. He was on a missionary journey in the northern part of Canada. As he traveled from community to community, any offerings he received were generally given to the needy along the way.

Mama deliberately set our table for Christmas. "But, Mama, will we have Christmas?" I asked. "Are you sure God won't forget us?"

She always answered the same way: "God never forgets and God never fails. Papa is in God's service and God takes care of His children. *Ja*, we have Christmas, Margaret. God will provide. We are warm and we have oatmeal and bread—even coffee and sugar lumps. Christmas? Of course we have Christmas." Her lovely face shone as bright as the Christmas star. "We have Jesus in our hearts. That is Christmas!" One old Norwegian song had become our theme song.

> *Heaven and earth may pass away*
> *Cliffs and fjords may disappear*
> *But the one who trusts in God*
> *Knows that God's promises never fail.*

Songs of faith filled the kitchen, the familiar Norwegian carols, including "Yule with Its Joy." Mama presented us with new clothes made out of scraps from the missionary barrel.

Mama was doing her part; if only I could have been sure God would do His. "But, Mama, we always have presents."

My memory of earlier Christmases in Winnipeg, with food and music, accented this Saskatoon holiday bleakness. Mama never wavered. "This is Christmas Eve," she reminded us, "a time to rejoice and praise God for the gift of His Son. See, we

36

have the table set for Christmas. We have the tree. We have our songs and stories, and you ask, 'Will we have Christmas?' We have Christmas!

"Come—a bath now, and then a nap. Then we dress for Christmas Eve." She jabbed at the big bone hairpin that held her figure-eight bun in place.

"Where is Papa?" I asked.

She paused, her slender hands on her hips. "God knows where Papa is." Her hands fell limp against the crisp starched apron that covered her plain dark dress. She smiled to reassure me. "A bath—come, we get the tub."

The round metal tub was for Saturday night baths when everyone got ready for Sunday. The only exception was the Christmas Eve bath—often in the middle of the week.

After the scrub in the tub we were clothed in our new long underwear that Mama had made. Then to bed for a nap—a ritual no one dared to break. "Sleep now!" Mama said.

We did! We dreamed of Christmas dinner, lots of people, and singing and marching around the tree. Always there was one present each. Tonight, only oatmeal—and no presents. But Mama said we would have Christmas. God and Mama never failed.

The house was still. Mama put on the coffee pot.

Soon, the house was stirring and Mama dressed her four children for Christmas. She didn't sing "Trust and Obey" or "Faith Is the Victory" without action. "If you pray for rain, you get the umbrellas out. If you pray for Christmas Eve celebration, you dress for the occasion." It was just that simple.

"Even if we have only oatmeal, we dress like true Norwegians. It is not what you have that is important," she said. "It is what you believe. God never fails. That we believe!"

I was proud, proud of the bright hair bow perched on my head. This was the nights of nights—Christmas Eve.

Mama gathered us around her rocking chair and told the story of angels and shepherds, wise men and gifts, but the greatest part of all was the baby in the straw. We sang the songs of Christmas and I looked longingly at the lonely tree in the corner.

Suddenly the sound of many stomping feet on our porch

followed by the shout of happy voices filled the winter night. "Merry Christmas!"

"Joy to the world, the Lord is come," sang the carolers. Mama opened the door to a group of happy young people from the First Baptist Church of Saskatoon and their pastor, Dr. Ward. He was grinning when he said, "We heard that the Norwegian missionary had not returned from his journey and since this is your first Christmas in Saskatoon, we thought you might enjoy a special Christmas from your Canadian friends."

"Come in! Come in!" exclaimed Mama. "Get warm by the fire!"

They came! Boxes of food and gifts poured into the little house. With shouts of laughter, the young placed the gifts under the tree and put food on the prepared table. Candy, fruit, and nuts were added to the bountiful supply.

Pastor Ward said, "Please accept our love, and may God bless you all. Now we will stop singing, and we will pray for your Papa's safe return."

Together we sang the carols of Christmas and once again the story was read of God's gift to man. A closing prayer was followed by an invitation to have Christmas dinner at the home of Dr. Ward. I was delighted! We always had the lonely people to our house, and now we were invited out as "company."

I wondered how Pastor Ward knew about us since we were not members of his church. We attended a small Baptist mission near our home. The Scandinavians met in our home for weekly Bible study and prayer meeting in their own language. At that time there was no established Norwegian church, but there was a close affiliation between the Norwegian Baptist Conference and the Canadian and American Baptist Convention.

The songs of Christmas echoed across the snow. The prayers ascended to God's throne. Mama's face was aglow. Her faith had been rewarded. She had known we would have Christmas!

We rushed into action. The butter, salt and pepper, water in the glasses, roast chicken, even cranberry sauce—there was no end to delicacies—cookies, fruitcake. But best of all, no lutefisk! (It was a true-blue Norwegian dish, but I didn't like it!)

Suddenly boots again stomped on the porch, but now a single pair! With a burst of joy, the door flew open!

There stood Papa!

His place was already set at the table. "Faith and works go together," Mama said.

Papa rubbed his cold hands to warm them. "I was lost in a blizzard, but now I am home—safe and warm," he said.

The joy of Christmas filled the house with laughter and songs. Faith filled my heart.

Seated around the festive table we bowed our hearts and heads in thanksgiving to God. "*Ja*, Mama, I was lost in a blizzard."

The story unfolded that Papa had been engulfed in a swirling Canadian storm. His eyes sparkled as he spoke. "The snow whirled around me in blinding fury while the wind beat against me. I was all alone, felt totally helpless, lost in a world of white. I stood still. Then I cried to the Lord, 'God, I am lost, but You aren't. You know where I am. Please guide me to a safe place.'"

With awe in his voice, Papa told how a warm Presence drew close and he followed the warmth to a cabin nearly covered by snow. "*Ja*, Mama, we had to shovel a path to the barn to feed and milk the cows. We lived on oatmeal and milk." He helped the pioneer family gather eggs and cut wood for the stove. The family and Papa cared for each other until the storm passed.

On Christmas Day we sang "Joy to the World" in the First Baptist Church, and then we were dinner guests in a parsonage other than ours. Mama had dressed us girls in made-over silks and satins, trimmed with lace. My dress was blue satin, trimmed with fur. She had mended cast-off long white stockings and reserved them for such an occasion. Our shining blond heads flaunted bright hair bows, and our little brother looked like the famous "Boy in Blue."

We arrived at the parsonage looking like fairy princesses, holding our brother in a tight grasp. The Ward children were dressed in cotton dresses and black stockings. This was our day! We were rich! Papa and the ministry would not be disgraced.

Late into the night we listened to Papa tell of his journeys. After we went to bed, Mama and Papa sat alone by the warm stove in the quiet kitchen, drinking coffee together and catching up.

They were having their own private Christmas.

9

Mama's Lessons

We loved Saskatoon! Mama enjoyed the gardens and the shiny house with the red linoleum, the Quaker Oats castle, and fairyland of violets. We enjoyed the toboggan slides and the frozen river with the big ice sleds and horses.

People came to sing and pray, to find strength in Mama's kitchen where the coffee pot perked happily on the black cookstove. Papa traveled among the scattered settlers, and churches were organized.

At bedtime we heard songs and stories as we sat by the warm stove in our kitchen. Some songs came from Norway and told plaintive stories about the sea. One was about a little girl whose father didn't return from sea. She waited and watched by the sea to give him a birthday gift. Another song told of a crippled child who had no playmates, but he knew that when he got to heaven, the angels would play with him.

No one had to remind us to be kind to a handicapped child. Instinctively we would hug such a child and remind him how angels would play games with him in heaven. "In the meantime we will play with you."

"But Mama, why didn't the daddy come home for his birthday?" we would ask.

"Life is filled with many questions that can't be answered,

children, but we must learn early to trust God and obey Him. That is one reason it is important to obey your parents. If we can't obey them, how can we obey God? Joy comes from God inside you. Even the little girl who was sad because her daddy didn't come home could be happy in her heart if she thought about her daddy, lost in a storm, being with Jesus. There are times when I am sad when I think about Bernice [my sister, who died of diphtheria several years earlier] buried in New York; then I am happy when I think of her being with Jesus.

"There is a time to die, a time to be born, a time to weep, and a time to laugh. One day is never the same as the one before it or after it. But if we keep a thankful, joyful heart and learn to trust God, we will have peace all of the time."

"Mama, sing about the bird flying away."

Mama sang softly:

> *Flee as a bird to the mountain*
> *Ye who are weary in sin.*

"You can always fly like a bird when you think happy thoughts and believe that God answers prayer. Someday, girls, I will sew soft white nightgowns for you, out of lovely material, not rough feed sacks. On your nightgown I will embroider a bluebird, the bluebird of happiness. Always remember the bluebird, girls. Someday—not now, but someday."

Mama never lied, we knew. Over the years she repeated again and again, "Someday, I will sew you nightgowns from brand new, soft white fabric. They will have on them a bluebird of happiness. Someday."

We waited. Christmas after Christmas came and went, until, finally, the boxes under the tree held the reward of Mama's lesson in hope: those promised nightgowns, lovingly sewn in the middle of our nights.

"Mama, Mama!" shouted Papa one day. "Look at this letter. It is a call to Chicago!"

We had never seen Papa so excited! Later we learned how much he had missed New York, the libraries, subways, and universities. Little did we know that this would be Mama's supreme test.

"This is an answer to my prayer, Mama. This is God's will for us! Schools and libraries, Mama!"

Silence.

A storm was brewing.

"I am not going!" she finally said.

Shock waves swept through us—Mama had defied Papa!

"I cannot give up this house—and my red linoleum. Chicago is full of gangsters, full of ugly noise and dirt. For the first time we have a home of our own, a garden. The children are happy. If you want schools and libraries we have some right here in Canada. I am not going!"

Late that night I overheard the same conversation. "I shall not be moved!"

Papa pleaded and argued, and then played his last card, "Mama, this is God's will!"

Defying Papa was one thing, but defying God was another.

"All right, Papa, if this is God's will, then He will have to tell me. If it involves me, I have a right to know!" Mama had stood up for herself, and she would on other occasions. We would hear that statement often in the coming years.

"Without a clear order from Him, God cannot expect me to give up the only home I have ever known. I won't move until He tells me as clearly as He told you."

"*Ja,* Mama, we agree! Now let us have a cup of coffee before we go to bed."

Mama sang happily as she polished her linoleum, worked in her garden, and baked her bread. God was a good God, and He wouldn't take this precious house from her. She had never been happier as she sang "Trust and obey, for there's no other way."

She placed her fleece before the Lord. "Now Lord, I want to obey Your will, but I must be sure it is Your will. If someone comes to buy this house, without any sign or advertisement, and if that same person wants to buy the red linoleum for what I paid for it, one dollar, then I will know it is Your will. I must be sure."

Since few houses were selling, Mama was confident no one would be looking at her small house. She sang happily.

"Excuse me, please." A pleasant lady stood in the doorway, viewing the flowers and talking to Mama. "I just passed by this darling house. Would you consider selling it?"

"Oh no," Mama answered. "I could never sell this house. Oh, just a moment. Please come in and have a cup of coffee."

"What a beautiful linoleum," the smiling lady continued. "Would you sell that linoleum to me? I always wanted a red one!"

Quietly Mama folded her hands over her starched apron. It was time for her to give up. "Yes, we will sell the house, and the red linoleum."

With her lips she said "Yes" to the smiling lady. With her heart she said yes to the will of God. God had spoken! She would trust, and she would obey!

And so it came to pass that the house on Avenue J, and the red linoleum, were sold. We were on our way to Chicago.

God had shown Mama His will as clearly as He had shown Papa.

10

$1 a Day

One day our eleven-year-old granddaughter, Sarah, cried, "Oh, Grammy, Kathryn is making fun of my big feet."

"Big feet? Let me look," I said. "Oh, my, you have princess feet, long and narrow, like your cousin Heather and like Princess Diana. Yes, princess feet. That's what you have."

"Well, what kind do I have?" Kathryn, nine years old, held up her sturdy foot.

"You have queen's feet, good sturdy feet. Yessir, Queen Kathryn."

That did it! I began to call them "Princess Sarah" and "Queen Kathryn." We even watched for sales and one day found a $100 pair of Evan-Picone shrimp-colored shoes on a clearance table for $15. Princess shoes! Sarah was elated. We also found an inexpensive matching sweater. The princess had her day!

Then it was Kathryn's turn. She came bounding in the room one day excitedly calling to Papa (Harold) to look at her shoes. "See the tag?" she asked. "One hundred and twenty dollars! Black patent leather with a bow!"

"One hundred and twenty dollars?" Papa slipped into his best horror act.

Kathryn giggled delightedly. "Look, Papa, my mom found these ladies' shoes for $15 on a clearance rack. I'll have them for next Christmas. They're too big for me now, but just right for queen's feet."

A little proppin' up on the leanin' side never hurts.

A similar situation occurred one time when a lonely girl in leg braces came to me with tears in her eyes. "I've been invited to a wedding and I hate my braces," she said.

"Oh, honey," I responded, "get someone to make you a long skirt and wear a beautiful blouse. No one will see anything but your beautiful face."

Later I received a picture of a beautiful girl in a long dress. Sometimes it takes so little to be sensitive to someone's need.

My mother knew the importance of responding to the circumstances of a child. It happened sixty years ago, but I remember it as though it was yesterday. The ad in the newspaper read: "Mother's helper, $1 a day." I was elated!

If there was anyone with experience, it would certainly be this fourteen-year-old preacher's daughter who had helped her mother since the age of two. Five younger sisters and a brother stuck in the middle qualified me for the job. A telephone call confirmed the fact that I was hired. I figured one dollar a day meant six dollars a week. A fortune in Depression days!

I boarded the Diversey Avenue bus to the affluent part of Chicago, close to the lake. The view from the second floor flat was magnificent. I stood in awe of the spacious, carpeted rooms and the beautiful furniture. Exquisite lamps and pictures gave the flat an air of elegance and extravagance. The china cabinet was filled with sparkling crystal and beautiful china. I couldn't imagine how anyone could have so much.

Then reality came!

"I want you to first clean the kitchen," instructed the mother. I wondered where the children were. Wasn't I a mother's helper?

Oh, yes, the kitchen. There it was, a sink full of dirty dishes, not only today's, but apparently from two or three days. I shuddered! Mama had never allowed dishes to stand in the sink. You wash, rinse, dry, put away, scour the sink, sweep the floor, and take out the garbage. That's what Mama meant about washing dishes.

(I remember visiting with my mama when I was very young.

46

"When he has brought out all his own, he goes on ahead of them" (John 10:4).

The Savior waits ahead

You're preparing for a trip to a city you've never visited. You pull out the road map to find out how to get there. Anxiety is replaced by confidence because you know *someone has already gone before you.*

Suppose you've been transferred to a new city. You must leave friends, routines, personal ministries, perhaps even family. Does that thought produce an anxious feeling of launching out unaided into the unknown?

It needn't. Jesus said He's gone before you. And if He has called you to a new environment, then He is already there waiting for you. Frances Havergal examines this comforting thought.

Walk with Frances Havergal

"What gives the Alpine climber confidence in wild, lonely, treacherous passes or ascents when he has not passed that way before? It is that his guide 'goes ahead.'

"It is to Christ's own sheep that this promise applies—simply those who believe and hear His voice.

"Perhaps we have been in a sheltered nook of the fold and we are sent to live where it is windier and wilder. The home-nest is stirred up, and we have to go (it may be only for a few days, it may be for years) into less congenial surroundings to live with new people or in a different position or in a new neighborhood.

"We do not put ourselves forth; we would rather stay. But it has to be.

"But Jesus 'goes ahead.' He prepares the earthly as well as the heavenly places for us. He will be there when we get to the new place.

"He is not sending us away from Him, but only leading us forth with His own gentle hand, saying, 'Rise up, My love, and come away with Me.' "

Walk Closer to God

Wherever you may be, if Jesus has brought you there, then He has prepared the way for you. And He has a purpose for your being there. Ask Him to show you what that purpose is.

Worship from the Heart

"Lord, sometimes I have the feeling that I, only I, have walked this troublesome path. Your Word teaches otherwise. Let me trace Your footprints along the sea of sorrow. Let me be as a child who steps into a father's warm footprints in the wet sand, always aware that the fresh prints indicate Your presence just up ahead."

Walk Thru the Word

New Testament Reading
John 10
Old Testament Reading
Deuteronomy 31:1-8

While the women drank coffee in the parlor I noticed a sink of dishes. Since Norwegian honor was at stake, I pulled up a stool and proceeded to wash them.)

My mistress continued, "When you finish the dishes, clean the stove."

The stove was filthy!

I knew about cleaning old gas stoves. Mama had us clean and polish ours every Saturday.

"Oh, yes, the ice box," she added. I knew to empty the water pan underneath and scrub away the mold.

"I have to go shopping, but there are a few things I couldn't send to the laundry, like linen and underwear and stockings. You can wash them in the tub and hang them on the back porch."

I watched my new employer reach for her pocketbook and move her large frame toward the door. *Strange that someone so large and strong can't clean the kitchen,* I thought. Her soft hands certainly didn't look like Mama's hands. The diamond rings sparkled on her hand and a gold watch reminded her that she was late.

Mama had one gold band on her finger, no watch. Her strong hands smelled of Fels Naptha soap and were so gentle when she held us.

"Oh, a sandwich, you can fix for lunch. We go out to dinner so no one will be cooking. The children are with my sister. Her maid takes care of them today." (Well, that answered one question.) Then she was gone.

While the dishes soaked I dismantled the stove. The oven had to be scraped with a knife and S.O.S. Then the dishes—wash, rinse, dry, put away, scour the sink, take out the garbage. While the pots and pans soaked I gathered the garbage that was stacked all around the kitchen and took it down two flights of stairs to the incinerator. Back to the pots and pans. Mama's never looked that black. I scraped and scoured with S.O.S. until my fingers were raw.

Next the floor! How could floors be so sticky? With scrubbing and scraping it finally looked like Mama's kitchen floor.

I was so tired I wanted to cry, but the thought of that dollar bill gave me new energy. Two cheese sandwiches and a glass of milk helped ease my hunger and I was ready to tackle the bathtub of laundry.

What a shame that anyone could leave soiled underwear in a tub. No one saw Mama's underwear. It was discreetly laundered and hung in faraway places. Her corset found a safe spot behind the stove, hidden from view. But the only place to hang clean laundry that day was on the back porch for all the world to see—bloomers blowing in the wind, petticoats and nightgowns. Was there no shame? When the tub was scrubbed I tackled the rest of the bathroom. Finally it was clean!

When the door opened, my buxom mistress came in with boxes from Marshall Fields. Since Mama only went to the Logan Department Store for sales, I didn't know anyone could buy so much, especially from Marshall Fields.

"What a day," she moaned. "I didn't even finish. Now, don't forget to polish the furniture. The children's rooms could stand a little cleaning, too."

It was 6 P.M. and she left to go out to eat. Hungry, and oh, so tired, I knew I had to finish. Then it was 8 P.M. I had worked for twelve long hours.

When my mistress returned she handed me a dollar bill and with a flourish announced, "You won't need to come back tomorrow. My maid will be back from her two-week vacation."

Too proud to cry, I boarded the Diversey Avenue bus for home. When I stumbled into Mama's kitchen, hungry and weary, I could only cry, "Oh, Mama, I'm so sorry. I thought I had a job for all summer. She never said it was to clean the whole house before the maid returned from a vacation."

Mama quietly wiped my tears and prepared some food. I could tell she was deep in thought.

"Come, Margaret, you and I are going back."

I sat in awe beside Mama on the bus. It cost ten cents in carfare, now thirty cents out of that precious dollar.

With quiet dignity Mama confronted the powerful mistress of the lakefront flat. "I believe you took advantage of a young girl who was hired as a mother's helper. I expect you to give her another dollar and our carfare. And don't you ever take advantage of a young girl again."

The large woman seemed to shrink in size while Mama's dignity made her seem ten feet tall. Without a word, the woman handed me the dollar and carfare, and Mama said good night.

Once again we were on the bus, going home. Mama was quiet, but there was a twinkle in her eye.

That was the unforgettable day when Mama made me feel like the most important person in the world. Mama responded with sensitive determination.

Mama's kitchen was warm and clean, the coffee pot was on, and we sliced her homemade rye bread and cheese. Papa chuckled delightedly!

"*Ja, ja,* in all the world there is no one like Mama."

I fell asleep secure in the order of things.

11

The Picnic

During the warm summer months Mama's Monday wash was on the line early. White sheets, embroidered pillow cases, linen tablecloths, and napkins whipped in the morning breeze. Papa's Sunday shirt bowed stiffly while underwear clung together in a less conspicuous place. Mama's intimate apparel, including a boned corset, with laces, hung in seclusion on the porch. Towels were clipped together according to size, while the Chicago wind rattled through thirty-five starched dresses, the aprons, and the embroidered luncheon cloths used for afternoon coffee. The sun filtered through the hazy day.

Tuesday we would tend the basket of ironing, but Monday was picnic day. Papa, relaxing from the strenuous "day of rest," packed his Bible and one of Spurgeon's books and hurried everyone along in his usual, impatient manner. For him the shortest distance between two points was *action*. We moved! The house had been put in order, and the food had been prepared. Before 10 A.M. we were standing on the corner of Wrightwood and Kimball, waiting for the Diversey Avenue bus. We hoped there would be seats.

One large bag contained meatballs and gravy in a covered kettle, wrapped in towels to stay warm. Another bag included waffles with melted butter and sugar, also wrapped in a towel.

Rye bread, cheese, jam and cookies and cake filled a third container. Dishes and tablecloth went into still another bag. Mama's mending was included with jars of milk and coffee. Bathing suits were tucked into empty places.

Papa, holding Joyce Solveig and his books in one arm, the meatballs in the other hand, managed to steer Mama and her children, who were holding blankets, a pillow, and the bags, into the bus. With a sigh of relief, the driver finally called out, "Diversey Beach," and Mama counted heads and bags, accounting for all that she had meant to bring.

We promptly forgot the second-floor flat and the Chicago heat when we saw the waves rolling in on the shores of Lake Michigan. A blanket cabana facilitated our speedy change into swim suits. Papa walked the shoreline, reading Spurgeon aloud, while we raced into the waves. Wistfully, Mama looked across the water and remembered her home by the sea, the cliffs and fjords, her land of the midnight sun. When the lake breeze blew through her brown hair she felt again the wind of the prairie and remembered her very own house. With a settled sigh, she picked up her mending bag and slipped the wooden egg into the toe of another needy stocking. A poetry book propped up before her, her darning needle flew back and forth, powered by her determined fingers. While she worked, the beauty of words refreshed her soul.

By noon, Papa wandered back from his rendezvous with Spurgeon and signaled his dripping enthusiastic brood to follow him. (We always suspected that he knew more about Spurgeon than he did about any of us.)

The starched tablecloth was spread, and napkins, made of feed sacks and personalized by varied embroidery thread, were set out. With dignity we asked the Norwegian blessing and then Mama served meatballs and gravy over boiled potatoes and carrots. Thin slices of buttered rye bread supplemented the menu. Sponge cake and a part of an apple finished the meal off. The Good Humor ice cream cart jingled in the background, but there was no need to look longingly at the chocolate-covered delights. The pennies had been counted out to cover the bus fare. We drank our fill from and washed the dishes in the water fountain.

"For everything there is a season," and now it was time to rest. In the midst of a noisy beach, Mama cradled Joyce Solveig in her arm and took her usual nap. Doris and Gordon sat quietly, looking at a book, while Papa read his Bible. Grace and I watched the crowded beach.

A mother, screaming at her children, waved frantically, "No, Sammy, no, you don't wee in the water." She turned to her neighbor, "So I told him already, but do kids listen? Rebecca, come back. Don't drink the water. Sammy weed already!" She turned to her friend on the next blanket, "A little peace I come to get, and what do I have? A headache and indigestion! In my coffin they'll see me."

Mama sat up, smiling, "That was a good nap."

"*Ja*, Mama, but now it is time for coffee." Out of one of the bags came a jar of coffee, still warm from towel wrappings, and a sugar lump. There was time for another splash while Papa walked the beach—but only after a trip to the rest rooms. No one disgraced the ministry, in or out of the water.

Suppertime came too soon. A quick change out of bathing suits brought us all to the spread table again. Meatball sandwiches, warm waffles with sugar, cookies, and apples emptied the bags and filled the table. Nothing was left. Washed dishes were packed away, so were the blankets, suits, and towels. Mama tucked away her mending and another poem in her memory. Traffic was less congested; soon the buses would be empty. The waves splashed over the rocks and sand and from the bus windows we watched the sun slip behind skyscrapers, saying good night to the windy city. The bus stopped.

Papa led the way up to the second-floor flat. Everyone helped to get the clothes off the line and then, in the tub, the children washed off the sand. I helped Mama sprinkle clothes for tomorrow's ironing. Papa played the piano and, with his usual gusto, sang "Standing on the Promises." While Mama put on the coffee pot, I took my bath and slipped into my side of the bed. Grace slept by the wall, Doris in the middle, and I, being the oldest, slept on the edge. I could wash out the sand of Diversey Beach, but I could never erase the memories.

The music stopped, for coffee was ready.

I fell asleep thinking how rich we were. Some people had vacations once a year. We had one every week of the summer: the Monday picnic.

12

Brooklyn, America

The train wheels clicked and clacked over the rails. Villages and fields were discarding drab winter covering for bursts of color and splashes of rain and sun. It was April, 1938. The New York Central was leaving Chicago behind, delivering a homesick daughter to New York for a family visit.

Again I relived the train ride from Canada and longed for the wind of the prairie and for a time that would be no more. Settling back into the plush seats, I rolled with the motion of the train as scenes from the past rolled together like the fields and towns outside my hazy window.

I chuckled to myself as I remembered a handsome, married minister from Norway and his "prayer meeting" with a farmer's daughter. I had inadvertently stumbled into the room in the middle of a not-so-holy kiss. One word to Mama sent an S.O.S. to Norway, and the secret code between wives resulted in action. Sooner than expected, the minister's adorable wife arrived on the scene. The curly-haired, saucy-eyed wife charmed her way into the hearts of everyone, especially Mama. The wife never made reference to the reason for the surprise visit, except to let the farmer's daughter know how much the wife had missed her charming husband. Chuckling over a cup of coffee, Mama and the wife agreed: "You do your part, God will do the rest." The subdued husband and his sparkling wife blended together like coffee and cream. When Papa spoke highly of that devoted couple, Mama smiled over her coffee cup.

"There are some things you tell, and some things you don't tell," Mama had said to me when I told her of my abrupt interruption of the hungry kiss. Her look told me that I had been entrusted with a secret—that we were to keep this as ours.

I wondered what had happened to another girl, Karen, who had loved Lars, a tall, curly haired immigrant. Out of a sense of obligation, Lars had married Bertha, a shy childhood friend from Norway. I remember Karen's sad face in the crowd at the wedding. Coming down the aisle Lars met Karen's eyes. I often wondered what Mama said to Karen after the wedding, when Mama stroked her soft golden hair and whispered in her ear. Perhaps she said, "Love suffers long and is kind." Karen folded her love like a tent and let it slip quietly into the midst of memories. She grieved quietly, then moved away.

There was another night in Canada when Papa took a young husband aside and urged him to take his beautiful wife away from the source of a problem—a handsome young man from Norway, who loved her. Mama took the wife aside also. No one but those two knew what was shared over afternoon coffee. The wife returned her loyalty to her rightful lover, her husband. Years later Papa found them in another town, happy and prosperous. "We never make a mistake to do what is right in God's sight. God honors obedience," Mama had reminded me.

The conductor interrupted my thoughts with a cheerful, "Hope you are enjoying the trip; the dining car is open."

"Thank you, I am enjoying the trip and I would love a cup of coffee."

The white linen cloth, polished silver, and starched porter reminded me of home. I soon forgot the menu, but the memory of people in red plush seats, dignified, starched porters carrying white linen napkins, the sound of cups and silver, and a current of conversation between strangers still blend in my mind—a page out of another time. Through smoky windows the world rushed by, and with it that mystical girl and boy land fled, never to return. Just as the landscape of rivers, trees, villages and people, clouds, and sky blended into one moving picture, so the scenes from home blended into one picture—Mama.

That must be why Papa needs her so desperately, I thought. *She is his home, his roots, his source of life meaning, for she continually directs his steps back to faith in God.* "God entrusted Papa to me," she would say. "God knew I would love him, care for him, believe in him—and always understand him. In turn God made a promise to me—that all my children shall be taught of the Lord. God never fails."

I saw the endless stream of lonely ones that Papa brought to Mama, the universal mother. Since she was his harbor, she could harbor all the human driftwood he found along the shore. To every problem there was one answer: "God and Mama." To every grief, one solace: "Mama will understand." God had given him someone special and he had to share her with the world.

There was that Wednesday service after which the visiting speaker came home to spend the night. While we girls were setting out our floor pallets, Mama asked the gentle white-haired Pastor Anderson what he would like to eat before retiring. "Oyster stew," he announced confidently.

We gasped! No one had seen an oyster in our house, much less eaten one.

Without flinching, Mama went to the kitchen and toasted her homemade bread, cut pieces in small squares, and poured scalded milk over the toast. Seasoned with salt, pepper, and butter, she placed a china bowl full of her "oyster stew" before the elderly guest.

"This is the best oyster stew I have ever eaten," he boasted on Mama's behalf. "Now I would like a cup of silver tea."

Into a fine china cup Mama poured boiling water, with cream and sugar: her own concoction for children and the elderly. Pastor Anderson enjoyed his "silver tea" while Papa drank his coffee. I still remember the look of admiration and wonder when Papa's eyes met Mama's laughing eyes. He was remembering her maxim: "It is not the problems, but how you meet them that counts. You do your part and God will do the rest—even in making oyster stew."

I wondered if I would be able to do my part as well as she had. My marriage to Harold Jensen (a Dane who knew how to celebrate a Norwegian Christmas) was fast approaching. Our good friend Barney had married Mildred, his anchor in the time of storm. The fires of romance and dreaming had burned out, at least for a time, and Barney had settled into a comfortable marriage of stability and companionship. I toyed with the idea of moving to New York, to be near my family, but I had made a commitment. With it came the knowledge that this bird couldn't return to the nest. One by one Mama's children would learn to fly. As the sentimental eldest I sighed for a time that would never be again—the simple days of childhood when Mama had been able to fix anything and everything.

"Grand Central Station!" Like a snorting horse the train thundered into the station. On the platform stood Papa, handsome as always, and impatient to get me home to Mama and a cup of coffee. Happy and talkative, he seemed pleased to have his first-born again under his roof.

"Come to New York, Margaret! You will love it. There is so much to see. Tomorrow I'll take you to the library, then to Carnegie Hall where Grace takes her piano lessons. You must see it all, the Statue of Liberty, the harbor and ferry boats, the great churches, Wall Street, Fifth Avenue, Radio City, Coney Island, Brooklyn, and the church on Fifty-seventh Street. You will love the people. You still want to marry a Dane? Oh *ja*, Harold is fine—could be taken for a Norwegian. Come, run and we catch the subway." Even the suitcase couldn't slow him down until we were seated, breathless, on the subway heading to Brooklyn. He continued, "Mama is very popular—and very beautiful. She wears the pearls," he chuckled.

As the subway thundered through the underground, I remembered the pearls: The Depression had been in full swing. The cupboard had been bare and we were anxiously awaiting Papa's payday. Instead of giving the money to Mama, the church treasurer had given it directly to Papa. What a tragic mistake!

57

Mama was the one to dole out streetcar tokens and an occasional nickel for a cup of coffee, but Papa was noted for his liberal "giving freely all things." He had no concept of what feeding his family involved—nitty gritty scrimping and saving. Walking past a jewelry shop he saw a lovely string of pearls. At the same time, he felt the money in his pocket. Overjoyed at discovering his wealth, he purchased the pearls.

Bowing low, in great respect, he handed her the gift. "Mama, I suddenly realized I had never bought you a present. You have such a beautiful throat, you should wear pearls."

Mama never flinched. Tenderly she thanked him for the generous gift and promised to wear them always. She did! Later she told me, "There is a time and place for everything. Sometimes we need pearls more than potatoes. That was the time for pearls." Mama somehow saw that we survived until next payday.

"Next stop, Margaret." We emerged from the tunnel and walked past row houses, side by side, like children's blocks. Every plot of ground was neatly planted full of shrubs and flowers. On the front steps sat mothers and grandmothers keeping a watchful eye on all the neighborhood young playing on the one-way streets.

Soon we were sitting in Mama's kitchen drinking coffee, laughing and talking—all at the same time. Starched lace curtains covered shining windows, and, in its proper place, the round mahogany table stood with the crystal vase. The upholstered furniture had been recovered, and a new carpet lay on the parlor floor. The dining room table was set for supper. Soon the family would be coming from school and work. Grace worked for the Y.M.C.A., earning thirty-five dollars a week. Doris and Gordon helped to carry the load with after-school jobs. Gordon had survived five sisters and a preacher-father, and had become one of the Brooklyn boys who played stickball in the streets. Joyce was cute, lovable, and sassy. She livened up her world with her own renditions of modern-day songs. Papa only heard her angelic voice—not the words of the songs. So if her voice were magic it seemed to make Papa blind to the lipstick, and deaf to her flirting phone calls that drove the boys wild. She even won a jitterbug contest. "*Lilla Solveig*" just had to sing for Papa "Flee as a bird to yon mountain," and his restless spirit quieted.

Jeanelle, the baby, was everyone's beloved. She was the joy of Mama's heart and the pride and delight of Papa's life, yet she managed to grow up unspoiled by it all. Years later she told me she once came home singing a popular tune, "A Little Bit Independent," and convinced Mama she had learned it in Sunday school.

Grace was Papa's church pianist, secretary, and confidante. She was his bridge over troubled family relationships. Grace set the pace in fashion and became a link between Mama's structured world and the cultural advantages of New York. Music was the common denominator in the family—just as long as it wasn't too "vorldly." Watching her so poised and self-assured I could hardly believe she was the mischievous sister who had gotten me into trouble as a child. It had been her idea to put soap on the kitchen floor, making it a skating rink or dance floor. That was fine—until I waltzed into Papa.

I was told how Barney miraculously walked in, out of the blue, during several stormy sessions. One such incident involved Papa discovering that Doris was in love with the Italian boy who worked at the local fruit market. Barney stepped in and kept Doris from running away from home. She had hidden under the porch, waiting for Papa's fury to subside. When she heard Barney's songs and laughter, she knew it was safe to "come home." It was good to know that Barney, with his Mildred, was still a part of our family: in Canada, in Chicago, and now in Brooklyn.

One by one, I watched the family gather around the table for supper, and, in unison, we asked the familiar Norwegian blessing. We eagerly passed the old bowls, full of meatballs and gravy and mashed potatoes, sculptured and decorated with parsley. The creamed cabbage, peas, and carrots followed close behind. Lemon pie with whipped cream topped the dinner, and the endless cups of coffee completed the festive meal. Papa retreated to his study, while we children washed the dishes and chattered above the clatter. When we had put away the last dish and cleaned the sink until it sparkled, we all gathered in the parlor for music. Before retiring, we enjoyed a last cup of coffee and a quiet time of talk.

Mama was happy. God had allowed her to be close to Bestemör Bertilda, who lived in a small apartment within walking distance. Bestemör, who had known unbearable loneliness, was now surrounded by her children and grandchildren.

Some years later, on Easter Sunday, Bestemör sat down, folded her hands, and died. In quiet dignity, and dressed in her church-going best, she said a temporary "good night" to her precious children, Elvine and Joe, but a glorious "good morning" to her Lord—and Bernice. Jeanelle was the only one who overheard Mama sobbing out all her hurts and griefs when Bestemör died. Perhaps it was all the loneliness of her childhood that surfaced—but not for long. Mama washed her face, combed her hair, tied on a starched apron, and put on the coffee pot.

The Sunday after I returned home we all walked to church. Papa, with reverent dignity, announced the opening hymn, "A Mighty Fortress Is Our God." Every head turned to nod to the pastor's daughter who was visiting from Chicago. There was a depth of understanding, compassion, and mutual love that held these people together in an ever-increasing faith in God—and America. No one was allowed to be disrespectful to authority. They stood up for the National Anthem—even in the bathtub.

At the conclusion of the service I was welcomed into the family of Papa's church on Fifty-seventh Street.

During the week I was introduced to Brooklyn's Fifth Avenue, lined with small shops representing all the nationalities. I pushed Mama's cart to the fish market, where everyone spoke Norwegian. Each member of Mama's family and then each member of the proprietor's family had to be accounted for. The Danish bakery was fragrant with Danish pastry, and the displayed wedding cakes were works of art. It was obvious that the Polish storekeeper kept up with the neighborhood children. We got Kosher dill pickles from a barrel in the Jewish delicatessen. The Italian fruit stand was a gathering place for everyone—especially the young.

"This is America, Margaret," exclaimed Mama, as if I didn't

know. "No place in the world like this." Mama beamed, for she loved her international neighbors and stopped to visit along the way with all of them. "A little visit, Margaret, sometimes catches a problem before it is too late. Besides, I learn whom to invite for coffee. A little talk with someone, and a little talk with God—it all helps to keep the wheels of the neighborhood running smoothly." Mama had her own way of curbing my impatience to get the shopping over with as soon as possible.

Weddings, births, music lessons, and report cards were duly reported along the way. Such topics make conversation flow in any language. The immigrants shared a mutual interest in each other's children, the first generation of Americans.

Over coffee cups I heard stories from Norway. From Mama's girlhood friends, whom I had never met before, I heard old tales about their fears of the unknown land, their dreams for their children, and their struggle to learn the new language. I sensed the treasure of friendships, deeply rooted in mutual respect and need, but matured with the sun and rain of joy and sorrow. The tapestry of lifelong friendships was made with the perfect blend of brightly-colored threads and pastel shades of patience and thankfulness.

Before returning to Chicago, I took one last ride on the Staten Island ferry. Across dark waters I saw the Lady with the Lamp looking out over the harbor. A lonely fog horn woke the lure of the sea that had slept deep within me. In my heart I crossed the Atlantic to the fjords and cliffs I had never seen. Someday I would. Wrapping my coat around me I wondered how the fifteen-year-old Elvine felt when the ocean liner eased into the embrace of the Lady with the Lamp.

I was about to venture into my own new world. My trip would not take me across the ocean, but down the aisle of Papa's church to take my place beside Harold who would there, in front of all these Brooklyn witnesses, to become my husband.

I yearned to complete my journey as well as Mama had hers—both her journey in the new land and her journey beside Papa. I trusted she had taught me well.

And so it came to pass that I married Harold in Papa's

61

church on June 30, 1938. Gordon and all my dear sisters stood with me, facing Papa and hearing his solemn words.

After our honeymoon trip to Cooperstown, New York, Niagara Falls, and down through Canada, we returned to Chicago where we began our new life together. I continued nursing while Harold completed his graduate degree at Northern Baptist Theological Seminary.

13

"Love It Back to Life, Mother"

"Standing on the promises, watching all the girls go by."

The five-year-old singer stood in the reception hall, feet firmly planted and arms folded across his starched white shirt and bow tie. His polished shoes shone on the soft carpet, and his blond hair, parted on one side, was slick and trim. He sang with all the confidence of a seasoned performer and enjoyed the applause of his amused audience—the guests attending the annual open house. This was his first day in the Norwegian Children's Home, Brooklyn, New York.

After ten years in Chicago, and in answer to "the call," Papa and Mama had moved back to Brooklyn. I had become a graduate nurse and stayed on in Chicago to work at the Lutheran Deaconess Hospital.

Mama, unaware of the "one-man show" in the reception hall, was giving her full attention to the last-minute details of hosting the children's home open house.

Enjoying a brief visit to New York, I followed Mama around and was utterly amazed at her ability to attend to innumerable details when she was continually interrupted to answer a child's question or to make an important decision. She flowed through the days like a river, bringing refreshment to many a dry bank. She reminded me of the man described in Psalm 1, who was "a tree planted by the rivers of water."

Mama also had received a call. "The board of directors asked me to be the superintendent of the children's home, a place for homeless Norwegian children. The parents of some are very ill. Others are missing or dead. The children from a family are kept together, so, here I am, a mother again."

The wise men behind the scenes saw the compassionate heart of a universal mother, and an ability to discipline and motivate others in love. God saw an obedient child, walking out her loving faith in Him who could do anything, who would never fail her.

So, Mama accepted the call to become the superintendent of the Norwegian Children's Home. Papa served as chaplain and social worker. They relinquished the pastorate at the First Norwegian Baptist Church to serve together in the children's home, but the fellowship and worship in their local church continued.

Today was open house. The warm sunlight cast a glow over the neatly trimmed gardens. Every room in the beautiful brick house was in order. The children had been rehearsing songs and readings, and, of course, proper manners. Bright hairbows and matching socks complemented polished shoes, ruffles, and lace. The boys stood like starched penguins in dark suits and white shirts. Every hair rested in place. Only mischievous eyes refused conformity.

Johnny, the new boy, had arrived in time to be scrubbed, combed, and outfitted in a new suit. He had been told that visitors were coming to see him. He was to stand still and watch. He stood still, but couldn't resist putting on a show.

Within moments of his rendition of standing and watching, he was gathered into perfumed arms and smothered with kisses. When an older boy led him away, Johnny waved happily to all the new-found friends who had come to see him.

Yesterday he had been alone. His mother had been taken to King's County Hospital, and no one could find his father. A distant relative brought him to the "home," where he discovered a new family life.

The ruffled girls swished alongside their guests and excitedly showed them their treasures—quilts they had made for their beds and stuffed animals that kept a silent watch over the neat dormitory. Mama insisted that each child have a box of his or her own in which to store personal treasures. I overheard one girl: "I never had a treasure box before, and no one can peek. I made my quilt. Debbie is five. She is my little sister and I take care of her. I help her dress and lay out her clothes for kindergarten. I braid her pigtails and match her socks and ribbons. I taught her to tie her laces and the bow on her dress. Each one has a brother or sister. Like a family, you know. Some have visitors, but I have no one. Will you be my visitor?"

An older woman, plump and silver-haired, squeezed the girl's hand and, in her soft Norwegian accent, promised to be her visitor. She opened her purse and pulled out a perfumed handkerchief, "Karen, put this in your treasure box, and next time I'll bring you a picture. Perhaps we can take a picture of you, for me to keep." That was the beginning of a long friendship.

"Young man, I understand you'll soon be eighteen and leaving the home."

"Yes, sir, but I don't know where to go," Tom answered the distinguished white-haired executive he was escorting on the tour of the boys' dormitory.

"I'll be your friend and help you get to college or find a job. Here's my card, just call me anytime. We can always find time to talk things over. By the way, what happened to you, young man? The last time I was here you were skipping out at night and having problems at school. In fact, several of you boys were about to be sent to correctional school. What happened?"

"Mother Tweten, that's what happened.

"I'll never forget the first night she came to our dormitory. We had planned some bold adventures and waited for her to make her rounds. Instead, she sat down on Bob's bed, sang Norwegian songs, and read the Bible and prayed for each one of us by name. She got up and kissed us all good night and told us she loved us. When she left she stood by the door and said, 'God bless you, *my* boys.' We couldn't carry out our plans. The next night she sat on Ted's bed, told a story, read, sang, and prayed. She kissed us good night and said 'God bless you, *my* boys.'

"Then one night she came in and sat on the wrong bed. Bill jumped up and said, 'You sat on Ted's bed twice. It's my turn tonight.' None of us went to reform school. The tough guy, Bill, got saved at the Billy Graham Crusade in Madison Square Garden. The next night he made Bob go forward, 'Get saved or I'll beat you up!' he said."

Downstairs in the dining room an air of festivity reigned. The older boys cared for the younger and the guests were served by happy children. Church groups and women's clubs mingled with dignitaries from government and businessmen, along with news reporters. The children sensed their importance and rose with honor to the occasion. This was a special day; Mama had made them a part of the festivities.

No one had believed that forty to fifty children could be beautifully disciplined in gracious courtesy. But they didn't know Mama!

Papa, handsome as ever, enjoyed the guests and with great flourish practiced all his old Norwegian jokes. The businessmen who had founded the home looked at their fulfilled dream.

Mama saw the thread of love that had been interwoven between frightened children and these adults—lonely immigrants who had persevered at building schools, hospitals, even the children's home. Mama was proud of her children. When they performed before their enthusiastic audience, a sense of worth crept into their once frightened, empty hearts. They basked in the love and approval of their mother and felt safe within the walls of their home.

To conclude the day's program, Mama told the story of the dead plant.

"One day Susie came in from the playground, holding a broken pot with a wilted plant in her muddy hands.

"She begged me, 'Please don't throw away the plant.'

"'But Susie, the plant is dead,' I said.

"'Then you must love it back to life, Mother.'

"She thrust the wilted plant into my hand and skipped away, completely confident that its life would return. I placed the remains of this plant in a new flower pot filled with fresh dirt. The sun filtered through the Brooklyn skies and warmed the lifeless plant that sat on my windowsill. Every day I watered my little wilted garden and waited. One day a green shoot appeared, and now a lovely green plant thrives on my sill.

"When someone brings us a frightened, wilted, hurt child, I hear my Susie say, 'Love it back to life, Mother!' So many human relationships can be loved back to life. For me the most rewarding relationships are those one has with children, who have been wilted and abandoned in a broken flower pot or home. For a child who then is thrust into my hand, 'Love him back to life' is my highest command. You people of Norway gave me a flower pot, this lovely home, and God pours His love through us—to love them back to life.

"I thank you."

The sun set over the gardens and brick walls. The children were tucked in their beds. The steps of the guests had echoed down the walk. The door had closed behind them. Mama sat down to a quiet cup of coffee. The amber glow of love had laid a warm blanket over the weak and strong together. She opened her Bible and read, "Inasmuch as ye have done it unto one of the least of these my brethren, ye have done it unto me" (Matthew 25:40).

14

Someone to Come Home To

Mama closed the door to her office and slumped to her knees in utter exhaustion. "I can't go on! I can't!" She wept into her folded arms. "My strength is gone! I cry to Thee, oh Lord, for Thou alone are my strong tower. Even Moses cried to You when the task was too great. You said, 'Moses, there is a place by Me, in the cleft of the rock, until the storm passes by.' I know You are Creator of heaven and earth—a God of miracles. Today I ask one special thing: Please send me a cook."

Homesick for her beloved land, the cook had left suddenly for Norway. In addition to all the administrative duties, Mama had to fill the void in the kitchen, cooking for forty-five children.

Days, months, and years were speeding out of control, like a train that wouldn't stop. She tried to get off some place, to acclimate herself to life on solid ground, but the train moved faster.

She arose quietly and opened her Bible. "They that wait upon the LORD shall renew their strength; they shall mount up with wings as eagles; they shall run, and not be weary; and they shall walk, and not faint" (Isaiah 40:31). "Come unto me, all ye

that labour and are heavy laden, and I will give you rest"
(Matthew 11:28).

As she did every day, Mama spoke to the silent pictures of
her own children. All but Jeanelle had flown Mama's nest;
Mama prayed for us across the miles. "Oh, my children, God is
your refuge. He never fails." Turning the pages of her Bible, she
read again, "I will never leave thee, nor forsake thee," and "I can
do all things through Christ which strengtheneth me."

Quietly, softly, the Word became a living sound. By rote
Mama repeated verses that floated randomly through her mind.
"The Lord is my light and my salvation." "God is my refuge and
strength." "Casting all your care upon Him for He careth for
you."

The quiet was broken by an insistent knock at the door.
"There is someone to see you, Mrs. Tweten."

Pausing for a moment, Mama breathed in the strength that
God had renewed in her. She allowed the mantle of love to cover
her with the "peace that passeth understanding." She closed
her Bible and went to the door to greet her visitor.

Before her stood a plump Norwegian woman. In broken
English she said, "I don't speak much English, but I need vork.
Could you use a cook?"

"Before they call, I will answer," came to Mama's mind.

A few days later a distraught mother with six children came
to Mama's waiting room. "Please take my children!" she pleaded.
Huddled in silent fear, the children clung to their mother's skirt.
"I can't go on! My strength is gone and I can't manage another
day!"

"Come, let's have a cup of coffee, and we can talk," comforted
Mama. The children ate cookies apprehensively and watched
quietly. "I recently said those same words," continued Mama,
"but God gave me an answer. Let me read it to you. We'll pray
together and ask God for a miracle. In the meantime, just hold
on for one week. Keep your children with you. They need you.
Trust Him for a miracle, and see what happens."

"Yes, I'll try a little longer," she answered. She gathered her
children and returned home.

Weeks passed before Mama remembered the distraught

woman and decided to visit her. When she saw the abandoned rat-infested basement flat she had sent the woman back to, she wept. No wonder the woman had given up—or had she? Where could she have gone?

An elderly man, leaning on a cane, called to Mama, "Hey, lady, they ain't here no more. She was going to put her kids in an orphanage and then she decided to try one more week. You know something? The old man got a real good job in Chicago and came for her and the kids. He had a nice clean flat—an upstairs flat with steam heat—waiting for them. It happened so fast, lady. In a week they were gone."

"Oh, thank you, sir, and God bless you. I'll come back to visit you." Mama remembered, "Who comforteth us in all our tribulation, that we may be able to comfort them which are in any trouble, by the comfort wherewith we ourselves are comforted of God" (2 Corinthians 1:4).

Returning to the children's home, Mama opened the door humming softly one of her favorite songs, "Be not dismayed whate'er betide; God will take care of you."

The nurse met Mama at the door. "Bobby is sick."

"Not Bobby!"

Impulsively, Mama picked a flower from the patch by the porch and took it to Bobby. His fever was high and he breathed heavily. Within moments Dr. Fanta was on his way and four-year-old Bobby was taken to Lutheran Deaconess Hospital in Brooklyn. In his hands he clutched the wilting flower.

Mama went with him, but she couldn't stay away from the home all day.

"I'll be back, Bobby. I have work to do, but I'll be back to see you later. Just hold the flower and let it remind you that I'll be back." With these words Mama left to attend to administrative duties. In the meantime the nurses talked amongst themselves, "Too bad his mother is dead," commented one. "He has no one, you know."

Half-asleep Bobby overheard the words that floated through the door, "His mother is dead. He has no one." He drifted into a semi-coma, and some time passed before he was fully con-

70

scious again. Suddenly he sat up. The first thing he saw was Mama holding fresh flowers.

"You're not dead! You're not dead!"

"No, Bobby. Of course I'm not dead. And you are my boy. You'll always belong to me, no matter how old you get."

He fell asleep, clutching a fresh flower, and Mama sat beside him, praying and singing.

Everyone needs to belong to someone, Mama thought. *God says we belong to Him. He bought us with His Son.*

One day when the "big boys," fourteen- to sixteen-year-olds, were helping in the kitchen, Mama overheard their conversation: "When we become eighteen we have to leave the home," one boy said.

Another commented, "I'm going into the service."

A third boy said, "I'm going to college."

The fourth boy was quiet.

"What are you thinking about?" Mama asked Tommy.

"Mother, who will we come home to when we go away?"

"Boys, you can come home to me!"

"Will you always be here?"

"You can come home, wherever I am."

The boys finished their chores. Giving Mama an impulsive hug, Tommy reassured himself, "We have to have someone to come home to."

Mama remembered Psalm 90:1: "LORD, thou hast been our dwelling place [our Home] in all generations."

We all have Someone to come home to.

15

St. Olav's Medal

It was a beautiful November day in Georgia. Red and gold leaves outside my kitchen window looked like a patchwork quilt. Kennesaw Mountain loomed in the distance, a sentinel against the blue sky. *Tomorrow*, I thought, *I will rake the leaves, but now I will enjoy a cup of coffee and look over the morning mail.* There it was—a letter from Mama, in her own characteristic handwriting (which we had, over the years, learned to interpret).

Sunday, November 16, 1951

Dear Margaret, Harold, and children,

Thank you for your letter, and I am glad all is well.

Tonight I have extra news! I was decorated last night with the St. Olav's Medal from King Haaken of Norway.

We had our annual banquet—set for two hundred people, with outstanding speakers and a fine program. The Norwegian consul, who has been our guest speaker for the last five years, was here last night. At the close of his speech he asked me to come forward. Then he spoke of the work I had done at the home and recommended that I get the St. Olav's Medal. (The king had been told of my work.) He pinned the medal on me and gave me a diploma with the king's seal and signature. All the people stood. I just could not talk, but I had to say something, so I said, "I only wish my six children were here. I do not deserve it, but I take it. Grace and love from God." The photographer was there and pictures will be in the *Nordisk Tidende* (Norwegian Times). I will send you the paper. Fortunately, I had on a beautiful black velvet dress, made to order for the banquet.

When I was in the hospital last year, the president of the children's home came to see me and we had a long visit. He asked about the family, past and present—where we had lived, what churches we had pastored, and where all you children are now.

I suppose the record is with the king. Something for the children and grandchildren to remember. You know this is next to the highest honor given by the Norwegian government. I still can't believe it. I wonder what Dad will think, when he hears. It is already in the papers in Norway. If I lived there, I would have to go to the king and thank him personally, but here I will do it through the consul. Well, I thank the Lord for it all. I know I now have a greater responsibility and I need the Lord all the more. Don't forget to pray for me.

I wore the new velvet dress and medal to church this morning.

Doris, Gordon, and families are coming for Thanksgiving.

> With love to all of you,
> Your loving mother

My coffee was cold, but warm tears fell in my lap—tears of gratitude for the honor Mama so richly deserved and tears for all of us who hadn't been there to rejoice with her.

I knew no photographer could have caught the wistfulness of Mama saying, "I wish my children were here." I thought about "the children"—Grace, working in New York, Gordon, married and teaching in New York. Doris was graduated from Wheaton

College and married to David Hammer. Joyce Solveig was married to Harold's brother, Howard. Jeanelle, the baby, was studying at Columbia Bible College.

I found myself back in the Norwegian diary reliving the fright of a fifteen-year-old immigrant girl, determined to find her mother. I saw her as the faithful servant in a Jewish home, using her leisure hours to probe libraries. I was back on the Canadian prairie, listening to the promise: "The bluebirds will come; just wait and see." Humility and dignity walked with her as the garment of praise covered her. "Always keep a thankful heart, Margaret." My mind's image of the coffee pot sitting on the cookstove reminded me to refill my cup and look ahead. Mama would go to see the king. Of that I was sure!

I was also sure that when the day came for her to stand before the King of Kings, she would proudly say, "I am glad my children are here."

Three years later, in July 1954, Mama boarded the *Stavangerfjord* and visited her beloved Norway. She traveled with Papa, visiting his homestead, their relatives, and friends. They kept his speaking engagements. She saw the country, the cities, even the palace and the king, with whom she had a fifteen-minute audience to thank him for the medal. What a thrill that was for her. He made her feel as though she were sitting in her own parlor and talking to a good friend.

She and Papa saw the church of Norway firsthand and rejoiced in God's work among His people.

The letters winged back and forth to us children. When I read the reports of her activities, I marveled at her endurance and wondered at the grace of God, who chooses His vessels, not always the great and powerful, but even this small, humble, obedient, faithful child of His.

She came home in September, returning to her forty needy charges. But we, her six children and twelve grandchildren, had missed her as much as those who lived in the children's home.

She settled back into her mothering duties and God continued to bless her faithfulness. Early in 1959 she sent me a copy of the children's home annual report, showing God's presence.

Annual Report To
The Norwegian Children's Home Association
January 20, 1959

"They that trust in the LORD shall be as mount Zion, which cannot be removed, but abideth for ever. As the mountains are round about Jerusalem, so the LORD is round about his people from henceforth even for ever" (Psalm 125:1-2).

It has been a blessing all through the year to know and realize this truth, that as mountains are round about Jerusalem, so the Lord is round about His people. We have felt it as a large family. The Lord has been round about us. He has protected us from sickness and sorrow. He has guided us through our problems and has supplied all of our needs and blessed us with His own presence.

We started the year with thirty-six children. Ten have been admitted and eleven discharged, so that at the end of the year we had thirty-five children, twenty-two boys and thirteen girls.

Some time ago, I was telling the Christmas story to the nursery group—how the shepherds were out on the field taking care of the sheep and the lambs, and how the angel came from heaven with the good news that the Baby Jesus was born—a Savior was born—and the whole choir of angels came and sang, "Glory to God in the highest." When all the angels went back to heaven, the shepherds said, "Come on, let us go to Bethlehem and see this thing—let us go and find the Baby Jesus," and so they went to Bethlehem to find Jesus.

One little boy spoke up and said, "Who took care of the sheep while the shepherds went away?" Well in all my days, I had never thought of that before. Just who did take care of the sheep while the shepherds went away? You have to answer a child, and I think I said something like, "God would take care of them." Anyway, the child was satisfied, but later I started thinking. Who takes care of our homes and our children while we go about our duties? We send thirty children to school every morning. They go to five different schools, in five different directions, so it would be impossible for me to follow them and watch over them. Who takes care of them? God.

I pray every morning, "God bless the children as they go to school; watch over those at home." The Lord is round about His people, and we humbly bow in thanksgiving and praise.

As I continued reading the ten-page report, I was amazed at the variety of cultural and stimulating activities scheduled for each month.

The report concluded with:

We fixed up a party for New Year's Eve, and as the hours grew late, we sat around the table and read part of Psalm 92, then thanked the Lord for His faithfulness and many blessings. "It is a good thing to give thanks unto the LORD, and to sing praises unto thy name, O most High: to shew forth thy lovingkindness in the morning, and Thy faithfulness every night."

Thus we entered prayerfully into the new year of 1959.

"For everything there is a season." The days and months added up to seventeen years of loving service at the Norwegian Children's Home. But now it was time to softly close that door and reopen another. Papa returned to his first love, the pulpit of the church on Fifty-seventh Street. Together they walked through the old door, a little slower, but in step with God's plan for the years ahead.

King Haaken could be proud of his people. One day his son Olav, the new king of Norway, would visit the Norwegian Children's Home in Brooklyn and pay tribute to the hard work and warm hearts of those people. They came to America, not only to be blessed, but to give back blessings with good measure and running over.

16

The Dress

Older now, Mama sat rocking gently, the bright wool afghan wound around her bony knees. Staring out across the quiet lake below our house, she sang softly to herself. A faraway look filled her eyes; her mind was somewhere in the "long ago." Janice, who had come for a visit, heard her murmur, "Love and forgive. Love and forgive."

"Bestemör, you are talking to yourself again," Jan laughed as she pulled up a stool to snuggle close to her. The house was quiet with the contentment that comes when those you love have returned home and are close by your side.

Pressing Mama's thin, blue-veined hand against her own soft, younger cheek, Jan asked, "What were you reading?"

Mama stroked the open Bible lovingly. "When ye stand praying, forgive" (Mark 11:25).

"But, Bestemör, there are some things you can't forgive."

I knew Jan was in for a story.

Stroking Jan's soft blond hair, Bestemör rocked a little slower and added, "I'll tell you a story, Janice. We'll call the girl Mary and the man John.

"It happened a long time ago." I reached for my coffee cup and listened from the kitchen. I had heard the story a few days before, but had promised not to tell it.

Bestemör's white hair framed her gentle face, and her blue eyes held that distant look. Jan waited. These were moments she would hold in her heart forever. She would remember, and tell her children.

Mary was young, filled with dreams of love for her husband, John, and her love for God and His service. John, restless and impatient in his new pastorate in the farmlands of Wisconsin, longed for the libraries and action of New York City or Chicago, where he had attended seminary. John's brilliant mind craved books. Mary saw beauty in everything—the smell of the freshly plowed fields, the song of a bird, the first signs of spring, crocuses and violets.

She tied her tiny daughter to her lap while she drove the horse and buggy to the country church. John would ride with Deacon Olsen to gather parishioners along the way. Mary sang to the wind and laughed with the birds. But she had one secret longing . . . a new dress for spring. Not the somber brown or black that befit a minister's wife, but a soft voile billowing dress with lace around the neck and sleeves, and a big sash.

There was no money!

Carefully she laid plans: She would put pennies into a box until there was enough money to buy a new kerosene lamp for John and material for a new dress. She would reuse the lace from an old velvet dress in the trunk. Someday she would make a blue velvet dress for baby Louise.

The day came when the treadle machine purred like music while Mary sang and sewed. Golden-haired Louise played with empty spools and clothespins. The small house shone clean. She had managed to save enough money, and the new lamp had a place of honor on John's reading table. Violets filled a bowl on the starched tablecloth, and cups were placed for afternoon coffee when John would return home.

A young preacher in his first church, John raced over the country roads on his horse. He was always in a hurry to fulfill his tasks. One day, he was as restless as the wind. He was remembering his boyhood days in Norway: cows and chickens, horses and pigs, crops and weather. In Norway, after early morning chores, he had run the four miles to school, over the rocky mountain roads to the place of books and learning. Always he dreamed of a time he would have books and more books to study, and he would learn all he could.

Then that time had come! He had come to America, and at seventeen years of age, he enrolled in the Baptist Theological Seminary affiliated with Chicago University.

Now, in Woodville, everything within him cried out for the throbbing city of Chicago. As he rode, he remembered sleeping in the furnace room and being the automatic stoker for the huge furnaces. Mr. Anderson, the cook, had brought waffles and coffee to keep him awake.

John had his books, the vast resources of a great library. There were other scholars with whom to enjoy stimulating discussions and share ideas. There were museums, art galleries, parks, concerts, and people of all races with differing views.

And there was the great Moody Bible Institute with its scholarly Bible teachers, and its access to his favorite reading—Spurgeon's volumes.

John's horse trotted along the country road in Woodville, keeping step with thoughts that went stepping into the past. He felt a twinge of regret at the memory of selling Mary's piano for books. He knew it was Mary's own upright piano, bought with her own money before their marriage—money earned as a maid. It did not seem important that she had not run her fingers over the keyboard once more before he sold it. *But surely any sensible woman can see the value of books,* he argued with himself. *The piano can wait.*

The horse raced faster and the restless rider became more frustrated. "I must have books!" he shouted to the wind. "I can't live without books! Surely there must be a way to save money—and I need a new lamp for reading late at night."

In a playful mood, Mary pulled down her long brown hair, brushing it in the morning sun. Then she put on her new dress, soft pink voile with violets and lace. She tied the sash in the back and swung around to the delightful squeals of Louise. It was spring! She was young, just twenty-three, with another new life within her and Louise to rock and love. The wilderness church, the somber immigrants tilling the land, and the severe harshness of long winters had isolated the young wife, and she had furnished her world with poetry and song. She grew to love the faithful people and shared their joys and sorrows.

But today was spring and she danced with unbounded joy in her new billowing dress.

The long winter was over. The breeze blew softly through Mary's starched curtains. She was tired of the black and brown dresses befitting the ministry, tired of having her hair up in a bun. After all, she was only twenty-three. And it was spring.

She couldn't wait to show off for her handsome, unpredictable husband. The baby within her stirred. She sang joyously.

When John rode along the road, he stopped at farms, listened to the farmers' daily woes, read Scripture, prayed for the families, comforted the lonely and sick, and brought news from town to town. There was always time for a cup of coffee and for some stories to bring laughter and joy to the homes of this strong, productive community. He loved all those people and was a part of them, but that day he felt like a dry well. His usual ruddy complexion was pasty, his quick smile restrained.

He wondered if anyone really understood the time and effort he put into his sermons, the planned outlines, the research into Greek and Hebrew. Still, in church, the farmers nodded and the women and children listened politely. Then there was Mary's face in the audience. Her glowing expression never wavered, her eyes brimming with pride and her hands folded in prayer. To her, each sermon was his best.

But he was dry. He needed fresh springs of water—books! That was what he needed! His restless spirit mingled with a complaining spirit. Self-pity edged in with cruel cunning. Now he was angry—angry to be without a challenge, cut off from stimulating resources. And now there was a new baby on the way and that meant even less money.

Wasn't this how it was when he was a child in Norway? Sickness and death, hard work, loneliness, and fear. But he'd had his schoolbooks—his best friend. And his guitar. Even that was gone, though, given to his sister when he left Norway for America.

John felt empty! This wasn't how he dreamed it would be. He dreamed of greater opportunities, universities, perhaps teaching. He dreamed of challenging audiences, travel—and more books!

The horse trotted at an even pace but now John was angry. Angry at circumstances. Angry at God.

"After all, I have given my life to serve You, God, and now I am back where I used to be—crops and cows."

Sadness engulfed him. He would go home—home to Mary for a cup of coffee. Perhaps Mary had saved some money and he could get books. That was it. Perhaps Mary would have the answer, the money. He turned his horse around, but the anger mounted within him.

Before Mary realized how time had flown, she heard the galloping hoofs of John's horse. The door opened and her heart leaped. John was home, and she twirled around in the swirling softness of voile and violets.

But suddenly, without warning, the storm broke! Blinded by fury, John saw only that the last hope for books was gone.

With the flash of summer lightning, the frustration unleashed the fury within John. He whirled Mary around to face him, shouting, "Foolishness, money for foolishness when I need books! No libraries, no books, no one to talk to about anything except cows and chickens, planting and harvest, and now this foolishness!" Erupting with rage, John ripped the dress to shreds. Just as suddenly, the storm was over, and the galloping hoofs of John's horse broke the quiet terror. As he rode into the wind he unleashed the remainder of his unbridled anger on the passing fields and their wide-eyed cows and clucking chickens. He longed to gallop from Wisconsin to the heart of New York to his beloved library.

Huddled in a corner, Mary clutched Louise and the shredded dress. Trembling with fear and anger, she remained motionless.

Like a wounded bird, Mary moaned in agony of soul and body. Then she gathered the tattered dress, folded it in a small

81

package, and hid it in her trunk. This she would never forget! Too drained to weep, she was sick with an emptiness and an unutterable longing for her mother in New York. There was no one to turn to in that lonely farmland. She remembered Psalm 34:4: "I sought the LORD, and he heard me, and delivered me from all my fears." Then she wept, long and deep, and cried unto the Lord.

Bestemör paused. "Be slow to cry to man, Janice, but let your cry be unto God." She rocked slowly, then continued.

Mary set her heart to seek a way of escape. She would make a pallet up in the loft and take Louise to sleep with her. John would sleep alone.

Pastor Hansen was coming to visit the rural churches and Mary decided to bide her time, to quietly wait and show the dress to Pastor Hansen, then ask for assistance to leave John and return to New York. With quiet determination she put on her dark dress and combed her long brown hair into a severe knot, befitting a minister's wife.

When night came she put John's supper in the warming oven, gathered the baby, and climbed to the loft. With her child in her arms, she curled up on a pallet and made her plans to leave John—for a season. She would return to the security of her mother, Bertilda, in Brooklyn. She knew she would never leave John permanently, but she needed time to let her wounded spirit heal.

When John returned late in the night Mary was asleep in the loft with Louise curled in her arm.

Quietly John ate his supper and looked for Mary. When he found her in the loft, he ordered her back to their bed. Mary gently tucked Louise into her crib and obediently took her place beside John.

John's storm had passed, but he was unaware of the debris in its wake.

Life went on as usual, but the song was gone and Mary's heart was weighted with bitterness. She put one foot ahead of the other, doing routine tasks as a God-given blessing for survival.

82

There were floors to scrub, clothes to wash, endless meals to cook, not only for the family, but also for Pastor Hansen. She quietly waited and thought out her plans.

The arrival of Pastor Hansen brought a new exuberance to John as the two ministers discussed books and theology and the work of the church conference. Mary served quietly. Her sparkling windows were covered with starched curtains, the embroidered tablecloth was set with dainty coffee cups, a happy child played with a string of empty spools of thread, the smell of freshly baked bread filled the house, and Mary wore a crisp apron. The message came across that all was well.

No one would have guessed the anguish behind her gentle face as she worshiped with the faithful congregation but heard little of the sermons.

She waited for the moment to show Pastor Hansen the dress. Then she could go to Brooklyn!

The final service was drawing to a close and, as yet, Mary had not had the opportunity to see Pastor Hansen alone. She had to find the opening, perhaps this Sunday afternoon, when John would visit a shut-in member while Pastor Hansen would meditate on the evening message. With a quickened mind she decided to listen to the sermon and perhaps use his comments as an opening.

"The text this morning is found in Mark 11:25: 'When ye stand praying, forgive.' Forgiveness is not an option, but a command. Forgiveness is not a feeling, but an act of faith, a definite act of the will to forgive, in obedience to God's command. The feeling comes later, the feeling of peace. When we offer to God our hurts and despair, God will pour His love and compassion into the wounds and His healing will come."

"No! No!" Mary cried inside. "I can't forgive! And I can never forget!"

The sermon continued, thundering in her ears. "Someone may be thinking 'I can never forget, even if I could forgive.' You are right, you can't forget, but you needn't be devastated by the remembering. God's love and His forgiveness can and will cushion the memory until the imprint is gone. When you forgive you must destroy the evidence, and remember only to love. 'For God so loved the world, that He gave His only begotten Son, that whosoever believeth in Him should not perish, but have everlasting life.'

"In closing, let us stand and say the Lord's prayer. 'Forgive us our debts, as we forgive our debtors.'"

John and Pastor Hansen rode home with Deacon Olsen. Mary stepped into her buggy, tied her wide black hat with a scarf, and carefully secured Louise around her waist. As the horse, Dolly, trotted briskly down the country road, Mary's scalding tears poured forth.

Louder and clearer came the words that burned into her soul: "When you stand praying, forgive."

Back into the hidden recesses of her mind came the distant memories of her mother and grandmother making difficult choices. They chose to leave the scene of heartbreak and discover a new life. Was that the choice for her also? Should she leave John?

"Oh, God, where do I go, except to Thee? Out of my depths I cry to Thee. Lead me in Your way, the path of trust and obedience; the way of love and forgiveness—unconditional love and forgiveness." *Only within me can God bring a new beginning,* she thought. *There is no place to flee—only to the rock of ages.*

She knew what she must do. She would obey God. Without waiting to unhitch Dolly, she fled from the buggy and placed sleeping Louise in her crib. With trembling hands she took out of the trunk the package with the torn dress, but she couldn't let go. The Sunday dinner was in the warming oven; Mary poked the fire and added more wood. Automatically she put on the coffee pot and set the table. "The evidence must go" rang in her memory.

"I forgive you, John." She finally picked up the tattered dress and, holding it to her tear-stained face, she offered it to God, a sacrifice of the heart. "For You, dear Lord," she whispered. She opened the lid of the stove and held the dress above the flame. "When you forgive, you destroy the evidence," sounded within her.

Tears splashed on the fire and the dress began to burn slowly.

She heard a familiar step behind her. She turned. There stood John, a bewildered expression on his face. "What are you doing?" he asked.

"I am burning the evidence!" Mary dropped the tattered dress into the flame. Mary had made a choice—to obey God!

Then John remembered! Pale and shaken, stunned by the sudden awful realization of what he had done, he murmured, "Please forgive me, Mary."

Bestemör rocked quickly.

"Please, Grandmother, what happened?" Jan begged. Bestemör waited. Her eyes followed the ducks on the lake, but her heart was somewhere else. Softly she continued: "Now John has gone home. Fifty-eight years together, and I miss him."

Wide-eyed with understanding, Jan wrapped her arms around her beloved Bestemör! "That was you and Grandfather!" The chair rocked slowly in the quiet room as Bestemör's loving hand stroked the bowed head.

I slipped quietly down the path of fallen leaves to the lake to feed the ducks. The four white pet geese honked majestically across the lake as I drank deeply of the cool autumn breeze and felt the burden of old hurts slowly ebbing away. God's cushioning love heals old scars.

P.S. A few days later Mama had a dream. Three angels appeared to her and said, "Come, we are going to a celebration." Over the arm of one angel was draped a beautiful new dress for Mama.

17

The Golden Wedding

The first Norwegian Baptist Church on Fifty-seventh Street in Brooklyn, New York, was ablaze with light. It was June 18, 1965. People came from every direction to attend the golden wedding anniversary celebration for Pastor and Mrs. E. N. Tweten. The Polish storekeeper, the Italian fruit stand owner, the Jewish merchant, all a part of the "Oslo Boulevard" (Brooklyn's Eighth Avenue), closed their shops early to join their neighbors: the owners of the fish market, the delicatessen, the gift shop, and Christiansen's Bakery. Mingling accents from the old world joined the Scandinavians in the happy occasion meant for all of them.

Tonight Mama's children and grandchildren would pay their tribute of love by doing what Papa told the world his children could do—sing and play music. With Grace and Jeanelle at the organ and piano, Gordon directed the rehearsals. There was no doubt about it. Mama's children would sing. With her usual efficiency, Grace coordinated the festivities.

The music poured forth as visiting dignitaries joined members and friends in the pews of Papa's church. A pause—then the majestic wedding march brought every person to his feet. Mama in her golden dress came down the aisle on Papa's arm. Behind them marched friends who had attended their wedding fifty years before: Uncle Joseph Johnson, Nick Olsen, Ida Breding, Olga Bjornsen, Marie Anderson, Fred and Oline Johnson, Aslak and Ingeborg Halvorsen.

Songs from the grandchildren brought smiles of approval. Tears came to many when Mama's children and their families sang "God Leads His Dear Children Along."

When we sang in Norwegian "He the Pearly Gates Will Open," everyone smiled and nodded approval, especially Mama.

Gordon presented Mama and Papa with a large picture of us children and our families.

Papa, white hair glistening, looked at his old friends and chuckled, "*Ja,* there is only one Mama!" Mama's soft gray hair framed her glowing face. "Papa, in spite of all your faults, you have been a faithful lover." That brought down the house and paved the way for the reception that followed.

Hot coffee was poured into countless cups as guests came to the beautiful table laden with international delicacies. In the center was a large Danish layer cake, with fresh strawberries and whipped cream.

Visiting among the guests, and shaking hands with every-one, was the state senator, who was a frequent guest at these celebrations. He brought his coffee cup over and joined me for a brief visit. With a sweep of his hand, he looked over the crowd: "This is America, and I love it! This is where I get my faith in people renewed. Margaret, you must write it down, all the stories and traditions. We all need to be reminded of our heritage and what makes America!"

During the reception Mama disappeared for a few moments. She returned wearing her original wedding dress. An Italian photographer, standing close to me, exclaimed, "My God, she is simply beautiful!" Tears fell on his cheeks as he snapped pictures. Mama, whose silver hair looked like a halo and whose blue eyes brimmed with happiness, stood in her lace dress and posed for her wedding picture. Fifty years ago there had been no picture. Papa bought books instead. Tonight she had her wedding picture.

Now it was my turn to gather the memories of the past.

Fifty Golden Years

They walk in beauty from the night
To golden sunrise,
Not the sundown.
Ahead the glory of Eternal Light,
The welcome skies
And jeweled crown.

Two hearts were born from fjords and cliffs,
The midnight sun
And snow-filled dale.
Across the foamy ocean crest
A new world begun,
By God's grace blessed.

Two lives were blended into one
To give the glow
Of human touch.
Not counting cost—His will be done;
The world must know
God gave so much.

Youth with courage born of surrender,
Strength from submission
To lose, not gain,
Wove golden cords of love made tender,
Earth's highest mission,
Giving life again.

Canadian blizzards and wind-swept field,
Midnight's lone hour,
The heat of day:
Outstretched hands, humble hearts to yield
To God's power
Life—Truth—The Way.

Cold hands warmed by the open hearth,
A rocking chair
And coffee cup.
Heavy hearts turned to God's love and new birth,

A humble prayer
And a welcome sup.

The children grew with sense of belonging
To the Master's Plan,
Children of God.
To trust, obey, and serve without yearning
Ambitions to scan,
Worldly fame to plod.

Memories come with haunting remembering
Of humble fare,
A warm loaf of bread.
With love, mirth, and time for singing,
A table to share,
White linen spread.

Dad preached with fervor God's matchless grace
On wind-swept plain,
Pulpit or mission.
Mother saw the searching, lonely face,
The hidden pain
Or lost ambition.

Together they gave, no thought of gaining,
Love to a child,
Hope to mankind.
They took human driftwood without blaming
Those sin had beguiled
Or darkness made blind.

The old hymns echo through turbulent years
Of war and plunder;
Depression's hour.
God's promises stood—faith dispels fears.
Men's schemes torn asunder
By God's mighty power.

For fifty years two hearts bent tender
To give, not gain;
To lose, not win.

For greatness comes in complete surrender
In service, not fame,
God's peace within.

They walk in beauty from the night
To glorious sunrise,
Not the sundown.
Ahead the glow of Eternal Light,
Golden skies,
The Father's home.

18

The Envelope

"Don't forget the envelope, dear." Grace eased Mama's frail form against the soft pillows, and covered her cold hands with the lacy wool stole Joyce had sent from Chicago.

"No, Mama, I won't forget."

The snow swirled around the house, piling drifts along the street, which brought traffic to a halt. It was Sunday, January 9, 1977, when Greensboro, North Carolina, was engulfed in a record-breaking blizzard.

Jeanelle, notified of Mama's weakening heart condition, was flying from sunny Florida. Joyce, with her son Steve who was returning to the University of North Carolina, was coming for a planned visit. Doris had arrived earlier, before the storm. Grace, who lived nearby, made it safely to our home before the streets became impassable. Tonight Mama's children would try to be together. Since the airport was closed, power lines down, and phone service disrupted, we could only wait and pray.

Harold kept the logs blazing in the fireplace and wood piled high on the porch. The power lines held and the house was warm. Doris kept the coffee pot hot.

Grace continued to rock quietly and hum old familiar hymns while the oxygen bubbled softly to ease Mama's difficult breathing. How thankful I was to be a nurse and able to care for her in our home. How good God is to allow each of us to hold a piece of her care.

Jeanelle and her husband had held a part in Florida when Papa went "Home." Doris and David had built the dream house in Stoneville. Grace managed the details of practical business affairs.

With a warm fire and a cup of tea, Harold had opened his arms to our gentle Mama. Howard had sent Joyce on her mission of love to each home. She had quietly helped out wherever needed. Whether weddings or funerals, Joyce had been there, a present help in time of need. Now we would all be together.

Christmas had been a joyous time with family and friends. Messages from grandchildren winged their love across the miles from Germany, Oklahoma, New York, Massachusetts, Arkansas, Chicago, Virginia, and Florida. The highlight was a Christmas luncheon we had for the senior citizens of the First Baptist Church of Stoneville. The Reverend Mr. Ward Burch led the delegation and Mama rejoiced with her church family by giving her Christmas reading and sharing stories from Canada. The final carol, "Silent Night," echoed long after Mama waved to the last car turning the road and crossing over the bridge on the lake. Mama knew in her heart there soon would be another crossing for her and many of her friends. "Lead me gently home, Father," she added softly.

"Just finished my rounds at Wesley Long Hospital and decided to check on Mama before going home." Mama patted Dr. Bruce with a "Thank you, dear," while he listened to her heart.

"She is about the same, but keep her comfortable, and don't forget, this jeep gets through anything." Then he was gone into the swirling snow.

My thoughts went back to Christmas again and I could hear Mama in times past, "No one celebrates Christmas like a Norwegian." Mama had sent two hundred Christmas cards, with a picture of her and her open Bible, to friends and family in Norway, Canada, and America. Each envelope contained a personal note.

Gifts had been planned for everyone in the family: afghans, shawls, quilts, or a piece of china. Birthday cards, each with two dollars enclosed, had been put aside for birthdays ahead. Thank you notes had been written. Each drawer was neatly arranged. Her desk was in order and her knitting basket closed. The open Bible, with a marker, lay by her bedside. She knew where the next reading would begin. During the past year Mama had read her Bible through four times. When I read out loud to her, she was aware of any skipped verses or words, even the "begats."

In her Bible she kept a letter which I had written to her a long time ago, and yet, it seems like yesterday:

For her birthday,
March 3, 1952

Darling Mother,

Can it be another birthday? And with that special day there comes the long, long trail awinding into the land of memories.

It seems only yesterday that hushed, excited voices whispered in corners about that present for you. The long, happy hours of roaming through dime-store counters, with only a few pennies to spend, can't be so many years back.

Remember the smudgy cards with all our names in childish scrawl? We promised you pink silk dresses and satin shoes. No wonder you smiled. You knew that life is made of cotton and leather, and that dreams don't always come true.

Perhaps your eyes will never see a home of luxury, but across the miles you see your children standing in their places, strong in body and serving your God. Your ears may never wear diamonds, but always you'll hear words of love and devotion. The ermine wraps may fall across other shoulders, but you'll always know the strength of young arms when your shoulders stoop. The pink silk dress will some day be the robe of righteousness in all its beauty. Could diamond rings make a mother's hand more beautiful? That hand so steady to guide, so tender to love, and strong when other hands were weak. Somehow, the memory of those hands folded in prayer brings renewed courage for the days ahead. But what about those tired feet in satin slippers? The miles are endless, the walks to church and visiting the sick, the round of shopping with only pennies to count, the tread of sorrow and nights of sickness. Still the feet go on, in countless ways of walking through valleys of disappointment and up the hills of hope and climbing the mountains victorious. And when those feet get too tired, there will be six rocking chairs and satin slippers by the fireside of six thankful children.

So, today is Mother's birthday, and what can we send? With God's help we'll send six Christian children, loving and serving the same Jesus Mother loves and serves.

Your Margaret

The storm continued with unabated fury and sent pines crashing into the woods, breaking the eerie silence with loud cannon-like booms. We kept our watch, and waited. The hours seemed endless. Suddenly the phone shattered the silence, and Grace shouted, "They are safe in Raleigh, and special transportation has been arranged!" Four hours later we heard the sound of a vehicle and saw the welcome headlights coming over the bridge of the lake.

Jeanelle, in Florida clothes, was shivering and Steve was bursting with the story of Jeanelle and Joyce's surprise meeting in the airport.

"Believe me, Aunt Margaret, the entire airport could hear them running to each other, shouting, 'How did you get here?'" It was 10 P.M. They had been en route for twelve hours. But now they were safe and warm. Doris had supper waiting.

Mama looked up to see her five daughters. With a "Praise the Lord," she dozed off to sleep, while the fury of the storm increased.

The upstairs of my home looked like a college dormitory with quilts, blankets, and open suitcases covering the entire floor. We somehow knew this was a special time and sensed that cord of love drawing us close. We agreed to take turns watching over Mama. I took the night watch.

The house was quiet, broken only by the sounds of logs crackling in the fireplace. Harold continued to pile up wood in case the power went off.

I held Mama tenderly and prayed for her, then tucked her in like a fragile child. The medication and oxygen eased her discomfort and she slept peacefully. I sat in her chair and rocked. Night duty was no stranger to me.

I had spent countless hours at the bedside of critically ill patients and I realized how few of them made preparation for their journey Home. But I thought of the envelopes that had winged across the miles carrying messages in familiar script, adding a dimension of faith for Mama's children. I thought also about the envelopes she had mailed to each of her grandchildren:

December 1969

Dear Dan,

Grandpa and I thought that this Christmas season would be a perfect time to give all sixteen grandchildren, as well as Heather Dawne, the first great-grandchild on her first Christmas, the little inheritance we have planned on for some time. The enclosed bond is not much, but with it we want you to know that we love you and wish the best in life for you. The very best, always, is to know the Lord Jesus as your own personal Savior and to live for Him.

Put the bond away in a safe place—at least until its maturity date—and then use it for something special. When I was four years old my grandmother died, and she had put away some money for me which I used for my wedding when I was twenty-one. Proverbs 13:22 says: "A good man leaveth an inheritance to his children's children." Keep this letter with your bond. May God bless you always.

Lovingly, your grandma,
Ella Tweten

Then there was the evening, not so long ago, when she asked us five sisters to sit down. We knew she had something special to say when she handed each one of us another envelope. "It is good to leave an inheritance to your children," she said. Each envelope contained five hundred dollars. "It is good to follow God's order."

Although Gordon was gone, Mama included Alice, his wife, in the inheritance. Mama shared the response from Alice.

Brooklyn, New York
November 1976

My Mom,

Your letter, with the check, was read and became a benediction on our Thanksgiving gathering. A picture at that time of the face and reaction was beautiful to see. What the Lord said to me was, "Do you see, Alice, love is eternal? You have known human love. Human love is fleeting. My love is eternal through My Son."

So thank you, *Mor*, for the love of Jesus flowing through you. It touched the hearts of our family. Only God knows what your love gift meant to them.

Jeg Elsker Dey (I love you),
Alice

I opened Mama's Bible and read:

But continue thou in the things which thou hast learned and hast been assured of, knowing of whom thou hast learned them; And that from a child thou hast known the holy scriptures, which are able to make thee wise unto salvation through faith which is in Christ Jesus. (2 Timothy 3:14-15)

For I am now ready to be offered, and the time of my departure is at hand. I have fought a good fight, I have finished my course, I have kept the faith. (2 Timothy 4:6-7)

I closed the Bible and opened yet another envelope I had found.

Mother's prayers for her children,
November 1975 (by Jeanelle)

Mother and I were enjoying a quiet morning together in her home. We had had an early breakfast and then moved on into the living room where she settled in her rocking chair and I settled comfortably on the floor near her. We talked of many things, especially that she would probably be going "Home" soon. We discussed the Old Testament patriarchs who seemed to know when it was time to leave their earthly dwelling. They made preparation for their families by praying for each other and bestowing a special "blessing" upon each one. As we talked together, I believe God was motivating us to think in the same direction because when I said, "Mother, wouldn't it be something if God would give you a special prayer or a special blessing for each of your five daughters?"

She immediately responded with, "Wouldn't that be wonderful? Yes, yes, I somehow believe He may want to do that."

Like the patriarchs of old, Mama also bestowed her own special prayer of blessing on each daughter. Mama, in her orderly way, had not only placed an earthly inheritance in our hands; but in our hearts she placed her blessing of faith.

Long before the dawn came quietly over the frozen lake and cast streaks of light over the snow banks, Grace slipped downstairs to take my place. I slept soundly until the dormitory upstairs came to life and I could smell the coffee and bacon in the kitchen. Joyce was serving Mama's Norwegian pancakes. That was motivation enough for action. The storm shut us in from the outside world.

After a restful night Mama was strong enough to be propped up in bed while we brought our coffee cups to sit beside her. We took turns reading the Bible and singing her favorite songs, some in halting Norwegian. We thanked her for the gift of love to us and once again the stories came with tears and laughter. At one time she looked up at us, "My escort to heaven." Another time she said, "I love him," and we quickly added, "Oh, we know you love the Lord, Mama." With a twinkle in her eye she said, "I was talking about Papa."

There were joyous hours around the piano, quiet times of reading to Mama. We bathed and dressed her in her soft pink gowns and propped her up with pillows. She automatically folded her hands in a blessing when we held a cup to her lips. There was a rest for her in the love from her children.

By Thursday the streets were clear enough for Pastor Wilson Stewart to visit and hold a Communion service. In conclusion we sang: "Surely goodness and mercy shall follow me, all the days, all the days of my life."

During the night watch, when Harold was sitting with her, Mama called out, "*Mor, Mor,*" with the cry of a child. At other times she talked to the children at the children's home. Friday morning she was weaker, but aware of her children kneeling by the bed expressing our love to God and to her for our beautiful mother. There was a hush in the winter wonderland where the snow was piled in drifts over fences and bushes.

Toward evening our youngest son, Ralph, slipped in quietly with a gentle kiss and said as he stroked her forehead, "This is Ralph, I love you, Grandma." She murmured softly, "*Ja, ja,* praise the Lord."

We sang an old song from the church string band days, "I will meet you in the morning, just inside the Eastern Gate." And then another song in the Norwegian language, "He the Pearly Gates Will Open."

A quiet peace settled over the house, and we were wrapped in the amber glow of love. Softly, gently she entered His presence. We felt the touch of the Master's hand as we rose to our feet. With hearts and hands united, we sang: "Praise God, from whom all blessings flow."

Mama had gone to meet her King.

Sunday morning the church bells rang out across the frozen snow. Huddled in woolen scarves and coats the worshipers braced themselves against the icy winds to attend the worship service at First Baptist Church, in Stoneville.

Joyce and Grace sat quietly in Mama's pew, while Pastor Ward Burch made the announcement.

"Our beloved friend, Elvine Tweten, went home to be with the Lord, Friday, January 14, at 7:45 P.M. The memorial service will be held here, at the church, at 2 P.M. today. We offer the family our love and prayers at this time."

When the ushers moved down the aisle to receive the Sunday morning offering, Joyce remembered Mama's clear instructions to Grace, "Don't forget the envelope, dear."

With quiet reverence Joyce placed Mama's church offering in the plate. Her offering to God—a life of faith. Her offering on earth—the work of her hands.

"Verily I say unto you . . . she . . . did cast in all that she had, even *all her living*" (Mark 12:43-44).

Going Home

Walk a little slower, Child,
The pathway shorter seems.
I long to smell the flowers wild
Beside the flowing stream.
Sing a little louder, Bird,
As squirrels chase in play.
In the dawn your song is heard
As night shadows steal away.
Stay a little longer, Sun,
For nights are often long.
For me the sunset-time has come
And I must journey home.
Bloom a little longer, Rose,
As breezes kiss your cheek.
Too soon the strength of youth goes,
My trembling hands grow weak.
Stop a moment, Beloved One,
I need your strong firm arm
To hold me close within your love,
Sheltered from fear's alarm.
Sit awhile, Lovely Girl,
I'll tell you how time has flown,
For I, too, raced in life's mad whirl,
Tell me—where have years gone?

Slow your pace, Tall Lean Youth,
Bend your ear to hear,
For age speaks forth wisdom's truth,
Perfect love dispels all fear.
Stop your play, Little One,
Stand beside my rocking chair,
Together we'll watch the setting sun
And say our evening prayer.
Wait a little longer, Dear,
See the sun set o'er that hill,
Let me feel your warm hand near.
The evening breeze grows chill.
Wait a moment, Silver Cloud,
Don't pass before the sun,
My steps are slow, my head is bowed,
My race is almost run.
Turn a little slower, Earth,
From space I watch you pass,
Fjords—mountains—place of birth,
Oceans, rolling fields of grass.
Come a little closer, Lord,
Let me feel Your hand.
I staked my soul upon Your Word,
On Your promises I stand.
Hasten now the perfect dawn,
Goodbye to shadows grey,
I leave you not to grieve or mourn.
Come quickly, Glorious Day.
I leave earth with a gentle sigh,
A caress for those I love,
As my spirit soars beyond the sky
With Him—Oh, perfect love.
The lights of home, the open gate,
The song of angel band,
Beloved faces there await,
And the touch of the Master's hand.

Papa

19

Bernice

1919. It was a long time ago and I was very young, yet I remember it.

Standing up in a crib behind a glass partition, I watched Papa's sad face. His black coat and scarf hung on his thin frame. He clutched his black hat in his hand, his face etched in grief. I reached out to touch him. "Hold me," I whimpered. He reached impulsively for me. But the glass partition kept us apart.

I remember standing alone in my long white gown, watching him wipe his eyes as he walked away.

The setting was the contagious ward in a New York City hospital where I was isolated in a glass cubicle, recovering from diphtheria.

Day after day, Papa came and stood behind the glass partition, his strong, firm hands pressed against the window in a perpetual wave. Somehow, as young as I was, I understood I shouldn't cry.

Finally, the day came when the nurse dressed me in my own clothes. Then Papa wrapped me in a blanket and took me home on the streetcar to Grandmother's house. The wind was cold. My head hurt. I held my ears in pain. But I was going home!

With unbounded joy I kissed my sister Bernice. We clung to each other in a joyous reunion.

Bestemör Bertilda moved about her flat and cared for us all. Mama, great with child, patiently awaited the day of birth. Bernice and I played games, hiding in the velvet drapes that partitioned the living room from the kitchen.

Jule Kakke lined the pantry shelves as Bestemör prepared for Christmas. The excitement in the air was not only for Christmas, but also for the new baby who was coming.

December 23, 1919, Grace was born—our Christmas angel. I helped Bestemör with the new baby, put cups on the table for coffee, and made sure Papa had his sugar lumps.

When evening came, Bernice and I curled up together in our bed, secure in our family's love. We had Bestemör and a new baby. We had Mama and Papa. We were all together in Bestemör's Brooklyn flat.

I couldn't remember exactly how it happened, but we were in Woodville, Wisconsin, where Bernice and I were born, and then next we were on a long train ride. Then suddenly we were in Bestemör's flat in Brooklyn. If the memories were there at all, they were only vague ones—of Papa preaching and Mama burning her dress. All I knew was that we were all together and Mama sang songs and told stories, and Bestemör took care of all of us. Papa didn't talk much. He slept in the daytime and went out to a watchman job at night. Mama still sang about how God would take care of us.

It was many years later when I learned what had happened to Papa. It all stemmed from the burning of Mama's dress. After the tempestuous storm of anger had swept over the souls of Mama and Papa, there came a quiet peace to Mama. "When we obey God," Mama said, "we find a rest in our souls."

For Papa, the quiet became a deep, dark chasm of guilt—and God's seeming silence. With no one to confide in, Papa rode the country roads engulfed in the dark night of the soul. He was losing his voice and the brown taste of fear brought the blackness of despair.

He had two young children to feed—Margaret (me) and

Bernice—but he couldn't preach. With his voice gone, he had to leave the pulpit. He had failed!

Practical Bestemör Bertilda, who had ridden through the storms in her own life, offered the obvious solution—come home to Brooklyn.

So it came to pass that we arrived in Brooklyn. Again there was the stoic, practical advice from Bestemör: "If you can't preach, Elius Tweten, then do what you can do." That's why Papa took the job as a watchman, the guardian of a building during the long shadows of the night.

His books were set aside. His dreams were gone. Despair replaced hope. In God's apparent silence, Papa lost not only hope, but also his faith in God. Everything he had preached seemed meaningless. Each night became just one step after the other—without purpose, without meaning. Papa's Bible lay untouched on the desk.

The battle to believe was lost.

One night Mama turned the pages of her worn Bible and stopped at Job. "Lift up thy face unto God . . . make thy prayer unto him, and he shall hear thee" (Job 22:26–27). "He knoweth the way that I take: when he hath tried me, I shall come forth as gold" (Job 23:10).

Turning familiar pages again she read in the Psalms, "My soul, wait thou only upon God; for my expectation is from him. . . . My rock . . . my salvation . . . my strength . . . my refuge, is in God" (Psalm 62:5-7).

The house was still. Bestemör and the children were asleep. Papa was at work. Wrapping a robe around her, Mama fell to her knees. "Lord Jesus, You said, 'If ye abide in me, and my words abide in you, ye shall ask what ye will, and it shall be done unto you'" (John 15:7).

While the world was wrapped in darkness, Mama stayed on her knees until the beams of the morning sun dispelled the darkness and the light of God's promise broke through her despair.

She had battled against an unseen enemy who was waging a war to destroy God's servant. But Mama had a covenant with

God—a covenant to walk in obedience—and God's covenant with Mama was that her household would be taught of the Lord.

She knelt beside the bed and would not give up until she heard God speak to her through His Word. "If you can believe, you'll see the glory of the Lord!" (See John 11:40.) "The LORD your God which goeth before you, he shall fight for you" (Deuteronomy 1:30).

The Word of God was welling up within her soul. She had meditated on the Word night and day, and now the Word was returning to renew her faith. "When the enemy shall come in like a flood, the Spirit of the LORD shall lift up a standard against him" (Isaiah 59:19).

"As for me, this is my covenant with them, saith the LORD; My spirit that is upon thee, and my words which I have put in thy mouth, shall not depart out of thy mouth, nor out of the mouth of thy seed, nor out of the mouth of thy seed's seed, saith the LORD . . . for ever!" (Isaiah 59:21). Deep within her, Mama heard the words of Jesus when He stilled the storm on Galilee: "Peace be still!"

Mama rose from her knees, dressed quickly, and put on the coffee pot. The battle to believe had been fought and won!

When she turned around at the sound of footsteps she saw Papa. His face was glowing! For the first time in weeks, he stood tall and erect, head held high.

He spoke in a clear voice, "Mama, I believe God! 'Though he slay me, yet will I trust in him' [Job 13:15]. In the night God spoke to me: 'Fear thou not; for I am with thee' [Isaiah 41:10]. Mama, all the words I have given to others came flooding back to me. I know God will guide us, and I will proclaim God's Word as long as I live! My books, I must get back to my books, and my Bible, the Book of Books!" He was smiling when he added, "'For ever, O LORD, thy word is settled in heaven'" [Psalm 119:89].

Papa's faith—and Papa's voice—had returned!

So that, as it was told those many years later, was why we had gone from Woodville, Wisconsin, to Bestemör's flat in Brooklyn.

Now I was remembering again those long-ago days when I

came home from the contagious ward in the hospital. I was three and a half years old. My head hurt and the pain in my ears increased, and Bestemör rocked me.

Golden-haired Bernice, two years of age, slipped into Papa's study and made uneven rows of his priceless books, then she quietly crawled up into Papa's lap and begged to be rocked to the accompaniment of a Norwegian lullaby. Munching on a piece of Bestemör's delicious yule cake she mumbled her approval, "*Godt, godt* (Good, good)."

One afternoon after coffee, Bernice crawled up into Papa's lap again. She dipped her sugar lump in Papa's coffee and laid her head against his shoulder.

Terror gripped him when he felt her hot cheeks against his face. Shortly he was on his way to the contagious hospital with two-year-old Bernice wrapped in a blanket.

Bestemör moved quietly about and put on the coffee pot. She, too, was feeling the fever and the choking pain in her throat, but with a fierce determination, she doctored her throat with Lysol and peroxide and willed herself to live.

This was no time to die, not now. She had left her own young children in Norway many years ago when Joe was five and Elvina four. Now she had them near her. Elvina needed her. This time she would not fail. She would live! No one would know, until years later, of her battle with the dread disease. She moved through those grim days weak, sick, but with a passion to survive.

Day after day, Papa went to see Bernice behind the glass cubicle just as he had visited me. Then the day came when Papa came home from the hospital for the last time—alone. Two-year-old Bernice was dead.

It was January, 1920—a cold, bitter day—when they buried my sister. The winds from the cold Atlantic mourned across the graveyard where three lonely figures followed the tiny coffin. Mama was home nurturing new life, while Papa, Paster Otto Hansen, and Mama's brother, Joe, escorted Bernice to her rest. The men walked in silence, bracing themselves against the winds, their boots crunching across the frozen ground. One man stood on each side of Papa as the winds blew snow over Bernice's freshly dug grave.

Shivering in the cold, Pastor Hansen read John 14:1: "Let not your heart be troubled."

Joe stood beside Papa, quietly grieving. Papa seemed to relive hearing Mama's final instructions given through a dry sob: "Put the woolen socks on Bernice, and don't forget her blanket." Then she had turned to the wall and wept alone, baby Grace sleeping beside her.

Pastor Hansen continued, "In my Father's house are many mansions."

Ja, *that is true,* thought Papa. *I must preach more on heaven. Earth holds such sorrow.* He seemed to feel the soft, golden hair on his cheeks as he had rocked her. The socks? *Ja,* he had remembered the woolen socks and the blanket, for Mama's sake.

Joe's arm reached around Papa's shoulder, "Come, it is time to go."

Oh no, he couldn't go and leave Bernice alone in the wind. He had to rock her in the warm blanket.

Paster Hansen's voice overwhelmed Papa's thoughts: "'I am the resurrection and the life.' She is alive forevermore." He had heard the same words at another graveside many years ago. The pain of loss was the same and it never went away: the loneliness of a nine-year-old boy calling across the valley for his mother who had left his world to join another.

"Come," repeated Uncle Joe. "We must go home now. Mama is waiting. Bernice is with Jesus."

Like silent shadows the three walked across the frozen ground as falling snow blanketed the tiny grave.

The kitchen was warm when Papa came home. Bestemör had the coffee pot on and Papa's sugar lumps ready. He didn't seem to notice. His eyes went to Mama rocking quietly in the corner. Mama looked up questioningly at Papa, but her words didn't come.

"*Ja,* Mama," he said softly. "I put the woolen socks on Bernice—and the blanket."

She nodded, overcome, then turned to nurse baby Grace.

107

Papa went to his books and wept softly when he viewed the uneven rows.

Mama's young face had quiet peace, for she was dealing with her grief at the throne of grace. God's promises would never fail! She had looked unto the hills and found, in God, a very present help in her time of trouble.

Some travel the high road in the hills, from peak to peak, where light lingers longer. Some travel in the valleys where they walk in the darkness of their own shadow. Mama would choose to walk the high road with God. She would walk in the light of His grace.

I sat by the window, my face pressed against the windowpane, staring up into the evening sky, yearning for my sister.

Taking Bestemör's hand, I pointed to the sky and gave my own grief to God. "God made an exchange. He took Bernice and gave us Grace."

Grief-stricken, Papa immersed himself in his books. Deep within he never really forgave himself for his uncontrolled anger that might have reached Bernice, the unborn child in Mama when he ripped her new dress. The golden-haired Bernice would be a constant reminder of heaven—and man's frailty, as dust, on this earth.

Mama, too, grieved alone with her face turned to the wall. Slowly, through prayer, she climbed the mountain of faith and knelt at the cross, crying out, "My help comes from the Lord."

Bestemör, was acquainted with a lonely, hidden sorrow of her own that was shared with no one. Always before, she had willed strength within herself to fight life's battles alone. She did so once again.

All these things I understood much later, but, I, too, grieved alone. My sister, my best friend, was gone. As I sobbed in my pillow, the pain in my head increased.

Finally, a quiet peace fell over the household, the kind of peace only God can give.

Yet the pain in my ears continued, until I was once again wrapped in a blanket and on my way to the hospital. My severe ear infection resulted in a mastoid operation and many painful visits to the doctor's office.

I remember the cold rubber apron on the doctor's lap when he irrigated my infected ear with a solution.

Night after night Papa walked the floor with me, preaching and singing, until I fell asleep, until I was finally well.

It was more than a year after Bernice's death when we waved good-bye to Bestemör. We were leaving New York City and catching a train to Winnipeg, Manitoba, Canada, where Papa would preach again.

20

The Asian Angel

Tomorrow the plane will take me back to the sunshine of Wilmington, North Carolina. Today, in Bloomington, Minnesota, 1986, I watch the snow swirling outside, beyond the reach of the cozy corner where I write. From my window I see the blanket of snow that covers the brown grass of fall. Barren tree limbs stretch toward the soft snow flurries that are already hiding their leafless branches. The world all around me is dressed in a coat of diamond-studded white ermine.

Last night I told the stories of my childhood memories of Christmas in Canada to an audience in the beautiful Blue Room of Northwestern College in St. Paul, Minnesota.

A mellow tenor led us in singing, "I'm dreaming of a white Christmas." I'll remember that song when I get back to North Carolina. The tenor and I laughed together over the Christmas traditions of lute fisk and rice pudding. I admitted, "It is a shame for a good Norwegian like me to dislike lute fisk—but I can't stand that slippery fish!"

I took the audience back to the Canada of 1920 and told them how Papa welcomed the lonely immigrants at the train station in Winnipeg and invited them home for a Norwegian Christmas Eve—with lute fisk!

Following the festive meal, we marched around the Christmas tree singing the carols in Norwegian and English. While we were singing, Johnny and *Bjarne* stumbled into the parsonage after walking eighty miles in the freezing Canadian winter.

I told them about Papa becoming a missionary to the Scandinavian settlers in the province of Saskatchewan. They listened intently to the story of the Tweten trek from Winnipeg to Saskatoon where we encountered an Asian man and a small restaurant in an open field.

I was ten years old, Grace was six, Gordon was four, and baby Doris was two. Papa had purchased a small house that came with monthly payments.

God and Mama would take care of the payments.

The journey grew long. The missionary and his family had already devoured their lunch. Mama was weary, and she wistfully mentioned how much she would enjoy a cup of coffee and a bowl of soup. Wanting to please her, when Papa saw a white cottage in an open field, he stopped to ask about a cup of coffee.

We were warned that there was no money so we had to be content with homemade bread and some water.

While Papa inquired, we waited. In just a minute Papa and a smiling Asian man emerged from the cottage. He urged us all to come into his restaurant and be his guests for dinner.

Papa protested, "Thank you, but we have only money for a cup of coffee."

The smiling man insisted. He would hear nothing of Papa's argument. He would serve us dinner.

With quiet awe we followed the charming host into a small restaurant, where we were seated at a table covered with a spotless white linen cloth. We had never been in a restaurant before. Mama sat like a queen. For once she was being served. We were the only guests present; even so, we were especially careful not to disgrace the ministry. We promptly asked a Norwegian blessing.

Our smiling host gave us his undivided attention, and he served us a delicious meal.

After the dinner we each solemnly shook hands with the man and said "*Takk for matten* (Thank you for the food)."

"Someday, I shall return to repay you for your kindness," added Papa. "May God's richest blessing be upon you." Then we were on our way.

Many years later, Papa told me that after we were settled in our four-room yellow house, he returned to repay the man for his kindness. But he found no restaurant, and no man, just an open field. Intent on finding the man, Papa made inquiry in the community. The neighbors assured Papa there had never been any Asians living in the vicinity. There had never been a restaurant, not even a house, on that property.

Puzzled beyond understanding, Papa went back for Mama.

"*Ja*, Papa, I know exactly where the place is and I will show you," she told him. But there was only a breeze blowing gently over the empty field.

Papa told us, "To Mama and me it was such an awesome thing. We were too full of wonder to speak of it. As the years passed we became convinced that our host was an angel."

God had sent an Asian man with a smiling face to feed the Twetens.

21

So Many Books to Read
. . . and Write!

Mama packed a box with clean clothes, carefully folded, so as not to wrinkle my starched dresses and petticoats. Two were for everyday; one was for Sunday. Papa's white shirt lay on top. Then she picked up the box and I followed her outside where Papa was cranking up the old Model-T Ford with its thin tires and snap-on curtains. With a quick smile, he kissed Mama, Grace, Gordon, and Doris good-bye. As Mama held me tightly, the lump in my throat grew bigger. My younger sisters and brother lined up to kiss me and stood in awe of this astonishing occasion.

I was going with Papa on a missionary journey!

We were leaving our home at 510 Avenue J, Saskatoon, Saskatchewan, to drive on the open roads through the Canadian prairie.

Papa and I drove over the dusty roads in silence. Communicating with his children was not Papa's place. It was up to God and Mama to bring up Mama's children. He had the Lord's work to do. Papa taught theology; Mama taught the living.

Mama was like a harbor, safe and secure, like a river deep and flowing. Papa was like a restless sea, with sudden flashes of temper like a summer storm. Then, as suddenly, Papa's songs and laughter came back, like sunshine after rain. When the storms came we ran to Mama, who explained that Papa never understood children because he had never been a child.

Softly she would remind us, "Papa's parents died when he was very young. He never had a real childhood." She would hug us and add, "When he was seventeen years old he came to America to study." Perhaps Papa didn't understand children, but Mama said that he understood loneliness and fear.

It seemed that Mama understood everything—most of all, Papa. She loved him.

Papa seldom showed affection to Mama's children. We obeyed his stern commands—quickly! Mama was perfect; her children should be likewise. But he loved Mama, too, in his own way. She knew his heart and understood. Understanding for us would come with the years.

One afternoon when I returned from school, my eyes saw the most wonderful thing in all the world—a piano stood in our living room.

"Margaret," announced Papa with a flourish of triumph, "You will learn to play the piano! Tomorrow I will get you a teacher. Education is not complete without music. Books and music go together."

The teacher came—a young, handsome son of another minister. I practiced!

Later I learned that Papa had sold some of his priceless books in exchange for the piano. I, too, learned to understand the heart. He gave to us the only way he knew how, and, although we didn't then understand him, I eventually saw that the piano and our music (we all learned to play the piano and we all attempted to sing) was a bridge of communication that linked Papa to his children. With the wonder of a child, he listened with approval.

The waving fields swept by now while Papa sang old Norwegian songs. I remember another time, when I was six years old, a long time ago. It was the time Papa threw my rag doll, Big Jack, into the furnace.

I wept for my well-worn doll, my only one. But Papa thought

it was part of the debris he swept up in the Winnipeg parsonage basement. Always in a hurry, he shoveled the contents into the furnace.

It was then that Mama explained, "Papa never had a toy and doesn't understand the ways of a rag doll and a six-year-old girl." She wiped my tears. "I will make a new rag doll for you. You must forgive Papa." I tried to forget about the rag doll, but I always remembered the little boy who didn't have a toy.

Unaware of me, Papa continued to sing the old hymns in his clear tenor, and he practiced his Norwegian sermons in English since he preached in both languages.

I clutched my clean handkerchief and sat up straight. This was a moment to remember. Once or twice I stole a glance his way. I was in awe of my handsome father in his black suit and high starched collar. Papa was a clean-shaven man with a full face and high forehead and bushy blond eyebrows that over-shadowed his piercing blue eyes. He was slender, barely six feet on tiptoe, but to me he was tall, a tower of strength.

I tried to remember Mama's instructions. "Keep Papa's clothes clean and be sure he has the starched white shirt for Sunday meeting." Mama had hugged me again and whispered, "I'll miss you, Margaret, and I'll miss you helping with the children." The lump in my throat came back.

"*Ja*, Margaret, we stay at the Thompson's house this time," Papa said, "and you will help Mrs. Thompson with the chores and housework. Deacon Salen's daughter Cora plays the organ at the tent meeting, but if she can't come, then you will play the hymns you have learned."

I promised to help Mrs. Thompson and play the organ. No one argued with Papa!

I stole another glance at him sitting up straight and tall, his broad hands on the steering wheel. He turned to me with a chuckle. "*Ja*, Margaret, so what do you think, going with your Papa on a missionary journey—like Paul and Timothy?" He laughed with joy and sang "Standing on the Promises." He loved the freedom of the open road and his Model-T. And he loved the journey he was taking. This was Papa's parish—the scattered, Scandinavian immigrants of the province of Saskatchewan. The farmers lived miles apart, but that didn't bother Papa. "When I come they get together for meetings in the schoolhouse," he said, "or they pitch a tent in the summertime."

As though talking to himself, he mused out loud, "The Scandinavian settlers are strong and full of faith. You'll see, Margaret. They learn to live with a new language, blizzards, even crop failures. But their greatest test is loneliness." His smile faded for a moment. "Some wait for years for their families to come from Europe. Some families never come. We are blessed, Margaret. We have Mama . . . there's no one like Mama." I turned. His blue eyes were on me. "The first time I saw your Mama I said, 'That is the wife for me!'" Papa chuckled delightedly. "I even forgot my sermon—but in three months I married Mama."

Some time later, Papa pulled off the main road, his excitement mounting. "Look, Margaret, there is the Thompson farm. Good people, quiet, hard-working. They have two sons, Trygvie and Seivert. Fine boys."

We settled in with the Thompsons and became comfortable with their daily routine. When one of the days came to a close, the farm seemed to settle into the stillness of the night with sounds from the chicken house blending into the darkness like a gentle lullaby.

Mrs. Thompson, a quiet woman with a warm smile, patiently washed the supper dishes while I dried them and kept up a running conversation about life with Mama and the children. Mr. Thompson, still dressed in his work boots and overalls, chuckled as he stacked the wood behind the cookstove in preparation for the next day's early breakfast. Finally he stretched, caught his thumbs on his shoulder straps, and peered at me over the tip of his glasses. "Margaret, Margaret, such a life in the Tweten house."

I turned away shyly. The cows had been milked, and I had helped to wash and scald the separator. Freshly churned butter stood in a crock. Loaves of bread lined the pantry shelf. Jars of homemade strawberry jam stood in rows. Mama would be proud of me.

I filled the water bucket at the pump and hung up the dishtowels to dry. Chores were done and the evening meal was over.

The Thompson boys, Trygvie and Seivert, discussed tomorrow's work with their father. Finally Mr. Thompson pulled off his boots and said good night. Mrs. Thompson took off her starched apron and with a weary sigh followed her husband to the loft.

It was still early, but quiet, gentle, hard-working Trygvie stifled a yawn. Soon he, too, said good night. Papa had gone to visit a neighbor and would be home later. It never occurred to Papa to go to bed before midnight. "So many books to read," he said.

That left only Seivert and me. Seivert, the youngest, seventeen years old with merry blue eyes, seemed to be the only one with an adventurous spirit. He had big-boned, Norwegian features, yet his unruly brown hair framed a boyish face. Seivert had boundless energy and seemed to work effortlessly all day.

He lit the gas lamp on the round table and handed me a book—a paperback novel with a hero, heroine, and villain. Seivert's deep blue eyes sparkled with mischief as he confided, "This is what I like to do when everyone goes to bed—read!" An old Victrola stood beside the table, and he put on the only record he owned—"Beautiful Ohio." When the record player ran down, Seivert cranked it again and went right on reading.

I had grown up under the protective banner of the parsonage and was well-versed in theology, but the novel offered me a new burst of excitement. I was totally absorbed in Mrs. Southwick's classic—my eyes glued to the pages as the characters, particularly Jack the villain, came alive for me. Too late, a step behind us alerted me to Papa's presence. He was reading over my shoulder. He snatched the book from my hand. Papa glared at Seivert, then back at me. "Margaret, God gave you a good head to read good books. This is foolishness." When he took the book, I was right at the best part, where the hero rescues the heroine.

117

Years later I asked Papa how the story ended. Before he realized the trap I had set for him, he told me.

There were more paperback books to read that summer, but I made sure I had a "good book" handy, just in case Papa came home.

I was glad when Mrs. Thompson allowed me to take coffee and bread to the men in the field. I would sit under a tree with Seivert where we shared coffee and a piece of bread. Seivert was my first love. We talked about the big world beyond the farm.

I wanted to be a missionary nurse and see the world and write stories. Seivert shared his dream of a big farm of his own.

In my own heart and mind, I reasoned that if I couldn't read novels, then I would write my own stories and poems, and no one would know. Besides, since I was going to be a missionary nurse and see the world, there would be much to write about.

I didn't tell Seivert that I cried in my pillow when people laughed at my missionary dreams and jokingly teased that I'd probably be an actress. Papa was always shocked! He assured me that it was his place to keep foolish ideas like acting out of my head. And Mama saw to it that I practiced the piano and read good books.

22

Anna

The 1985 Writer's Conference at Gordon College in Wenhem, Massachusetts, had come to a close, and I was enjoying a relaxed evening with my two eldest grandchildren, Heather, fifteen, and Chad, twelve. Their favorite dinner of southern-fried chicken, mashed potatoes, hot biscuits, and cherry pie was ready to serve. I was stirring the milk gravy when the telephone rang.

Janice, our daughter, answered. She turned to me and said, "Mom, it's for you. It's Jud."

Dr. Judson Carlberg, Janice's husband and dean of the faculty at Gordon College, was hosting a consortium of college educators from across the country and tonight was their kick-off banquet. A prominent speaker from the West Coast had been scheduled to speak on the theme "The Integration of Faith and Social Action."

Jud's voice came over the phone, "Mom, the guest speaker missed his plane. Could you be ready in thirty minutes?"

Jan answered for me, "Of course she can be ready."

And so it came to pass that my favorite son-in-law introduced me to a bewildered audience of educators as the "Speaker of the House."

I would probably never address a more profound-looking

gathering; nevertheless, I began, "Tonight you can become children again, for I am just a storyteller." Pens and notebooks disappeared.

"Your theme intrigues me, and the idea of revolutionary ideas sounds exciting. I grew up with revolutionary ideas. My father was a stubborn Norwegian and he seldom did anything the orthodox way.

"Now Mama would like the title, 'The Integration of Faith and Social Action,' only she would say it like this:

'Ja, ja, *faith and works all go together.*
You do what you have to do.
It is simple—just not easy.
You trust and obey God,
Love and forgive, do what is in your hand to do.
It is simple—it is just not so easy.'

"As for Papa, he did it his way. He probably invented brown-bagging." I saw my dignified audience relaxing. I was at ease myself. After all, it was a privilege to tell the stories of Mama and Papa, even the stories of the Great Depression.

During the Great Depression some of Papa's church parishioners were patients at the Cook County Hospital in Chicago. They were terrified, not only because of their illness, but also to be considered charity cases. Depression years brought changes to these proud Norwegians.

"Oh, *ja,* it won't be so bad," Papa cheerfully assured them. "I come with Mama's soup."

The story was so familiar to me. He took a jar of Mama's homemade soup, wrapped it in a Turkish towel, and placed it in a brown bag. So began the daily trek of Papa's brown-bagging.

An hour's ride on two street cars brought Papa to the County Hospital. There he read God's promises from the Bible, offered prayer for health and courage, then calmly spoon-fed Mama's soup to the frightened patients. Years later these same people told how they waited for Papa's brown bag and Bible.

Integration of faith and social action? "*Ja, ja,*" Mama would say, "Faith and works. It goes together."

One day during the Depression, after a hospital visit, Papa passed by the dejected wrecks of humanity huddled in the outpatient clinic. Many had been brought there by the police. Suddenly Papa heard someone call out hysterically in Norwegian.

Papa stopped at the desk, "May I help?" he asked. "I am a Norwegian minister."

"Oh, can you ever help!" the nurse said in a disgruntled tone. "We have a wild woman the police brought in and no one can understand her." She nodded toward a large, blonde woman in the corner. "Perhaps you can reason with her. We are getting ready to transfer her to a mental hospital."

"Let me see what I can do first."

When Papa spoke to the frightened woman in her own language, she calmed down enough to tell her story: "I went from door to door asking for work. I work," she said. "But when one resident discovered her jewels were missing, she called the police and told them, 'A crazy-looking woman came here looking for work. She has to be the thief!'"

Unable to explain in English, the frightened woman had become hysterical as the police dragged her to the station for questioning. She finally became unmanageable. She was taken from the jail to the Cook County Clinic where plans were made to transfer her to the mental hospital.

Papa listened patiently as he gathered the bits and pieces of the story. When he heard all of it, he strode over to the director of the clinic, his blue eyes blazing, "I will tell you one thing. This voman is not crazy. She is Norwegian!"

"Will you sign for her release?" the director asked.

Papa grabbed the pen. "Of course, I will sign!"

In the meantime at home, Mama had supper ready. "Margaret, look out the window and see if Papa is coming." The worry lines on her face deepened.

I looked. "He's coming, Mama, but you should see what he has with him!"

Mama shook her head. "Put another plate on the table, Grace. Papa has company."

Moments later, Papa stood before us, tall and dignified in

his black suit, black hat, and high starched collar. Clinging to his arm was a large woman, her coat bulging at the seams, her slip sagging. I stared at her. High above her forehead, on top of her blond hair perched a hat with a feather sticking up, and on her bare, squatty legs, cotton stockings were rolled down around her ankles.

She clung tenaciously to Papa's arm. "This wonderful man!" she exclaimed in Norwegian, "This wonderful man! They said I was crazy but he told them I was Norwegian. How did you ever find such a wonderful man?"

Mama hid a smile as if to say, "Oh, we'll talk about that wonderful man later." (We had all thought it was the other way around.)

We stared open-mouthed at the apparition before us. With steely blue eyes, Papa glared at us, "Say hello to Anna, children!"

Quickly recovering, we all shook hands with a formal "*Velkommen, Anna.*"

We sat down at the table and we asked a Norwegian blessing in unison. After the meal Mama asked Papa quietly, "Well, Papa, what do we do now?"

Papa frowned; then his bushy eyebrows arched. "Anna will stay with us until I can find another way. I'll think about it tomorrow. We take one day at a time."

So Anna slept on the parlor sofa. The next day Papa took two street cars to see Mrs. Farmen, who had clothes large enough for Anna. Finding a home for Anna took longer. Finally Papa came home with the announcement that he had found a home for her.

Anna became the dishwasher in a Norwegian mission house for immigrant girls. She had her own room, and, best of all, a family. She spent her life there, productive and happy.

When Sunday mornings came, she sat in the front of the church, never taking her eyes off that "wonderful man."

The parlor sofa was empty once more, but not for long. Papa would come again and again with someone for the sofa. My eyes swept over my audience of profound and learned educators. With my heart I saw caring people who longed to reach

122

out to a crying world of Annas. "But we must do it God's way," I concluded.

"When our boats are loosed from our moorings in Christ Jesus, we become victims to the tide of man's philosophy. But if we follow Mama's faith, Mama's philosophy, we can say,

'Ja, ja, *faith and works go together.*
Trust and obey God.
Love and forgive everyone.
Do what you have to do.
Do what is in your hand—
Just do it!
It is so simple—it is just not easy.'

"God bless you all."

The following day I was on my way home to North Carolina. Within a few weeks the family would gather for a happy reunion at beautiful Wrightsville Beach.

The weeks flew by and once again that summer of 1985, we enjoyed our shrimp and cornbread, garden vegetables, and homemade ice cream. When we watched the suntanned grandchildren race down the sandy beach and jump into the sunlit waves, we were remembering our own children when they were young. It was as though we were seeing Jan, Dan, and Ralph race ahead of us to hit the beach first.

Wasn't it only yesterday?

Staring at the waters at Wrightsville Beach, past and present merged again. Somewhere on the backroads of my mind, I heard Papa's church singing: "Wonderful the matchless grace of Jesus, deeper than the mighty rolling sea. . . ."

23

I'm Crying, Lord

The glow of sunset casts a blend of shadows and golden light across beautiful Lake Barkley, nestled in the hills of Kentucky. From my lodge window I look longingly at the rocky island in the center of the lake. In my mind I see a "safe place." I have just closed Gordon MacDonald's book, *Restoring Your Spiritual Passion.* How easy it would be to sing "Holy, Holy, Holy, Lord God Almighty!" on that "safe" island.

If I could row a boat to the island, then I could find that "still" place. MacDonald had said, "By laying an adequate roadbed in the inner spirit, we can prevent the hostile elements that cause fatigue."

I am fatigued.

Too soon the shadows creep over the golden shafts of light and my island is shrouded in a blanket of night. The world around me sleeps.

Finally, I fell asleep hearing 350 women singing the Women's Retreat song—"Holy, this place is holy. Come now and feast on His Word." It had been a beautiful time of sharing with God's precious people. Now it was time for a "safe" place.

David the psalmist said he didn't understand the evil around him until he went into the sanctuary, then he saw from God's perspective, in the light of eternity. I was to walk by faith, in the light of His Word.

After a night of rest I awakened to a new day and pulled back the drapes. A thick wall of morning mist covered the outside world.

I sat by the window and wrote words, but my mind kept reaching for the hidden island. I wrote: "I know it is there. I saw it yesterday!" In my heart I was saying, "Great is Thy faithfulness today, O God, because I knew it yesterday."

Now I found myself thinking of another yesterday, when I spoke at a retreat in Palm Springs, California.

As I faced eleven hundred black women, my white hair stood out in sharp contrast to the beautiful color around me. Their songs of praise filled the ballroom of the luxury hotel and "Amazing Grace" took on new meaning.

Out of my heart I told about Lena, my lovely black friend, who had said, "Unclog the channel, Margaret! You can't see God for all the long hair and bare feet clogged up in the channel."

Back then my channel was clogged with unanswered questions: "Why is our son a prodigal? What did we do wrong?" The cares of this world—with long hair and bare feet—kept my channel clogged. I wanted "out of the storm." I wanted to go home.

Eleven hundred women listened intently as I told them about Lena and our son.

"If God had wanted you to die for that child, He would have asked you," Lena had scolded. "Who you be to tell God Almighty He didn't do enough when He sent Jesus to die for that child? Jesus came to give life and that your joy be full. Now I asks you, Margaret, where is your joy? Your joy is Jesus. Your peace is Jesus. Your life is Jesus, and it does not depend on answered prayer or your family being right. You must get the joy of the Lord in your soul, Margaret. Leave the rest to God."

I looked over that sea of shining black faces. "Lena was right, you know. She made me realize how praise unclogs the channel and, like a detergent, cleanses the cobwebs from the mind. With the channel clear I saw a sovereign God at work, bringing 'all things together for good'! Praise was the believing *before* the seeing. God promised, 'If you can believe, you'll see the glory of the Lord.'"

I continued, "Our children—yours and mine—are held hostage by the enemy. We as God's children, the church, must put on the armor of God and stand in the gap to intercede for these imprisoned children of ours. They are held hostage by America's permissive society that defies God rather than man, and that has given the enemy free reign through drugs, alcohol, and unbridled promiscuity. God's laws have been broken and 'the wages of sin is death; but the gift of God is eternal life'" (Romans 6:23).

Now and then a dark head bobbed with understanding. Momentarily my eyes locked with the deep, dark eyes of one lone woman. *Did she have her own prodigal?* I wondered. "We don't wrestle against a drug pusher, but we wrestle against the powers of darkness." My voice was firm. "A real Satan seeks to steal, destroy, and to kill, and comes 'as a roaring lion seeking to devour' our children."

Out of my heart I told the story of our prodigal son who came back to his heavenly Father's house. The battle to believe had been fought—and won! Eleven hundred women stood to their feet to rejoice over one sheep who had returned to the fold.

It was a high moment of faith.

The following day a message was given by another woman, a tall, dignified black woman who was known as one who interceded before the throne for the broken, wounded ones.

This woman of prayer faced the crowd with words, "When you pray, forgive." It was Lena's same theme of unclogging the channel.

With tears, the woman spoke of broken hearts and lost dreams and cried out to the sea of faces before her, "Many of you have known rejection, abuse, molestation, beatings, and rape. You have lived with guilt and deep bitterness because life was unfair."

She held us spellbound. "Many lost our innocence as very young children and saw too much sin for our young years.

Many went from house to house and never knew a home. It's time to cry! Cry to the Lord! Pour it all out! Be healed by your tears and cleansed by the precious blood of Jesus."

There was a rhythmic beat to her voice. "Jesus came to set us all free—cleansed, forgiven, healed, and free. We begin again, for in Christ all things become new. Cry unto the Lord! He hears the cry of the humble in heart."

Then I heard a sound I had never heard before—the sound of crying unto the Lord. "Tell it to Jesus," she continued. "Cry it out to the Lord. Forgive everyone who harmed you. Don't hold the hate—cry it out. Everyone has something to cry about. God hears your cries."

The sobs filled the ballroom of the luxurious hotel. Outside, the palms waved in the California sun while the birds sang. Inside, it was like the sound of the mourning of the ocean rolling on the beach. Wave after wave washed on the shore of memory. Above the sobbing came a lonely cry, like the cry of a wounded animal. "Cry, my sister. God is listening. Forgiveness is the only way—love and forgive."

I felt my own tears washing my cheeks. "Oh Lord, I'm crying, too. I'm crying with my sisters and I'm crying to You. I'm crying because I don't want to go back to the past. I only want to walk with You into the future, secure in Your love."

I, too, was remembering and weeping for the fallen leaders, oaks that crashed in the forest. Satan shouted, "Timber!"—and they fell. Dry rot was hidden in the heart of the oaks. Truth, not acted upon, had become dry rot.

I cried as I remembered angry Peter cutting off a man's ear in the garden. "The man refused to hear what You were saying, Jesus." But then Peter didn't hear either, that is, until the rooster crowed. Then he wept.

How many of us really hear You, Lord, I wondered, *or do we cut off the ears of those who don't listen to us?*

I was crying for leaders who, like Judas, turned away from walking with the Light of the world, only to go out into a night of darkness. How could love of money be so overpowering? And my tears were for their children who stumbled in the shadows.

I heard the speaker say, "Cry to the Lord."

127

"And I cry, Lord, to You, for the great men who sold their souls to their Bathshebas and turned to passion, forgetting the wives of their youth. Their children cry in the night.

"How are the mighty fallen so deep! I weep for those who once held high the Word of God, who walked with true wisdom, then turned aside to walk with vanity of pride in man's knowledge. Their children wander, without a sure compass for life's journey.

"Oh, Lord, I don't want to remember the past because I know You have forgiven and forgotten. But I must go back and perhaps help some who can't forget. Only when I walk into the past with forgiveness can I walk into the future with understanding love."

I can hear Lena singing: "So many falling by the wayside; please help me to stand."

Tears stain this page, Lord, so take my hand and let us remember together—with love.

Out of the past I allowed myself to see my brother Gordon coming home—a twelve-year-old boy, hair disheveled, coat buttoned wrong, holding out fifty cents in his grubby hand. His eyes were shining with pride, head held high. The money represented his worth for that moment, his offering of love from the sale of the newspapers. His sisters crowded around him proudly. This was Gordon's moment in the sun. Not only was he on the honor roll as a student, but he also paid for his violin lessons by cleaning the basement for his music teacher. At 4 A.M. he was up and out on the Chicago streets to sell newspapers.

Now he stood facing Papa with his fifty cents gleaming in his newspaper-stained hands. Without warning, the storm broke! Papa saw only the grubby hands and disheveled appearance. Papa didn't see the worth of his son. He couldn't tolerate the lack of neatness. Papa could not risk Gordon's appearance disgracing the ministry. With uncontrolled rage, Papa's hand came down and Gordon's fifty cents flew across the room.

Then the silence!

Bruised in spirit, soul, and body, our brother Gordon retreated to the only corner he knew—a cot in the dining room, with a brown box that held his earthly treasures.

The sisters clung fearfully to one another, silently screaming, "I hate you, Papa!" It was the inaudible scream of the wounded.

Papa whirled and retreated to his study. Lost in his books, his storm passed with the night.

But the storm still raged for Gordon. Beaten, bruised, but not broken, Gordon rose the next morning to the sound of horses' hoofs and the rattle of the milk wagon. Quietly he went out into the semi-darkness to deliver his newspapers. Bitterness crept into his soul.

Sunday morning came and Papa was in his place, faithfully preaching the truth of a heavenly Father's love. Mama's children sat in a row—but they couldn't hear Papa's words.

Back in the ballroom in Palm Springs, the focus on Gordon blurred. "Oh, Lord, I'm crying out to You again, but not just for Gordon. I weep for all the leaders' broken wives and children who have been beaten with slashing words as cruel as rods. There are tears also for the leaders, those who have toppled in the forest because of slashing wounds from family or associates.

"Words have the power of life or death. Words can make men soar to heights, or can cause them to stumble, wounded, by the wayside. So many of Your children, Lord, wait for the oil and time to heal the hurting places."

I had experienced so much of the oil and wine of healing for my own hurts. Perhaps it had been easier for me, the oldest Tweten, because I became a committed Christian at six—not perfect, but committed. As I grew older, I stood up to Papa's anger, gutsy and confident, but all the while loving him. I could forgive Papa's anger because I had learned at Mama's knee to keep short accounts with God.

The lovely black leader was closing the Palm Springs meeting in prayer. With my eyes shut, I thought, *I should cry for You, too, Lord. You were counting on Your servants, weren't You?*

Tonight I pray for the children who lost their faith along the road. Tonight I thank You for helping Mama's children to go back—and now we can bring the healing we received to others. We love You, Lord.

Thank You for listening. You understand. You were beaten, too. With words and with rods.

24

I'm Singing, Lord

The mist lifts slowly over Lake Barkley, bringing to my island visibility in the morning sun.

In my mind I row out to the rocky island to a make-believe hideaway. It is in the still place where I see from eternity's point of view. It is in the still place where I can hear, then my heart can sing, the "song of the soul set free."

Because I sing from a heart of joy, I can return again and again to another time with deep thanksgiving in my heart. I'm going back, Lord. Clinging to Your hand, I'm going back.

It was a lovely summer afternoon in 1946. I had taken our young children, Jan and Dan, for a walk in the park. Upon returning, I spotted a strangely familiar figure that came right out of my childhood, sitting on the porch. With a cry of joy, I recognized my old friend. "Uncle Barney!" I called.

He was one of the Christmas wayfarers who received the touch of divine love through Mama and became a permanent family member. When Barney had first stumbled into the parlor, he had handed Mama his whiskey bottle, then knelt in repentance while Papa prayed for his soul. Mama never told us what she did with the whiskey the parlor converts gave her.

Barney was a big, balding man—still a handsome romantic

with bright brown eyes. In our carefully guarded Tweten home, Uncle Barney became our link with "the world out there," where people were brave and cowardly, strong and weak, loving and hateful, great and small, noble and mean. Barney brought us reality and humor. Often he would wear a hat slouched to one side like a gangster and flash us an impish, wicked grin as he spun his yarns and sang his songs in his rich tenor voice.

Within moments today we were all laughing and talking together. Jan and Dan were on his knee and he was singing, "I'm coming back to you, my hullabaloo."

Uncle Barney and I laughed at the memory of Mama kneading her bread faster and faster as the songs became "too worldly." When Mama's glasses fell down on her nose, Barney knew it was time to softly croon a Norwegian song. The tempo of kneading slowed down as the Norwegian song blended with Mama's memories of her oceanside home at Lista, Norway.

Jan and Dan clamored for more songs, just as Mama's children used to do. Uncle Barney sang.

While the coffee pot perked on the stove and Mama kneaded dough for the next day's bread, Barney strummed his mandolin and sang the folk songs of Norway. Barney had the power to persuade Papa to leave his books and dance a polka as we clapped in rhythm. The agony and ecstasy of life was always with us; we learned to capitalize on the joy of any moment.

Barney told stories of his life as a newspaper man in Oslo. As a boxer he had been wild and rebellious, but finally tamed by a beautiful golden-haired, blue-eyed fisherman's daughter. One day she had gone to sea with her father. The fishing boat never returned. He searched the seashore and called to the waves, but only silence greeted him.

In desperation he had come to America—to forget. "Out of all things, God works together for good," Mama repeatedly reminded him as she baked her bread or cooked her famous vegetable soup.

There was always a wildness about him as he winked his brown eyes at all the pretty girls. *"Bjarne* (Barney), you must get a good wife and settle down," Mama would often say.

132

"How can I help it if God gave me such a big heart with room to love them all?"

When he saw an injustice he exploded, "Lucky for you I'm not God!" As we grew older he followed "Mama's girls" around at church picnics in case the boys had a few ideas of their own. When there was no money for an ice cream cone, Barney managed to dole out a few nickels. Years later when we fell in love, he listened. When Papa's unreasonable demands made life difficult, Barney talked to Papa. His mandolin played "Just Molly and Me," or "I'm Coming Back to You," and the girls fell in love with him and his music.

Heeding Mama's admonition to "settle down with a good wife," Barney finally married a comfortable friend, Mildred, who was solid, faithful, and strong, and became his harbor in the storms of life.

Within him still pounded the restless waves that batter Norway's rocky coast, the waves that had buried his love. Walking the New York City seacoast, or the trails of Central Park, he was an easy victim to passions hidden within. Black despair engulfed him until he found himself on the Brooklyn Bridge, looking for an escape.

Unnoticed in the shadows, a silent figure, who had stood quietly waiting, saw the stooped figure of despair. Suddenly Barney felt an arm around his shoulders, "Let's go home to Mama for a cup of coffee." In silence Papa took Barney home to Mama.

Later Barney found his harbor, Mildred, waiting and forgiving. The storm had passed. Barney was safe in the arms of the Lord who said, "I love you with an everlasting love." Together Mildred and Barney served the Lord for many years and became a harbor for others.

While I prepared supper, Uncle Barney spun his make-believe stories and the children begged for more. Harold returned from the church office and we sat around the table, once again sharing the memories of another day. Long after Jan and Dan were asleep, we still recalled that other day.

"Your father was a great man, Maggie," Uncle Barney told

me. "Few understood him. Perhaps I love your Papa the most because he had the capacity to forgive the most."

A lonely sadness seemed to linger in our old friend and the lyrics from an old familiar song—"Someone slipped and fell. Was that someone you?"—seemed to haunt me. Uncle Barney leaned forward. "My life was a total disaster when I came to your home in Canada. Margaret, it was your father who prayed for me, and I surrendered my life to Jesus Christ. Your home became my home. I loved you Tweten children more than anything in this world."

"I know," I answered, "and at one time or another we all wanted to run away with you, especially when Papa's temper exploded." I paused. "Doris was always ready to run away."

Barney was pensive. "Perhaps I knew him better than anyone, yet there was a part of your father he never shared with anyone. He spoke very little about his childhood and always kept the deep things of his heart hidden."

"Did that explain his temper?" I asked.

"Temper?" he mused. "Maggie, I've been a wild one in my day, and I know the world, the flesh, and the devil. But I must say that I never knew a man so untouched by the evil in the world. Your father was a pure man, a godly man, and a man of great compassion."

I nodded. I knew Papa was a godly man. *But why that temper?* I wondered again.

"Your Papa never condoned sin, but he never condemned the sinner. I know, I know—you could never understand his uncontrolled temper. Neither could I." Uncle Barney looked away for a moment. "When I tried to talk to him, he changed the subject, or suddenly had to go someplace. He was a restless man, Maggie. I could never understand why. He had a wonderful wife—an angel—and you children were good, obedient, and studious. None of you caused grief in the family. Oh, you were all very independent and probably could have gone in many directions. Now, I don't understand much, but perhaps the fear of your father kept everyone in line until you were old enough to be wise and choose God for yourselves.

"Then again, your love for your mother kept you all close.

134

Few families are as closely knit as the Tweten bunch." Uncle Barney smiled at Harold and me. "You can see I loved him. Your Papa saved my life, you know."

Harold and I waited quietly for Barney to go on.

"Every one of us fights a lonely battle—some a power battle or an emotional battle like your father did, and then some of us mortals have the conflict with a beautiful Delilah. We all have our Bathshebas, one way or another. I thought I was strong, but I, too, came to the place of such guilt that I couldn't face living another day. Your father understood me."

Uncle Barney looked directly at me. "That night on the Brooklyn bridge, with the blackness of despair all around me, I knew I couldn't live with my agony of soul. It was then that your father came.

"We walked off the bridge together. There was no condemnation from your Papa, only love and a new beginning." Uncle Barney wiped his eyes. "You see, I loved him. He saved my life. That is the part of him you must hold to."

I never saw Uncle Barney again. He and his wife Mildred continued to minister with their special love until Barney died years later in a tragic fire.

But he helped me to remember to "hold to the good," and to leave the mystery of life's battles and question marks in God's hands.

Again as I look longingly across Lake Barkley to my rock-enclosed island, the sun rises over the hills in triumph over the darkness. Just so, each one of Mama's children came through their own darkness to rejoice and to start singing that song of the soul set free.

When I was a young child, Mama would sit beside my bed and ask, "Margaret, is there anything you need to ask forgiveness for?"

Then we would pray together over the little sins that so "easily beset us." I learned early to keep those short accounts with God. I also learned, very early, to forgive—especially to forgive Papa in regard to the rag doll. Mama taught me a bedrock foundational truth that I have since learned to understand in even greater measure.

I recall one event when Papa's unreasonable anger was vented toward me. I was a high school student and the anger rolled up into a flame within me. For a moment I had only one desire—to lash back in fury at Papa.

But when I saw the tears running down his cheeks, the fury in me left. Slowly, I put my arms around him and said, "Papa, I love you."

But the ability to forgive had begun long before that. As a six-year-old child I walked the aisle in the Winnipeg auditorium to stand before Dr. R. A. Torrey. "I want to give my heart to Jesus," I told him.

The reality of God's love for me never has left me!

From Oswald Chambers (*My Utmost for His Highest*) I read: "In external history the cross is an infinitesimal thing; from the Bible's point of view it is of more importance than all the empires of the world. We have to concentrate on the great point of spiritual energy—the cross—to keep in contact with the center where all the power lies, and the energy will be let loose."

One by one, Mama's children came to the cross where the redemptive love of God through Jesus Christ became a reality. There were still unsolved mysteries, but the one thing we understood was that each one comes to the cross alone to make a personal decision to accept God's "so great salvation," regardless of the messenger. God's plan is perfect. Somehow it comes through, even through imperfect messengers.

Each one of the Tweten children had to face the truth of God's Word and make a personal decision. At six I believed that God so loved Margaret that He gave His only begotten Son, that if Margaret believed in Him, Margaret would not perish, but Margaret would have eternal life.

Belief also came to each of the others—for God so loved Grace, God so loved Gordon, God so loved Doris, God so loved Joyce, and God so loved Jeanelle.

That is just the beginning for all of us. After that we build ourselves up in the most holy faith. Then the battle begins!

One by one, we come to understand what Paul prayed for in Ephesians 1:17-19: "That the God of our Lord Jesus Christ, the Father of glory, may give unto you the spirit of wisdom and revelation in the knowledge of him . . . [to know] the hope of his calling . . . riches of . . . his inheritance . . . exceeding greatness of his power."

Into each of Mama's children came a hunger and thirst for knowing God.

St. Augustine, after his conversion, saw that the Scriptures were not words to be interpreted; they were words that interpreted their reader: "There can be no holiness apart from the work of the Holy Spirit—in quickening us by grace to Christ, and in sanctifying us—for it is grace that causes us to even want to be holy."

Because Mama's children searched the Scriptures, they desired only to walk in obedience to God.

Grace, always composed and efficient, came through her battle with darkness into the glorious light of a soul set free. Because of her struggle, she reaches out to others to show them a better way.

Gordon grew in knowledge and the wisdom of his world—a scholar in Greek and Hebrew, successful in business, but with a cool cynicism and aloofness from Papa. Gordon's heart was still numb with hurt from his childhood. He was young when he met Christ, but he came home from the military service with spiritual indifference. When God marked a miracle in our own prodigal's life, Gordon was deeply influenced.

Then the mystery of the grace of God, the work of the Holy Spirit, exploded into reality in Gordon's life. Love and forgiveness swept their way across the years to the heart of Papa when Gordon said, "I forgive you and I love you." That love poured out into every area of Gordon's life and reached out to bless his sisters.

A reunion with Gordon and his wife Alice became a praise gathering. In my mind I can still hear him singing a song from Scripture:

The Spirit of the Lord
Is now upon me
To open prison doors
And set the captive free,

137

To open blinded eyes
And cause the blind to see.
The Spirit of the Lord
Is now upon me.

Our theme song became, "Oh come let us adore Him!"

Gordon sang the song of the soul set free!

Doris, with her spirit of determination, went off to Wheaton College with one hundred dollars in her purse.

"I need work now, or I won't eat!" she declared.

So she cleaned the homes of the faculty.

"I need a winter coat now," she declared.

Doris found fifty dollars in her mailbox for the material, and while others made pajamas, Doris's Home Economics teacher helped her sew a winter coat.

Doris marched to her own music of dedicated determination.

Then came the day when she sang a new song—the song of the soul set free—free to love and forgive and reach out with compassion. "I can do all things through Christ" is now her theme.

Joyce Solveig, the insecure, frightened one, was sensitive to the storms around her but secure in Mama's lap. Finally, she turned to her own refuge in the time of storm—the Word of God. "Fear thou not; for I am with thee" (Isaiah 41:10).

Today her song is "Through it all, I've learned to trust in Jesus. . . . " Now she sings the song of the soul set free.

Jeanelle, the youngest, was the one closest to Papa's heart. She was the child he held on his shoulder through her nights of illness.

When the rest of us left home, Jeanelle stayed close to Mama's heart in a covenant with God. Together Mama and Jeanelle believed God for miracles. Jeanelle held Papa's hand with quiet understanding but grieved over what he could have been. Through shadows and valleys, Papa's youngest has learned a deep walk with God, and she, too, sings the song of the soul set free.

Each one of us has come through dangers, toils, snares, and tears, as Uncle Barney had. But we all arrived safely through

God's matchless amazing grace. North, South, East, and West, you can hear us singing our song—the song of the soul set free. Hallelujah, hallelujah! The song of the soul set free.

The Children's Uncle Barney

Some leave monuments of fame,
A sweeping sunset done in oil,
A bridge to span the ocean wave,
An empire built from common toil.
But down life's road there comes but one
Who spins his magic on a child,
That bit of gold when day is done,
Weaver of stories, sweet and wild.
His wide brown eyes of mystery,
Enchanting smile that children know,
He drew them close upon his knee
And sang sweet songs of long ago.
This one—a part of life and daring
Who loved, not wisely, but too well—
Came from the cliffs and fjords, bearing
Tales from craggy coast and snowy dell.
With battered mandolin and plaintive tune,
He sang of lovers lost at sea—
Golden hair, a windswept dune,
The ocean crossing over the lee.
With him we climbed the rugged cliffs
Or sailed the seas across the foam
And fought great storms in iron ships,
But never failed to come back home.
And always there would be tomorrow
Dime store trips—a lollipop,
An ice cream cone for childish sorrow,
A splash of sun on a small raindrop.
This world of dreams and make-believe
Belongs to children, full of wonder.
The years find time enough to grieve;
Let childhood keep the right to ponder.

139

Hand in hand, he walked with us;
Bending low, he wiped a tear
Side by side he talked with us
And listened to each childish fear.
"Some day they'll say old Barney's gone.
Don't you believe it—no grief for me.
I'll be singing a glory song
With heaven's children round my knee."
Some build monuments of fame,
A life of victory and power
But one walked gently childhood's lane
And left us with one shining hour.

25

Life's Cedar Chest

At 6 A.M. we were at the Wilmington Airport again. This time I was heading for the snow-covered plains of Minnesota. My husband Harold checked the bags and waved good-bye as I boarded the jet. Harold would turn homeward to the typewriter and table full of manuscript pages. I could visualize him praying for the gift of interpretation when he viewed my hasty scrawl.

Mama had always said, "*Ja, ja,* you do what you have to do." For me, that was writing on yellow pads in airports, on planes, or at a kitchen table at 4 A.M.! Even now a yellow pad rested on my lap as I leaned back against the cushioned seat. But I didn't write. My thoughts danced and sparkled like the shimmering waters of Lake Barkley where the rocky island lingered as a still place in my memory.

There was a time when Mama's children opened a cedar chest of memories, then closed the lid on the why of yesterday and opened the door on the how of tomorrow.

Each one of Mama's children knew what *atonement* meant. Being "at one" with God through Jesus Christ affected every area of our lives. We had heard Papa preach and Mama pray. The power of the Holy Spirit made us realize the redemptive work of God in our lives, and the Holy Spirit made the life of Christ in us visible in the marketplace. This we knew. This was the anchor, the absolute in our lives, from which we did not waver.

Oswald Chambers wrote in *My Utmost for His Highest*, "The Holy Spirit is deity in processing power, who applies the atonement to our experience." All Mama and Papa's children came to understand the processing power of God as we opened our chest of memories and allowed God's indwelling presence to bring renewal to our minds.

Looking back I marvel at God's processing power to bring to remembrance the things stored in life's "cedar chest."

I lift the lid slowly, cautiously, looking in my heart for a picture showing the family gathered for Thanksgiving dinner in Brooklyn Church on 57th Street.

Papa was closing the door on sixty-eight years of preaching the gospel. Mama had prepared her last family Thanksgiving dinner. Together we helped with the packing in preparation for their retirement in Florida where they would be near Jeanelle, their youngest child.

All day Papa had packed his books in boxes—some to be given away, others to be sent to Florida. Mama lovingly marked her earthly treasures with her children's names.

It was late when we said, "Good night, Mama. Good night, Papa." He was still in his study, surrounded by boxes and empty shelves. When morning came, Mama's coffee pot sent the message, and the sleeping household came alive.

But Papa, his face grey with grief, was sitting in his study— where his books were back on the shelf. Gordon broke the silence. "Just leave the books, Papa, and I will send them to you when you get your study ready."

Mama urged gently, "Come, Papa, it is time for coffee."

Later Papa shuffled back to his books while Mama and her children continued packing. Papa was in his place.

I put that memory back in its place. From the "heart chest" I drew out another picture.

During one of Papa's earlier visits to our home, he sat

playing the piano. His music stopped abruptly. "What's wrong, Papa?" I asked.

He shook his snow-white head. "Margaret, I just realized that I am seventy years old and I'll never play the piano any better than I play today. I always wanted to play well. And now the years have passed too fast. Too fast," he mumbled solemnly. "All my life I wanted to do everything better—to improve my English and my preaching. *Ja,* the time, it goes too fast."

He reached for his Bible, but he couldn't read. His eyes were filled with tears. I didn't know what to say, so I put my arms around him and pressed my cheek against his. He didn't seem to notice, he just turned to his Book.

I put that picture back in my "chest" and wondered if I could have said more—and did he notice?

Thirteen years before, when Papa returned from Norway, he had made one of his rare visits to Harold's and my home. He was vibrant, as happy as a little boy coming home from camp. We sat at the table drinking coffee and he recalled his visit to the old homeplace after forty years.

In glowing terms, Papa told about his beautiful sisters and their fine children. Knute, his older brother, a powerful, muscular man, lived alone on the Tweten farm in Bamble, Norway. Papa was proud of his family. We laughed when he told about Uncle Knute's straw bed, "*Ja,* Margaret, I burned Knute's straw bed and bought a real bed with a good mattress. Believe me, Knute wasn't happy about that, but I suggested to him that he should sleep in the new bed for one week."

Papa chuckled delightedly. "He never mentioned the straw bed again."

I listened to stories of bravery that came out of the nightmare of the Nazi occupation of Norway. The bunkers in the yards told the story of that tragic hour. But Knute, who lived alone in a remote area, had escaped German occupation of his home.

Papa sent frantic requests to Mama in America for coffee, linens, curtains, and even medication that was unattainable in Norway at that time. That morning as we sat at the kitchen table, I saw a practical side of Papa as he told of making repairs on the old family home and painting the house and barn. Joy and nostalgia blended as he told about getting new appliances into the old kitchen, even a radio. Knute, the recluse, got a view of the world through the eyes of his younger brother.

During his evenings in Norway, Papa sang and played his guitar and read the Bible to Knute. Uncle Knute gave Papa a black horse called Midnight. During the visit, Midnight and Papa were inseparable. I had visions of Papa riding in the valley through snow-covered woods. He told of sleigh rides and falling into snow banks, of green pastures and spring, of birds and flowers, of hills and mountains.

Every day Knute carried his lunch pail into the forest where he cut lumber for his livelihood. The two brothers, so different, were one in the old homeplace where once rang the laughter of father, mother, sisters, and brothers.

Papa sang the old songs while his older brother listened pensively about another world he would never see—America.

I had a picture in my heart of Uncle Knute sitting on the porch looking out over the fields and woods as the sun cast a glow over his world. He would never understand what a man could learn from books in a musty library, in America. Here in Bamble, a man walked tall like the towering timber of the woods. Grain from the fields and food from the gardens filled the barns. Besides that, hunting and fishing provided all a man needed. In the evening, a quiet contentment filled Knute's heart. What could a man find in books that he, Knute Tweten, didn't have? He had the majesty of mountains, waterfalls and crystal springs, animals for company, birds to sing in the early morning, and the song of doves in the evening time. Knute was content.

If there were the mystery of a woman's love in Uncle Knute's life, the secret lay buried within him. He communed only with God and His creation around him. Uncle Knute was in his place.

But Papa, the younger brother lost in his books, was also in his place.

I closed the lid softly. There would be another time to look into memory's cedar chest.

144

26

"Did I Miss Something?"

In March of 1973, Papa's children were gathered around the fireplace singing, "Surely goodness and mercy shall follow me all the days, all the days of my life. . . ."

Mama, her frail hands folded, rocked quietly and sang with us.

Across the road from Doris and David's home in North Carolina, the wind blew over a fresh, lonely grave. Near their place, a yellow house stood watch over the valley—the dream house where Mama and Papa had planned to move after spending some years in Florida. Inside, the study was full of Papa's books, a study he would never see.

Papa had gone Home!

Mama would make that final move from Florida into the yellow house in North Carolina alone—yet, not alone, for goodness and mercy would follow her.

My heart was tender as I heard Harold's words over Papa's grave, "Lord, Thou hast been our dwelling place to all generations. Thou art God. Lord, in Elius N. Tweten—'Papa' to all of us—was a man in whom there was no guile. A man who trusted God, stood up for Jesus, and believed and defended the Bible as God's divinely inspired Word. 'Blessed are the pure in heart.'"

Harold concluded with Papa's familiar benediction from Hebrews 13:20-21:

Now the God of peace,
that brought again from the dead our Lord Jesus,
that great shepherd of the sheep,
through the blood of the everlasting covenant,
Make you perfect in every good work to do his will,
working in you that which is wellpleasing in his sight,
through Jesus Christ;
to whom be glory for ever and ever.
Amen.

Papa had served the God of peace for many years. Now the man who had struggled with anger as his one prevailing flaw had been made perfect. We couldn't grieve, for somehow in our imagination we saw Papa in the libraries of heaven talking with his beloved authors, Charles Haddon Spurgeon and Matthew Henry. From out of the past came the lawgiver Moses, the prophet Isaiah, the poet David, philosophers, teachers, and preachers. The living Book was now alive to Papa. He left his books to meet the authors, particularly the Author and Finisher of his faith.

One by one, Mama's children took the journey into the past with its mountains and valleys, sunshine and shadow, agony and ecstasy. Each of Mama's children came through to view the yesterdays with love and understanding instead of judgment and condemnation.

The great Communicator, the Holy Spirit, had built a bridge from the minister in the pulpit to the father who had broken communication with his family because of one tragic sin—uncontrolled anger.

The very Word that Papa preached, James 1:19, warns us all to be slow to anger. Anger and wisdom seldom live together. Somewhere along life's way I had heard that "anger is a wind which blows out the lamp of the mind." With the passing of years, Mama's children could open the chest of memories and discard the wood, hay, and stubble, and remember the gold and silver of Papa's life.

We discarded the memories of how we all desired to take Mama out of the "winds of anger" and carry her to our "safe" places. Instead, we kept the covenant God had with Mama. Mama would trust and obey. God would keep her children by His power. Mama did not fail. God could not fail. We kept the gold and silver, knowing that the Lord was a strong tower; the righteous could run there and be safe.

Together we discarded the winds of anger directed at us in our youth when Papa's reason and wisdom's lamp went out. Together we kept the gold that came on the wings of love and understanding. The great Communicator kept building bridges for us.

Over the years, Mama had listened quietly while her children opened the lid on yesterday and watched as the balm of Gilead, the matchless love of God, the comfort of the Holy Spirit, brought healing to her wounded children. She knew. God could not fail.

Grace, the quiet peacemaker, had always typed Papa's sermons and helped him with his correspondence. Like David of old who soothed Saul's restless spirit, Grace played the music that was the one major area of communication between Papa and the children.

From the dark and dusty backroads of the mind, Grace discarded the stubble and remembered the gold—the trips with Papa to the great Moody Memorial Church to hear outstanding Bible teachers, the concerts in Radio City, and the visits to Calvary Baptist Church in New York. Papa was unashamedly proud of Grace's accomplishments, especially her work in Switzerland with the Billy Graham Conference. Before his death, the time did come—suddenly, like a flash of lightning—when Papa saw us as adults and expressed his delight in Mama's children. "*Ja, ja*, Mama, you did a good job!"

Joyce Solveig, who had cringed in fear during the winds of Papa's anger, remembered a childhood moment in his loving arms. It was during a seventeenth of May festival in Humboldt

Park, Chicago. In the excitement of the Norwegian parade, Joyce wandered away into the crowd.

Over the noise of the crowd came the booming voice on the loud speaker, "Will Reverend Tweten please come to 'Lost and Found' to get his daughter?"

Joyce shuddered. Knowing how angry Papa would be was worse than being lost. She saw him stride through the crowd, pushing his way free. The anger didn't come.

Instead Joyce was swooped up in loving arms and held tenderly as he cried, "*Min lilla Solveig, min lilla Solveig* (my little Solveig)."

"I remember feeling so safe and loved," Joyce whispered. "I wanted the moment to last forever."

Today, Joyce had discarded the fear of Papa and kept the gold of "safe and loved" in her memory chest.

Doris walked with Gordon through the winds of anger, gently leading him to unconditional love and forgiveness. They discarded the chaff and stubble from the storehouse of yesterday. For Gordon there was inner peace from the bitter memory of a shiny fifty-cent piece rolling across the floor. Together, as Doris and Gordon thought of Papa, they clung to the gold and silver of unconditional love and forgiveness.

Peace had come for Gordon long before Papa's death, and with tears of joy, the beautiful reconciliation between father and son was fully realized through the power of the Holy Spirit. On that grand occasion, they had faced one another at the table—two stubborn, independent men—weeping, hugging, forgiving, loving. The love of God was shed abroad in the hearts of all of Mama's children, and they chose to live in obedience to God. God would keep their children, and their children's children, from generation to generation.

Doris and I attended the James Mason prayer meeting on Tuesday nights where we saw the miracles of God's so great salvation, and the salvation of my son, Ralph.

This godly, white-haired man, James Mason, had become the spiritual father we never knew. From him we learned that love never fails. We learned to discard the why of yesterday and to turn to the how for tomorrow. Paul and Silas hadn't cried why and like them Mr. Mason moved on to the how—singing praises to the God of his salvation.

One night, two years before Papa's death, Doris and I took Papa to hear Mr. Mason. Music burst forth from the piano, organ, and other instruments, blending with the voices of praise of the people in the room. These people had been set free from the bondage of the past and were singing songs that the world could not understand. It was the sweet sound of "Amazing Grace."

Papa listened. He heard the same message he had preached, yet he sensed a spirit of love and praise that was deeper than he had ever known.

Late that night, he looked at me with misty eyes. "Tell me, Margaret. Did I miss something? In all my years of preaching, did I miss something?"

He was eighty-three years old, still ramrod straight. I answered gently, "Papa, you have faithfully preached God's Word all these years according to the light you had."

"*Ja, ja*, Margaret, I have been faithful." He ran his hand through his snow-white hair. "That I know, but Mr. Mason has something, a love, that I have missed."

Inside, I wanted to cry out, *You did miss it, Papa! You missed the love and communication with your children. You missed walking gently with Mama.* I almost choked thinking, *You missed the worth of your son, Gordon. You missed the victory over the sin of anger.* I could have lashed out at him so easily saying, *You never realized that the power of God in you was greater than the anger that came from the enemy. Satan wanted to destroy you, Papa. But the enemy didn't win—for you were kept by the power of God. You were kept by the same power that raised Jesus from the dead and was able to make you more than a conqueror over the winds of anger. You did miss a lot of things—but you didn't miss God's unchanging love!*

I wanted to cry it out, to tell him at last—but after all these years I couldn't say it. Papa stood before me, his white hair framing his sad, tear-filled eyes. I could only put my arms around him.

Tonight, two years later, Jeanelle remembers the outpouring of his heart before God took our father home.

It was as though the Holy Spirit, the great Communicator, had brought to his memory all he had missed. Then like sunrise after a long dark night, God let Papa hear the song of the soul set free: "Amazing grace! how sweet the sound. . . ."

Once again Mama's children looked into the chest of memories, and piece by piece we put the gold and silver back into the treasure chest.

With Gordon, we sang together, "Oh, come, let us adore Him. . . . For Thou alone art worthy, Christ, the Lord."

Oh so gently, we closed the lid. Jesus had spoken "Peace, be still!" to the winds of anger.

It was 1975 when Mama and her daughters stood beside the second grave on the hill. The wind cried in the valley as another sound echoed from the courts of heaven—the sound of a soul set free. Our brother, Gordon, had been cut down in the prime of his life with an aneurysm. The reunion between father and son was now complete. Through our heartache and tears, we joined in singing, "Amazing grace! how sweet the sound. . . ."

Like Papa, Gordon had a restless nature, an unquenchable thirst for knowledge, and a bent toward independence. He was an intellectual man—a man who could be both cynical and compassionate, stubborn and gentle. He was a good friend, a hard worker, a man given to laughter, and a man consumed with goals. Gordon had an unending love for books and music, New York City, and his wife and children. He was also Mama's "boy" and a brother adored by his sisters. But for years a distance existed between Papa and Gordon, father and son. Finally the seeds of faith that had been planted in Gordon in childhood, and had always been part of him, burst forth in his adulthood. He became a spiritual giant, a man who experienced and extended unconditional love and forgiveness. Gordon became outside what he had always been deep inside—a man with a warm, responsive heart.

If God had given us the choice, we would have said, "It's too soon, Lord. He's too young." But deep within we knew that

150

Gordon was free, at home with his Savior and walking the courts of heaven with Papa. We could not ask for more.

Gordon Lund Tweten

The sound of taps across the hill,
A silent pause,
And the world is still.
A swaying branch of scented pine,
Gentle breezes
Over the hills of time.
Light fills the glory of the dawn,
Eternal Home!
Glorious sunrise—earth's shadows gone!
Worship and praise around the throne,
Hallelujahs ring,
Worthy, worthy, worthy is my King.

"The blanket of snow covers the bleakness of winter," Mama had always said, "but when winter comes, the next thing to come is spring." Just so, the blanket of God's love covers the bleakness of sad memories. Mama had only a year and a half left, just one springtime, after Gordon's homegoing.

On January 16, 1977, at 2 P.M., with a blanket of snow outside covering the bleakness of winter, we gathered to say good-bye to Mama. The quiet memorial service defied the blizzard raging on the other side of the church walls. "Let not your heart be troubled" once again sounded across the pages of time.

A settled faith lingered in the hearts of the five sisters, Mama's daughters. We followed her grey casket into the icy wind—so reminiscent of the Canadian winters.

We buried Mama beside Papa and Gordon. The two older graves were covered with snow. Bundled in coats and scarves, we braced ourselves against the wind and huddled together around Mama's open grave.

Across the road Mama's yellow house stood empty and silent, the coffee pot cold.

Slowly we walked to Doris and David's big house where logs blazed with warmth and the coffee was hot. An amber glow of love engulfed us. We knew that Mama was safe in the house of the Lord forever. The restless stream, Papa, and the flowing river, Mama, were eternally united by God's amazing grace.

Papa, Mama, and Gordon—all in their place.

The winter of the soul will pass. The next thing to come is spring, for "some golden daybreak, Jesus will come!" Then we shall see Him face to face.

> *Dear Lord,*
> *Please take our reservation.*
> *Mark down the time and place*
> *Where we may walk together*
> *And talk face to face.*
> *We know there will be many*
> *Singing of Your grace,*
> *But—take our reservation.*
> *Mark down our time and place.*
> *—Margaret, Grace, Doris, Joyce Solveig, Jeanelle*

27

Papa's Homeplace

From Porsgruno, Rolf drove over winding roads, through valleys and hills until we saw a sign marked *Bamble*. Then, turning around the rocky bends, we saw where the road led to a mailbox: *Tveten*. My heart skipped a beat.

Following the lane from the mailbox we saw the white, sturdy house on the right, the barns on the left. "So this is Papa's homeplace!" I exclaimed as we walked to the house where Elius N. Tveten, one of nine children, was born on May 18, 1888.

No curtains hung in the windows. No flower boxes looked out on the overgrown gardens. The sounds of living had echoed into the past.

Harold and cousin Rolf walked around the barns while Jan and I followed a rocky trail to Papa's potato field. Nestled in the hills was a valley of rich soil where Papa had planted his gardens. Long ago, during one of Papa's rare sentimental moods, he had told me about walking hand in hand with his mother to the potato field. In the middle of planting, she had stopped and said, "Look up, Elius, and listen to the song of the potato bird." Hand in hand again, mother and son stood to listen.

I knew how Papa felt. My grandchildren enjoy working with

me in the garden. In the middle of work someone will say, "Look at that butterfly," or, "Watch the squirrels," and we stop to look. Then it's back to work and the children drop cut potatoes into the holes. Kathryn decides it is faster to dump a bucketful into a hole, and our dog Yenta, a yellow Lab, retrieves the hidden potatoes. We face a challenge, but the result will be potatoes for the whole neighborhood.

I could visualize my grandmother, Papa's mother, doing what I enjoy doing—walking to the garden with a child's hand in one hand, a hoe in the other.

As I stood at Papa's place looking over the valley, I saw a rocky hill, like a huge boulder. That had to be the place my father had wistfully described. To him it probably had a greater significance than we could know. But the fact that he mentioned a specific place gave it special meaning to me.

Standing there, Janice and I shared our thoughts about the places we had seen: the one-room, framed schoolhouse that remained unchanged; the Lutheran church with the steeple, where the Twetens were baptized, confirmed, married, and buried; the graveyard with its Tveten gravemarkers and memorials to past generations. We talked about the four farms where my father worked as a child attending school, and the four-mile, rocky, dusty road to the schoolhouse.

In my mind I heard, *You can't go home again.* But in my heart I knew *you can go home again.* I did! I came "home" to the roots where part of me belongs. I came "home" to learn a deeper understanding of how to bring the past into the present. In knowing the past, I can prepare better for the future.

The wind blew through the trees surrounding Papa's lonely childhood home. The barn was silent. The cows, chickens, and horses were gone. The overgrown gardens were a reminder of another time when fruit trees blossomed in the spring, flowers grew in window boxes, and the house rang with the sounds of living.

Now the wind sighed over the lonely valley as the sun lingered over the "rock" near the potato field. Reluctantly, we turned to leave. I took one final glance back over a time that is no more.

154

I settled back in Rolf's car and tried to imagine what life had been. Stories from the past come slowly for the Norwegian people. They carry their sorrows inside and move into the living present with patience and courage.

I was hearing stories that my father never told. Therefore, I knew the "rock" that he had mentioned had to be special to him.

Putting the bits and pieces together in my heart, I found my thoughts going back to a long-ago time, a time that could have been. I saw a young, golden-haired, blue-eyed boy running across the open field, thin coat open, hair blowing in the wind, to climb up on his "rock." With arms outstretched he shouted to the world, "I'm king of the mountain!"

I visualized him walking slowly beside his mother later as they followed a small coffin to the graveyard. One of his sisters, his playmate, had died with the Black Sickness, a type of influenza. Papa watched the family nail a black cross on the door. Not understanding any of it, the young boy, Elius, ran to his place, to the rock. There he sobbed alone.

When spring came, the gentle mother took Elius by the hand. "Come, we plant potatoes." Living goes on.

Another day came when another black cross was nailed on the door, then another, and another, until young Elius had seen four crosses, one after the other, nailed to the door of his home. The wind howled over the churchyard. Elius ran to his rock again and again and cried alone. Perhaps he wondered if he would be next to go into a box.

When spring came, as it always does, even after the winter of the soul, there was the cry of a newborn baby. Then a year later, there was another sound of new life.

Knute, the eldest son, helped his father till the soil and cut the timber. For Elius there was no time for play since his fragile mother needed his help to plant the garden, do the chores, and care for the little ones.

Then there came another time when from the top of his "rock" he heard the sound of death—hammers nailing another black cross on the door. This time, the strong father had died. The mother, a new life within her, held the young girls while

155

eight-year-old Elius and Knute, fourteen, watched in utter despair.

Knute tilled the land, cut the timber, and Elius tended to chores and gardens and watched over his frail mother. Once again the black day of sorrow came when the five surviving children stood around the grave of their mother. Knute was fifteen, Elius, nine, and the youngest of three little sisters was six months old.

Elius and the three sisters were taken into separate homes where they remained for several years. Elius was boarded out to four different farm homes where he had chores to complete before and after school. When he was fifteen he returned to live with Knute until he went to America two years later.

Knute, too old for his years, stayed on the farm to till the land and cut timber. He stayed until he died at the age of ninety. He had gone to the woods with his lunch pail and axe. They found him there, sitting on a log, at rest from his labors.

Years later, Papa told me how terrified he was of the dark woods around his temporary home after his mother's death. He had to carry two pails of water from the spring through the woods and couldn't run. The sounds were magnified by fear of imaginary animals and the unbearable loneliness of being separated from his family.

Papa seldom spoke of his childhood; but when he returned from his trip to Norway to visit his homeplace after forty years, he told me about the "rock" and the song of the potato bird.

"I was so lonely in those strange homes, but when I could get away, I ran for miles to go up on the rock. Then I would call out over the valley, 'Mor, Mor (Mother, Mother),' but the echo returned." I can still hear Papa saying, "I longed for the time when we planted potatoes and listened to the song of the bird. I went back to that spot when I visited Norway, and looked out over the valley. Margaret, for a moment the old grief returned," he admitted. "But suddenly, from out of the sky came the song of a bird. It seemed that the bird sang just for me. Then suddenly, it disappeared into the blue sky."

Is this when his anger built? I wondered, *back then in his lonely childhood?*

I wanted Papa to tell me more about his childhood, but he shrugged his shoulders. "*Ja, ja,* life is a mystery," he mused. Then quietly he returned to his books.

I leaned back against the seat of Rolf's car. For days now I had traced the roots of my beginnings. But had I not also traced the roots of Papa's anger? A boy orphaned early and tossed to and fro in foster homes, a boy too old for his years? Had the anger built in his soul as each family member died, as each black cross was nailed to the door of his childhood? I thought of Papa and his fear of the dark woods after the death of his young mother. No wonder he had learned to escape into books. No wonder he didn't go on to the university to study more, to teach. His early years had been years of responsibility. He wasn't accustomed to following his dreams, only his chores.

But even in his childhood Papa had a rock to run to—it had set a pattern for his life. No wonder it was so easy for Papa to run to the Rock of Ages.

Before we realized it, Rolf was turning into the driveway of cousin Ella's lovely home. Inside, rustic walls held the trophies of her husband's hunting trips and the aroma of coffee already filled the room.

Beautiful handiwork and her gourmet cooking showed Ella's creativity. Around the table we enjoyed the delicious food and the love and warmth of family and friends. We shared our faith in God, and when I sang an old Norwegian song, Ella reached for her guitar. We sat together singing, Ella strumming the guitar, "*Himmel og jorg kan brenner.*" It was a song about everything disappearing—the heavens and the earth, cliffs and valleys—but the one who believes God will know that His promises never change.

When the song ended, Ella gently handed me the guitar. "This was your father's guitar," she said softly. "When he went to America, he gave it to my mother. Before she died, she gave it to me. Now, Margaret, I give it to you."

Her beautiful expression stays before me even now. I can

still see her clearly as she took my hands and said in Norwegian, "You pray for me and I will pray for you."

You can go "home" again. Back to your roots, your heritage, your beginning.

I did!

Gently, I close the lid on the treasure chest of the past. We have traveled far—from the tent on the Canadian prairies back to the homeplace.

Now it is time to move toward the tomorrows that are in God's hands—just as the yesterdays, with their winds and storms, sunshine and peace, were in God's faithful hands.

From the past we learn that God is faithful and the faith of yesterday rekindles faith for today. We can trust Him with the depths of our sorrows, for He is acquainted with grief.

We also learn that God even trusts us, with all our frailties, to be the bearers of His love.

God's covenant and our obedience will move into the tomorrows, from generation to generation. My heart is full of praise.

Somehow, throughout the courts of heaven I hear the sound of "Amazing Grace."

Papa, do you see this other young man? Across the miles from glory, can you see him so like you, Papa? Blond hair blown by the wind. Clear blue eyes. Strong and sturdy—a true Norwegian. Do you see him, Papa, as he looks out over his congregation? Do you see him step behind the sacred desk?

From the open Bible, do you hear the sound of "Amazing Grace," or "For God so loved the world"?

Do you see him now, Papa—this young preacher behind the pulpit—one so like yourself? The Reverend Mr. Robert Keiter. He's your grandson, Papa. He followed in your steps.

28

Papa's Bible

I am home again where the sun shines on the pampas grass and the ocean rolls over the sandy shore. The Minnesota snow is a fading memory. But the love and warmth of friends stay gently on my mind.

This morning my "still" place is in the kitchen with my books and yellow legal pad pages strewn over the table. It is early and the world is asleep, but my coffee pot is awake.

In my hands I hold two books. One is my father's Norwegian Bible; the other, his Norwegian songbook, *Evangelisten*. The note in the Bible says:

Dear Margaret,

This is for you, in loving memory of your father.

Love, Mother
1973

Turning the yellow pages of the songbook, I read the words of the familiar lullaby that I used with our children. Now I sing the same song to my grandchildren:

Sangen om Jesus
Syng den igjen, igjen.

(Songs about Jesus, sing them again and again.)

Sermon notes are tucked between the pages of the Bible and the songbook. Some are written in Norwegian, others in English. My childhood language returns with the help of a Norwegian dictionary as I look at one of Papa's sermons on the "Grace of God and Reasons to Believe." The sermon closes with Romans 11:33: "O the depth of the riches both of the wisdom and knowledge of God! how unsearchable are his judgments, and his ways past finding out!"

I reach for the books on my shelf—Papa's worn *Treasury of David*. (It has taken me four years to get to Spurgeon's fourth volume.)

The marked pages in Spurgeon read, "The Bible should be our Mentor, Monitor, our Momento Mori, our Remembrance and the keeper of our conscience."

My sister Joyce Solveig has a favorite picture of Papa, with his snow-white head bent over the open Bible. My mental picture is one of Papa meticulously dressed in his striped trousers, swallow-tail coat, and high starched collar. (Mama alone ironed Papa's starched shirt for Sundays.)

When Papa stood behind the pulpit and opened his Bible, it was with a sense of awe that Mama and her children knew that Papa was in his place. To Papa, the pulpit was the sacred place from which mortal man proclaimed, "Thus saith the Lord."

It is through this memory that Mama's children are able to leave the quicksand of human speculation as to the why of Papa's winds of anger. From this we are able to move to the higher ground of God's divine love and matchless grace.

To all of us who have been wounded by winds of anger, in whatever form the storms come, there is only one place of surety—the cross. "The cross," according to Oswald Chambers, "is the point where God and sinful man merge with a crash, and the way to life is opened—but the crash is on the heart of God" (*My Utmost for His Highest*). Only at the cross can we realize how much we have been forgiven; then we can cry out, "I forgive as I have been forgiven."

In Harry Dent's book *Cover Up*, he deals with the Watergate in all of us, the desire to cover up. For me, it would have been easy to cover the winds of anger, but in my travel, I have heard the cries of many who have been wounded by life's storms. The storms of anger can damage all of us, but the stagnant pool of unforgiveness will destroy us.

Only when we are uncovered to the grace of God can we be covered by the love of God. There is no firmer ground than forgiveness.

All through the pages of Papa's sermons I read the message of God's grace and mercy—and "God is faithful." Today I finally see Papa as a man hungry for God, the way God must have seen him. Yesterday, I saw only the storm in the man.

Through the ages God's perfect plan has been carried out through imperfect people. Looking through the notes, I smiled at Papa's three-point sermons. One caught my attention:

> *A Formula for Duty Living:*
> 1. *Prayer—Motivating force.*
> 2. *Pluck—Impelling force.*
> 3. *Perspiration—Accomplishing force.*

I think back, remembering the day when Papa took me to Paul Rader's tabernacle in Chicago to hear Gypsy Smith.

"Listen to Gypsy Smith's words, Margaret," Papa told me. "He paints pictures with words like an artist paints with oil. Every time I hear Gypsy Smith he makes the gospel fresh and new. Margaret, we must never lose the wonder of the cross."

I read from the marked Spurgeon volume: "It is not enough to read the Bible. Meditation assists the memory to lock up the jewels of divine truth in her treasury. It has the digesting power to turn special truth into nourishment. It helps to renew the heart to grow upward and increase in power to know the things freely given of God."

Again I am reminded that we must act upon truth or it becomes dry rot within us.

161

While I was sorting through Papa's papers, the phone rang. It was Monroe Holvick, an old friend of the family. After their fifty-one years of happy marriage, his wife Leona had died at the age of ninety-two. Monroe was remembering their years as rural American Sunday school missionaries.

"I was led to the Lord in your father's church," Monroe choked, "and your father baptized me and married Leona and me."

Moments later he said, "Leona and I read *First We Have Coffee* three times and we laughed and cried together, remembering many happy hours in your home."

"Monroe, tell me, what do you remember the most about my father? I'm writing a sequel to *First We Have Coffee*, a book called *Papa's Place.*"

"Oh, how wonderful! Your father? The Bible, Margaret. He was a man with the Book. How he loved the Word of God!"

"Do you remember his explosive temper?"

A quiet pause followed, then gently Monroe answered, "I loved him too much to remember that part. I only remember how much your Papa loved God and people in need. Every time he preached, we went home with something to remember."

Kindly he added, "Even Moses had a temper, Margaret."

When our conversation ended, I realized again how much love covers and I prayed, "Lord, help me to see others through eyes of love, rather than of judgment."

I reach into Papa's sermon notes again and see this:

> *Amazing Love:*
> 1. *Nature.*
> 2. *Object.*
> 3. *Gift.*
> 4. *Blessing.*
> 5. *Terms laid down by God.*

How Papa loved oratory! He practiced for hours to improve his English. His notes to himself read:

> 1. *Don't argue—persuade.*
> 2. *Move toward a decision.*

162

3. *Have a key sentence.*
4. *Phrase with care—phrase simply.*

The more I read, the more I realize what a great teacher he would have been. From my perspective now, I can visualize him in a classroom, fulfilling his lifelong dream, teaching all that was stored up inside of him.

I recall how Papa told me, in one of his wistful moods, that he had a secret dream to go to a great university and get his doctorate in theology. But someone had suggested that he has needed to minister to the Scandinavian people. The dream was buried.

Was he thinking of that dream as he prepared for his ordination? He had written: "Man comes to a sense of his own greatness only after he has humbled himself in the dust before the majesty of God. God does not want man to obey out of fear and cringe before Him. He wants man to stand up, a new creation in Christ, and God can speak to him. Man must stand erect, girt and ready to obey. There is no room for pride, since we are not our own. All power is given."

Perfection was important to Papa. I recall how angry he became when we didn't enunciate words properly. "Speak up! Stand up straight! Look people in the eye when you shake hands!" he told us.

Now I can smile, but it wasn't humorous at the time.

"Go polish your shoes! Brush your hair! Don't disgrace the ministry!" It was always "the ministry."

I continue reading from Papa's notes: "People can only be induced willingly to do what they want to do. A good speaker clears the mind of the audience from previous thoughts; then the hearer can be introduced to your message."

When I turn the page, I read:

1. *How do you go on when no one is listening?*
2. *Why am I sent to work where circumstances are adverse?*
3. *Am I merely a man exposed to conflict, pain, and failure?*

Papa answered his own questions, saying, "The answer is that life is a campaign, not a holiday. We go on because a prophet is sent by God with a message. It is in the battle where we prove our mettle."

At this point I stop to ask myself the questions, *Do I really listen? Do I wait to hear from God before I speak? Do I hear what people really say, or do I hear words?* And then I pray, "Spirit of the living God, fall fresh on me."

In the morning stillness I turn to Psalm 18 where David remembers the blessings of the Lord. Spurgeon suggests that, like David of old, we should publish abroad the story of the covenant of the cross, the Father's election, the Son's redemption, and the Spirit's regeneration. Write a memorial of God's mercies, he says, not only for our comfort, but for our children and grandchildren. Then our children will also rejoice in the Lord. In the margin I wrote: "Take heart, Margaret, and write."

Somehow it seems that I am discovering Papa's depth, touching his soul as I read his sermon notes.

> *Sins of Civilization:*
> 1. *Spiritual ingratitude.*
> 2. *Moral corruption.*
> 3. *Spiritual pride.*
> 4. *Ecclesiastical complacency.*

Beside the fourth point, he had written: "There can be no religion where human rights are not recognized. The day of Jehovah is a day of searching—judgment. We could change human lives by persuading them to believe that by the grace of God their lives could be changed."

Over and over Papa wrote his sermon points, asked heart-searching questions, and wrote his answers.

> *Knowledge of God Gained From:*
> 1. *Notice.*
> 2. *Scripture.*
> 3. *Observation.*
> 4. *Experience.*

"Son of man," Papa wrote, "stand upon your feet! *Why?* 1.

God asks you to. 2. You are a man—erect. 3. God wants to speak to you. 4. So—listen. 5. Look. 6. Go. 7. Prove yourself a man."

Great expository preachers inspired Papa, men like G. Campbell Morgan. According to *A School of Christ* by Nathan Wood, Morgan's weekly convocation lectures at Gordon College, Wenham, Massachusetts, in 1920-1931 are remembered as some of his greatest work. Morgan left a lasting impression on generations of Gordon students. He brought an example of expository preaching with vivid phrasing, logic, and diction, and a voice ranging from confidential whispers to deep, organ-like tones.

Dr. Harry A. Ironside, another man that Papa admired, completed the exposition of the entire Bible during his seventeen years as pastor of the great Moody Memorial Church in Chicago.

Perhaps because Papa never reached his own theological goals, he wanted us to hear great preaching from outstanding men of God like Dr. R. A. Torrey, Dr. Ironside, Dr. Will Houghton, and Dr. V. Raymond Edmman. Papa greatly admired Dr. Scarborough and Dr. R. G. Lee from the South, and Dr. William Ward Ayer, the pastor of New York City's Calvary Baptist Church.

When the young men came on the scene, Papa rejoiced to see the great evangelistic emphasis by Dr. Torrey Johnson, founder of Youth for Christ; Dr. Robert Cook, President of King's College; and Billy Graham.

During Billy Graham's first New York Crusade, Papa was deeply moved. Later he told me, "I found myself weeping as I watched humanity coming like mountain streams from the balcony and moving toward the river of life. Margaret, I'll never forget what I saw with my own eyes. The simple message of the gospel is still the power of God to change lives."

As I read Papa's notes, I see his struggles and convictions. "When the hearer in the pew hears from the pulpit 'Thus saith the Lord,' he has a choice to make. Either the hearer chooses to obey or he chooses to disobey."

Again he wrote: "Obedience to truth is the simple way. Most of us know what to do, but would rather spend hours discussing the *why* of the situation rather than obey God's *how* to move to higher spiritual ground. So simple—just not easy."

Mama's quiet walk of obedience brought a steadying factor into a household's encounter with "storms." God had His own way of weaving a tapestry of "all things" for good.

When I recall bits and pieces of conversation with Papa, I can now sense his frustration at being ahead of his time. He was hemmed into one sphere of service when his outlook was ecumenical. He longed for the fellowship of all believers in Christ, longed to escape being bound by diverse doctrinal barriers.

Today I see the crumbling of the divisive wall and I rejoice in the fellowship of oneness in Christ Jesus. How Papa would rejoice to see me tell the old story of Jesus and His love to a Catholic audience, and then share the same message in a Baptist church.

In a formal setting of robes and candles, I tell the simplicity of "God so loved the world," and we kneel together. In the informal setting of drums and guitars, we also praise the Lord together.

Someone once came to me and said, "You are doing all the things that were in your father's heart to do." (Thank You, Lord!)

Then there was the night when 7,000 people at the Book-sellers Convention gathered in Kennedy Center to praise God. When we stood together, representing all denominations, and sang the Hallelujah Chorus, I thought the heavens would open. (Didn't I hear Papa shouting all over God's heaven?)

I close Papa's Bible and put his journal notes and song book away. I have just had a fresh glimpse of my Papa—a glimpse of his own searching heart, that poured a fresh healing balm on my own memories. I sense his frustrations, his insatiable quest for books, his unfinished theological dreams and goals.

I had seen Papa stretching tiptoe toward his God, and I had seen him silently weeping, struggling with his winds of anger. A proud man. A godly man.

From his journals, I knew him with a new intensity. How much Papa had loved God and Mama and his children. Again

I realized that Papa had bypassed his own childhood. He was a boy grown up too soon, a young man thrust into responsibility before his time. Papa had suffered great losses as a child—his siblings, his parents. At seventeen, he had struck out alone for America.

In Mama and in his God Papa had found strength and sure footing. In his books and in his preaching he had found acceptance. One thing I knew as I closed his journals—something I had always known—Papa loved his children. Perhaps he left the rearing of the children to Mama in order to keep a safe distance, to veil his fear of losing us as he had lost his siblings and my younger sister, Bernice. From his children he had sought perfection, demanded it. But from his journals I knew that Papa, too, had sought to be God's perfect man.

Somehow it seems that Papa must be looking over my shoulder, saying, "*Ja, ja*, Margaret, so you are reading my notes?" I can almost hear him chuckle. "*Ja*, now maybe you will listen."

Then again I can almost see him with a tear in his eye. "Someday, Margaret, we'll talk it over. It is good to write the joy and sorrow of life. But above all else, write about God's grace and mercy."

Margaret

29

Miss Rosie

An early morning sun tried vainly to filter through the cold, predawn darkness of Chicago. The radiators crackled and popped with a vengeance, sending steam upward from the drying underwear spread over the towel-covered radiators.

Hertha and I dressed quickly in the cold dawn, pulling on new underwear, long cotton slips, black cotton stockings, and shiny oxfords. With a sense of awe, we slipped into our blue-and-white-striped uniforms. Over those long uniforms we awkwardly fastened our starched white pinafores and buttoned on stiff collars and cuffs. We were excited, nervous, giggling.

I brushed back my hair in a soft bun and the waves stayed in place. Hertha's curly dark hair framed her round cheeks and mischievous brown eyes. She shifted her ample frame into the snug pinafore.

I inspected my carefully trimmed and cleaned fingernails, wound my shiny new wrist watch, and clipped a fountain pen in place in my pocket beside the bandage scissors and clean handkerchief.

We checked our room to see that all was in order: bed made, sink cleaned, wastebasket emptied. During the week, we would get a dust mop from down the hall to dust the floors and on Saturday we would scrub our room. But not today.

The sound of laughter and footsteps erupted in the hall. We stepped from room 200 and followed the older nurses to the chapel. The ones with three black bands on their starched caps were seniors and they went first. The two-black-stripers were second-year students and the one-stripe cap meant a one-year student. Plain caps were given after the three-month probationary period. We came up last—all the new students—with bare heads. Our starched uniforms rustled in tune with the others and we quietly filled the chapel.

Miss Rosendahl, director of nurses, seemed majestic—tall, broad, overpowering. Her flaming red hair was piled high on her head, a starched cap on top of that. She wore a long, stiff uniform and a wide belt around her ample hips. But it was the way she stood—like a general, with folded arms, feet apart, and her clear blue eyes taking in every minute detail. I knew right then and there that no one missed chapel.

In her commanding voice, Miss Rosendahl announced a hymn. Miss Johnson, a petite blonde called Johnnie, sat at the piano. Miss Rosendahl's voice rang out with one of her favorite hymns:

Holy Ghost with light divine,
Shine upon this heart of mine.

When she came to the part, "Bid my many woes depart," I somehow sensed she meant us. She never quite made the high notes, but she made up for it with her fervor. Chapel ended with a Scripture verse and the Lord's Prayer, and we moved out, according to rank. This time "Miss Rosie" marched in the lead and I had a feeling that we should be singing:

Onward Christian soldiers
Marching as to war.

The rustling probationers—the new "probies," without caps—brought up the rear.

Breakfast was eaten hurriedly since the nurses reported on their floors at 7:30 A.M., but our capless band headed for Miss

Rosendahl's office where we met the director of nurses personally. A former war nurse, she looked at us as though we were still at war. I suspected that underneath that stern exterior was a dedicated nurse whose goal in life was to send forth the Florence Nightingales of tomorrow. That day, though, we young students saw "Rosie" as the general, and ourselves as the war zone.

With arms folded, she met our fears with a firm gaze. "Discipline, my children [I was seventeen!]; yes, my *children*, discipline! You must learn to take orders and follow them." Her eyes met mine. I wanted to say, "Haven't I lived with Papa?"

I sucked in my lower lip as she continued, "Lives are at stake in this hospital and you hold those lives in your hands. By one error you can send a person into eternity. Yes, girls, discipline is what I will have!"

I shuddered! A life in my hand was awesome.

"I will stand for no nonsense," she said firmly. "And the breaking of rules will send you packing—yes, I mean packing! Home in disgrace!"

I visualized my box being repacked and me heading home to face Papa. Oh, I would obey the rules. No mistaking that!

Our first assignment was to clean the closets on different floors. Hertha and I rearranged linens and scrubbed shelves as though our lives depended upon those linen closets. Then we were taught how to make beds, and we practiced for hours until the corners could pass Miss Rosie's inspection.

During one boring session of making and remaking beds, Hertha picked up a book and read to me about "Anthony whispering sweet nothings into Cleopatra's shell-pink ear." With all the drama of a Hollywood star, Hertha was acting out the dramatic scene—and Miss Rosie came in to check the corners.

I never did find out what "sweet nothings" went into Cleopatra's shell-pink ear, but I still remember the lecture on discipline versus nonsense.

In between the practical work assignments, we attended four hours of classes a day. With our new books and notebooks tucked under our arms, we marched to class to hear lectures from doctors and to learn "practical nursing" from graduate nurses.

Dr. G. taught Materia Medica and he promised to fail any student who did not know the measurements "frontward and backward." We dreaded his exams, particularly those on measurements, but no one ever failed them. His students were known to score high on state board exams.

The days moved quickly through three months, and then came the capping ceremony when Miss Rosie planted our plain starched caps firmly on our heads. At last we were called student nurses, not just probies. We had arrived! I had missed picking springtime violets with Mama and the children, but I had a cap on my head.

Unexpectedly, one day I was in trouble with the director of nurses. "Miss Tweten, come into my office at once!" she ordered. I looked at Hertha. I was terrified. What had I done? Hertha's sympathetic gaze followed me, but then the door closed and I was alone with Miss Rosie.

"You know the rules, Miss Tweten." Her voice rose. "I have a good mind to call your father—and you a minister's daughter."

I shuddered! *Papa? What did he have to do with this?*

"You know the rules," she thundered again and I nodded miserably.

"There will be no lipstick! No rouge at the Norwegian American Hospital. And to think you have lipstick and rouge on, Miss Tweten. You should be ashamed!"

"No. Oh, no," I protested. "I never wear rouge or lipstick. Papa won't let us."

"Now you are lying! I will call your father."

"Oh, no! I'm not lying. I don't even have any lipstick or rouge." My cheeks felt hot.

"We'll see!" Miss Rosie towered over me now as she grabbed a washcloth and proceeded to scrub my face. I felt my cheeks burning but the cloth was clean. A frown split her brow. Her expression seemed puzzled as she looked at my red cheeks and red lips and muttered, "I can't believe it—it looked like lipstick." She squared her shoulders even more. "Well, well, well," she added in conciliatory tones. "What kind of soap do you use?"

"Anything Mama finds on sale," I stammered.

"Now you are impudent!" Her eyes blazed.

"Oh, no, Miss Rosendahl, I really mean it. Mama likes Palmolive, but she will get other soap on sale." I was trembling inside. I didn't want to pack up and go home. Awkwardly I said, "Dr. Thornton says I have a good complexion because I walk all the time. I walked to Carl Schurz High School from Logan Square and on my afternoon off from the hospital I walk home."

"My gracious, child, that is four to five miles."

I winced. She had called me "child." Didn't she know that I was seventeen? Meekly I said, "I enjoy walking, Miss Rosendahl. Besides, I don't have five cents for carfare. Papa brings me back, so that saves ten cents."

She looked away. "Well, time's wasting. Get back to work, Miss Tweten, and no nonsense."

"Oh, no, Miss Rosendahl, no nonsense." I almost danced back to my room, though that was against the rules, too. But all I could think of was, *I don't have to pack! I don't have to pack! Oh, glory! Life is good!*

Later, behind closed doors, I gave a one-woman show, and Betty and Hertha rocked with laughter. Word soon spread throughout the dormitory that Rosie had washed my face.

Later in the week when I had my half-day off, I walked through Humbolt Park and once again found myself in Mama's warm kitchen. The children gathered around me and Papa was quietly impressed as I told about the classes and floor training—and Miss Rosendahl.

Mama's hot meatballs and gravy, her mashed potatoes, creamed peas and carrots never tasted so good.

30

Tweedlededum

By the time I was assigned to Fourth Floor Annex, I had the one-year stripe on my cap, and routine days of floor duty and study had blended into months of discipline and learning. With the discipline came a degree of responsibility, a growing confidence, and a sense of pride in my work. I loved what I was doing. I was an idealistic, romantic eighteen-year-old "child" according to Miss Rosie, but I loved people and I learned from them even though they demanded much from me.

One morning I had four patients to tend before my ten o'clock class. While my other patients finished breakfast, I bathed Miss Kari who was slowly dying. Her distended abdomen looked like a full-term pregnancy; blue-grey pallor colored her clammy skin.

I gently swabbed her parched mouth with some glycerine and lemon, and coaxed her to swallow a few drops of water. Her haunted dark eyes followed me. While I bathed her, I softly sang some old hymns and assured her of God's love. Then I turned her on her side, placed a pillow behind her back, and brushed her long damp hair. I found a ribbon on a plant in the hall and tied her hair with a bow. I took her hands, one at a time, and trimmed and cleaned her fingernails. Then I put her rosary in her hand. She smiled and clutched it to her breast. She moaned in pain, and I administered morphine sulphate.

I went to the door and nodded to the off-duty policeman waiting in the hall. "You can come in now," I whispered. He eased his six-foot-six-inch frame into a chair beside Miss Kari and spoke softly to her in Polish as he took her hand and held it tenderly in his big hand.

He looked up, almost apologetically. "My sister," he said softly, "we came from Poland together." I knew he would still be sitting there at the close of the day. Miss Kari dozed, comfortable and secure in the love of her only relative. I closed the door.

After gathering up the remaining trays, I bathed a nineteen-year-old boy with a severe tooth infection, gave him aspirin to reduce his fever, and applied saline packs around his red, swollen jaw. "You must drink," I urged him, placing a pitcher of juice on his bed stand. He nodded, his eyes glassy.

By the time I reached Mr. Joe, he was trying to pull out his catheter and yelling for the toilet. "I'll wet this d— bed if you can't get me to the toilet," he scolded. Finally he was bathed and quieted. Still he glared angrily at the contraption that spilled urine into a bottle. "Fool thing if I ever heard of one," he muttered.

I agreed.

"Blondie! Help me! Help, Blondie!" screamed Mrs. Goldstein down the hall. "Tweedlededum, where are you? Oh, Blondie, help! Help!"

I hurried to Mrs. Goldstein's room with a basin and bedpan in my hands. Her abdomen was distended, too.

"Oye, oye—a doctor you should be getting, Blondie. Call Dr. Finklefish . . . oye, Dr. Finklefish!" she yelled. "Help!"

"Shhh . . . it's not Dr. Finklefish. It's Dr. Finklestein. Dr. Fishskin is the lab extern."

"So? What does that matter, Tweedlededum?"

"Shh. Miss Rosendahl should hear you. Tweedlededum— such a nickname for Miss Tweten."

She ignored my reprimand. "Get Dr. Fishfinkle—or whatever," she persisted. "Can't you see I'm dying?"

176

The intern, Dr. Finklestein, was down the hall. I hurried to him with Mrs. Goldstein's request. "Please, I have to get to class!" I told him.

When we reached her room, he said, "All right, Mrs. Goldstein, what have you been eating?"

"Choking, I am! Can't you see the cast is choking me? From my legs to my breast, this cast is choking me. A hip I should break—oye, oye! No one should suffer like this. My mother died with a broken hip. But I won't!"

Her distended abdomen had made her hip cast tight as a drum.

"Come on, now, Mrs. Goldstein, be honest. Tell me what you've been eating."

"Isn't it enough that I am dying with a broken hip? I should go to my grave with the malnutrition, too?"

I peered into her bedside table. The doctor's gaze followed mine, settling on the rye bread, chicken bones, jars of pickled herring, and cheese and pickles.

Dr. Finklestein moaned, "Oh, no! And how many times have I told you not to eat anything besides your diet? These foods make so much gas, and you'll gain too much weight."

"So . . . a little bite now and then to keep up my strength?" She moaned miserably to emphasize her plight.

Turning to me, he ordered, "Give her the three H's." That meant a soapsuds enema—high, hot, and a "h" of a lot. I wouldn't dare use the word Papa used in his sermons.

I ran to the utility room, leaving Mrs. G. muttering about it being bad enough to have a broken hip but now she'd go to her grave with the malnutrition.

I recruited some help, and we turned the mountainous body (cast and patient) amid screams of, "I'm dying! Help! Help!" I held up the white enamel can filled with soapsuds made from leftover scraps of soap, and inserted the long red rubber tubing—high, hot, and a "h" of a lot.

We planted the still screaming Mrs. Goldstein on the bedpan and used newspaper to protect the linens. I prayed, "Please, Lord, not the entire bed. I have class in twenty minutes."

While she sat on the bedpan, I ran to check the other

patients, then back to Mrs. Goldstein in response to her cry, "Blondie! Blondie!"

Sure enough, the distention was down, and Mrs. Goldstein decided to live. One of the nurses came in to help, and between the two of us, we got Mrs. G. bathed, powdered, and into a clean bed, with a silly ribbon in her hair for good measure.

"So . . . a nap I'll take," she said, patting her cast. "You'll be a good nurse someday, Tweedlededum."

Back at the nurses' station, I scrubbed vigorously, then gathered up my books for class. It was ten o'clock. I had made it!

After lunch I had two more classes, then back to the Fourth Floor Annex for scheduled afternoon care. Basins came out again. Faces and hands were washed. Beds were straightened. Back rubs given and supper trays cleared. Then, bedpans before the visitors came.

As the night crew came on at 7:30, I took my charts to a corner and sat down. But how do you chart a dying woman, a frightened teenager with a severe tooth infection, or old Grandpa Joe still hollering for the toilet? How do you ever chart Mrs. Goldstein? They just stay etched in your memories.

Thirty minutes later I put down my charts and wearily headed for my room on the second floor of the dorm. The nurses lived on one side and the interns lived on the other side. A wide hall—and honor—stood between us. Someone in the kitchen made a pot of tea and Hertha and I had a party. Then we studied for Dr. G.'s exam on Materia Medica to the sound of waltz music. Mama might not have approved of all the waltzes, but then it was Hertha's radio and Hertha didn't have to listen to Moody Bible's radio station.

31

Traumas and Trust

I awoke out of a sound sleep, aware of a menacing form leaning over my bed. I froze, my face hidden in the shadows. At first I thought one of the interns had come into the wrong hall. But the street light revealed an intruder. I lay motionless and prayed.

My roommate, usually a light sleeper, was sound asleep that night.

Suddenly I jumped up and screamed, "Hertha!"

She rolled over in her bed and answered, "That's all right, Margaret. I know all about it." She had been dreaming! The intruder fled out of the room and down the fire escape. Apparently a latecomer had left the fire escape door unlocked after Miss Abrahamson's nightly check.

I screamed again! "Hertha! There was a man in here."

"Good," she mumbled. Then suddenly awake, she screamed too!

We ran down the long hall to make a report to the telephone operator.

Within moments, Miss Rose appeared, with curlers in her hair and dressed in a big bathrobe. Other supervisors came as well. Seconds later, several interns and externs were on the scene, and finally, the Chicago police arrived.

Hertha and I were still shaking. "Now, now, Miss Tweten," the director of nurses said accusingly, "are you sure it wasn't your boyfriend, Harold, sneaking up the fire escape?" Miss Rosie glared at me.

One policeman offered his suggestion. "I know there's a tall young man who stands under this window to say good-night." He smiled directly at me!

"That is my friend, Harold Jensen," I blushed. "Harold always waits to see if I get to my room safely." They all smiled—except Rosie.

The police sent the interns to search the empty rooms and to check the bathrooms.

Miss Rosie stood motionless, arms folded, glowering at me. I shuddered. I was sure she'd call Papa and he would somehow blame me for all this commotion.

Hertha and I huddled together. When everything was clear, the police wrote up the incident and promised to guard the dormitory area. Everyone left except one young extern.

"Don't go," Hertha pleaded, "I have to go to the bathroom, and you are coming with me with that flashlight." The doctor obliged and flashed his light into the bathroom, then gave Hertha an "all clear."

"Margaret, you might as well go now, too, while I'm here on guard," he offered. I was too embarrassed and said, "Oh, no. I don't have to go."

The extern disappeared with his flashlight, and suddenly I had to go to the bathroom. It seemed that the long hall had no end, and the empty stalls looked threatening. Hertha stood in the doorway of our room and called out her encouragement. I came back safely and we finally got to bed, but not until Hertha checked the fire escape door and then locked our door. She piled up chairs and moved a desk in front of the door. No one would ever enter that door again uninvited!

The interns teased me saying, "The preacher's daughter had night visitors." I tried to laugh with them, but for years the fear could be tempered only by my stubborn trust in God.

One day, long after the night visitor, Hertha walked into the room. I was packing my brown box. "What in the world are you doing?" She asked.

"I gave the wrong medicine," I sobbed. "And Miss Rosie said if we ever, but ever, gave the wrong medicine, we might as well start packing."

"What did you give?"

"I gave milk of magnesia instead of cascara. The patient had been on cascara before and I didn't see the change. Oh, I don't know what to do."

"Does Miss Hanna know?"

"Of course. I told her right away. She said that we could not afford to make errors, even small ones. Someday it could be fatal." I kept packing.

"Telephone for Tweetie," someone called out.

I just knew it was Miss Rosie! I could hear her now . . . but it was Miss Hanna. I was to report back to her.

"Miss Tweten, you are a good nurse," Miss Hanna said, her expression almost kindly. "But sometimes you try too hard. You do more than you should, and you try to protect those who don't carry out their duties. Now, I want you to remember that you can't be responsible for everyone. You do your work, and I will see to it that the others do their share. I just wanted you to know that I think you are becoming a fine nurse."

"But, Miss Hanna, what about the medicine? I told you I gave milk of magnesia instead of cascara."

"Oh, yes . . . I talked to the doctor, and he said that he was putting the patient back on cascara. The milk of magnesia was ineffective. I am sure you will never give a wrong medicine again—if you carefully read the orders each time. Take nothing for granted, Miss Tweten. You must check your orders. Now get to class."

"Thank you, Miss Hanna. Oh, I do thank you." I started to reach out to hug her, but drew back. "I want to be a good nurse," I whispered.

I was surprised to see a tenderness in her eyes, a haunting longing. Many years later I learned that she had loved, "not wisely, but too well."

I thanked God for His boundless grace, and I unpacked my

box. Hertha and I went to class. I never forgot to check my medicines three times in accordance with Miss Hanna's rules.

On another day, when exams were coming, Hertha and I sat on the fire escape stairs at dawn. We were memorizing our notes from Dr. G.'s Materia Medica. The sun rose over the skyscrapers of Chicago, and down on the streets, we heard the welcome sound of horses pulling their milk wagons. The rattle of the bottles heralded the entrance of the new day.

Before long, we were pinning on our long white starched pinafores and fastening our caps in place, ready to march in order to chapel. This time we led the line, and the capless probies brought up the rear.

When I reported for duty later that day, I saw five tall men pacing the hall, their fists clenched in anger. Their weather-beaten faces and large rough hands told me they were farmers. They looked miserable in their Sunday clothes and polished shoes.

"What's wrong?" I asked the night nurse.

"A beautiful girl is dying in that room, apparently from an induced abortion. You're assigned to her."

I walked into the room with a basin of water to bathe my new patient and caught my first glimpse of the dying girl. Black curls clung to her forehead; her body was feverish, and her eyes were glassy.

The five brothers followed me into the girl's room. "Please, Sis," they said to her, "tell us who he is. Please!"

They turned to me with a helpless, desperate look.

"She's our baby sister," one of them said. "She's only nineteen. She came to visit our aunt who took her to the ballroom to see how exciting Chicago is compared to the farm back home. Some man at the ballroom sweet-talked her, and no one knew about it until our aunt found her bleeding. She called the ambulance."

"Now Sis won't talk to us," the older brother added. "Mama and Papa don't speak English and have never been off the farm, so we had to come. Poor Papa, he's left with all the chores." He shook his head.

"If only Sis would tell us who . . . we'd kill the guy. We owe her that much. She's Mama's baby girl."

I ushered the five brothers back into the hall and the pacing with clenched fists began again. I went back into the room and quickly bathed the girl. As I cared for her, I prayed for her. "Oh God, she's so young!" I said. She was nineteen . . . and so was I!

She died quietly that day and the nurses wept openly with the grief-stricken brothers. One brother spoke through taut lips, "Now we must tell Mama and Papa our sister is gone. She never told us who he was."

I watched them walk slowly out like old bent men. Their grief was too deep for words.

That night I read in my Bible:

For ever, O LORD, thy word is settled in heaven.
Thy word is a lamp unto my feet, and a light unto my path.
Thou art my hiding place and my shield: I hope in thy word.
Order my steps in thy word:
and let not any iniquity have dominion over me.
(Psalm 119:89, 105, 114, 133)

I kept thinking about Papa's sermon on "The wages of sin is death; but the gift of God is eternal life" (Romans 6:23). Deep within me I felt a new respect for God's protective laws. I also experienced a sense of awe at the consequences of taking God's laws lightly! I wondered how many people suffer as a result of disobedience to God. Where had this girl gone wrong? When she left the farm for Chicago? When she went to the ballroom with her aunt? When she yielded to the sweet talk of a stranger? When she tried to rid her body of an unborn child? Or was she solely the victim of a man bent on sin?

Even if Papa was unreasonably strict with us Twetens, I sensed a new security in the admonition: "Honour thy father and mother" (Ephesians 6:2).

"But Mama," I used to say, "Papa is always so unreasonable."

"*Ja, ja.* Who doesn't know that? But I don't read in my Bible

183

anywhere 'Honor your father when he is reasonable.'" She would smile patiently. "Now, if Papa is unreasonable, he will answer to God. But if you don't honor Papa, who do you want to answer to?"

"But, Mama, you mix it up."

"No, you mix it up. The Word of God is very plain. It is very simple—just not so easy to do."

I thought about the five brothers going home to tell their mama and papa that their sister was dead. Suddenly I could hardly wait until time to go home tomorrow—just to be at the table, to feel the security and love of a family. It was true Papa was stubborn and unreasonable at times, but obeying him brought a sense of security. We can trust God's laws; they bring order. Man's laws, without God's order, bring confusion.

In spite of what had happened. I fell asleep in a settled peace that night, thinking, *The LORD shall preserve thy going out, Margaret Tweten, and thy coming in* (see Psalm 121:8).

32

Trials and Triumphs

From my tenth-floor room in the nurses' dorm, I looked out over Cook County Hospital, a massive complex of brick and stone, a medical city within a city. Far below me, the roar of Chicago's elevated trains, clanging street cars, and automobile traffic mingled with the wailing sirens of ambulances and police cars.

I was one of many student-affiliates at Cook County Hospital for six months' special training in pediatrics and contagious diseases. These nursing specialties were lacking in the smaller, private hospitals.

I wondered if I would ever find my way around this vast expanse of buildings as I headed for pediatrics, but I needn't have worried. When I entered the building, I met my supervisor, Mrs. Schroeder, a calm, quiet, self-assured woman whose very bearing said, "Everything is in control."

During a children's feeding period on pediatric rotation, I met Gladys Thompson, a student from Lutheran Deaconess Hospital. A warm, lasting friendship developed from that casual meeting. Looking back now, I know it was part of a divine plan!

Gladys and I worked together on the tuberculosis ward. We moved cribs and beds out to the roof garden where the patients could see skyscrapers etched against the high, smoke-filled sky

185

and benefit from the sun as it filtered bravely through the haze. We fed the children between-meal snacks and read to them, and then we settled them down for extra naps. Rest, food, fresh air, and love were the prescription for these fragile children.

On another floor, far from the garden roof, I donned gown, mask, and gloves to irrigate pus-filled eyes and to cleanse open sores—caused by venereal disease. This encounter with the wages of sin was particularly trying for me; this fresh, agonizing realization of how the innocent suffer. I knew from childhood that blessings flow from generation to generation; but here on the pediatric wing, I learned how the destructive wages of sin also pass from generation to generation.

One nurse wanted to adopt a beautiful child who had been abandoned by her parents. But the child tested positive for syphilis and gonorrhea, and her prognosis was hopeless. The nurse wept—her dream of adoption shattered—but she continued to buy clothes and toys for that lonely child.

One day a policeman brought five children from the same family into the pediatric admitting room. Their bodies and hair were soiled with feces and vomitus. Diagnosis: typhoid fever. They had been found alone, deserted by their parents, and they were covered with lice.

One by one, I bathed them on a porcelain slab, using a shower-type hose, a soft brush, and Lysol soap. After their heads were shaved, I scrubbed them with a cleansing solution and wrapped their heads in towels. They sat in a row, silent and terrified. Clean now in white hospital gowns and wrapped in warm blankets, their faces were still pale. Their haunting, solemn eyes followed my every move as I tried to get them to sip some weak tea. We nurses adopted them and showered them with love until the smiles came and the hair grew back. Through the years I have wondered what happened to those frightened children who had to learn about love from strangers in white.

The contagious wards never had enough beds. During the years of the polio epidemic, disease victims filled every available space. Tragedy and heartbreak surrounded us. Bodies were crippled for life. Some children would never walk again—others

186

would never grow old. Diphtheria patients cried in fear; scarlet fever patients filled many cribs. Even one of the interns died.

One day, as I finished bathing a beautiful child who had a high fever and rash, she impulsively pulled my mask down and kissed me on the mouth. Her arms wound around my neck, and she clung to me, begging to be held. I desperately tried to replace my mask.

"I love you," she whispered.

When the long day drew to a close, a deep weariness settled over me. It was difficult enough to care for adults who were ill, but my encounter with wards of sick children seemed unending.

Tomorrow I was going home—home to Mama's kitchen, to health and cleanliness, where simplicity and order were a way of life. I prayed for the wisdom to be thankful for the simple things: home, family, a warm fire, a loaf of homemade bread, and a cup of coffee.

The next day when the Fullerton Avenue streetcar stopped, I stepped off and trudged heavily to the flat on Ridgeway Avenue, arriving just in time for Mama's afternoon coffee. To think I could spend the night and have all the next day, too!

The kitchen was warm and the hot liquid was delicious, but I couldn't swallow much of the coffee cake. My head ached, and I dozed in the rocking chair.

I awoke and realized that I had to go back to the hospital. I longed to stay home, but the way I was feeling, I had to report to the infirmary in case I couldn't return to work. The rules were strict. Mama looked anxious as she secured my scarf and whispered, "I'll pray." Her comforting words rang in my ears.

Papa walked with me to the street car. I shivered in the cold. "*Ja*, Margaret," he said tenderly, "we will get you to the infirmary and perhaps you can return home tomorrow." On the streetcar he tried to read. I kept shivering. When we reached the infirmary, Papa said, "Good night," and I was admitted. We were both sure that a good night's sleep would be the cure.

Two nights later, I opened my eyes and saw the white face of my father staring intently at me, with a look I remembered from many years ago.

I was three years old then, standing behind a glass cubicle in the New York contagious hospital. I had diphtheria. I reached out my childish arms to be held, but the glass partition separated us. I remember just standing there, not crying, as I watched Papa's sad white face through the glass.

The memory blurred! I was no longer a child, but I saw him again looking at me with that sad, white face. Mama stood beside Papa, looking anxiously at me—and Harold Jensen, my friend from the Northern Baptist Seminary, was with them. Why were they there?

"We are praying for you, Margaret. You will be fine." Mama's words seemed far away.

I tried to focus on Harold. So young. So strong. His lips moved. "You have been very sick. The hospital called your parents and I brought them over," he said. "We've been here all night, but, Margaret, you are going to be well." Harold seemed far away, too.

Faces and sounds blurred again: "A strep throat, temperature of 105 . . . didn't think she'd make it." Papa's white face . . . Mama's tear-filled eyes . . . Harold's worried expression.

I remembered the nineteen-year-old boy who had died from an infected tooth. Then I remembered the child, the one with scarlet fever, who had pulled my isolation mask from my face and kissed me. My thoughts slowed and stopped, and I fell asleep.

Our six-month rotation training was almost finished, so when my infection was gone, I returned to our infirmary at Norwegian American Hospital.

Miss Rosie thought I could be up and going, but our old family physician, Dr. Thornton, said, "Not on your life. This child needs rest. She has been very sick."

He winked at me as Miss Rosendahl walked stiffly away in her starched uniform. He left his blue and pink pills, told me fish stories from Alaska, and promised oranges and grapefruit in the morning. "You'll be fine," he called back as he lumbered down the hall.

He was right! He usually was.

It wasn't long before graduation day came, and so did state

board examinations. Thanks to Dr. G. and his tough rules, we made high grades in Materia Medica. My lowest score was in dietetics. I had boiled oysters in milk for *an hour* to prepare oyster stew. No one let me forget that one!

On graduation night, Miss Rosie was in her glory! So was Papa! Papa gave the invocation, and in glowing terms thanked Miss Rosendahl for her contribution to society.

Mr. Hartsmire tiptoed through the tulips and led us to the lovely amaryllis. He waved his baton as though we were the St. Olav's chorus. Life was beautiful!

We stood in shining white, from starched caps to polished shoes. Our striped uniforms and black cotton stockings were packed away. Forever. A shiny gold pin held the memorable date: N.A.H.T.S. 1937 (Norwegian American Hospital Training School).

After the graduation ceremonies came a reception for families and friends. Papa and Mama enjoyed the event to the fullest, especially the stories from former patients. There were many, like the Polish policeman, who remembered. And came!

Mama was deeply moved when an elderly doctor made a great effort to attend the ceremonies, defying his own doctor's orders.

"I had to come," he insisted. Turning to Mama, he added, "I remember the day I came to the hospital with a serious heart attack. When I was placed in the canvas oxygen tent I knew I was dying. But this child," he turned to me, "put her head in the tent and smiled at me. 'You are going to be all right,' she told me. 'I'll take good care of you.'" He looked back at Mama. "I thought, *If that young girl can smile, I can't be dying.* So I determined to live to see her smile again." I kissed his wrinkled cheek and thanked him for coming.

After graduation, Gladys Thompson, my friend from Cook County Hospital, and I worked together at Lutheran Deaconess Hospital. Life was still beautiful—but it was changing.

Floor duty hours had dropped from twelve a day to eight. After duty I changed into street clothes since rules forbade uniforms outside the hospital.

I saved every dollar I earned, eager to repay the $300 cash

Mama had drawn from an insurance policy to buy my books and uniforms when I entered training.

Soon Papa no longer shook the stove at 5 A.M. in the cold water flat on Ridgeway Avenue. The flat was empty. Grace and I watched the train leave for New York where Papa was to pastor Norwegian Baptist Church in Brooklyn. Then Grace left to work in New York.

I was alone, yet not really alone because Harold Jensen and I were planning our wedding for June 1938.

After our wedding in Brooklyn, we settled into a cozy apartment on Central Park Avenue in Chicago. Harold still attended Northern Baptist Seminary and I worked at Lutheran Deaconess Hospital. Life was really beautiful then.

33

Violets for Mr. B.

The doctor's phone call was on my mind as I threw a white sweater over my new uniform. "A prominent man has returned from New York to his hometown to die," the doctor said. "He desires no visitors, flowers, or conversation. He is a bitter, lonely man—and gravely ill. Do what you can, Margaret."

I gathered my nurse's bag, bulging with credentials, equipment, New Testament, *Reader's Digest*, pen and paper.

Traffic was light at 6:15 A.M. I gave myself enough time to park, register at the hospital office, and get a report from the night nurse.

Inside the gloomy room, a gaunt, hollow-eyed man was propped up in bed with a book in front of him. With a curt "Good morning," Mr. B. resumed his reading.

I sat in a corner and quietly read the chart, trying to get my bearings as to how to care for this independent, brusque man. *Help, Lord!* I prayed silently.

Within a few days we had set up a comfortable routine. At first I tried conversation that stemmed from the *Reader's Digest* or current books—a good beginning, I thought. He knew most of the writers. Then I decided to brighten his day with some stories from the *National Geographic*. He said he had already been to those places. I bit my lip.

He seemed to enjoy my discomfort. Once he offered a suggestion: "Don't try so hard, Mrs. Jensen."

I burst out laughing and agreed just to be his friend and do things his way. The tension lessened.

When ministers or boyhood acquaintances came to call, he insisted I observe the "No Visitors" sign. The only visitor he received was his sister, who came every day to relieve me for lunch. She and her brother rarely spoke. She would sit quietly beside him and just read.

One day she said, "I can do so little for my brother, Mrs. Jensen. He was so assertive and successful, and I'm just a quiet wife and mother. I wish I could be more like him, yet I'm really content to be what I am."

"Oh, if you only knew how much gentle people can bless others," I said to her. "They're refreshing, like quiet streams and green meadows. Your actions speak louder than words when you come day after day to sit with your brother. You communicate your love, and he hears."

She stared out the window, her lower lip trembling.

My conversations with Mr. B. became more relaxed as I related humorous incidents from my family. One day I told Mr. B. about my son, Ralph, and how during his childhood he once came running in from play and said, "Mommy, Mommy, how do I explain to God why I was bad when I should have been good?"

"Oh, you don't have to explain to God," I told Ralph. "He knows all about us. Remember that song in Sunday school that said, 'Jesus paid it all, all to Him I owe'? When we confess our sins, Ralph, He forgives us."

"Oh, good!" my son said. "I forgot that part." Then he ran out to play.

It soon became routine to see Mr. B. look over his glasses and say, "Well?" That meant he was ready for another story, usually a humorous one about Ralph. I was on familiar ground there, and I realized my stories opened a new world to my cynical patient.

One morning he did the routine, "Well?" but he added, "What does the theologian, Ralph, say today?"

"Come to think of it," I said, "he did make a theological observation yesterday. When we passed an old Model-T Ford, he said, 'Well, Mom, it's not the car that counts, it's the driver in it. That car won't go far without a driver. Kinda like us, huh? Our bodies wear out, but we live on, right? It's the soul that counts.'"

Later, I even ventured to take my record player and some classical records into Mr. B.'s room. He listened patiently for a few days, but finally, in exasperation, he exploded. "I enjoy music only in concert halls—not canned!"

I dragged my *canned music* to the parking lot.

One day he was holding his book upside down and I realized he couldn't see well enough to read any longer. Ever so gently, I offered to read to him. Instantly offended, he sputtered angrily, "Can't you see I am reading?"

I felt a deep sadness. *Not by might nor by power, but by My Spirit,* I seemed to hear the Lord remind me. Again I prayed silently, as I so often did.

When a card came from New York, I read the verse and note from his former secretary. She said she had paid to have prayers said for him.

Mr. B. struggled to maintain his composure. "She thought enough of me to pay for prayers?"

"God thought enough of you to send His Son to die for you," I said softly, then slipped out of the room before he could argue. When I returned, he was holding the card.

Looking out the window, he swept the view with his thin blue hand. "All of this used to be woods," he said. "We used to pick violets in the spring. Now the woods are way out there, beyond the parking lots, and I can't even see the violets. I'm glad I can still see the birds and squirrels, though."

His tone had lost its bitterness. Only sadness remained. I told him about gathering violets with Mama in the springtime. He nodded solemnly.

After a while, each day found him weaker, and he had to be turned in bed. He no longer held his book.

One day a gentle knock on the door interrupted my thoughts. When I opened the door, a beautiful woman stood there, holding a bowl of violets. "Would you tell Mr. B. that I'm one of those children who used to play in the woods when he did, and pick violets? I know he doesn't want visitors or flowers, but I thought he might like these."

I thanked her and took the flowers from her. I placed them on the windowsill and turned Mr. B. to face the sky and woods. When I told him about the visitor at the door, he stared at the violets.

"The violets were dead last winter," I said, "but now it's spring and these are alive. Jesus said, 'I am the resurrection and the life; he who believes in Me shall live even if he dies.' Do you believe this?"

I went about my duties. I knew he heard me, but I didn't wait for an answer.

A day came when I sat beside Mr. B. and held his cold, frail hands. Softly I said the Lord's Prayer and his lips followed my words. Again I said to him, "Jesus said, 'I am the resurrection and the life; he who believes in Me shall live.'" I looked into his face. "Do you believe this, Mr. B.?"

"Turn me to the window," he whispered. After turning him, I put a pillow behind his back to prop him up.

Looking at the violets, he whispered, "I believe."

I sat back down beside him. Tears blinded my eyes.

"It's all right now," he said. "I believe."

Quietly, gently, Mr. B. slipped into his final sleep—out of the wintry darkness and despair of his heart into joy and everlasting life.

34

Night Watch

After getting our 7:30 report and checking the medicine lists, our nightime cares began by emptying wastebaskets and passing out fresh water until the visitors left. Then came back rubs, and we changed draw sheets, washed each patient's face and hands, and helped each one with oral hygiene. The cart with bedpans rattled down the hall toward the utility room where the pans would be emptied and washed. I ran through the halls, trying to keep up with the demands of forty patients, most of them on complete bed rest.

Medicines, including sleeping pills, were carefully checked and administered. Most of our patients had been cared for in their homes until they became too ill, and now the hospital was a place of fear for them. So part of our care was to tuck the more frightened ones in for the night. Lights were turned low and the flowers and plants were taken out of the rooms and placed in the hall to be watered and returned before the morning shift.

One particular night, Miss Hanna urged me to hurry. A new patient was in the corner isolation room: diagnosis—erysipelas. I knew what that meant—an acute infectious disease of the skin or mucous membranes caused by a streptococcus and characterized by inflammation and fever.

I put on my isolation gown, mask, and gloves and entered the room to care for my patient. She was in pain as I applied fresh dressings to the oozing lesions that covered her face and body. It was lonely in her room. The patient—her face wrapped in gauze, her eyes full of pain—haunted me. So I stopped long enough to tell her one of my stories about Mama and Papa, and the Tweten antics.

I already had become known at the hospital as the story-teller, often entertaining my patients while I cared for them. As I told my isolation patient one of those stories, I soaked all her linens in a tub of diluted Lysol. In the morning I would wring out the sheets and place them in a special bag marked "Soiled Linen" and send it to the laundry room.

I made certain my "mummy" patient was as comfortable as she could be and promised to come back and tell her another Tweten story before going off duty. As I stepped from her room, I faced a hall full of blinking lights—all calling for attention at the same time. I was alone on the floor now, except for periodic checks by the night supervisor. Where should I start?

When I saw old Zeb leaning over the fire escape rail, his open gown blowing in the breeze, I knew my first responsibility. He was cyanotic, his face etched against the street light.

"No, no, Mr. Zeb, you must not get out of bed!" I cried out.

"Had to get some air! Can't breathe in that danged tent; so I climbed out. I want to go home and sit on my porch and get some cool night air. It's too hot tonight!"

It was hot all right, and humid—Chicago in July. I carefully helped my cardiac patient back to bed and urged him to stay in the cool tent—a large canvas contraption, with only a peep-hole for the nurse to look inside. No wonder he wanted "out" to his porch.

When Mr. Zeb was settled, I ran to put saline packs on nineteen-year-old Bill's face.

His mother's eyes filled with fear as she watched her son's fever soar. More aspirin and liquids! I sponged him with cool water and urged his mother to force the liquids and keep sponging his hot body.

Across the hall Mrs. Olsen couldn't sleep so I warmed some

milk for her and talked for a few minutes to reassure her that the long night would pass and by morning she would be better. I was trying to reassure both of us. The mustard plasters were bringing results and her pneumonia-filled lungs were relenting at last.

The elevator door closed and I heard the ambulance attendant announce, "Hey, Nursie, you have a new patient."

"Diagnosis?" I asked.

"Observation," he grinned.

Together we got her into bed and put the side rails up. The incoherent speech and jerking motions warned me of a long night with an advanced alcoholic.

I closed the fire escape, the only source of a breeze. The whir of small fans mingled with the snores. For a brief moment I wiped my perspiring face and stopped for a cracker and a cold drink of milk. Before I could finish the milk, my new patient started yelling about the rats in her room. There she stood, all two hundred pounds of her. With the open hospital gown in perpetual motion, she walked on her bed, bumping the side rails and yelling, "Get a broom to chase the rats!"

I ran to the phone. "Please send an intern—I can't handle her!" Grabbing a broom I began to "chase rats" at my patient's direction.

"Over there!" she yelled. "Get that rat! You got him! Now get that one!"

I kept the broom in perpetual motion while my cheerleader waved me on with her flapping gown. Out of the corner of my eye I saw the interns in the hall, watching the performance, nearly overcome with hysterics. That moved me to chase the interns with the broom.

Mercifully they calmed down long enough to push the needed hypodermic needle into the patient's exposed posterior. The sedative took effect and before long her snores joined the others. The interns spread the story that they weren't sure who the new patient was that night.

One gentle intern, Dr. Gibbs, checked Grandma Olsen and saw that she was still awake. He warmed another cup of milk for her and sat beside her until she fell asleep, holding his hand. That memory stays on the backroads of my mind.

Four A.M. came too soon! The sound of bedpans and wash basins rattling on the cart was loud enough to wake the dead. Sleepy-eyed patients brushed their teeth and slurped pink mouthwash, while I washed other faces and hands. Some of them fell asleep on their bedpans. Grandpa drank his mouthwash.

There were urine samples to gather, insulin shots to give, temperatures to take, saline dressings to apply, and the isolation case to care for. And there was Mr. Zeb and the fire escape!

A private duty night nurse had asked me to check on her patient while she went for a cup of coffee. "He's sound asleep, side rails are up, and I'm sure he'll sleep until I return."

The patient was another "observation case"—he had a history of delirium tremens.

When I settled Mr. Zeb again, I looked down the long dimly lit hall and saw the private duty patient busily urinating in all the flower pots down the hallway.

"Glad I found the bathroom," he slurred, and proceeded back to his room and climbed over the rail. I tucked him in and said "Good night."

When his nurse returned he was sleeping peacefully and she said, "I'm glad he didn't give you any trouble."

"None at all," I answered. She never knew how the flowers got watered that night.

Before dawn, it seemed that the long, hot shadows kept trying to close in on me like a heavy mantle. My eyes drooped. My legs ached. Wearily I reached for the chart to record temperatures and medicines. I turned at the sound of footsteps.

Coming down the hall in the early dawn was the familiar figure of Dr. Thornton with his Abe Lincoln appearance and a sack of oranges on his back. Unpressed clothes hung on his gaunt frame, but his keen eyes were filled with compassion and humor. "Just thought you might need a good orange to keep you awake for the day crew," he chuckled.

I hugged his stooped shoulders and kissed the cheek of our family's beloved physician. How often Mama had brought sick, suffering humanity to Dr. Thornton's office. His roll-top desk could never close and neither could his heart.

Without even glancing at the charts, he ambled into his patients' rooms with his pocket full of blue and pink pills. "Now, honey," he told Mrs. Olsen, "it's not so bad. You'll be home in no time."

Then disregarding isolation techniques, he pushed aside the gown and gloves—in order to visit the new isolation patient. "Foolishness, foolishness," he muttered, pushing the bandages aside. "Nothing like soap and water—good old soap and water."

"Now, now, young man," he said in Bill's room. "You look better already. A few more days and the infection will be gone. Reminds me of a story I heard on a fishing trip in Alaska. . . ."

When Dr. Thornton left, pink and blue pills were on the bedside table and Bill was laughing. "I'll be back this evening—and it will all be all right," he told the boy. And I knew it would be!

I never found out what the blue and pink pills were, but they worked! With a chuckle, Dr. Thornton moved on to the other floors, his bag of oranges over his shoulder. He had come into my darkness and brought light.

35

Home

I rocked in Mama's rocking chair and watched her roll out pie crust for the Sunday dinner lemon pies. In the quiet of Mama's kitchen I drank in the peace of belonging and sipped a cup of coffee. This was my first weekend at home in many weeks but it was as though I had never been away. On Monday, after a month of night duty, I would begin the morning shift again, but tomorrow I would attend the regular Sunday morning service in Papa's church.

The long hours of night duty had left me weary and I fell asleep in Mama's rocker. When I awakened, I saw that Mama was looking at me anxiously. Quietly she reminded me, "Your strength and help come from the Lord. He will never fail you, Margaret." Her words filled my heart, and the familiarity of the room brought refreshing to my soul.

I knew from Grace that a lot of the family meals these days consisted of potatoes fried in lard. The Depression days brought a number of people to seek food and shelter at Mama's table. But she declared stoutly, "I have never seen the righteous forsaken or His seed begging bread." For Mama, God's words were a fact of life.

Everything in the kitchen was in preparation for the next day. The homemade soup and freshly baked rye bread were for

Saturday's supper but the meatballs and lemon pies were for Sunday's dinner.

I was home—and a part of the Saturday night ritual of shampoos and baths. Clean clothes were laid out for the morning and shoes were polished. The dining room table was set, potatoes peeled and carrots diced. Meatballs were ready for the frying pan; apple sauce cooled in a bowl.

When the younger children were finally tucked into bed, Mama and I closed the day with a cup of coffee and a sugar lump. For the special occasion of "Margaret is home," she managed day-old sweet rolls for a penny apiece. Life was good!

That night I was back in our bed—Doris in the middle, Grace by the wall. I took my place on the edge. We laughed and talked until sleep tucked us into a land of dreams.

Papa greeted the day with a rousing Norwegian hymn: "Early now on Sunday morning we lift our songs of praise to God." Nothing had changed in the Tweten home!

Mama's meatballs were sizzling in the frying pan. Hot coffee, toast, and oatmeal waited as the Tweten clan emerged from the bedrooms.

I fell into the routine as though I had never been away— dishes done, beds made up, and everything in order before Sunday school.

Scrubbed and dressed in our best, we walked down Wright-wood Avenue to Logan Square. Papa strode ahead of us in striped trousers and swallow-tailed coat, his coattails blowing in the wind.

Mama had happily nodded her approval when she checked his high starched collar and white shirt. There was no doubt about it. Papa was a handsome man!

The church family greeted me warmly and assured me of their love and prayers.

"Did you know that your father cried the first Sunday you were in training?" our friend Leona chuckled delightedly. "He actually cried—and said, 'You must excuse me. This is the first Sunday Margaret hasn't been here in church.'"

"You mean he missed me? I didn't think he knew I was gone!"

"Oh, he misses you. He just won't tell you. But I saw him cry. Your father loves you all very much—he just doesn't know how to show it."

I watched Papa in the pulpit, but I couldn't think of anything else. Papa missed me! He really missed me!

I was home!

At dinner we sat down at Mama's table covered with a starched linen cloth. The familiar menu of meatballs and all the trimmings blended with the stories from Barney and Leona who sat with us around the table.

When the table was cleared, Mama brought in her famous lemon pies and coffee. I knew that the potatoes fried in lard would come later—probably the rest of the week—but today was a time of feasting and joy.

Papa dipped his sugar lump in his coffee and exclaimed, "*Ja*, Mama, that was the best pie you ever made." He always said that and we all always agreed.

Sunday afternoon was a time for naps or long walks. Night duty had exhausted me and I was ready for a nap. I had walked in the hospital corridors.

The house became quiet, the Sunday kind of stillness. Dishes were done, and Mama and the children were napping. Papa had gone into his study for his quiet time before the evening service and Barney, Leona, and Grace went for a walk. I quickly fell asleep in my old room.

The next thing I knew, Mama had the coffee pot on. Leona and the others had returned from their walk and Papa came out of the study. It was time for afternoon coffee.

By five o'clock, we all marched down Wrightwood Avenue again to the Logan Square Church. It was time for B.Y.P.U. (our Baptist Young People's Union, but the ages ranged from one to 100—we were all young). After the various "youth groups" met, the Ruth Society served refreshments. We ate open-faced limpa bread sandwiches with goat cheese, hard-boiled eggs with anchovies, spiced cheese and mutton roll. Coffee cakes and gallons of coffee with thick cream were added—then the sugar lumps.

By 7:30 we had gathered for the evening service. The choir sang and the string band played, and then Papa preached.

At the close of the service, good-byes were exchanged. At home I picked up my brown bag and Papa and I walked to the streetcar together. He read the Bible and I watched the city from the dusty window until we left the streetcar and walked through the doors of the Norwegian American Hospital.

I kissed Papa on the cheek and thanked him for bringing me safely back to the hospital. I knew that the extra five cents for carfare was a sacrifice.

I felt particularly blessed—I had a haven to go to when I was so exhausted. Many of the trainees I knew were from out of town and could not go home. Some didn't even have a home to go to. Being able to come home and get into the same familiar setting and the same routine was especially important to me. It had given me a needed sense of security. It restored my perspective, refreshed my sense of personal identity, and renewed my strength.

36

Love Stories

One of my favorite places is the ocean, especially when I'm there with my grandchildren. With an eye for beauty, my grandsons were watching Heather and her friend, Kris, jog on the beach.

"Heather wants to be a doctor," Chad said proudly of his sister.

"Wow!" Eric gave a long, low whistle.

Shawn's answer was equally as expressive. "Hey, she could be anything—writer, lawyer, doctor, or . . . a model!"

"So could you boys," I interjected, my hand firmly on Chad's shoulder. "Chad, you won first place in an art contest. Besides, you're a good soccer player, and a writer!"

Eric grinned. "Looks like you have some competition, Grammy!" With a quick hug, Eric joined the others and they ran down the beach, the rest of their remarks lost in the wind.

I found myself watching the children—and talking to myself. "Oh, you beautiful children, each of you is so different with a unique creative talent from God. Keep thankful hearts—remember, every perfect gift comes from above." My words raced on the wind behind them to the water's edge.

The ocean waves rolled over the sand. Fishermen were bringing in their boats. I found myself humming an old song:

Shrimp boats are a-comin'. . . .
Gotta hurry, hurry home. . . .

I did. It was supper time!

Having all the family together during these sunny days was a gift from God. I thought of my grandchildren growing up and being able to go into various fields of work armed with wonderful new technology. I remembered a long ago time and our lack of modern medicine, and when the prescription of love and prayer sometimes overcame that lack.

I was a young R.N. and had been assigned to a four-year-old girl who was fighting for her life. Diagnosis: ruptured appendix, peritonitis. The dressings on her enlarged abdomen had become saturated with purulent drainage.

She was the youngest of a large, devoted family who all called themselves the "Knights of the Round Table." Each child had been given a knight's name in addition to his or her real name. The eldest was called Sir Dependability, another Sir Sincerity, a third Sir Kindness . . . this young girl was named Sir Love.

Sir Love's anxious parents took turns at the bedside of their beautiful, dying child.

The slow drip from a proctoclysis can sent fluid into her rectum. Needles under her skin sent fluid into the thighs from the hypodermoclysis method. Aspirin and cool sponging helped to lower her high temperature caused by the severe infection.

I gagged inwardly when I changed the abdominal dressings. Nevertheless, I smiled and told stories to Sir Love and her parents as well. Stories about the Tweten family. Stories about Jesus.

Sir Love named me Miss Tweedledeedee. "Come change my dressing real fast, Miss Tweedledeedee," she would call. She wanted to get it over with.

Whenever her doctor, a tall, gentle man, came, he held back his tears and handed her a lollipop. "Try to suck this, Sir Love," he would say. "You need the glucose."

One day she was too weak to suck the lollipop.

When I reached the hospital the next morning, the cleaning maids were huddled close together in the hall, crying.

"What happened?" I asked.

"Sister told me not to clean her room, not to disturb the family, because Sir Love is almost gone."

For a moment, the world stood still while doctors, Deaconess nurses, and the cleaning staff prayed for one small child. Then I went into the room to change the dressings and sponge Sir Love. Her body was cyanotic. My heart ached. Her parents held hands and quietly prayed.

Day turned into night. Sir Love was still alive. I said good-bye to the parents and left.

In the morning, Sir Love was still alive. The cleaning woman cleaned the room. I bathed Sir Love and changed her dressings.

Her doctor came with a lollipop, and she sucked it. We dripped water into her mouth, and she swallowed. Color crept back into her face. Shouts of joy spread through every department of the hospital. Sir Love was alive!

Gradually she began to eat the special meals the kitchen staff prepared. One day I took her in a wheelchair to visit the people who had wept and prayed and showered her with their love.

Months later, I was a guest in the home of the "Knights of the Round Table." Sir Love came in from the street where she had been riding her tricycle. Her grubby arms flew around my neck and I was smothered with sticky lollipop kisses. "Miss Tweedledeedee! You came!"

I smiled, remembering Sir Love. Perhaps one of my grandchildren would become a doctor. They would never have to administer lollipops for glucose and there would be miracle drugs to treat infections. But even with all the modern technology, the power of love and prayer still tips the scales.

Another four-year-old child, the youngest of thirteen, fell into a washtub of scalding water. The entire family came to the Emergency Room with him. No one expected the child to live.

I recall holding him—he was swathed in gauze with only his eyes visible, peeping through the mask of bandages. Intravenous fluids dripped into his small veins.

He became the hospital pet, surrounded by love from every department. Dr. Al was his doctor. Usually brusque in his manner, Dr. Al, we knew, was a teddy bear—especially where children were concerned.

Under Dr. Al's care, "Wonder Boy" slowly improved, and eventually he was given the freedom to roam the hospital halls.

He visited nurses and patients, but Dr. Al was the one our bright-eyed Wonder Boy loved. He even followed him on rounds and called him "My Dr. Al."

One day there was a medical meeting in the conference room. Wonder Boy was roaming the halls and happened upon the door to the conference room.

The men attending the meeting looked up when the door opened and saw Wonder Boy, in his little hospital gown, searching the faces around the table. Suddenly his eyes lit up. "There he is, My Dr. Al!" The little boy ran to the doctor, and love had a shining moment in that conference room.

Love had its way again some years later when I was on a private duty case. My patient was in a coma, his condition critical. There seemed to be little hope for recovery. But, just as I always did, I spoke softly to him, and assured him he would be better in the morning.

I told him what I was doing for him, saying such things as, "I'm changing your I.V."; or, "I have to turn you now." In between, I repeated Scripture verses of encouragement, verses like: "Fear thou not; for I am with thee: be not dismayed; for I am thy God: I will strengthen thee; yea, I will help thee; yea, I will uphold thee with the right hand of my righteousness" (Isaiah 41:10).

One day my comatose patient opened his eyes. "Mary. You must be Mary."

"No—but you are close. It is Margaret."

"I heard you; I heard your voice. You sound just like Mary."

Later, his story came in pieces. Mary was an army nurse he had loved, but both their parents rejected their idea of marriage because of religious differences.

"I loved her," he said softly. "We parted, but I never forgot her. I had made plans to find her—then I became ill. I need to find my Mary."

I waited, then answered quietly. "I have watched your lovely wife sitting here day after day. I know devotion when I see it, and believe me, that kind is rare." I patted his hand. "You must not allow a dream from the past to cloud what you have in the present. You have been a gravely ill man, but your health is being restored. You must trust God to take care of your Mary. By coming into her life at this time, you could destroy both her and her family if she has one. Then what about the one who loves you now? Why don't you close the door to the past and give yourself to the present?"

Slowly he recovered enough to go home. Before he left he turned to me and said softly, "Thank you, Mary—thank you for everything."

Many months later I met his lovely wife again.

"Oh, I'm so glad to see you. My husband is a changed man since his illness. He decided to go to church with me and it is as though we are newlyweds. He used to be so quiet, but our lives are so full these days. Strange what a serious illness can do! I guess coming close to death made him realize how precious life can be. I'll tell him I saw you."

A thankful heart stores up past mercies to feed faith in dark days. I heard that someplace—I think I'll try to remember it.

My romantic roommate was always in love with someone or something. When the soft music of "Speak to Me of Love" came on the radio, someone shouted down the hall, "They're playing your song, Hertha!" Then all the dormitory radios were turned up together for Hertha.

We teased Hertha about her "chicken farmer" whom no one had met. But then she met Thor, and they lived happily ever after. Her song is still *her* song.

One day, I met a real chicken farmer, not in a romantic setting, but in the hospital.

He stood in the corridor, outside the door where his wife lay in a coma. His weathered face reflected the sun and wind; his thumbs nervously pulled at his overall straps.

"Proud to meet you," he answered politely when I told him I was the morning nurse. Then he nodded toward his wife's room. "My woman's in that. . . ." His voice choked up. "Cain't run no chicken farm without her."

I assured him that we would all take good care of her. The patient's room was quiet; the intravenous fluid dripped slowly into her veins. The doctor warned us not to move her, due to an embolism (an obstruction in a blood vessel). Constant care was needed to monitor medication and vital signs. She was cold and clammy.

One day I asked the doctor if we could lift her so I could put a warm blanket under her. Reluctantly he agreed, "Only if four of you nurses lift her carefully." We did! I placed a warm blanket under her.

I talked to her quietly, cared for her, held her hand, and quoted the 23rd Psalm. There was no response.

Her husband came to see her early each morning; then he returned home to care for his chickens and twelve children. The eldest daughter, eighteen and newly married, helped care for the family.

One morning the farmer met me in the hall as he was leaving. "I got a pot of coffee perkin' in the room. Just had to do somethin' and I saw how all you nurses drink coffee. Just had to do somethin'."

I thanked him and took a cup. He smiled, then returned home to care for his chickens and children. Each morning it was the same routine. He was waiting for me with a cup of coffee, saying, "Not much, mind you, but I just bought the coffee pot and figured how to make the coffee—my woman always did it—I just had to do somethin'."

He brushed a tear with the back of his work worn hand, and continued, "Cain't run no chicken farm without my woman— and all those young'uns to tend."

Day after day I cared for "his woman," and spoke softly, "Don't be afraid, you will make it. God will take care of you. Your family is fine. People are praying for you."

Once again I quoted the 23rd Psalm—and there was a stir. My patient's eyes opened. "That voice . . . I . . . know that voice," she faltered. "I heard someone talking. *You are the voice!*"

"Yes," I answered with a lump in my throat. "I am the voice!"

She continued, "One day I felt like I was going through a long dark tunnel; then through cold, black water. I was so cold. Someone lifted me up and put a warm blanket under me." Her lip trembled. "Then I heard the voice saying, 'Though I walk through the valley of the shadow of death, I will fear no evil, for thou art with me.' I felt a warm hand pull me back. *I heard you!*"

Gradually the patient improved until she was able to sit in a chair. Until then only her husband was allowed to visit her, but with Christmas coming, her children were to be allowed to visit two at a time on Christmas Day.

Her three nurses from the three shifts bought her a beautiful pink stole for the occasion. When Christmas morning came, my chicken farmer was there with the cup of coffee. By the time her children came, my patient was sitting in a chair, her long black hair parted and braided—with a pink bow in each braid. The soft stole around her shoulders covered a warm flannel robe. She was beautiful!

The farmer gave her an approving glance, then joked tenderly, "Now, now, we cain't be lettin' you git used to them fancy things."

She understood—and smiled up at him. And then her children were there. Her dark brown eyes filled with tears as the first two came through the door of her room. They came at intervals, quietly and in awe. Her married daughter and the young husband lingered the longest. Finally they left to take the younger children home.

"Your daughter is lovely," I said, when we were alone. "She seems to have a nice husband."

"He is a good boy," the mother answered; then quietly added, "He just walks soft-like through life."

The day came when she went home to the farm.

Months later I had a surprise visit. There stood my chicken farmer in his clean overalls, his patient wife beside him. She was wearing a plain cotton dress and flat shoes. Her long black hair was pulled back into a bun. They stood hand in hand.

"Farm's goin' good, ma'am," he told me. "Young'uns all in school. Right smart, too. It's good to have Ma home—just cain't run no chicken farm without my woman."

Her smile said it all—and somehow the memory goes "soft-like" through my life.

37

No Big Deal

Beverly bounced through the kitchen door, laughing delight-edly, "Aunt Margaret, wait until you hear this one!"

I put my pen down and in the dining room Harold stopped typing. It was time for a break anyway.

Beverly, a petite blonde, is married to Steve Jensen, our nephew. "Benjamin's first-grade teacher just called and I thought, 'Oh, no! What's he done now?'"

Benjamin had not been feeling well one day and he had asked his teacher to call his mother. There was no answer. "I can't reach your mother right now," the teacher told Benjamin, "but we'll try again later."

Benjamin looked out the school window, then his face brightened. "Oh, do you know Aunt Margaret, the author?" The teacher nodded as Benjamin continued. "She wrote *First We Have Coffee*—that book is about her mother. Then she wrote *Lena* and that is about Ralph. *First Comes the Wind* is a love story and *Papa's Place* is about Aunt Margaret's father. She's writing one now about nursing. Do you know my Aunt Margaret?" he repeated.

"I have read two of her books, but I certainly have learned something today."

"You have?"

"Oh, yes," the teacher told him. "I have learned about your Aunt Margaret, the author."

"Oh." Then he grew quiet. "Oh, well," he sighed, "when you get to know her, it's no big deal."

No big deal—he was right. Sometimes, when we think the agony of life is overwhelming, God allows the ecstasy. Somehow it all comes together, the rain and the sun, the smiles and the tears—all a part of life and not always the big deal we make it out to be. Mountains and valleys—no big deal.

"Kathryn," I asked my granddaughter recently, "what do you want to be when you grow up?"

Katie's bright blue eyes twinkled and the bow seemed off balance in her tousled blonde hair. She said, "A nurse, like my grammy. Then when I'm too old to do anything else, I'll write books—just like my grammy."

She blew me a kiss and skipped happily on her way. I wondered if she sensed at all how important nursing had been to me. It always was, even when I was six—like Kathryn.

I remembered one Sunday afternoon at the old parsonage on Ellen Street in Winnipeg, Manitoba. The house was quiet because everyone was taking a Sunday nap, including Papa.

My nap was always short, so Papa had given me instructions to be very quiet and wait for a guest who was coming sometime that afternoon. "His name is Dr. Orchard," Papa said, "and he is the president of the Canadian Baptist Convention, so be sure you open the door, shake hands, and welcome him nicely. Can't forget your manners. Show Dr. Orchard a chair, and then come and get me. You don't need to say we are taking naps. Perhaps Canadians don't take naps on Sunday like Norwegians."

I promised!

Tired of waiting, I decided to play hospital. I got a couple of Mama's white sheets, put one on the parlor floor, and covered the sofa with the other. Diapers made up the beds—all in a row—where imaginary babies were sleeping. I pinned a diaper around my waist and tied one around my head for my nurse's cap. With chart in hand, I went carefully from bed to bed, checking temperatures and duly recording the results.

During my routine hospital visit, a knock came at the front

door. Suddenly, I was face to face with the president of the Canadian Baptist Convention.

I shook hands and told him my name, just as Papa said, and invited him to sit on my sheet-draped sofa. Proudly I told my guest, "Everyone except me is taking a nap"—then clapped my hand to my mouth—"Oh! Papa said I shouldn't say that. But that's what they are doing—taking naps. I don't like naps, but I had to take a little one!"

He was studying me seriously, his eyes sparkling.

"This is my hospital and I am the nurse. You see, when I grow up I'm going to be a nurse. And I'm going to write stories." My audience of one nodded his approval as I chatted on. "Papa thinks I tell too many stories, but I tell stories to all my children."

Again, he nodded his approval.

"I have to pretend they are children. I don't have many toys. Papa threw my rag doll, Big Jack, in the furnace. Big Jack was so old, and Papa didn't know he was my only doll." I was standing directly in front of Dr. Orchard.

"Mama said I had to forgive Papa because he never had any toys and didn't know Big Jack was my friend. Poor Papa . . . no toys. I don't have toys, but I make up toys."

Dr. Orchard's voice was deep when he said, "It was good that you forgave your father." He smiled at my hospital. "So you are going to be a nurse, Margaret?"

I nodded my head confidently. "Oh, yes. See, these are all my sick children. Come . . . visit them," I urged. I tugged at his hand and together we made hospital visits.

Then Papa came downstairs! I had forgotten to call him! Papa's steely blue eyes looked straight through me—but Dr. Orchard saved the day!

"Pastor Tweten, you have a remarkable young daughter. She'll make a fine nurse, I'm sure."

I was still clutching Dr. Orchard's hand firmly. I needed a friend. I looked up at him and he winked.

"We have had a delightful visit and now we will close the hospital down, Margaret, so your father and I can visit."

Together we folded the diapers and sheets and we talked

about sick children and nurses. Then I ran upstairs to tell Mama all about it.

Papa never mentioned the incident, but one day he returned from a Canadian Baptist Convention with, "Dr. Orchard sends his greetings to the little nurse, Margaret. *Ja, ja*, I wouldn't be surprised if you do become a nurse."

I watched my little Kathryn skipping happily in front of me—and I wondered, *would she really follow in Grammy's footsteps?* That *would* be a big deal to me.

Real importance, the really "big deals," grow out of love and commitment, the kind one elderly couple shared. A light rain drizzled on the metal awning outside the Emergency Room door of Kennestone Hospital. The earth was damp and the budding branches on the big oak reached out toward North Surgery. The hospital grounds were splotched with green, and friendly clouds hung close by.

It was almost time to go off duty and head for home. It seemed like a good day to transplant flower beds and dig in the moist earth. It certainly didn't look like a day for tragedy—but suddenly, there it was, sinister and black. A frightened old man shook with sobs as he was lifted gently from the ambulance. His little home, with all his worldly possessions, had just burned down. Tears streaked the soot on his cheeks. Ma stood quietly by—her grey hair, tied in a knot, framing her wrinkled face.

"Now, Pa, ain't no use in carryin' on so and gittin' yerself plumb tore up. I reckon it could be worse."

Pa sobbed, "But, Ma, you and me got nothin' in this world except what we got on our backs."

Ma's chin quivered; tears made a path in her furrowed cheeks. Her small gnarled arms wrapped around Pa and she buried her weary head against his whiskered chin. In a moment she suddenly straightened. "But, Pa," she said tenderly, "you got me and I got you, and we can work together. I still got strength in my legs and as long as I can stand up, I can work." She turned to me. "Work's a blessing, ma'am."

I nodded slowly, thinking how love suffers long and is kind,

215

endures all things and always hopes. And another familiar passage came to mind: *I will never leave thee nor forsake thee.*

The doctor's kind words reassured the couple, and after a while they left the Emergency Room, hand in hand, walking into an unknown future.

The rain had stopped. The buds were dripping. The earth was soft. The clouds had lifted and the sun shone over the top. Love would find a way.

Commitment and covenant—*no big deal.* No, not when the heart settles it into the will from the very beginning.

38

Private Duty Nurse

"No one laughs anymore!" the young modern-day nurse declared.

She wearily complained to me how paper work and red tape, rules and regulations had the medical profession living on the ragged edge of frustration and burnout.

An elderly doctor spoke of the days before Intensive Care or Coronary Care units, when bedside nursing brought patients through crisis situations.

"We need both," he complained bitterly, "the new technology, *and* the personal touch. Too often the disease is treated but not the patient. When you 'old' private duty nurses are gone, Margaret, it will mark the end of an era of old-fashioned, bedside nursing. I am glad I practiced medicine when I did," he told me. "Somehow I don't fit into this age of computers and transplants, to say nothing of sex changes. I'm overwhelmed with the moral issues of abortion and surrogate mothers. It seems to me we are complicating the living and robbing the dying of dignity."

He moved sadly down the hall to visit an old friend, a medical colleague of many days.

I knew what he meant. I've thought about it often. He wore the unmistakable look of dignity that marked the doctor of yesterday: dark suit, polished shoes, white shirt and tie, his silver hair neatly parted. With a calm, unhurried pace, he nodded his greeting to orderlies, janitors, nurses, and doctors. Gracious manners and courtesy walked with him.

Change must come, I realize, but it is never easy.

I sighed and went to my patient's room. I had been called to nurse an elderly patient who was blind, and this would be my final case. After I met the patient and family, I went to the desk to check the doctor's orders. I asked for the head nurse. Before me stood a young woman in a blue turtleneck sweater, slacks, unpolished shoes—and no cap to identify her rank.

She looked at me as though I had arrived from outer space. I was starched from cap to shoes.

"*I am the head nurse!*" she announced.

Then I saw her pin on her sweater.

Aides and orderlies were laughing down the hall. A young man in blue jeans and a sweatshirt came to the desk and wrote orders on the order sheet. He asked for a prescription pad, and the nurse, still seated, just pointed to the drawer—she didn't even look up.

As I turned down the hall, I realized, *I've been around too long.* Then I met a friend from long ago. Her shoulders were stooped from years of nursing, but her cap was starched and her uniform crackled with stiffness. Her shoes were immaculate but her steps were slow as she moved softly down the hall.

"I'm nursing an old friend of mine," she confided. "I helped with all the babies in the family, and I nursed the old folks through the flu epidemic. Now old Grandpa is dying and the family refused intensive care. They want a familiar face around him—so here I am; can't even retire." She chuckled.

"Did you see that head nurse?" I asked.

My friend nodded and whispered, "Remember how it used to be when the doctors came on the floor to make rounds? We all stood up and then the head nurse made rounds with him and took notes, and we had the dressing cart all ready."

"Believe me, I remember! Miss Rosie didn't miss a shoelace. What would she have done with a turtleneck sweater?"

We laughed together, and then went our separate ways.

During the quiet of night duty, I looked out over the parking lot. A light rain was falling over the world outside. In the morning someone was to come and take my patient home. This would be my last night in the hospital where I had nursed for so many years. I would be packing my uniforms away.

The supervisors and head nurses I had known were all retired. The older doctors had young assistants. One by one the older physicians were closing the doors of their medical practices. In several cases a Doctor, Junior replaced the Doctor, Senior while the father beamed with pride. I wondered how many times I had heard a doctor say, "Nothing makes a father more proud than to have his son in the same profession." I agreed.

One by one, the private duty nurses were retiring; the young chose more dramatic areas of nursing. I was nostalgic by the time morning came. With the change of shifts (one old man called it the "swapping of the mules") I was fully prepared to go off duty for the last time. I passed the dining room on my way out and saw the long table where the private duty nurses used to eat together. Now aides and orderlies were drinking coffee there together.

I paused in the doorway, remembering. When we were on the day shift, a family member usually relieved us at 11:30 for lunch. That gave us time to get back before the patients' trays came.

For the moment I relived the storytelling that went on around that table. In thirty minutes we could eat lunch and hear a new story every day.

One elderly nurse told her own story. It happened during a serious flu epidemic when she was a young nurse. She went from case to case with little sleep. She barely had time to wash her uniforms and polish her shoes. The housework had to wait. Dishes piled up. The bed was left unmade and dust rolled without interruption.

One day she returned to her home and knew she, too, was very ill. She had the flu! She had seen several patients die. After weeks of nursing others, she was sure her resistance was too low to recover. There were no more doctors and nurses to call on. Everyone was exhausted.

She was going to die! She knew it.

Then she saw the disaster in her home.

"I will not have the women from First Church come in here and find me dead in this dirty house," she declared to the empty room. "This house will be put in a dying-clean condition!"

She prayed for strength to finish the job before she died—then proceeded to clean the bathroom, scrub the floors, wash the dishes, take out the garbage, and clean the refrigerator and stove.

Dragging herself to the bedroom, she changed the bed and put on her best sheets and embroidered pillow cases. She placed her soiled laundry in a laundry bag. Finally, everything was in order. After she bathed, she put on a warm flannel nightgown, brushed her hair, took some aspirin, and sipped some hot tea.

"Now, I have this house in dying-clean condition," she declared. "Let the women of First Church come!"

By this time, her fever was soaring and she had chills. She crawled wearily into her clean bed. She folded her hands and prayed. She was ready to go.

Morning came! She was still in the same position, hands folded across her chest. The bed was drenched, her embroidered pillow cases damp from perspiration. But her fever was gone. She opened her eyes. She was still alive!

I could hear again our laughter as we filled the elevator. We all vowed to go home and put our houses in "dying-clean condition."

A young nurse who had been sitting at another table pushed into the elevator with us.

"You always have something to laugh about at your table," she said wistfully. "Everyone is so serious at our table. I don't see anything funny."

I replied, "That is sad! Life is filled with agony and ecstasy, but laughter is like a detergent. It clears the cobwebs from our minds. We see that for every thing there is a season: a time to weep, and a time to laugh.

"Make the most of your moments of laughter," I encouraged her, "for those moments will live in your memory."

The people in nursing homes often show a keen sense of humor. During one Sunday morning chapel service, as the wheelchairs rolled in, one little old lady yelled to another, "Your wheelchair touched mine!"

"No, it didn't!"

"Yes, it did!"

"Move over, then!"

An attendant moved the chair, and I chuckled to myself, thinking, *They sound like my grandchildren.*

Mama used to say, "We need one good laugh a day." In a nursing home, you can't miss.

Miss Ruthie, for instance, was ninety years old, more or less, and moved about in her wheelchair with skill and ease. Her white hair was tied in a bow on top of her head; her grin revealed the humor in her heart.

A piano player often entertained the residents, and Miss Ruthie's feet kept time to the music.

"We ought to get married," she announced to the pianist one day.

"Well, Miss Ruthie, we all know how much I love you," answered the young piano player. "But there is a problem; I have a wife."

Miss Ruthie thought for a moment, then her toothless smile lit up her face. "Hang her!" she announced—and wheeled herself down the hall.

I left the hospital and moved toward my car in the parking lot. For the last time. An era in my life had come to an end. I heard a door close behind me.

39

Today and Yesterday

"Grammy, you write your stories and I'll write in my diary."
While I sat at my desk, six-year-old Kathryn took her pen in
hand and sat beside me. She looked thoughtful—then began
to write.

As I picked up my pen to write, too, I thought of Mr. B. and
the violets on his windowsill.

I glanced down at my grandchild, eager to tell her about him,
but she was intent on the work at hand. She had her own
stories to write—mine could wait. Someday I will tell her about
the man who lay so near the edge of eternity, about the violets,
and about how they were Jesus' special way of inviting a dying
patient to "come to Me."

In a few moments, Kathryn tired of writing and dropped her
pen. "Come on, Grammy," she urged. "Let's play dress-up."

Hand in hand we went to the old family chest. I took out
some baby clothes. As I held up one tiny garment, I told her,
"Your daddy wore this."

She eyed me skeptically.

Then she spotted something else. She frowned. "Grammy,
what in the world is that?"

I leaned back. "That, my dear, is my nursing uniform from
when I was a student nurse."

She stared at the uniform, then back at me. Picturing her daddy as small enough to wear a baby garment was tough enough. But picturing Grammy in that outfit was even harder.

She put on the blue and white striped uniform and time-worn apron, now yellowed with age. My cap was limp and grey—but I put it on her blonde head.

"You wore this?" she giggled.

Then we took pictures! Soon it was bedtime. She curled up with her stuffed animals and I tucked her in. I wondered what she had written in her diary.

As she slept, pages from past years rustled in the dusty cupboards of my mind. On the bookshelf my textbooks stood in a row. *Anatomy* and *Physiology* (Kimber, Gray, Stackpole, 1934). I wondered what my grandchildren would be studying in the future. *Surgical Nursing* (Eliason, Ferguson, Lewis, 1934). I marvelled at the advanced technology of today.

I recalled the time when I was six, and I helped the doctor fix my blanket on the kitchen table. I climbed up on the blanket. Papa gave the chloroform and my tonsils were taken out—all on the kitchen table.

I opened the *Principles and Practice of Nursing* (1933) and saw a note from Mother Jensen (Harold's mother) that I had never noticed before. In her large scrawl she had written:

Life is a desert of thirst—
But there are oases, and signs
enough to find them.

A second note read:

How confused the motives that guide our lives!

I wondered when she had written those notes—and why I hadn't known her better. *Is it always so,* I asked myself, *that we fail to know each other?*

Another note said:

One can come into a room and it is as if another

*candle is lighted. Another comes—and we see the
smoke and darkness.*

In still another, she had written:

*Joy and exaltation, a white light on faces turned
up to someone they adore. It is like the second movement
of the ninth symphony. The music gets it clearer.*

The last note read:

*Only one life, t'will soon be past;
Only what's done for Christ will last.*
—Mother Jensen

In her large handwriting she had penned these words—so
long ago—and I was just now discovering them!

She died in 1963, but before she went home she saw the
heavens open and heard the music of angels. She was smiling
when she closed her eyes. "Oh death, where is your sting?"

I turned the pages in my nursing book, and I stopped at the
topic Pneumonia. I remembered the twenty-four-hour-duty
nurses who stayed with their patients for twenty-four hours;
then they would be relieved by a family member for four hours.
Many of these patients had pneumonia.

Now I wonder how either the nurse or patient survived.
Pneumonia was the most fatal of acute diseases and nursing
care was the most important factor in caring for these patients—
with mustard plaster paste, cupping, strapping the chest, and
in some cases with venesection (blood letting; phlebotomy) and
oxygen. The canvas tents they used were heavy and depressing.

The cold-air treatment was also used: The patient was
wrapped well, including a hood—only his face exposed—then
taken outside or into a cold room. A hot water bottle was placed
at the feet. It almost reads like fiction today, but yesterday it
was a frightening reality.

I remember when my one-month-old baby sister, Jeanelle,
lay dying from pneumonia. Dr. Thornton's craggy face looked

sad. "Give this one back to God, Mama," he advised. His shoulders sagged when he left. Grief is a heavy burden.

Leona, our nurse friend, took that blue baby and rubbed her with warm oil, suctioned out the mucous, and *willed* that child to life. Today, Jeanelle is a beautiful grandmother.

It was time to leave the books until another day. The principles remain unchanged, but the methods of practice change continually. Tragedy comes when principles change. Modern technology without eternal principles would bring malnutrition, starvation, and death to the soul. In the medical world of yesterday or today, healing of spirit and soul as well as body is vital.

One case that defied medical explanation stands out vividly.

My cardiac patient was dying. The family was present and the intern had called the family physician who was already en route from his home.

The patient's son had returned from military duty and sat weeping in the utility room. I reached out to comfort him, and he sobbed out his confession on my shoulder.

"Nurse, I kicked off family teaching . . . turned my back on my Christian training . . . just threw my life away. Now I realize what a fool I've been . . . and I want God's forgiveness . . . and my father's forgiveness."

We prayed together, amid the clatter of that utility room. Then he said, "Now it's too late—if only my dad knew. But now he's in a coma."

"Come on," I urged, "put your head in the oxygen tent and tell your father."

The son leaned into the tent, close to his father's cyanotic face. "Dad, Dad, I've come home—really home. I asked God to forgive me . . . and I want you to forgive me. I turned my life over to Jesus Christ. . . . I love you, Dad!"

By the time the physician arrived, the patient's color was almost back to normal and he was calling out his son's name.

Months later I met the son again. "Guess what? I married a beautiful girl, and my dad is doing great!"

That memory from yesterday still brings joy today.

The morning after Kathryn had written in her diary, she sat

down to enjoy a cup of milk and coffee with Papa, and she handed her diary to me. "Wanna see what I wrote, Grammy?"

I read, "I love you, Mom," on one page. The next page, "I love you, Dad." The following pages—"I love you . . . I love you . . . I love you . . ." She had named us all.

I opened God's diary. I turned the pages. His Word said the same thing to me: "I love you."

40

A Raccoon and God's Care

Keith and Kevin, brothers, were two who came to our home in Greensboro to see what had happened to Ralph. There they stood—cut-off jeans, sandaled feet, beards, long blond hair, and vacant blue eyes—and a tiny raccoon on Keith's shoulder.

A raccoon?!

"Hi. This is Jeremiah," Keith said to me. "I found him in the woods, and it's up to me to keep him alive." Keith's dull blue eyes stared into space.

"Oh, I see," I answered.

I didn't see, but Ralph warned me that Keith's mind was strung out on drugs and that Keith believed his mission in life was to care for the baby raccoon whose mother had died.

"Where shall we put Jeremiah?" I asked.

"Oh, he stays with me."

We sat around the dining room table and Harold asked the blessing—with one eye on Jeremiah still sitting on Keith's shoulder.

We passed the meatballs and mashed potatoes, standard fare at the Jensens', while Keith fed Jeremiah from a doll's bottle filled with milk.

I had been warned to "play it cool"—drugs did strange things to young people.

When they came to our door with vacant eyes, I just hugged them, then fed them. Words couldn't be heard anymore. They knew some of the words, the Scriptures, the admonitions. They had memorized Bible verses in Sunday school and had heard enough preaching to convert the world.

Ralph taught me well. "They only understand love, Mom—that's all."

Did love include a raccoon? I had to learn to love Jeremiah. When I found "marks" on my carpet I bit my lip—and scrubbed. I almost lost my cool when I put my foot into a wet shoe! Ugh!

Jeremiah even slept with Keith. I prayed a lot!

Dan showed the boys the farm, and together they cut down brush, washed up in the cool mountain spring, bunked in the cabin, and pitched in with the building of the Shalom Valley chalet.

My faithful blue Datsun carried a trunkful of food to Shalom Valley. We camped and picnicked there, and the guitars were strummed into the night.

Jeremiah found a home and became a favorite pet. Eventually even the dogs tolerated him.

In the hot summer when I gardened in shorts and a sleeveless top, Jeremiah would sneak up behind me and climb to my shoulder. His cold, finger-like paws climbing up my bare legs sent chills up my spine. One day I scolded him. "Jeremiah, you should be ashamed, scaring me to pieces like that."

Jeremiah looked at me and talked back, "Brrrr."

I asked, "What do you want?"

He jumped down and ran over to a large tin that contained marshmallows.

"Now Jeremiah, you know those are for a wiener and marshmallow roast tonight. You should be ashamed, eating my marshmallows."

He cocked his head and with his little "Brrrr," almost said, "Please?"

I yielded and tossed him a fat marshmallow. He looked at me, gave me a quick "Brrrr" thank-you, and ran to the creek.

That's when I forgave him for all the wet shoes and spots on the rug.

Keith and Kevin were getting brown in the sun, eating, sleeping, and loving the land. Their expressions were no longer vacant.

Even now, these many years later, I can hear the whippoor-will, see the stars over the valley, and smell the hot dogs and marshmallows at the open fire. I can still picture Keith strumming his guitar and hear his plaintive songs winging into the night.

Another young man, Rob, handsome like Michelangelo's *David*, with dark curly hair and soccer-toned muscles, came with bitterness and anger. Gradually God's Spirit worked on the inside while we opened our arms on the outside. The bitterness left and love replaced the anger. Rob became a new creature in Christ.

Back then we spared the words and lavished the love. God was at work.

On Tuesday nights we beat a path to the Masons' prayer meeting. Young people sat on the floor and the music flowed into the streets. They came to see what happened to Ralph—and stayed for six months. We took care of the outside; God's Spirit worked on the inside.

One Saturday night I was home alone. Harold was out of town and everyone else had gone to a prayer meeting. I was scrubbing the kitchen floor on my hands and knees. (My Norwegian mama never believed in mops. She's in heaven now, and I do use a mop now and then.)

I had been to the grocery and used practically all my meager paycheck for the boys' groceries. While I was scrubbing, I mentally figured my bank balance and realized I was overdrawn $50! Everything wrong happens when Harold is away.

I fell apart! It's strange how we brace ourselves for the great calamities of life but often fall apart at some small crisis. Right then $50 seemed to me like an unscalable mountain.

I slammed the scrub brush on the floor and cried into my bucket of sudsy water. "It's not fair, Lord. It's just not fair. All

I do is work, cook, scrub, and take these kids no one wants, and then I make a mistake—fifty lousy dollars! It's just not fair!"

I had a good cry as I finished the floor and emptied the bucket of water. I dried my hands and brushed back my stringy hair, but I couldn't stop the tears. I was angry. "Don't You care, Lord?" Just then the doorbell rang.

"Oh, no. Somebody's kid needs a place to sleep! I don't want to see anyone. I'm too upset."

I took a deep breath and went to the door. There stood our friend, Bob Adams.

"Margaret, I was at the meeting with all the hippies and the Lord spoke to me and said, 'Go, give Margaret $50 for groceries.'"

I didn't answer. I just stood there with my mouth open as he told this story.

"She surely doesn't need $50. Besides, Lord, I'm in a meeting."

"Go! Now!"

"Yes, Lord!"

I finally found my voice. "Oh, Bob, I'm overdrawn $50. Harold is gone and he'd be disturbed if my check bounced. I was convinced God had forgotten me."

We rejoiced together. Bob had obeyed and I had been shown God's care for His weary child.

I was reminded of how we are all overdrawn at times, not always $50, but sometimes we find ourselves short of faith, creativity, hope, or courage. We feel empty, alone, and in despair, with simply nothing in our account to draw from—overdrawn in energy, strength, or the ability to know how to put one foot ahead of the other. Someone once cried on my shoulder, "I am not a victorious Christian, I am just surviving." That's the way we feel.

Then, in those darkest hours, God's messenger comes: a friend with $50, or someone with a song, or we read or hear a Bible verse, or feel the warm clasp of a hand that strengthens, or hear a word of hope, or even receive just a smile or a hug from someone—just enough to enable us to take one more step.

The old song comes to mind: "Just when I need Him, Jesus is near." It is really true. Jesus never fails.

Fifty dollars wasn't the only blessing that night. Before they came home, Keith and Kevin each experienced God's transforming power through His amazing grace. "Great Is Thy Faithfulness" became Keith's theme song. Keith was faithful to the raccoon, and God was faithful to Keith.

Come to think of it, that song is my theme song, too.

41

Great Faithfulness

January 15, 1973. Keith was getting married in a few days.

What meant so much to me was meeting Kevin and Keith's parents. Their mother, a warm, plump farmer's wife, hugged me. With tears streaming down her cheeks, she turned to her stoic German husband and said, "This is the mama who took our children in."

His eyes moistened as he shook hands with me. "Thank you. . . ."

We couldn't speak.

Later that night the doorbell rang and there stood Ralph, Chris, and baby Shawn. "Hi. We came to spend the night, and besides we don't have homemade cinnamon rolls for breakfast. Can't stand to miss anything. Dan's here—we can all go to church together."

Chris and I prepared food and the men huddled together to talk "farm." What a family! I love it!

You'll never guess what happened. The next morning I stayed home to prepare a roast for the gang and take care of Shawn. The men, laughing and talking (and full of coffee and cinnamon rolls), piled into the car to go to church—and *forgot Chris!*

Mama and Papa Tweten, Brooklyn, New York

Golden Wedding Anniversary

Mama Tweten (1974)

Papa, Mama and Baby
Margaret (1917)

Papa and Mama Tweten

ABOVE: Harold and Margaret Jensen
(1938)

RIGHT: Harold and Margaret's
50th Wedding Anniversary

The Tweten family—(top) Gordon, Grace, Harold Jensen, Margaret, Doris; (bottom) Joyce, Papa, Mama, Jeanelle (1938)

The Jensen family—Jan, Harold, Margaret, Ralph, Dan (1950)

Dan, Ralph
and Jan Jensen

Dan Jensen

Chris and Ralph Jensen

The Carlbergs—Judson, Janice, Chad and Heather

LEFT: Original wedding party at 50th anniversary (clockwise from left) Grace, Joyce, Jeanelle, Doris, Howard, Harold and Margaret (1988)   RIGHT: Margaret with the grandfather clock—a gift from the children for her Golden Anniversary (1988)

The Sisters—Margaret, Grace, Doris, Joyce, Jeanelle

Lena Rogers Leach (1970)

Last family picture with Harold (1991)

Harold with the grandchildren (1979)

Margaret with the grandchildren—(top) Chad, Sarah, Shawn, Margaret, Heather, Kathryn (floor) Eric (Christmas 1993)

Margaret in her new office (1988)

Margaret

Cousin Ella, Margaret and Papa's guitar
(1986)

Margaret

I said, "Chris, this is the time to pack your bag and go home to your mother!"

"Forget it," she announced. "I'm staying with you."

You should have seen those four sheepish men when they returned from church, all mumbling their apologies. Chris said, "It's good to have something to hold over your heads."

She's one in a million!

On the Saturday evening of Keith and Barbara's wedding, a blanket of snow covered the quiet college campus, but the candlelit chapel invited the guests into its warmth.

The college president sat in one row; jean-clad youth with dull boots and long hair, from another generation, sat in another. Fur-wrapped, bejeweled women of society walked down the aisle on the arms of lanky youths (who looked a little uncomfortable in their tuxedos) to be seated with the other guests.

Warm, friendly faces of the Pennsylvania farmers nodded and smiled to young and old as they, too, joined the other wedding guests.

Dignified Hunter Dalton, owner of the Snow Lumber Co., took his place. He had given the "hippies" jobs—with some persuasion from his beautiful mother, Frances Dalton. Frances loved "my boys," and Hunter never regretted his decision. He came to love my boys, too.

Businessmen, musicians, a nightclub entertainer, the settled elite of the establishment, and those from the country and town, young and old, filled the pews of the college chapel that snowy night.

To me it was beautiful—flowers and candles, and an array of informal youths, some hidden behind palms. Ken Helser's music came softly—guitars strumming to the slow, gentle beat of drums and whispering overtones of the organ. The sound was like the sighing of wind through tall pines or waves rolling on a sandy shore.

The ministers stood in their places. Then came Keith, the groom, and Kevin, the best man, dressed in tuxedos—tall and smiling.

I reached for my evening bag and grabbed a lacy frill to dab at the tears stealing down my cheeks.

Harold nudged me and offered me a mint.

These were "my boys," boys who had come to me with bare feet, cut-off jeans, beards, and long hair—and a raccoon named Jeremiah. They had blank stares and hollow eyes then.

Through my tears I watched my own Ralph, tall and confident, escorting Sandy, Keith's sister. Her long, dark hair fell softly against the back of her green velvet gown. Her life, too, had been made new. Lisa, blonde and fair, her face sparkling with joy, stood next to Rob, the once-bitter young man, now so gentle and full of love.

The music swelled and the words rang out as a slim young girl stepped to the microphone and sang a love song to Jesus:

> I'll never be able to pay the debt I owe.
> It was paid long ago
> By Jesus' own precious blood.

My lace handkerchief was soaked. I needed a whole box of Kleenex. Harold reluctantly released his pocket handkerchief.

Voices blended as the congregation sang,

> There's a sweet, sweet spirit in this place;
> And I know that it's the Spirit of the Lord.

The candlelight fell on faces: ruddy, lined faces, fresh from the farm; young faces filled with love; dignified men; others misty-eyed and humble.

The groom's mother and father reflected thanks to God since five of their children had been changed in that wonderful summer.

The music swelled, the organ pealed, drums rolled, guitars burst into waves, and the trumpet sounded as Barbara came gracefully down the aisle, beautiful in a white satin gown and flowing veil. Her soft brown hair framed her lovely face, and her large eyes were filled with love and tears as she looked at Keith.

Then came the words, "Dearly beloved, we are gathered here.

. . ." (Oh, God, how we are gathered here—from New York, Pennsylvania, Massachusetts, Maryland, the Carolinas . . .). The ceremony continued. "I now pronounce you man and wife."

Communion followed. "This is My body . . . this is My blood . . . for you."

Then the pastor announced, "The bride and groom have requested that anyone who wishes to join them in prayer may come to the altar."

The pews emptied. After the prayer, the guests quietly returned to their seats.

"Thank You, Father, for hearing Your children," I whispered.

Softly a soloist sang,

O happy day that fixed my choice
On Thee my Savior and my God!

The bride and groom, hand in hand, walked down the aisle swinging to the song's upbeat tempo.

O happy day, O happy day,
When Jesus washed my sins away!

The guests followed, also singing, "O happy day!"

Two short years later, the wind blew cold over the tombstones of the village cemetery.

Once again we gathered from the East and West, young and old, furs and army coats. The college chapel filled with mourners. "Dust to dust. Ashes to ashes. . . . Our beloved Keith is home with Jesus."

One by one, they stood to tell of Keith's shining faith, full of the love of Jesus, only three short years—the same amount of time for ministry that Jesus had!

Keith, the outdoorsman who loved animals, had cared for famous racing horses owned by a neurosurgeon. One day Keith fainted. The cautious eye of the surgeon made the diagnosis after tests: a brain tumor. Keith survived the surgery four months, then God had taken him home suddenly.

Beautiful Barbara stood by the flower-draped casket and smiled through her tears, "Keith saw Jesus just before he died—then Jesus took him home."

They played a tape of Keith's voice, out of the past, telling of his love for Jesus.

"I want to sing my song for you . . .

Great is Thy faithfulness,
O God my Father.

That was when I broke down and wept, remembering. Night after night, when Keith couldn't sleep, he used to strum his guitar and play, "Great Is Thy Faithfulness." God had reached down from glory and taken Keith home. In faithfulness. In love.

I wondered what would happen to lovely, gentle Barbara. Slender and graceful, that day she moved among family and friends bringing faith and comfort to others. Several years later she remarried.

I have that tape, and whenever I listen to it, I'm impressed again with God's great faithfulness.

For everything there is a season. The nonconformists, called "my boys," were returning to school, getting established in the marketplace, beginning their own families, and settling back into the traditional churches. Then they began bringing new life to others, life without legalism or the bondage of powerless tradition.

"For I am not ashamed of the gospel of Christ" (Romans 1:16) became their theme; the method of sharing their faith was through unconditional love.

One day, Kevin, neat and trim, was in the post office when an unkempt, barefoot hippie walked in.

When the young man left, an irate woman shuddered, "Ugh, I hate hippies!"

Kevin turned quietly and faced her. "Do you know that God loves hippies? That's how my brother and I were until Jesus changed us. Now he's at home with the Lord."

The post office became quiet, and tears of remorse stung the haughty cheeks.

236

We watched the young families grow in wisdom and in understanding. Although separated—sometimes by miles, sometimes by death—love drew us close. We would all meet at the throne of grace. "Great is Thy faithfulness, O God!"

42

The Uprooted Dream

On my fortieth birthday I had written a letter to myself, a letter filled with dreams for the next forty years. I was counting on going beyond the biblical three score and ten. The letter was to be opened on my fiftieth birthday, then on my sixtieth, and seventieth—just to mark off the dreams that came true.

Now I am in my seventies and the letter is still with me—but the dreams? That is another story! Most of them rolled out with the tide, washed away like sand castles on the shore.

My childhood memories of the Canadian prairie had placed a dream deep inside me of a farm. In my letter, I drew up plans for the farm: cows and chickens, gardens and flowers, shade trees and swings, verandas and rocking chairs.

The letter was filled with the laughter of children and grandchildren, along with the song of birds, barking dogs and meowing kittens, and wobbly legged calves. Through the words I saw a movie in living color, with green pastures and grazing brown horses, and children riding bronze ponies. Throughout the years I had filled wastebaskets with my poems about *my dream farm.*

Then crashing into my dream came the nightmare of war in Vietnam!

By this time, Janice Dawn, our firstborn, was happily

married to Judson Carlberg. Our younger son, Ralph, was in school. Harold traveled throughout many of the Eastern and Southern states, and I was the infirmary nurse at Greensboro College.

With tears in our hearts, Harold and I watched our lanky, blue-eyed Dan, our elder son, board a train in Raleigh—destination: the Far East.

"Don't worry about me, Mom," he had told me. "I have the armor of God over my army uniform. I'll be home again!"

With a chug of its engine and a clang of its wheels, the train pulled away. It was Sunday morning and we found ourselves driving teary-eyed toward church.

During the communion service someone sang, "Fill my cup, Lord. I lift it up, Lord. . . ." I felt drained and empty; doubt fought to remove the faith I struggled to keep. Yet soon God's peace quietly filled my cup and His love enveloped me in His presence. I was in a safe place.

While letters and packages flew across the miles, I marked the days on a calendar. Each month I embroidered a square for a quilt, marking Dan's year in Vietnam; each square had a message of hope. My journal began to fill up with God's promises.

All thy children shall be taught of the LORD;
and great shall be the peace of thy children. (Isaiah 54:13)

I will contend with him that contendeth with thee,
and I will save thy children. (Isaiah 49:25)

Lena Rogers Leach, the beloved maid who worked with me in the infirmary at Greensboro College, joined me in the battle to believe. Lena, with her shiny ebony skin and wide, dark eyes, had fought more than one spiritual battle for the college students at Greensboro. Now her heart of love included my sons.

The battle was fought not only for Dan in Vietnam but also for Ralph. He was held hostage by the enemy in a war zone of rebellion against God's authority.

Dan's war was fought with guns and tanks; the war for

Ralph, a spiritual war, was not fought with conventional weapons but with the sword of the Word of God and the shield of faith.

My dream of a farm was held suspended between these two wars.

Then in November 1969, Dan came home. His war was over. He came home with a dream like mine—a dream of a farm where all the family could come, for reunions, or even to live. While Dan taught school in the mountains, he drew up plans.

"Just listen to that child talk!" Lena threw back her head and laughed joyously as she listened to Dan spill out his dream. "'Families should not be separated.' That's what our child says. 'God never intended folks to be torn apart.' Lord, have mercy!" Dan thinks Lena is coming to that farm to cook cornbread and fry chicken for all the Jensens coming down the road!

Lena and I plastered pictures of farms all over the kitchen walls of the college infirmary. "We have the farm in our heads. Now all we need is some land to put it on," I sighed.

Laughter filled the infirmary kitchen and hope flooded our hearts.

One day Lena picked up the newspaper on her way to the college. Over a cup of coffee, we began our Bible study and prayer. Then Lena opened the paper.

"Look at this, Nurse Jensen. This could be Dan's land. Sixty-six acres near Stoneville, that little town thirty miles from here. Just wait till Dan comes from school and we show him this paper."

Lena got a beat, then hummed a tune; soon the words came:

> *Go out there, Dan,*
> *Possess the land.*
> *We move one step at the time.*
> *We walk by faith,*
> *Not by sight.*
> *We move one step at the time.*
> *The Word's a lamp;*
> *The Word's a light.*
> *We move one step at the time.*

> *We walk by faith;*
> *Not by sight.*
> *We move one step at the time.*

We had our theme song!

Then Ralph came home! Our tall, lean son—our handsome, Southern, blue-eyed boy—had gone off to a Christian college with the seeds of rebellion stirring inside him. We almost lost him to the quicksands of sin. He came back as a stranger—gaunt, bearded, long-haired, hunched over in his fleece-lined jacket. Then in the midst of the rebellion, God worked His miracle in Ralph's life, turning him around and really bringing him home—home to God, home to us. The war had been won and heaven and earth rang with "Amazing grace! How sweet the sound!"

Out on Dan's farm near Stoneville, which was now expanding to include a place for the boys' hippie friends to come for food and lodging, with machete in hand, Ralph carved a path through the brush to the gurgling spring. Dan bulldozed the scrub fields and made a pasture for Ginger, the horse, and perhaps the wobbly legged calves I saw in my dream. Together we planted fruit trees and gardens while the valley rang with the sound of saws and hammers.

The log cabin at our farm was to be replaced with a chalet-type lodge house, which Harold and Dan designed and began building. It had cedar siding and open beams. A wide stairway brought us to the second and third floors where the view stretched to hazy blue mountains and Hanging Rock, a favorite scenic ridge. It would be a place where hippies were welcome to come for food and lodging.

One by one, Ralph's old friends came to see what had happened to Ralph and if, indeed, he was a new creation. They saw the valley and stayed; later, they saw the miracle of God's love.

Guitars strummed into the night accompanied by whippoorwills calling to each other while stars watched.

"Families shouldn't be separated," Dan had said.

Lena nodded. "Too much hurt in the world. Folks need each

other, and a place to come to—a time for healing from this hurting world. Why, Dan child, you be like Moses fixing to bring us all into the Promised Land."

Lena's laughter rang out while we watched the lodge develop and the land overgrown with scrub trees and weeds bloom into a beautiful valley of flowers and gardens. The freezers were filled.

After Harold helped Dan acquire the sixty-six acres, Harold and I purchased the adjoining thirty-eight acres. Across the valley, Doris and David Hammer, my sister and her husband, built their beautiful colonial home overlooking the valley. Across their road stood a yellow house built for our Norwegian Mama and Papa.

But Mama came alone. Papa never saw the desk and books in his new study. God took him Home to meet the Author of his faith—and the authors of his treasured books.

Once again I read the letter I wrote myself on my fortieth birthday. Twenty years had passed, and at long last it seemed my dreams were coming true.

Dan marked off building sites. Jan and Jud would have a place to build a house or a cabin for summer vacations, and even for their retirement in years to come. There would be room for relatives on plots of ground in our combined acreage.

My dreams soared. All my life I had moved from place to place, never having a place or being close to any people I could call my own. As a child I envied my friends with relatives so I called older friends "aunt" or "uncle."

Now Uncle Howard, Uncle Jack, and the sisters could all come. No one would ever be lonely again.

Doris and Dave had 150 acres. Combined, Dan and Harold and I had more than a hundred acres. My brother Gordon from New York bought adjoining property.

For five years our family poured strength, creativity, and money into our dream. Dan's chalet neared completion and our house was sited on a knoll. No one would be separated again.

"We all need a place to come home to," Willie from the children's home had told Mama.

I was confident that love would cover the valley with a blanket of peace.

"Missionaries on furlough should have their own home, a place where they can spend time with their families and where they can share in Bible study and prayer with other families," I suggested.

"We need recreational facilities—tennis courts and a swimming pool," Ralph insisted. "Even a lake, stocked with fish."

The ideas flowed like mountain streams, fresh and challenging. Dan named the place Shalom Valley Farm, the place of peace and wholeness. Shalom Valley was carved in wood and etched in our hearts.

And then, suddenly, in 1978, before the chalet was completed, the dream was gone!

Our sky turned black for us. Thunder rolled, and in fury a cold wind swept darkening clouds across the valley. The trees bent in sorrow and the valley seemed to weep while the uprooted dreams perished in the storm of life.

Today the unfinished lodge, still empty, stands alone on its sixty-six acres. The fruit trees we planted are withered and the fruit on the vines has died. The wild grasses grow again over the valley and the lonely cry of the whippoorwill calls into the night. Standing guard over the lonely house, towering pines reach to the skies as the valley sobs out its sorrow. The dreams are dead, and the song is not sung.

"Where are You, Lord?" I cried over the valley in the day of destruction. "No! No! My dream can't die! The music can't die now! For fifty years I've held this dream in my heart. No, no, not now, not when it finally seems to be coming true. Now it is gone!" My anguish was unbearable. "Why, Lord?"

Sometimes God answers in silence. This was one of those times!

And so it came to pass that Dan went away. He took his beautiful bride to follow another dream, somewhere in the West, where they would build their own little nest. And our dream of a farm for the family was uprooted.

And then it also came to pass that Harold said, "Come, Margaret. I believe it is God's will that we move to Wilmington."

And Ralph said, "Come, Chris, for when God closes one door, He opens another."

He did!

Many months later, after the sharp pain had faded somewhat and turned to a dull ache that never goes away, Harold and I returned to Shalom. On a hazy fall day we walked hand in hand down the overgrown path to stand beside the foundation Ralph had begun for his home. The furniture shop was to have been down by the spring.

We looked at the knoll where we had marked off our house. My sister Doris and I had laughed about each having a flagpole so we could hoist a signal when the coffee pot was on.

We had said, "When our house sells in Greensboro, then we'll begin to build on Shalom." We wondered why our house didn't sell then—but God knew. God had a plan. Later, long after the weeds had grown back at the farm, when Harold said we should go to Wilmington, the first person who looked at our Greensboro home bought it. God's timing!

The valley was gold and red. A quiet peace covered the land. Harold and I wept as we stood beside the empty lodge that Harold had helped to build. Three years of his hard work. We could hear again the hammers and saws, the laughter, and the songs from our "hippie boys." We loved them "as is"—God changed them "as His."

Doris and Dave's colonial house still stands high on the hill overlooking the silent valley of Shalom. My brother Gordon died before he could come to his place. And the wind blows through Dan's unfinished lodge.

I remembered a verse I had written in my journal when I first saw the land:

A land which the LORD thy God careth for:
the eyes of the LORD thy God are always upon it,
from the beginning of the year
even unto the end of the year.
(Deuteronomy 11:12)

We turned to look again at the valley with its patchwork quilt

244

of gold, yellow, and red. The towering pines swept the sky—strong, green, and unbending. When we closed the gate, we wiped our tears and left the lodge—so alone—in the setting of God's surrounding beauty. "Keep Your eye on it, Lord; please keep Your eye on it."

A dream was marked, For Sale!

We didn't go back again.

43

The Troll

Our Norwegian Papa passed his favorite stories on to his children. In turn, each generation passes them on, and each new generation gets a revised version of an old text.

One legend is about an old farmer in Norway who was tormented by a troll. Now, in Scandinavian folklore, a troll can be a giant or a mischievous dwarf—but a troll always spells trouble!

Sometimes the old farmer's cow would refuse to give milk, the hens would stop laying eggs, and the gardens wouldn't produce. Only a troll could cause such disasters.

One day the farmer decided to take his family and his belongings in the old wagon and sneak quietly away in the dark of night. He would leave that troll behind forever!

The wagon moved slowly down the road and the farmer chuckled to himself. "*Ja*, now we will be free from that old troll at last."

The farmer's wife happily agreed. Their troubles were over!

Suddenly, from under the wagon, up jumped the troll with, "Moving, are we?"

Now, Ralph and I were moving!

Harold and Chris were in Wilmington, and Ralph and I had returned to Greensboro to gather up some odds and ends.

Plants filled the back seat of our weather-beaten car; yucca bushes were sticking out of the windows—even prickly leaves escaped from the trunk.

And our "troll" was with us!

Vicky, our black Labrador retriever, was curled up at my feet by the front seat.

From behind the wheel, Ralph verbalized my feelings when he said, "Well, Mom, we're leaving it all behind; we'll soon be on our way. I'm not sure if we should laugh or cry."

That choice was made for us. When Ralph started the car, our giant troll jumped up into my lap like a frightened kitten and refused to move. There she sat, all 100 pounds of her, looking out the window. Together we were framed in yucca bushes.

At the traffic light a trucker leaned out of his cab and burst into laughter. "Now, I've seen everything!" he called.

"The Beverly Hillbillies have got nothin' on us," I yelled back.

Between the prickly leaves and our troll with her hot breath in our faces, there was no time for tears.

When we pulled into our driveway in Wilmington five long hours later, Harold stared at us with his mouth open. "I can't believe you!" He wasn't laughing.

Harold unloaded all the plants and prickly bushes. I limped around to get circulation back into my legs. Vicky, the troll, was off looking for holes to dig and squirrels to chase. Ralph drove on to his home a block away.

When we viewed the challenge before us, Harold's "Moving, are we?"—taken directly from the troll story—brought the laughter. This was no time for tears, either.

I walked through the freshly painted rooms where love had prepared a way for dragging feet and a doubting heart. A new stove stood in the kitchen and I knew that signaled #1 priority. When I saw the bedroom in order, that was #2 priority.

It was the screened-in porch that challenged us. Furniture and boxes were piled high out there and somehow it seemed to me that my life consisted of boxes to be emptied. "I think that troll from Norway keeps them filled," I told Harold.

I viewed seven rooms of furniture to be placed into five small rooms, but decided, like Scarlet in *Gone With the Wind,* "I'll think about that tomorrow."

I heard again, "*Ja,* when you are dying—iron!" So I did! With that shiny new stove looking at me, I decided to prepare a special meal. Tomorrow was another day. Tonight we would enjoy steak and mashed potatoes, and be thankful that Ralph, Chris, and the children were only a block away.

The next day Ralph put a two-dollar ad in the paper, and, closing the door to security, he walked through the gateway to a challenging future. Turning his face to the wind, he fixed his heart on God and planted his feet on the firm foundation—God's promises.

The storms would come, the winds would blow, but his house of faith would stand. It was built on the Rock.

"A man has to have a dream. He can't live without a dream," Ralph told us. "God gave me a dream—*The Master's Touch.*" The dream began with restoration of two chairs. It lives on in homes enriched with Ralph's eighteenth-century furniture reproductions. The lessons of faith continue for a lifetime.

44

Hurricane Diana

Wrightsville Beach

Unending, grasping sea,
Forever reaching for the shore;
Is the sky not enough for you?
Yet, you reach for more.

Never ending, gently lapping
Billows, angry with the spray,
Reaching, grasping at the sand
While night follows day.

Sometimes laughing in the sun,
Then angry, with billowing foam
Breaking high to splash the clouds,
Then rolling back home.

Restless, rollicking, ruthless, rolling,
Tempting, tempestuous, tossing, turning,
Splashing with sunlight, crying with rain,
Playful or angry—always churning.

Sometimes I hate you, love you, fear you—
Held captive by your power;

Cold salt spray, relentless hold,
A willing prisoner by the hour.

The cold wind of October encouraged me to button up my jacket and tighten the scarf around my head. The beach was deserted again. Tourists had long ago picked up their umbrellas and blankets and closed their beach houses for the winter. College students were catching up from a long, playful summer.

I carried my familiar bag of bread and out of nowhere the sea gulls came dipping and soaring to fight over the scraps. When the bread was gone, they were gone, too, to faraway places.

There is something about the sea that calls us back again and again. When a storm comes up, so do traffic jams as the people in the cars try to get to the shore to see how high the waves are. Police firmly, continually, redirect traffic back into town.

Today the sea was peaceful and the sky was blue, but the wind reminded me that summer was over and winter was coming. I walked around the bend to the Coast Guard station, found a stump, and just sat.

Someone once asked an old woman, gnarled from farm work and sun, what she was doing in that rocking chair on her weather-beaten porch. "Well, I reckon I just sits . . . and rocks . . . and thinks. And then again . . . sometimes I just sits," she said.

So I just sat! It was difficult to believe that this peaceful ocean with its playful waves could one day have brought near-disaster to us. Besides just "sitting," I also allowed my thoughts to go back to that day of near-disaster.

It was a Tuesday morning in September 1984. Television and radio stations canceled regular programs to keep the public informed about unpredictable Hurricane Diana, which was blowing off the coast of North Carolina. It was the most massive and threatening hurricane since Hazel in 1954.

I remembered a story from Hazel about an old man who had lost everything. Searching through the debris of his home, the

250

man was surprised to find his fishing pole. He picked it up and headed for the now quiet beach.

"Where in the world are you going?" his distraught wife cried.

"Can't think of no better time to fish," the man answered, "and sort out my head." (Our fishermen love that story.)

Ralph and his family came to our house to wait out Diana with us.

The monstrous, angry waves of the storm roared and reached for man-made dunes, cupping up mounds of beach-front with giant fingers. The winds came in a fury, and the rain hammered our boarded-up windows.

We filled the bathtub with water and kept large kettles filled with drinking water. Long lines of people had waited in grocery stores to stock up on food supplies, flashlights, and batteries.

Before the power went off, Chris and I prepared a large kettle of soup, some coffee, and lots of cookies—emergency fare.

At 3 A.M. Wednesday, the ill-humored Diana was lashing to be free, yet she was held at bay forty miles off shore. At her appointed time, the leading lady turned to churn and roar her way toward shore. High tides and torrential rain continued.

On Thursday at 3 A.M., the winds struck the coast at 125 miles per hour; the pounding surf leveled the sand dunes and knocked out power lines.

Tornado warnings followed. We all wrapped ourselves in blankets and huddled on the screened-in porch and prayed. Trees swayed like grasses.

Back inside the house, we read Psalm 91 by candlelight:

Thou shalt not be afraid for the terror by night. . . .

Yet we shivered in our fear! Ralph's furniture showroom could be wiped out by the Cape Fear River rolling down Market Street. The factory with its expensive machinery and priceless woods and partially finished furniture lay in the path of the tornado. It could all be destroyed and priceless antiques wiped out!

We huddled together and read Psalm 93:1:

The LORD reigneth, he is clothed with majesty . . .

The wind screamed through the pine trees. It sounded like a freight train. The trees bent to the ground.

Thy throne is established of old: thou art from everlasting. . . .
(Psalm 93:2)

We cried out together, "Oh, Lord, our trust is in You. Stay the power of nature's fury. You alone ride upon the wings of the wind."

The roar of the wind drowned our voices. We kept praying until sparks of faith rekindled the flame in our fearful hearts.

I will say of the LORD, He is my refuge and my fortress: my
God; in him will I trust.   (Psalm 91:2)

The morning came, and the rain turned gentle. The trees shook off the terror of the night and stood tall again. Neighbors came with hot coffee prepared on kerosene camping stoves.

The sun came out to bring courage and warmth to a new day. With fear and trembling, Harold and Ralph headed off in the truck to view the damage at the shop. Wonder of wonders, the showroom was dry! The river had raged outside the door, but it had not entered.

Across the road to the sound, trees had snapped in the path of the tornado. Ralph eased the truck around the debris and got to the factory. All around the factory the trees had fallen, but *away from the building!* There was no damage!

O sing unto the LORD a new song; for he hath done
marvellous things.   (Psalm 98:1)

Across the ocean front, the sand walls had just crumbled. Deep within our family the walls of faith had grown stronger.

The memories wouldn't stop, but it was time now for me to go home. The sun cast a glow over the peaceful ocean, and fishing boats were returning to the shore, sea gulls following close behind.

The storm seemed so long ago; yet remembering, I realized afresh how fragile life is. "We have this moment to hold in our hands." I left the isolated stump on the beach and went to my car and drove home. Once there, I eased the car into its place, brushed off the sand, and put on the coffee pot.

Late into the night, I continued to ponder the storms of life.

The Storm of the Soul

I saw the storm—black, threatening clouds.
Salt spray with stinging sand
Beat at my heart and whipped my faith.
I covered my fears with my hand.

Doubts thundered with deafening noise,
So I ran from the threatening storm.
Stumbling and falling, I heard a voice:
"Turn in to the storm—to Me."

My eyes were blinded by salt and tears;
My faith slipped in the sand.
My heart was beating with unknown fears,
But I turned to the storm—and His Hand.

Over the noise of the angry storm,
I heard Him call my name.
"You are hidden with me—safe in My care
From eternity to eternity—I am the same."

45

The Blue Datsun

"When you die, Grammy, can I have the Blue Datsun?"

To five-year-old Kathryn, the Blue Datsun was the golden chariot that carried Cinderella to the ball, the Roman chariot in *Ben Hur*, or the old reliable that carried sand buckets, big towels, and excited young uns to the beach.

"The way it looks right now, Kathryn, the Blue Datsun will die before I do, but if she lives, you certainly can have her."

Kathryn was happy. The Blue Datsun would remain in the family forever.

For some reason the Blue Datsun was a "her"—a part of the family. We talked to her, pleaded with her, screamed at her—even cried over her. We sympathized with her as she aged and became increasingly bent, broken, and bruised.

The Blue Datsun hadn't always looked like that. At one time she was shining and new. One look at her and I knew I had a friend who could face the challenges of the roads of life with me.

The students at Greensboro College admired my excellent choice and she was the envy of the campus. Everything else in the parking lot paled beside her shining blue armor.

One day our elder son Dan took her into the North, and my Dixie Datsun collided with a Yankee Ford. She hadn't known the war was over, and she came limping home, wounded and depressed. Her battle scars healed eventually, though, and once again she gamely hit the road.

One Christmas Eve, Ralph and his friend Billy were crossing an icy bridge on their way home for our special Christmas Eve dinner. The brave little Datsun was hit again by an oncoming car. Apparently the driver was under the influence of the deadly enemy, drugs. The Datsun smashed into the railing, but it held fast, and the boys were kept from going into the frigid river below. The occupants of the other car also were spared, and Ralph and Billy shared their faith with them while waiting for the police to come. Our Christmas Eve dinner was a little late that night, but our hearts were filled with gratitude that all the lives had been spared.

The Blue Datsun proudly wore the "purple heart" awarded her for bravery and for injury in action, but the scars were beginning to show. Her rusted-out trunk held a board across the holes, and sand buckets and inner tubes (used as ocean liners) found a special place there. The plastic seats were held together with dark blue tape, and wet bathing suits, sticky fingers, and gum wrappers found a happy home there.

Her air-conditioning worked only in the winter, so in the summer all the windows would be open and the wind would blow on the children while they sang:

> *Sea gull, sea gull,*
> *Up in the sky—*
> *We can see you flying so high.*
> *Please, please, don't go away.*
> *We'll come back another day.*

When we reached home we would just sweep the sand out and I would put a clean towel over the front seat.

The time came when the Blue Datsun began to run down, and one day she came to a dead stop.

Earlier that day she had faithfully taken me to the hospital for the 3-11 P.M. shift. My starched uniform had a clean place, and an extra hair net let the wind blow on me as I drove.

During my shift, the Blue Datsun stood forlornly in an

255

obscure parking place, waiting, but at 11 P.M. she perked up, and we chugged home together.

Then she died! Right there in her own familiar place. Her days of being mended and patched were over—her heart had stopped beating.

That's when we hung our heads and cried over her. And then we buried her.

Yet the memories live on, and the stories will keep her in the family always.

Kathryn remembers the stories and someday she will probably write them in a book. "When I grow up, I'll be a nurse like Grammy," she has said. "When I'm too old to do anything else, I'll write books, too."

We can count on it!

Today we go to the beach in a 1984 Oldsmobile, but the trunk is covered with plastic and the seats are covered with plastic and towels—no wet bathing suits on these plush seats!

Gum wrappers go in containers and Papa's "wash your hands" keeps sticky fingers off windows. The air conditioner works and the tape recorder plays songs by Sandi Patti. And the car windows stay up.

Kathryn sits with her beach towel. Wistfully she mourns for the old days—the days of sandy buckets, dripping inner tubes, and open windows with sand and wind in the air.

Finally, Kathryn finds her voice and says, "I'll never forget the Blue Datsun, Grammy. Remember the funny noises she made when we went down Oleander Drive? Everybody looked at us because it sounded like—oh, I guess I better not say what it sounded like. Anyhow, I miss her."

We laughed together!

But there was another day I didn't laugh—a day when the old Blue Datsun was still running.

I had been invited to the Country Club for lunch. The Blue Datsun chugged along, funny noises and all. At one point she stalled in the Oleander Drive traffic.

I'll park this old relic far away so no one will see it, I thought to myself. I found a remote corner for the Blue Datsun and joined my friends for lunch, the car forgotten.

When it was time to leave, the hostess made the remark that she had to park her new Cadillac some distance away because of the limited parking space.

"So did I," I told her.

We walked together and I wondered when she would get to her car. I didn't wonder long. When we reached my Blue Datsun, there was the shining new Cadillac, perched right beside it! I wanted to die! It didn't help a bit when I saw the absolute pity in her eyes!

From somewhere in the past I heard my Norwegian mama say, "Pride is a terrible thing, Margaret. Wear your high button shoes with a thankful heart."

(Those high button shoes keep coming out of the barrel of life.)

"*Ja, ja*, Margaret, is not so important what you have on the feet, but is important where the feet go."

Mama was right, of course, but you're right, too, Kathryn. We'll always remember the Blue Datsun.

46

The Homecoming

While the other grandchildren compete in games, six-year-old Kathryn bounces and skips through life—and, like her grandmother, tells stories.

I decided to take advantage of a half-price sale at Belk's department store, and I took Kathryn with me. It was early in the day and the store was quiet. Kathryn saw her opportunity and asked the clerk, "Would you like to hear a story?" First thing I knew, she was well into a story about her Aunt Janice. The clerks listened and smiled as Kathryn said, "Well, one day when my Aunt Janice was a very little girl, she climbed high up in the cherry tree. She was hiding up there and eating the top ripe cherries. My Grammy kept looking and looking for her. All the neighbors were looking. Then Papa said, 'We will have to call the police.'"

Kathryn was doing a good imitation of both Janice and me.

"'You come right down,' Grammy said." (I cringed at the way Kathryn barked, "Come down"—because she was right. It was exactly the way I had said it.)

"'Promise not to spank me!'" Kathryn went on, repeating the cry Janice had made.

"'Come right down!'" (Me again.)

"'Promise?'" (How could Kathryn sound so much like Janice?)

"All the neighbors said, 'Oh, honey, you can come on down. Of course your mommy won't spank you.'" Kathryn sighed. "And Aunt Janice came down, and Grammy couldn't spank her." Her audience clapped enthusiastically!

It was time for us to leave!

With a smile and a happy skip, Kathryn called back, "I'll tell some more stories next time."

Later, when all the family was around the table (and not to be outdone by my granddaughter), I said, "Let me tell you a story about *The Homecoming*."

"Is it true, Grammy?"

Our children want true stories! Maybe I've spoiled them. Sometimes I change the names and places, but my stories are true.

"It happened when I was nursing a patient who suffered from depression. She was even more upset because we couldn't get a private room for her."

A new patient, a very old lady, was being admitted to the other bed, and we pulled the curtain for privacy.

"It's all my fault. It's all my fault," moaned Ellie Mae. All the old lady's family members were there. "She was sleepin' when I went to make coffee, and the next thing I knew Granny was on the floor. Didn't hear no bump. She just lay thar so still. Lordy, I done thought she was gone for sure."

"Hush, Ellie Mae," comforted an aunt. "You done the best you could . . . and you called the Rescue Squad. Now hush, child!"

Granny, ninety, more or less, lay quietly on the white hospital bed, the glucose dripping into her bony arm. I checked her blood pressure and said, "It's okay." And then I said, "The intern is on his way to get the family history."

By this time, Granny, wrinkled like a tree branch, her wispy hair tied in a knot on top of her head, was surrounded by her thirteen children. The fourteenth child, Willie, was on his way from a sawmill in Georgia. Three country preachers arrived and joined the family. Ellie Mae still sniffled into her Kleenex.

One preacher reminded everyone how much Granny loved the church Homecoming with dinner on the grounds.

Zelda, the eldest daughter added, "Remember? We put Granny on a chair under the oak tree. She was all dressed up with her new straw hat. She said, 'I'm too tired to go around that table like you young'uns, so go fetch Granny a little bite of each.'"

Everyone remembered how plate after plate had made its way to Granny's lap, how she sampled each one and made comments about the cooks: "The strawberry puddin's about as good as mine," she chuckled. "Gettis knows how to cure a ham. Mary Jo's pickles are not spicy enough, but good, mind you."

Granny apparently held court while all the kin paid homage, that is, all but Willie. "He took hisself off to Georgee and no doubt will end on the road gang. Rocky Creek is home, and folks don't need to go off with folks they ain't no kin to."

Then young B.J. reminded them how Granny was honored on Mother's Day, having the largest family. Everybody was there, that is, everybody but Willie.

"Stop that snifflin', Ellie Mae," one preacher admonished. "It's the Lord's will, that's what, and we can't argue with the Lord's will. Her time has come. What a pity, just before Homecoming. But you can be sure, it will be the biggest funeral in Rocky Creek county."

To all the family's anxious questions, I answered, "She's about the same—not responding, but her vital signs are stable."

"Do tell, Ellie Mae, these folks believe in signs. I told you to pay attention to Granny's signs." Zelda's voice was accusing. "She knowed her signs for plantin' and for deaths. Cain't see for the life of me how thet water in her arm does any good. Aunt Minnie got a cure that would put Granny on her feet in no time. I remember the day old B.J. fell. . . ."

On the other side of the curtain, the depressed patient listened intently.

For a few moments, the family ran out of memories. No one spoke. Then the quiet was broken by the sound of clumsy footsteps as a wide-eyed young man stumbled into the room. He leaned low over Granny's bedside.

"Momma, Momma, Momma, it's Willie, your baby boy. Oh, Momma, Momma, tell me that you love me."

Willie held one wrinkled hand in both of his and kissed her cheek. She seemed to wince, but just for a moment. "Oh, Lord—Momma, Ah done come home. Now speak to me," he pleaded.

I tried to quiet him, but he yelled, "Ah has to know she loves me." His glassy eyes were pleading.

"Just sit by her bed and tell her you love her," I said as kindly as I could.

"Oh, Momma, Momma, Ah love you. If you love me, Momma, please . . . squeeze mah finger." With a yell, he hollered, "She done squeezed mah finger, nurse. Momma loves me! She loves me!"

An attendant led Willie to the visiting room—and to a cup of coffee. On the other side of the curtain, the depressed patient almost smiled.

"Now, ma'am, I need some family history," the intern said as he pushed his way to Granny's bedside.

"Oh, Lord, Doc. Momma lived here all her life," Zelda told him. "We all knows her history."

"Yes, sir," the others added. "These preachers all know, too." The three preachers nodded in agreement.

The intern's face was expressionless. "How many children?"

"Fourteen, yes sir, all live in Rocky Creek. Momma saw to that—all but Willie. Ah reckon Willie better go home, Doc. You see, he didn't get to Homecoming last year, and his conscience is a hurtin'. It orter too! No one misses Homecoming in Momma's family."

"Does she drink or smoke?" the intern asked flatly, his eyes down.

Zelda drew up her shoulders and folded her arms, glaring at the intern. "Momma drink? No, siree, sir. Momma don't drink. A good Christian woman, she is, and nairy a drop in the house. Now Paw, it was hard to tell, had a still on the back forty, but Momma never knew."

The intern seemed slightly annoyed. "Does she smoke?" he droned on.

"You mean smoke them cigarettes, Doc? No fancy cigarettes for Momma." Zelda frowned. "Snuffin' she liked tolerable well. . . . Momma healthy? Got kicked by a mule oncet, and stun'd by a bee."

Granny lay still as her history unfolded. Zeb, the oldest son, wiped his eyes as he listened to the conversation.

Young Zeke, one of the grandsons, was telling the other children how Granny watched "Medical Center" on TV. "Granny would get excited and clap her hands when the ambulance raced through the big city streets. Just like Paw used to do," he chuckled. "That ambulance scats them cars like Paw did the chickens when he rode Nellie. Whee, they flew every which way. All them nice people in them white coats totin' that poor soul on that log . . . she gits to sleep on sheets she didn't wash . . . looks like Homecoming—folks all gatherin' round. Meet lots of new folks that-a-way.

"It was the ambulance ride she always clapped her hands for," young Zeke continued. "Every time 'Medical Center' came on TV, Granny would say, 'Wheee—hear that sireen, Zeke?'"

Granny's wrinkled face looked so peaceful. The glucose continued to drip into her arm as the kin from Rocky Creek kept watch. "Granny's in a coma," they'd announce to each newcomer, "and can't hear nuthin'." They talked on and on, that is, until Willie returned.

"Momma, Momma, it's Willie, your baby boy!" he cried. "Ah quit mah job at the mill, Momma. Made enough to git me a brand new truck. Ah'm comin' home to do loggin' in Rocky Creek. . . ."

Suddenly Granny sat straight up! "Take me home, Willie, in that new truck!" The voice was frail, but the command was unmistakable.

"A miracle!" Ellie Mae cried. "It's a miracle!" Everyone talked at once. The preachers all had prayer, and Granny's kin went home. I was not at all surprised to hear the depressed patient, on the other side of the curtain, laugh out loud.

Granny was wheeled past the emergency room to the discharge center. She waved her bony hand. "I thank you nice folks. Y'all come see me, hear? It was nice to sleep in sheets I

262

didn't wash. But the sireen was the best." She left behind a vision of a toothless smile in a strong face wrinkled like oak bark. The wispy knot on her head bobbed precariously as she was lifted into Willie's new truck. He tucked her hand-knit shawl around her shoulders and they were off.

The following Sunday, the folk from Rocky Creek stood to sing the closing hymn:

> *Coming home, coming home;*
> *Never more to roam.*
> *Open wide thine arms of love;*
> *Lord, I'm coming home.*

Willie had come back for homecoming.

47

Bargain Week at WMBI

As I share these stories of faith and humor from my childhood, I watch people whose lives have been shattered by the storms of life, bowed down by unbearable sorrow, bitter and brittle over cruel wrongs. They listen, receive, and yield to God's Spirit.

Often I hold them in my arms and pray for God to keep them in His care.

In between my travels, I keep writing and speaking. TV and radio talk shows and community projects have become other areas of communicating God's unconditional love.

In looking through one of my file "boxes" recently (I never seem to get them all emptied), I found a copy of a letter I wrote to my four sisters in June of 1987.

Dear Grace, Doris, Joyce, and Jeanelle,

I'm sitting on the runway—waiting for take-off to go back home to Wilmington.

Last Saturday when I arrived in Chicago, Jim Warren, host for "Prime Time America," met me, and I ate lunch with his lovely wife Jean.

Sunday morning Jim picked me up and we went to the Willow Creek Community Church where 9,000 people attend the two Sunday morning services. Streams of traffic flowed like a river while policemen directed the oncoming cars, an incredible sight. Literally thousands of young people packed the beautiful building that was surrounded by trees and lakes with ducks swimming in formation.

The music is sometimes contemporary, and the young pastor, a walking dynamo, gave a sermon on the subject of "Amazing Grace."

Dwight Ellefsen and his family picked me up after church and we proceeded to Rockford to the golden wedding anniversary of Gladys and Tom Ellefsen. Gladys, a nursing classmate of mine, was beautiful in a deep aqua and lace gown—lovely! Two bridesmaids made the celebration, and I was one of them.

Monday I began a most fascinating challenge, an unforgettable experience. As we drove through the city, the skyscrapers towered above us. All around humanity streamed in all directions. Then we came to tall red brick buildings, a serene monument to a man of God and his dream—The Moody Bible Institute!

To think, Grace, that when you and I attended evening classes at Moody, it cost only a nickel for carfare and a nickel for a bowl of soup! We were so rich, and now we realize it more than ever.

I was taken to the offices on the tenth floor and introduced to the staff of "Prime Time America." News reports came thick and fast, and I was suddenly a part of a world of communication that moves a hundred miles an hour.

Telephone calls to Boston, California, Atlanta—separating truth from rumors—also receiving an input of wisdom from great men. All this I was a part of (via phone) and I stand in awe of the behind-the-scenes work (sixteen hours a day). For Jim, it doesn't stop even then.

I also saw what it was like to scuttle about for one show. A half hour before air time, secretaries, producers, host, and even me, the cohost, scurried to the eighth floor studio, gathered books, notes, pens, and a glass of ice water. Then we stopped for prayer. The lights flashed on and it was countdown!

"Good afternoon. This is Jim Warren of 'Prime Time America' and, to my cohost, Margaret Jensen, welcome to Chicago!" The music came on, then news reports, and live interviews from Europe, Canada, and California. And I was on!

My mind went back to the five-cent soup and the five-cent streetcar fare—and now, here I was! The two and a half hours seemed to fly.

It was *Bargain Week* with Margaret Jensen. (Incidentally, I worked this out on the plane, and Jim okayed it.)

Monday, *The Bargain of Giving.* I used stories, of course, and last of all, my punch line: I gave my life to Jesus at six years of age. God got only me but I got God—a real bargain!

We had been through a very hard day. We had to deal with heartbreaking news from around the world, but we also heard accounts of God's faithful people sharing their love and faith with a suffering humanity.

Afterward the staff picked up papers and locked the studio. What a studio—so incredibly beautiful—with a wooden carving that says, "Let the words of my mouth be acceptable." They have the most modern equipment, and such talent! Jim is one of the most creative people I've met—music, art, drama, and a voice and presence that move people to action. I stand in awe that I could even be on his program, also in awe of the guests who appear on P.T.A. in person and by phone.

My first day came to a close and Jim and I were on the way to supper in his home where Jean was waiting.

We were in the Austin area, stopped at a red light. Traffic was heavy at 6:30 P.M. Suddenly we heard a *boom.* The window on my side was shattered into a million pieces (back seat window also) and someone snatched my purse. They call it "smash and grab." It took two seconds. Jim saw two teens running through the alley, so he jumped out of the car and took off after them. But then he yielded to wisdom and we took off to the police. It was so routine to the police—forms, questions, etc. There was no chance of recovery. My airplane ticket home, $125 in cash, all my identification, my glasses, and my keys—all were gone!

Just that quickly it came to me: "In everything give thanks." We were not hurt, even by the shards of glass. We had a sense of God's protection as we headed home to Jean and their son Randy and a wonderful supper; then back to other friends in River Forest to stay overnight. A quick call and Harold put everything in motion to arrange a new return plane ticket.

In the morning my new friend had a lovely purse ready for me. In it were a lipstick and a comb along with a change purse containing twenty-five dollars. How grateful I was—a woman without a purse and lipstick is really lost!

Tuesday—a new program for the new day. The theme was *The Bargain of Yielding.* I spoke of yielding the right-of-way at a red light, yielding to wisdom (a warning to hide purses and not to get out of the car), and yielding to God's will.

We did more. Jim called an inner-city preacher who gave a rundown of the work at his location, including a new gym, a health clinic, legal advice, and counsel for youth and church.

We used this story to make people aware of the needs in the inner city. We asked for ball teams and church groups to supply balls, bats, and basketballs for the gym. We also prayed for the two boys who had robbed me. I know God will turn it all for good.

While sirens cry into the night and the traffic jams pile up all day because of the people-to-people shuffle, the voice of WMBI reaches around the world.

Wednesday I talked about *The Bargain of Obedience.* Obedience *is* a bargain. Jean and Randy picked me up after the broadcast and we went back to the Willow Creek Church in the evening. It was packed with four to five thousand people, and most were young people. A dynamic message, electric music, praise choruses, and then a communion service.

Thursday was *The Bargain of Forgiveness*. God forgives us—what a bargain! This was another busy day filled with interviews with authors, executives, and missionaries.

Friday was the *Bargain of Love*. Nothing separates us from the love of God. Again, what a bargain!

Love, Margaret

If you ask me, a life given to God is the very best bargain of any that we can make!

48

Dark Powers

Outside, the rain drizzled drearily from the dismal sky, and an early morning mist shrouded the woods in a misty grey.

Inside, the coffee pot perked happily and my loaf of home-made bread stood on the breadboard waiting to be sliced and popped into the toaster. Real butter and strawberry jam would add the final touch. It was warm and cozy in the kitchen, and the coffee was good. Real cream helps!

When I opened my Bible, I noticed a date and a notation. Then scraps of paper fell out from the pages, notes I had written in airports and on planes. One was a reminder of my trip to Toronto, Canada in 1988:

It's a lonesome time tonight, I had written. The aircraft came to a stop and I picked up my carry-on baggage and followed the crowd to Custom Services. One woman had forgotten her passport.

With my customs slip filled out, I waited in one of the endless lines where I watched multiethnic groups move stoically through slips of paper, translators, and mountainous baggage. Their turbans and swirling garments added color and drama to the depressing routine of a long day.

Finally, I was out in the rain to pick a number for a cab. I was number ninety-three. It would be a long wait.

Cab after cab filled up with people from various parts of the world. I felt alone and isolated. Few seemed to speak English. I was only across the border, yet I felt like a lone English speaker in an international crowd.

The rain kept up a bleak rhythm on the pavement as cabs pulled up to the curbside pools, splashing water on us. A weary cabby yelled, "Ninety-three," and I was hustled into his cab. The driver was from India and spoke little English. He was not interested in conversation so I settled back to watch the rain and listen to the swish of windshield wipers.

The Holiday Inn loomed ahead like a familiar friend. I wasn't in a foreign country after all, just across the border in Toronto.

I emptied my pouch of Canadian money on my lap. Two large bills. In my relief to get into the warmth and security of a familiar hotel, I tipped the silent Hindu a large amount. His thank-you sounded genuine, and I smiled and wished him a good evening in the rain.

After I checked in, I wheeled my own bags to the elevator to go to the eleventh floor. A convention was keeping the bellhops hopping and one old lady didn't look too impressive to them. Weary, maybe, but not impressive.

I aired my musty room and placed my Bible, books, and yellow pads on the table. I opened my luggage and found hangers for my clothes. The open drapes allowed me a full view of the city. Towering buildings seemed to melt into the thick fog and the lights from a Chinese restaurant blinked bravely from the street below.

Across the Trinity Square the walks and gardens blended into the grey mist while Holy Trinity Church kept a silent vigil. At times the Eaton Department Store peeped through the fog.

I watched the rain and thought of Harold. "It's a lonesome town tonight," I mused and decided to shake that lonesome feeling and head for the coffee shop.

The multicultural city of Toronto met me again in the lobby. I wondered if anyone spoke English. After wandering aimlessly through the shops I moved toward the coffee shop, where I was seated by the window. Again I listened to the rain, and I experienced that empty feeling of eating alone. I thought about

270

my friends who had lost their mates. Tonight I could feel that barren lonesomeness that steals into your being like an uninvited guest and refuses to leave. I knew my loneliness would pass, but those friends faced empty years. I prayed for them.

It had been a long day with being up at 4:30 A.M. and the endless waiting in bustling terminals, customs, and cabs; but now, the day had come to a close. Back in my room, sleep was a welcome friend.

In the middle of the night I awoke suddenly with . . . a sense of . . . evil . . . in the room. Paralyzing fear gripped me! Was someone in my room? A dark foreboding cloud seemed to fill the room, and a frozen fear engulfed me. Deep within I cried unto God, and I called out the name, "Jesus!" Then I jumped out of bed and turned on the light.

Nothing!

"We wrestle not against flesh and blood, but against principalities, against powers" that we can't see but can sense (Ephesians 6:12). Perhaps previous occupants had been involved in the dark powers of an unseen evil kingdom; I didn't know. This I did know: I was God's child, and the name of Jesus is greater than any other name.

I sang "Power in the Blood," and walked the floor offering praise to our God who is greater than all the universe. I took authority in the name of Jesus over any evil spirit that had been in the room.

The old hymns of the church came to me: "A Mighty Fortress Is Our God," "'Tis so Sweet to Trust in Jesus," and "God Will Take Care of You."

I thanked God for the precious blood of Jesus that cleanses us, our homes, and even a hotel room from sin. The living Word of God came alive as the wonderful words of life came to mind: "Lo, I am with you alway[s]" (Matthew 28:20); "I will never leave thee, nor forsake thee" (Hebrews 13:5). I drew new strength from the fact that in the name of Jesus we have the victory (see 1 Corinthians 15:57) and from my confession that "Jesus is the Lord in my life."

The room was filled with peace and a sense of God's presence. I picked up my Bible and then wrote on my yellow pad.

After a little while I closed the Book, put down my pen, and went to sleep. God's love covered me like a blanket, and in the morning I awoke to a new day of blue skies and sunshine.

P.S. I was suddenly brought back into my cheerful kitchen of the present when the phone rang. I picked it up and a friend said, "Margaret, please pray! A young man who was in a drug rehabilitation program was brought to a class conducted in church. Trembling violently, he refused to go into the church. 'I can't! I can't!' he said. 'I sold my soul to the devil when I was in a rock group!' Oh, Margaret, is there hope for him?"

"Oh, yes," I answered. "There is power in the name of Jesus. There is no other name under heaven given among men that can bring deliverance to this young man."

We prayed together over the telephone and God will use my friend to give this young man someone who will hold him fast.

The unseen darkness around us is real, but so is

Amazing grace,
How sweet the sound.

49

"Diamonds and Mink, No Less!"

Suddenly our house was too small. The walls just seemed to close in on me. Five books had been handwritten on the kitchen table. Harold had typed those five books in the dining room. Boxes of notes and mail were jammed into a closet. It seemed the whole house had become an office.

My Norwegian heritage cried out for Scandinavian order!

Our organized daughter, Janice, shuddered at the boxes. "With all your speaking and traveling, you've got to have a place for files and desks."

Even Ralph recognized the need. "Mom, you just have to have an office!"

"I'll help you sort boxes when you get your room," Ralph's wife Chris offered.

Harold added sheepishly, "I already bought a four-drawer file and a new desk at an auction. But everything is stacked on the porch."

Our new friends, Bob and Lou Marbry from New Jersey, were in on the family discussion.

Larry, their son, chimed in with, "We can do it! You get the

273

material and I'll build. We can build a garage with an office in the back for Margaret. I'll draw up the plans."

Steve, our nephew, joined in, "Way to go! A room for the famous author."

"Well, Steve, if I'm so famous how come I only have one bathroom?" I stole a glance at Harold. I couldn't help it—I just had to say it: "I knew it! I knew it . . . I should have married Sammy!"

A long time ago when I was a young student nurse, I was assigned to a difficult patient who complained continuously.

"Oye, oye! Wash good between the toes, Blondie, not too often I get to the feet. Now my back—a good rub I should have. How I suffer with the back. Too much lifting I tell my Abie. But does he listen? All day I work in the deli, on my feet, no less, and who cares? I tell him all day my back hurts, but does he listen? So who listens?"

I would listen as I bathed her.

Then I would tell her stories. One story was about Mama and the red linoleum she bought for one dollar because the corner was torn. "Believe me, a red linoleum is next to heaven after getting splinters in your hands from scrubbing wooden floors."

The "Oye, oye" stopped. My patient was listening. I rubbed her back—and continued.

"We had a water tank in the corner of the kitchen. The water wagon came twice a week and we got fresh water for twenty-five cents a barrel." I tied the top of her hospital gown, stretching it across her broad shoulders.

"Then there was the outhouse! It was so cold in the winter," I told her. "Blizzards and sixty below in Canada!"

She was lying on her back now, staring up at me.

"One day, when I was watching the children while Mama pulled the sled to the grocery store to get a bag of flour, the little ones had to use the potty.

"It was my duty to empty the potty in the outhouse, then rinse it with snow." I straightened the covers around my patient.

"Since it was so cold, I decided to empty the full potty into the cook stove."

Her eyes widened.

"The odor was terrible, but the worst part was that the fire went out. I had forgotten to put wood on the fire."

"Oye, oye!" she exclaimed, squeezing her nostrils. "What'd your mama say?"

"I was only ten years old, but I knew better. Well, of course when Mama came home, the fire was out and the kitchen didn't smell at all like Mama's kitchen. But before she had time to say a thing, the younger children announced in unison, 'Mama, Margaret emptied the potty in the stove.'"

My patient eased forward expectantly. "Did Mama spank, Blondie?" she asked sympathetically.

I could barely force a smile, remembering. "No, Mama didn't have to spank. She just looked at me sadly and said, 'It is good when we can trust people, but it hurts when people don't fulfill that trust. You see, Margaret, disobedience hurts others. Emptying the potty in the stove may have seemed like a small thing, but it had big results. If you had put your coat on and gone out and emptied the potty in the outhouse, you might have remembered to get some wood for the stove.'"

The patient nodded in agreement, yet her sympathetic gaze never left my face.

"I learned a lesson that day when Mama said, 'Disobedience is never small in God's sight.' I understood, and I never emptied the potty in the stove again."

My patient's uproarious laugh split the air. "So now you empty bedpans!"

I didn't think she was funny at all!

Suddenly she sat up, and she was sympathetic again. "My Sammy, my wonderful Sammy! He is coming, and meet him you should. Och! So handsome! So smart! A lawyer he is—a smart lawyer. Every family should have a lawyer and a doctor." She looked long and hard at me. "And a good nurse!"

Clapping her hands together she closed her eyes, "Oye, I can see it now already—my grandchildren! What a beautiful couple you should make. Children you would have with the blonde

275

hair and brown eyes, maybe blue eyes and black curly hair—a little like my hair, maybe? Diamonds and mink you should be wearing, Blondie. So handsome my Sammy—and rich! Abie and I spend nothing, all will go to Sammy."

"I will be happy to meet your Sammy." I tucked a pillow behind her back, confident that she would go to sleep dreaming about grandchildren.

I had a class, so I took a hurried leave and joined Hertha. I told her about Sammy, and we doubled up, laughing.

"She has grandchildren already and I haven't even met Sammy. I can't wait to tell Harold—diamonds and mink, no less!"

Then I met Sammy!

He was obese, stuffed in the chair, peering into a law book. His thick glasses sat low on his nose. He didn't budge out of the chair. I'm not sure he could have.

Over his glasses, he scrutinized me, top to toe. With a leering smile, he announced, "Mama, I like!"

She beamed. "See? What did I tell you, Blondie? So handsome, my Sammy. He likes!"

I choked on my silent laughter. "Oh, yes, I am pleased to meet your Sammy." He was still jammed in his chair. "But, you see, I must finish nurses' training."

"Finish? What's to finish? Marry my Sammy and you don't nurse anymore. Maybe help in the deli—and give my back now and then . . . a little rub. Mink and diamonds my Sammy will buy." Sammy nodded.

"That is lovely, but I must go now. The hospital rules are very strict and I have a stubborn Norwegian father who insists that we finish what we begin."

Sammy sighed and bent over his law books; the light shone on his bald spot.

That was more than fifty years ago. And ever since then, whenever the budget looks lean and we need a good laugh, I only have to say, "I should have married Sammy. Diamonds and mink, no less!"

Now the hammers are heard, concrete is being poured, and walls are going up. By the time I begin my sixth book I will be in my own office with files in order and no boxes in the closet. And a special spot for Harold to type. I'll keep the coffee pot on—so come and see!

Diamonds and mink? Who needs them? Larry had promised me another bathroom—for the office.

50

A Present Help

The laughter and chatter of happy women mingled with the sound of coffee cups at breakfast. Then it was time to go in for the meeting. With notebooks and Bibles in hand, the women moved into the retreat center. Enthusiastic singing rang across the valley and an atmosphere of expectancy filled the air. Then I noticed one woman whose expressionless face seemed to call out for help.

I decided I must meet her. When break time came, I moved slowly to stand casually beside her. *I must be careful,* I thought.

"Hello. What a beautiful morning," I greeted casually.

A dull, listless stare looked back at me. I didn't know what else to say so I took her in my arms and held her. I wanted to weep. I just said quietly, "God loves you."

She stiffened. Then slowly, in the same flat voice without emotion, she began to speak. "I'm having a nervous breakdown. That's what my doctor told me. I don't know why I'm here. Someone paid for me to come and the doctor said it was a good idea. I'm falling apart."

There was silence for a moment and then she continued, "I have a retarded child who needs much attention, but my husband was good to help me."

Then came the blank stare again, looking off into space.

Oh, God, help her, I cried inside. No one seemed to notice us; they all appeared to be enjoying the coffee break. The curtain was opening on one of life's tragedies, and I wanted the drama to end. I wanted this to be a make-believe play. But it was real!

In a flat voice the woman added, "Now my husband is helpless. He had a stroke. And I am having a nervous breakdown. My doctor said so. Life is too hard for me now."

I felt myself crying on the inside, *It's not fair. It is too much for one woman!*

Then it was time to go. I had to speak in the next session. I told my stories of faith in trials, the humor and tears in my Norwegian immigrant family, and Mama's walk of undaunted faith. The audience cried and laughed with me. But my friend stared ahead without expression.

Lunch time came. I sat down beside her and we ate quietly. There are times when words can't be heard—the heart hurts too much, and the mind is numb with unanswered questions.

Before we left the table I asked her, "What will happen to your child and husband if you collapse?"

There was no response.

We went into the following session where I continued a theme of how God fastens us as a nail in a sure place. Corrie ten Boom was fastened in a concentration camp, Chuck Colson in a prison, Joni Eareckson Tada in a wheelchair. In these seemingly impossible situations the glory of the Lord shone through His special nails, tough and hanging in there, by God's grace.

Then I saw the tears trickling down the cheeks of my fragile friend. I knew God's gentle Holy Spirit was quietly at work. The Comforter had come.

The sessions continued for two more days. Before I realized it we had come to the closing prayer. I looked for my friend. There she was, coming toward me. Her face was alive. Strength seemed to flow from her being.

"That question, the one you asked, has been haunting me ever since. You know, 'What will happen to your family if you collapse?' It kept coming back to me. Then I saw it! I was the nail God fastened for them. He would not fail me now." She squared her shoulders and held her head high, "And I won't fail them!

"I'm going home refreshed in my spirit and body. There will be a way to get help and I've decided to go back to my church."

Then she threw her arms around me and we prayed together, cried, and laughed. We knew God would see her through.

Later, as everyone was saying good-bye, a small group of women came to tell me that the woman used to be in their church. They promised to help her. They had paid her way to come and had been praying for her. I was reminded that God has His angels all around, helping where needed.

My friend was one of the last to leave. She gave a "V for Victory" sign and laughed, "No way I can have a nervous breakdown! I'm the only nail my family has."

Later, when my plane soared over mountains and valleys, I put my head back on a pillow and closed my eyes. "Oh, Lord, thank You. The same comfort You gave my Norwegian mama, she in turn gave her seven children. You are the river of refreshing, the endless flow of love, grace, and mercy. Take care of this little lady, Lord; please put Your loving arms around her and wrap her in a blanket of Your peace."

Into my mind came the memory of another retreat where the wife of an airline pilot was surrounded by prayer. She had suffered deep depression when she discovered that their three teenagers were involved in drugs.

"Why weren't you here?" the frustrated mother complained to her husband.

"Hey, I'm giving you a good living. Can't you keep track of the kids?"

The bitterness mounted.

The church family rallied to the family's support, and prayer and counseling came to the children. Within a year they were back in school and doing well.

But the bitterness remained.

The mother wept most of the time. "What can I do?" she cried in my arms during a women's retreat.

"Praise," slipped into my heart and out from my mouth. I

always resent a glib answer, but somehow this was different. "I have an idea," I suggested. "Take your Bible and begin to write down all the 'praise Him' verses you can find. Before you begin, let's thank God for your husband, who is a good provider—and don't forget, he is hurting, too. Thank God that your children received help in time and are doing well in school. Then let's thank God for your new strength, the joy of the Lord."

She went to her room to write.

The next day she stood before the entire retreat group and said, "I began in Genesis to write 'praise Him,' and I couldn't stop. During most of the night I kept writing and I really don't know when it happened, but I started rejoicing and now I can't stop."

The prayer of praise was proppin' up her leanin' sides.

I was home from yet another retreat and while the coffee perked, I donned my baggy jogging suit and red kerchief, and I was ready for the clearing of the scraggly fall garden.

The empty suitcases were up in the attic and the clothes spun in the washer. In a few days I would be on the road again—to New England, then Toronto, Canada. But today I would dig up all the old zinnia plants and Harold would plow the garden for spring. It was a good day.

Everything looked dry and dead except the periwinkles and mums. They nodded at each other, reluctant to leave and determined to welcome the winter with a smile. Too soon, they also would be gone and only green brushes and pines would resist the winds of winter.

Today was warm, the coffee good, and I had set an extra cup for Chris, Ralph's wife. Sure enough, I soon heard the car in the driveway, and Chris bounced in.

"Just have a minute. Have to run errands for Ralph," she said.

We munched on raisin toast and drank coffee.

"You ought to tell Chris the story you told me," Harold chuckled delightedly. "I'm telling you, Chris, you never heard such counseling in your life. I think Margaret should stick to stories and let the Littauers counsel," he laughed.

Chris urged me on, so I told the story.

It began at the retreat. I wondered how I could listen to even one more heartbreak when a beautiful woman came sailing in. I instinctively liked her, with her flashing black eyes, curly hair, and expressive Italian gestures.

She fairly trembled, announcing, "I have a problem!"

I wanted to laugh, but I didn't. I waited. Harold told me to do that—wait and be quiet. ("You can't solve every problem, Margaret. Just let them talk and perhaps they can hear their own solution.") I waited and stayed quiet; besides, I was too weary to talk.

"I'm forty," she declared.

"Oh, *you* have a problem," I couldn't resist responding. "I'm only seventy-three."

"I was just born again," she continued. "It was a wonderful experience of being made new and knowing what it means to have right relationship with God."

That didn't sound like a problem, but I was quiet. Harold would have been proud of me.

She went on. "Also, we just started a new business. It's going great! And I have three beautiful children."

I wanted to laugh. She had a problem? So who needs solutions when you have such problems?

"It's my husband!" she blurted. "He is dull, and I mean *dull!*"

I was beginning to come to life. This ought to be good.

"I came from a noisy, happy, talkative family," she explained. "We get excited about everything. My husband doesn't get excited about anything. He just works and works—and is dull! I thought I should begin all over again. Here I am, forty years old, with a new exciting job, and I'm a new Christian, so I need a new husband to go with it all."

I tried hard not to laugh, but I couldn't help but enjoy the entire episode.

"Is your husband a Christian?" I asked.

"Oh, yes, the solid kind."

"Is he a good father?"

"Perfect father."

"Does he love you?"

282

"He's crazy about me. Gives me flowers and candy. But he's so boring!"

"Is he a good provider?"

"Terrific! We have a lovely home!"

I had to say it. "I think you need a new husband!" Harold should have heard that one. "You're right," I continued. "Let him go!"

She clapped her hands, "Oh, I knew you'd see it my way! Everything new!"

"My dear," I repeated, "let him go! I've just talked with a dozen gals who'd love a dull husband. Their men chase after butterflies—wine, women, and song. How these gals would love a boring man who comes home at 5 P.M., who is a good father and provider. I doubt if they ever saw a box of candy or flowers. These gals would stand in line for a dull guy."

By this time she wasn't too sure where we were going. So I asked, "What kind of childhood did he have?"

"Terrible! Could never please his father."

"Great," I said. "Now he can't please you, even with flowers. What was your family like?"

"Ah, music, laughter, fun, excitement—and noisy." Wistfully she added, "Oh, how I miss that."

"I understand," I told her. "There was nothing dull about my Norwegian family."

We were quiet a moment.

Then, "By the way, did it ever occur to you that God put you into his life to give him the joy he never knew?" I asked.

"Oh, no. I never thought of that."

Impulsively, I added, "I just love you! I wish you lived near me so we could have some fun lunches together!"

We quietly prayed that God would speak to her during the next sessions and give her the answers she needed.

"We have to go, but we'll talk later," I promised.

The retreat came to a close and she came to see me.

"Margaret, Margaret, I saw it! This guy is terrific! What a man! I've been so blind. I am to give the joy I had in my family to him and our family. Oh, I need this man and he needs me. Guess what? I called him and told him to get ready. *Mama mia* is coming home! We'll farm out the kids and take off for a fun time."

She laughed, "This guy won't know what hit him. Wow! Wait until I tell this dull man how much I love him."

We hugged and laughed together. The dozen other gals would have to wait!

51

"You V.I.P. and Don't Know It!"

The small clock beside our bed sounded its alarm, too big a noise for a pretty brass clock. It was 4:30 A.M. when my husband rolled out of his side of the bed and I sleepily headed for the coffee pot.

Why do we always have to catch the six-thirty flight to Chicago? I asked myself. Then the coffee began perking cheerfully and the day looked brighter. After all, my good-natured husband took it all in stride, humming along with the sound of the electric razor as it blended into the sounds of the morning.

After a quick cup of coffee, a verse for the day, and a prayer for safety, we got the bags into the car and were off toward the Wilmington New Hanover County International Airport. The streets were dark and deserted—even the dawn didn't want to get up at that hour. Before long, though, it reluctantly slipped around the edge of town, awaking the sleepy inhabitants.

The airport was teeming with passengers. The walk to B terminal was long, and my bag was heavy. *Next time I won't take so many books along,* I thought. *But then, I said that the last time.* A hug and a prayer, and I climbed the steps to the waiting plane while Harold stood waving in the early light. I was on my way to Chicago, my town for many previous years. There I would change planes and go on to a convention in California.

Waiting for my late flight in the Chicago airport, I settled down with an open book in my lap. A young black girl sat down next to me and began rustling the pages of a magazine. I looked at her over my book.

"Oh, I see you are reading a Christian magazine, a very good one," I offered.

"I know." She kept reading.

I turned back to my book. Curiosity got the best of me; besides, I should always be ready to witness about God's love.

"Are you a Christian?"

"Yes, ma'am."

"Oh, that's wonderful. So am I."

"I know."

Back to my book. I wasn't getting too far in this conversation, but I wanted to know more. "Where are you from?" I asked.

"I'm country, just got a box number," she replied.

I went back to my book again. Usually I am very happy to be in my book and I don't begin conversations, but this young woman intrigued me.

"Where are you going?" I persisted.

"California."

"Oh, isn't that exciting! So am I."

"I know."

Back to my book.

Then gently she touched my arm and spilled out her humble story.

"I'm so scared. I never traveled before. But my husband is a country preacher and he said, 'You go to the convention and learn something.' We are just country people, only have a box number. I'm scared to go the convention alone. Maybe I won't get the right plane. 'Just ask,' my husband said. 'We can't tell how God works, so just go.'

"I was so scared," she confessed. "I prayed, 'Please, God, let me meet someone I know.' Then I saw you! See, you are the speaker! Here is your picture!" She opened the brochure. "You

286

V.I.P. and I followed you all over the airport and sat beside you because I know you. Besides, that plane won't go down, no way, when you're the speaker."

I closed my book. I felt a lump in my throat.

"When we get to California someone will pick you up in a fancy limousine; you V.I.P.—and if I stick close to you, will you tell them I'm with you? Then I get to ride in the limousine with you."

We laughed together out of pure joy, and I told her (Mary, she said her name was) to stick with me. We would go to the convention together.

Sure enough, a limousine came and Mary stuck like glue. After finding the registration desk, we went our separate ways with a promise to meet later.

The bellhop led me to my lovely room. He also showed me an adjoining room with a magnificent view of mountains and palm trees. By the flowers and the basket of fruit on the table, I realized it was prepared for a special guest. So as I left I closed the door adjoining the rooms. Then it was time to unpack my clothes and iron them, shower, and stretch out for a short nap before the evening banquet.

The convention was great—a thousand happy, talkative women, and a number of great speakers. My beautiful Mary managed to find me even in that crowd. She was my shadow. Then it was time to leave, and while I was packing I heard a knock at my door. It was my Mary.

"Oh," I said to her, "let me show you the room with the view." Turning the knob, I was surprised when the door opened. "I don't know who was supposed to come here, but believe me, it must have been an important person. Look, Mary, flowers and fruit—and no one showed up."

Mary curiously peeked at the card in the flowers and burst into joyous giggles. "This room was for you! These flowers and fruit are for you!"

"What? A two-room suite for me?"

Mary laughed so hard she doubled up on the bed. Pointing her finger at me she finally managed to say, "You V.I.P. and don't know it!"

I gave her the flowers and fruit. She looked like a happy bride walking down the hall, chuckling, "You V.I.P. and don't know it."

On the heels of her joyous laughter I seemed to sense, deep within my soul, a loving Father with outstretched arms saying, "Oh, My children, you V.I.P. and don't know it. I have baskets of blessings for you and you don't even read the card. You close the door to My promises."

I seemed to hear the country preacher's admonition, "Go to the convention and learn something."

I learned something: Read the card. The promises are for us.

Thank you, my lovely friend Mary, for your encouraging words.

52

The Sisters Are Coming

My garden clippers kept singing a duet with Rudy's clippers. In the quiet of the morning my young neighbor and I clipped around the cedar trees and I filled a garbage container with prickly vines that had entwined their thorny stems around the tree trunks. The winter freeze apparently had destroyed our palm trees and Harold was sawing off the dead, brown branches.

"Don't cut your palms down," a TV gardener had advised. "There is a possibility of life in the depth of the trunk." We doubted that, but we followed his instructions and trimmed the branches but kept the palm. It turned out he was right.

"Whew, it's hot." Rudy stopped to wipe his face. "What in the world are you doing with those clippers, Miss Margaret?"

"I'll tell you, Rudy, why Harold and I decided to tackle this lawn: My sisters are coming!" We both had a good laugh.

"Nothing like company coming to get things done. My mother-in-law is coming!" said Rudy.

With the visitors in mind, we played our clipper duet while Harold mowed the spacious lawn and trimmed the edges. Then Harold and I inspected the flower beds. Each day I had spent one or two hours in a flower bed, and since I have six of them,

I had begun two weeks earlier to be sure the weeds were all gone. My sisters were coming!

In the house I had cleaned one room at a time—woodwork, windows, and curtains, and I even coaxed Harold to wash ceiling fans and put up sparkling light fixtures. He had groaned, "I know, I know, your sisters are coming!"

Then the day came! The guest rooms were ready, and my Norwegian tablecloth was on the breakfast table, which was set for coffee. The brownies and cookies were cooling and the bread dough I had set early that morning was . . . falling? Not rising? It was just a lump of dough refusing to budge!

"Oh, no! Five loaves of bread falling! Something must be wrong with the yeast," I moaned. My pride plummeted with the five loaves of hard bread that had to be thrown into the woods for the squirrels, raccoons, rabbits, and birds.

Then it was time to go to the airport. "Where are you, Harold?" I called. There he was on his knees in the driveway, not praying, but painting a huge sign on oilcloth. With great fanfare he hung the sign up on the clothesline. In bright blue paint, it read:

THE SISTERS ARE COMING! HELP!

They came! Jeanelle, the youngest, Papa's pianist, from Florida; Joyce Solveig, Papa's songbird from Arkansas; Doris, from Greensboro, who went to Wheaton College on a hundred dollars; and Grace, the secretary, accountant, and general manager. In Papa's words, "*Ja, ja,* there is no one like Grace. She should be secretary to the President."

Believe me, five sisters in noisy reunion in our small airport was news! And everywhere we went people continued to notice the joy of our gathering.

One clerk at the mall laughed and called wistfully, "Have fun!" She added, "I lost my only sister and now there is no one to tell the family jokes to."

Someone else watched us laughing together while Joyce told stories in a Norwegian accent. He came by our lunch table.

"Sorry to interrupt," he said, "but I just can't help noticing how much fun you are having."

A clerk in a gift shop said, "You ladies have made my day. Not many people have fun anymore. You can't believe the cross and unhappy people who come into our shop."

We had to pull Joyce away from the humorous card display. She and our daughter Janice and Ralph's wife Chris could spend all day laughing at cards.

"Do you remember . . . ?" someone started. And we all remembered.

Remember how Jeanelle begged Mama to let her take her cod liver oil with a fork?

Harold remembered when Doris wanted to run away with him because Papa was on the warpath.

When Grace was a young child someone invited her to spend the night with her daughter, and she said, "Oh, no! My mother needs me!"

I recalled when Papa shook the stove at 5 A.M., and I curled up close to my sisters Grace and Doris. He called, "Margaret, time to get up!"

The kitchen was warm in our second floor Chicago flat. Papa sat in the rocker reading his Bible. On the table was a cup of hot cocoa and six slices of buttered oven toast. I ate quietly. No one interrupted Papa when he was reading, and he always had a book in his hand.

With a "*Takk for maten* (Thanks for the food)," I buttoned up my coat.

Looking over his rimless glasses Papa said, "*Velkommen* (You're welcome)," and, "button up your collar. It's cold." He went back to reading and I set out on the three-mile walk to Carl Schurz High School.

That was all we said. Through the years how often I've wished I had said more. The warm kitchen, the cocoa and toast said what he couldn't say in words; "You V.I.P.; button up. It's cold outside."

We continued to reminisce as we gathered around the piano to sing old hymns and imitate the Norwegian string band. We could never tell if the band sang in Norwegian or in English.

Whenever we get together we usually recall the days we were with Mama. At the end we watched her spirit soar Homeward to be with Papa, Gordon our brother, and our baby sister Bernice, and we knew that Mama saw her Savior face to face.

A friend, observing our cheerful visiting, remarked how special it was to see five sisters so close and enjoying each other.

When an emergency arises, we start the sisters' telephone alert "to pray." When a special joy comes our way, we call "to rejoice." Each of us is a unique individual, but our mutual love for the Lord, for our families, and for each other binds us together as one.

When we were children Mama would say, "Always love each other." And as we grew older she reminded us, "Love each other and stay close in your hearts."

When the years turned our hair grey and the storms of life had left their scars, and Mama knew she was going Home, she looked at us five sisters and said, "What have I ever done to deserve such beautiful daughters?" Then she added, "Always love each other, stay close, and take care of each other."

Now we are getting older and through the years we have loved each other, and we stay close in our hearts even when miles separate us. Now is the time to take care of each other.

The days of joy came to an end. Too soon it was time to part. We huddled together as Harold lovingly prayed over the sisters, asking God to keep us all in His loving care. Doris and Grace headed toward Greensboro on Route 421. Jeanelle and Joyce winged their separate ways by plane.

The sign was still hanging there: "THE SISTERS ARE COMING!" I didn't want to take it down.

Our children and grandchildren are still talking about their aunts and the day the sisters came. Harold and I laughed together about the housecleaning (who noticed?), the mani-cured lawn, trimmed hedges, and weedless flower beds—even the five loaves of bread in the woods.

Somehow it really wasn't for anyone to notice. It was just our way of saying, "You V.I.P. and I want you to know it."

53

House Under Construction

It began in the fall of 1987.

The porch and carport walls had been torn down. Debris multiplied until the backyard looked like "Sanford and Son." The back steps consisted of cement blocks perched precariously on makeshift slabs. Our once cozy home looked like a bombed-out war zone. The only thing settled was the dust.

Larry Marbry, a young builder, had taken one look at my dining and kitchen tables piled with yellow pads and mail. He shook his head. "You need a room for writing!" he said.

Believe me, that was the understatement of the year.

I wrote in the kitchen. Harold typed in the dining room, which was also part of the living room. At the end of each day I cleared the tables, and the boxes went under the bed. I let the long side of the bedspread hang down on the side where the boxes were so they wouldn't show.

When the family came to visit, cots emerged from the utility building and lined the living room like a camp dormitory.

Larry was determined to do something about the mess. "I'm going to draw up plans to give you some room—and a special writing room. Margaret, if you and Harold will buy the material,

I'll do the building. We'll pay as we go and we'll look for bargains. This is my gift back to God, and my gift of love to you."

He grinned. "I can't sing like my wife Reneé or tell stories or preach, but I can build! Whatever is in our hand—that is what we give back to God."

And it came to pass. The plans were drawn and Larry took a hammer into his hand; the nails found a sure place.

Harold reluctantly cut down our productive pear tree. We all remembered how we canned pears during Hurricane Diane. Pears blew everywhere. That was the time for pears. Now is the time for writing. For everything, there is a season. Instead of pear blossoms, there bloomed a beautiful two-car garage with an office room across the back for writing.

Machinery filled the garage so the cars stayed outside. The sounds of saws and hammers blended with the laughter and the jokes. My camera caught pictures of Larry's eighty-seven-year-old grandfather on a ladder, setting the pace for the young. Harold kept supplies coming while Ralph, Steve, and the boys, Shawn and Eric, reviewed basketball scores and pounded nails.

Perfectionist Larry checked, measured, and rechecked plans and workmanship until phase one was completed. I could move my papers and boxes into the new office. I had a place to write!

Inside the house, sheets of plastic covered the openings where windows and doors had been. A bulldozer had removed the old porch and carport. Out of these ruins rose a dining room, a breakfast room with bay windows, a den, and a bathroom. And after fifty years of marriage, I had a laundry room!

Along with everything else, the attic had to be cleaned. More boxes came to light; some of them were marked "Miscellaneous." With Chris's help they found their way to the Salvation Army. Christmas decorations came down—we would be needing them soon; suitcases went back up—no travel for at least a month. We were too busy building.

There were times when delays and frustrations made us wish we had never begun, but Larry kept the plan before us. "We'll complete the job," he assured us.

God had given him a plan, a nail in a sure place, and the hammer was the will that nailed the plan to fulfillment.

At last the saws and hammers were laid aside. The trucks carried away the debris. The driveway's concrete was dry and the back steps had been transformed into a safe stoop with wide steps.

In the spring the flowers would come to cover the brown earth of winter. It was always so—spring follows winter, even the winter of the soul. I peered out my bay window and visualized a garden in bloom.

My dream of a Scandinavian kitchen became a reality too. Red-checked curtains blend with blue gingham wallpaper. A scalloped white organdy eyelet valance, embroidered with steaming white satin coffee pots and cups, reminded us of our new friends, Rut and Bjorn Langmo, who had sent this gift from Norway.

Jan and Chris had a beautiful basket of soft blue and peach silk flowers arranged for our golden wedding anniversary. During the sheet rock dust storms, I carefully protected this treasure until the buffet in our new dining room was ready.

Now it was time to select paint, carpet, wallpaper, and curtains. Limited finances and time made it imperative to find bargains—and find them fast!

With an "Onward, Christian Soldiers" determination, the girls and I marched off to our war, pocketbooks swinging from our shoulders, car keys ready for action. This definitely was the day the Lord had made, and no one had better get in the way. Even trembling traffic lights turned green when we approached.

At one store we spotted the sign: *Wallpaper Sale!* The magic words! And there it was, the color and flowers that would match the basket arrangement perfectly. Within five minutes the wallpaper—on sale—was tucked into the trunk of the car.

Like three conquering generals, proud and ramrod-straight, we marched into Kmart and invaded the curtain department. We bought our rods and blinds, then "Onward, Christian Soldiers" again. There was no time to waste.

J.C. Penney's department store had a sale on lace curtains. Once again the song of victory: The last curtains needed were in my safekeeping. Home we went and hung them in place.

"European lace?" someone asked, fingering the curtain panel gingerly.

It took all my integrity to answer, "No—on sale at Penney's."

There were still some purchases needed to finish our remodeling so Harold went one direction to get paint and brushes while the girls, Jan and Chris and I, went the other to the fabric center. Looking in the rear of the store for remnants, Janice spotted a bolt of material, another perfect match. "Mom, look. It's just right to cover that old chair and make a valance."

The salesman laughed. "Someone must be looking after you," he said. "Decorators spend days and weeks waiting for perfectly coordinated colors."

"Oh, He is," I answered confidently. "Believe me, He is!"

Harold gave the carpet man our colors and within fifteen minutes, that purchase was settled. We had chosen soft beige carpet to match the walls. It would replace the gold carpet, stained and worn from years of faithful service. I almost gave a salute when the old gold rug was carried to its final destination: the dump truck. Gold has never been my favorite color.

The Jensen war on clutter was about to be won!

Now the laundry room. After having the washer in the kitchen competing with the coffee pot and telephone, I really thought a dedication service would be in order. Imagine: shelves for soap and a clothes bar to hang Harold's shirts on. It made me realize what I'd been missing. If I catch the shirts in time, I can skip the ironing, and my Norwegian conscience is quiet. And that's not all: In my laundry room, no one trips over the ironing board (when I do iron) and there's a specific place for the iron itself.

Larry caught me staring into space. His brows furrowed. "Is something wrong?" he asked.

How could I ever explain that I was remembering how I would run out to the clothesline to beat the black clouds of rain, and then drape soggy underwear over the doors inside?

It was time to prepare for Christmas! Harold had finished all the painting, and the furniture was in place. I took the plastic off the beautiful blue sofa that Ralph had made, and his hand-carved table came out of a bedroom corner and stood in a place of honor.

The round mahogany table, Mama's wedding gift from the Jewish lady she served, the tabled I polished so carefully as a child, was given a prominent spot.

Above it hung Joyce Solveig's needlework of love for our anniversary:

I have loved you with an everlasting love.

The piano stayed where it had always been, and still was the focal point for all the family.

A place of honor had been bestowed on each piece of furniture that had endured years of living. Nothing was new, just restored. Then out came the old Christmas decorations and up went the tree. We trimmed the tree with the ornaments of fifty years, and each one held a memory. Carols, tree lights, and candlelight all blended into the magic of Christmas.

We celebrated Christmas Day with dinner in the new dining room! A royal blue cloth from Denmark covered the table. Christmas dishes matched it and red candles were set in the white candelabra from Sweden.

The family pictures on the wall smiled with us as we gathered to ask God's blessing on this house and to thank Him for the gift of His love.

The music of "Silent Night, Holy Night" filled not only the room but also our hearts. It had been a long, hard year of work, but today was a glad day of celebration.

"The beauty of a life is godliness and the beauty of a home is order." I heard that somewhere, and it has been tucked away in my heart. After fifty years of waiting, I finally have the room and order I have longed for. I have my place to write.

A quiet peace fills the rooms, and I am conscious that every good and perfect gift comes from above and that God uses our hands to extend those gifts to others.

Chad said it all. "Grammy's house small? No way! There's always room for us!"

You are so right, Chad. It's the same house, the same street, the same yard with the gardens and flowers. Love just stretched the walls.

P.S. Dear Lord, just as we took the clutter out of the attic, help us to take the clutter from the attic of our minds and bring the beauty of order to our souls as well.

54

Gifts of Love

The telephone lines were kept busy between North Carolina and Massachusetts. Heather, our eighteen-year-old granddaughter, had been taken to the emergency room at the hospital. X-rays, tests, and surgery became the topic of conversation. All else was put aside—even writing. Across the country, family and friends prayed while waiting for the medical reports.

Dr. Bill Wood, a noted surgeon, stopped his heavy schedule to sit and wait with the family. The gift of friendship comes in many wrappings.

Finally the sound of joy welled up when word came that Heather was going to be all right.

A family friend, Dr. Luke Sampson, stopped by several weeks later for a cup of coffee and a visit. He had recently lost his mother and now he also was reliving the death of his young son, Jonathan.

His question burned into my heart. "But what if the reports had not been good—as in Jonathan's case? What would you have done then?"

I thought for a moment. "Luke, a thankful heart stores up past mercies to feed our faith in dark days. We can't get ready for tragedy. We must stay ready. The sting of death is cushioned by the fact that we are made for eternity. We can't avoid suffering and death, but we must bring it all into the light of eternity. We are made for eternity," I affirmed. "This is just our training ground."

Thoughtfully my young friend responded, "We like to have control over our lives. And then something comes along that we have no control over. I'm beginning to realize that God in His sovereignty had a plan. Looking back, I can see in some measure how events can work together for good."

Faith is all that we can give to God, especially in the dark days. He gives us everything else—life, His covenant, the promises; above all, His gift of love.

After Luke left, I thought back to another day, to experiences of the past that rekindle my faith today, to a number of gifts of love.

Ruth Bremer's nursing office was bursting with the news. Someone called out to me, "Rosa's house burned down! All her Christmas presents are gone. Her tree caught fire—everything's gone!"

My heart went out to Rosa, our faithful maid, who worked so diligently to keep her family together. I immediately reached for the telephone and called Frank Owenby, chairman of the hospital board and owner of Owenbilt Mills. "We need help for Rosa. This is our opportunity to show that we are a family, and that we care. By the way, I have also been thinking about Christmas gifts for the children of the others on our housekeeping staff."

There was a low chuckle on the other end of the line. Finally, Mr. Owenby answered, "You can have anything you want, Margaret. Just go to the warehouse and R. H. Whitlock will show you the 'seconds' in clothes and you can fill the truck."

With a gentle laugh, he added, "Margaret, you'll get what you want one way or the other. I might as well give you the warehouse. You and Ruth Bremer—you're too much!" But his heart was as big as his warehouse.

We made a list of all the children: sizes and sex. We recruited help in finding a place and some furnishings for Rosa and her family. No hospital had a more exciting Christmas.

At the warehouse, I chose jackets and shirts, warm clothes,

and even some baby things for the new twins. R. H. Whitlock filled the truck.

We used a room at the hospital to wrap and tag the gifts. No one was forgotten. All was ready by the morning of Christmas Eve. It probably had never happened before and it might never happen again. But this was one moment in my life that keeps returning and rekindling my faith.

The smiles of joy, the heartfelt thanks, and the sound of laughter brought a hospital family together. What had begun as a tragedy ended as a triumph.

I still remember one janitor who laid aside his mop and pail to show me a picture of his children in their new clothes.

When I saw Mr. Owenby later, I said, "How can I ever thank you?"

With a catch in his voice, he answered, "I should thank you. It was the happiest Christmas ever."

All through life we have the mountain peaks that give us a glimpse of the overall view. But for the most part, life is lived in the valleys of everyday tasks.

One of my tasks was to make rounds in the B section, the lower floor where black patients were admitted.

When I passed Miss Lizzie's room I called out a reminder to give us a urine specimen.

"Oh nurse, I forgot again—just went to the toilet." Lizzie, a diabetic, always forgot her morning specimen.

"I just need a few drops for testing, so how about trying one more time?" I asked.

She succeeded! I jokingly stood at attention, saluted, and cheered, "Hurrah for Miss Lizzie! We did it!"

The ward burst into laughter, then I heard Miss Lizzie tell them, "Lord have mercy! Did you see how plumb carried away that child gets over a little wee? Ah do believe she's selling it!"

Across the hall was an elderly woman who had had surgery. I was trying to get her to sip a few swallows of ginger ale. "Come on now, Mammy, every little bit helps."

Sleepily, she answered, "That's what the old lady said when she wee'd in the ocean."

The men's ward was quiet with the stillness of death. Three

men in the four-bed ward were keeping watch. Uncle Joe, like fragile ebony, lay unconscious in the fourth bed, peaceful and quiet. His white hair framed his thin face. I checked his feeble pulse.

Uncle Joe, one hundred, more or less, was in a coma and dying.

The silence was broken by one of the men. "Old Uncle Joe taught us how to read."

The others nodded.

"Never can get no place if you can't read," he added.

They all agreed.

"Nurse," he said to me. "Uncle Joe, he taught us from the Bible, and all the young'uns around. He read from the Bible, he did."

Uncle Joe's bed was soiled and demanded attention so I pulled the curtains, bathed him like a baby, and changed the bedding.

When I finished, his frail, quiet form lay clean and powdered in a spotless bed. He looked like a peaceful child. I held his hand and quoted the 23rd Psalm.

I pulled back the curtain, and saw that the three other men were crying. "Thank you, nurse. The last wish Uncle Joe had was to be clean when he died. He said, 'I don't want to meet my Maker dirty.'"

The mountaintops in nursing were exhilarating, but the tasks in the valley brought peace.

Whenever we in the emergency room heard the wail of the ambulance, we braced ourselves for the unexpected. "Life is what happens to you while you are making other plans" should be inscribed over every emergency room door.

One day was quiet until we heard the wail, and we braced ourselves. A young husband had fallen asleep at the wheel of his car, and it hit a truck. His wife was admitted to surgery with severe lacerations. The two young children huddled beside their father in the waiting room, all in shock. They were en route to Florida from a northern state.

I called Harold, and he took the family to our home where they could wait more comfortably. They bathed and ate a good meal, and then fell asleep. Later, Harold retrieved the luggage from the wrecked car and called the insurance company for the worried young husband. When I got home we laundered all the blood-soaked clothes.

For a while I wondered what kind of people we had taken in—but not for long. Not when I overheard the four-year-old child tell the two year old, "Don't cry. Everything will be all right. I asked Jesus to help us, and *He did!*"

The young mother finally recovered and the entire family flew back home, but their gift of love—their friendship—remained.

Another morning, while I was arranging E.R. supplies for the day, I heard the screech of a car. A young girl dashed in, a limp baby in her arms. Sobbing hysterically, she cried, "She's dead! She's dead! Yesterday she was in a high chair and today my baby is dead!"

A little later, the young woman's brother came to take her home. After they left, the doctor asked me to get an autopsy form filled out. "She was too upset now, Margaret, but I thought you could go and get it this afternoon, and also see how she is doing."

Another nurse and I drove out to the little house in the country where the mother lived. We got there just in time to hear an older woman, with arms folded, thunder forth, "Be sure your sins will find you out. You just had to go off with that no-good tramp and get yourself in the family way. Believe me, no sin will I tolerate in my house, and I told you to go!"

Anger rose up within me. I ordered the older woman to "be quiet," and added, "I don't know what God you serve, but my God is a God of love and forgiveness. Your daughter lost someone precious to her, and I have come to see her."

The young mother fell into my arms and sobbed. After she grew quiet again, she signed the autopsy form. Cause of death: pneumonia. We talked about the future, and we became good friends. Later she went back to school, attended church and made new friends, took a secretarial course, and obtained a good job.

I'll always remember the kindness of this girl's young married brother who took her in when her own mother threw her out.

I will also remember a stormy night when Ruth Bremer was asked to travel a lonesome country road to a shack in the woods where a young girl was having her baby.

Ruth delivered what she thought was a stillborn. Then a faint gasp escaped from the tiny premature infant. Ruth immediately put the tiny baby inside her blouse and drove back to the hospital.

Somewhere today there is a black Ruth named after the Ruth who saved her life.

At the end of the hall in B section, I saw a doctor's mother sitting beside her black cook. The faithful old servant was dying and the child she had cared for was now her doctor, faithful in his care for her. The servant died peacefully, with her family around her, and the doctor's mother wept. Through her tears, she said to me, "You can't laugh together, weep together, pray together, and rear your children together and not love each other." She wiped her tears, saying, "I just lost my dear friend."

The time came when my days of nursing at that hospital were drawing to a close. Harold and I were moving to North Carolina.

On one of my last rounds, I saw the housekeeping staff of the B section gathered together. They seemed to be led by one of the janitors, who used to be a butler in a wealthy home. He had brought his impeccable manners into his hospital job. He would greet me in the morning, bowing low. "Nurse, may I help you get your patient well by cleaning his room?"

"I would be honored," I would tell him.

When he finished I would thank him, and his reply was a thank you in return. Bowing with great dignity, he would say, "I appreciate your appreciation."

Somehow I had the feeling that wherever he went, he would always manage to poke holes in the darkness and let the sun shine through.

I wonder why we so often remember the small acts of kindness while the big events slip away.

That day, I looked at the huddled housekeeping staff and I asked, "What's wrong? Did someone die?"

They sadly shook their heads. Tears glistened on their black cheeks. "We just heard you were leaving." I suddenly realized they were crying for me! I cried, too!

The segregating walls could never segregate love, and I knew that one day even those walls would come down. With hugs and promises we parted. I shall never forget the gifts of love from B section.

55

Pants or Plants

I shouldn't be thinking about gardening when I have to write, but Harold keeps all those seed catalogues around making my choices most difficult. So, just for a few minutes, I went out to check the bushes.

The red bush was putting out buds. The holly was loaded with red berries. Now I'm looking for the crocus bulbs to send their shoots through—a real sign of spring.

And then it will get warmer and I'll be out there bending over (and not on my knees) to dig up, plant, or transplant my garden.

One day Harold watched me. "Margaret, do you realize the neighbors have never seen your face?" he asked. So for Harold's sake, this spring I'll try to bend my knees more.

The day when Harold worried about my bending was my kind of morning to plant or transplant. It was a drizzly, misty morning and I didn't have to drag the hose around. I was up very early, routine for me, confident that no one would see me in my shower cap (to keep my hair dry), my old pants with the loose elastic, and my muddy garden shoes.

Oh, I was happy that morning. I had my scooper and hoe, a bag of fertilizer, and all those wonderful plants to put in the bare spots.

The rain came harder and my shower cap came over my eyes. For the most part, my hair stayed dry, but the elastic in my old paint pants didn't. I was determined to finish the planting, so I kept working.

Before long, Harold called to me. "Margaret, telephone. Long distance." That always gets me to the phone, but Harold says it even if Chris is calling from down the block.

It was still early. I figured it was my sister Doris. She's the only other one I know who gets up with the birds. As I turned to face Harold, he gave me an I-can't-believe-you look. He glared at my tilted shower cap and my sagging paint pants. "The phone, Margaret," he reminded me.

I stood there with my hands full of muddy plants and with my pants falling, staring back. "Who is it?

He simply said, "Margaret, the phone. Drop the plants."

Drop the plants? I thought. *What does he know about transplanting? He stands there, clean and spotless, holding a cup of coffee. He doesn't know what it means to plant in the rain so you don't need to drag the hose around.* But my pants were falling. I elbowed the waist band to secure them.

"Margaret, drop the plants!" he called again between sips of coffee.

I heard him. It was the choice that got me: *Either drop the plants or drop the pants.*

I chose! I dropped the soft, wet, muddy plants, grabbed my pants, kicked off my shoes, and rushed into the house to answer the phone.

It was Doris. She said she was praying for me—she usually does. I needed it this morning. So did my plants.

I told her it was the choices in life that were so difficult. She agreed, and then added, "The choices aren't always between good and evil; sometimes they're between good and best."

"I'll try to remember that," I promised.

A hot shower and a good breakfast ended my gardening for the day. It was still early, but now time to read God's directions for a new day. I read in my devotions that character is the sum total of our everyday choices. And I thought about Joseph in the Bible—he decided who he was before he decided what he would do. He lived out his choices.

Everyone around us is affected by the choices we make. Jesus says, "Come and learn," but we would rather "go and do."

God will not force His will upon us, but if we don't choose God's will, Satan will force *his* will upon us.

I remember the story Papa told about the farmer and the mule. The mule wouldn't move, no matter what the farmer did.

A bee came along and told the farmer, "I'll help you."

The farmer shook his head. "If I can't make that stubborn mule start plowing, how can you make him?"

"Oh, I can't make that mule go," the bee admitted, "but I sure can make him *willing* to go." The song says:

> *God never calls us to go gainst our will,*
> *But he just makes us willing to go.*

Sometimes it is hard to obey God—but it really is harder not to. God will take care of the consequences of our obedience to Him.

I turned to my favorite devotional, Oswald Chamber's *My Utmost for His Highest.*

The warfare is not against sin. We can never fight sin. Jesus deals with sin in redemption. The conflict is along the line of turning our natural life into a spiritual life—done by a series of moral choices.

In May 1988 near Carrolton, Kentucky, a pickup truck going the wrong way on Interstate 71 crashed into a church bus, and twenty-seven people were killed. During the funeral of the children who had died in that tragic accident one black woman stood up to sing, "I've come too far to turn back."

Her child was in one of the caskets, but the mother had already chosen. "As for me and my house, we will serve the LORD" (Joshua 24:15).

God had not forced this woman to sing. He did not force her to stay with a straight course. She had already learned the joy of obedience. Once again—although her heart was breaking for her son—she made the deliberate choice to obey, to sing, to not turn back. She would continue to trust the promises of God.

Her son would dwell in the house of the Lord forever because God had chosen to prepare a place for him. The woman was still growing, still learning to trust Jesus completely.

56

Ten Bushels of Corn

I finally learned my lesson about planting corn. The way I did it, each ear of corn cost about two dollars. "Leave it to the experts," was Harold's advice. So I backed my wounded pride into a corner and turned my attention to the flower garden.

One day our son Ralph came over with this great news, "Mr. G. has a wonderful garden and we can buy corn from him. How much should I get?"

"Just get all he can spare," I answered. Then Ralph was off. I should have been a little more conservative, but I didn't have any better sense just then.

Ralph came home with a truckload of corn—ten bushels!

It was Saturday and that meant we all had to get ready for Sunday.

Harold had been painting in 100-degree heat, so he had found a lounge chair under a tree and was clutching a cold piece of watermelon.

Then Ralph came with the corn! I called Chris and the gang came over. We set up a production line. The men shucked corn; Chris and I washed it, and Shawn cleaned off the silk. About then one-year-old Sarah got into the shed and helped herself to lime and fertilizer. We grabbed her before she ate any of it and washed her under the water hose.

The boys got into a fight over who cleaned the most corn, and then Shawn hurt his finger. He stretched out on the grass, like the athletes do, and waited for a stretcher to take him to the medical center. None came.

While Shawn lay "wounded" on the grass, Sarah decided to do a striptease. She wiggled out of her diaper and held up her shirt triumphantly to show her bare bottom. No one could stop to dress her. Eric turned on the garden hose and watered everyone, but not the garden.

Chris dumped the ears of corn in boiling water, then we iced them and into the bags they went. We ran out of ice! I ran out of room in the freezer. Chris jumped in the car, cleared space in her own freezer, and brought more ice. Having her live only a block away is wonderful!

But this was Sarah's day! She found the tomatoes and began tossing them, "Ball! Ball!" No one would catch. We caught her instead, but not before we were sliding in tomatoes. We managed to can the rest—nine quarts.

Sarah was still wired for action. She found the sugar bowl and managed to get up on the table to reach it. So between her tomato-juice bottom and sugar-baby top, we just had to throw her into the tub, but not before she dumped the hair shampoo. She was in her world—bubbles all over!

Clean and smiling, she looked like an angel, fresh diaper and all. That is, until she found a plum. We thought she was bleeding, but her happy smile gave her away.

Chris shouted, "Somebody get this child!" but no one wanted her.

Papa said, "Go to Gramma."

Gramma said, "Go to Papa."

Chris said, "Go to your sweet daddy."

Ralph said, "Can't you see I'm shucking corn? Go to your big brother Shawn."

Shawn held up his sore finger, holding her off.

Eric kept the hose going.

It took all of us, but we managed to fill the freezers with corn, can all the tomatoes, and clean up the kitchen by 10 P.M.

Sarah, usually in bed early, sat in the middle of the table, big as life, eating watermelon.

The children were given another "sloshing" and wore Papa's T-shirts. The boys wailed, "We want to spend the night."

Chris wanted a cup of coffee, and so did I.

By then, Sarah, thumb in her mouth, had her head on Ralph's shoulder. This had been her night out and she wasn't about to forget it.

Neither would we!

I read someplace that life is what happens to you while you are making other plans.

Believe me, this was one day we didn't plan, but if you laugh as hard as we did (when it was over), perhaps it was in "The Plan." The whole day was just another reminder that out of all things, even ten bushels of corn, God works together for good. At least the freezer is full, and Sarah had her moment in the sun.

P.S. Today, Sarah is ten years old and plays basketball with a ballet twist. She dresses in ribbons and lace for a piano recital, squeezes close to her Papa in church, and rides up front to the family Sunday dinner.

"I just love Sundays," she announced happily the other day. "I love sitting around the dining room table, all crowded, and everybody talking at the same time. I just love!"

Harold smiled at me and I answered from my heart, "So do I. So do I!"

57

Jimmy's Song

While some people race over the highways of life in the challenging pursuit of power or pleasure, others take a country lane and walk a little slower. I have noticed that often, when the end of the road is reached, the ones who move in the slow lane win the race of life.

My friend Jimmy walked soft-like through life. When overcome with grief over the loss of his father, he retreated into a lonely world of doubt and unbelief. How could a good God take his best friend?

Music was Jimmy's great love and his understanding family provided a soundproof room where he played recordings of the great artists. Jimmy's beautiful tenor voice blended in unison with the performers until it was difficult to tell the difference. Since an audience intimidated him, he sang alone for hours.

One day a soft-spoken, gentle girl named Margaret heard him singing and she became his audience. During the days of music a friendship formed; then he sang the love songs, from his heart right into her heart. "Be my love," he sang, and she became his sweetheart wife. Through her gentle ways she shared her unshakable faith in God and took him by the heart to lead him back to the faith of his childhood, to the reality of God's love for him.

"I'll never be lonely again. God loves me, and my beautiful angel loves me," Jimmy said.

Harold and I visited Margaret and Jimmy in their cozy home, and we drank tea together. Then Jimmy gave us a concert. With a recording of Ed Lyman singing the songs of faith, the two voices sounded as one. It was one of those wondrous moments that come, never to return again.

Through the years our paths separated and we didn't hear Jimmy sing again, although news came across the miles of how he worked faithfully every day.

"I have to take care of my angel," he said.

He not only had the practical qualities of faithfulness and dependability, but he also moved through life with the courtesy of a Southern gentleman.

Hand in hand, Margaret and Jimmy served God and people faithfully. The living Christ who enables us to do the impossible gave Jimmy a new boldness and love for his Savior. He shared his gift with the lonely people in nearby nursing homes, singing of his faith in a loving God, and he shared the story of God's great salvation. From his heart of love, he shared with lonely prisoners behind bars, singing and preaching about God's freedom through Christ. He was a frequent soloist at his home church, and at office Christmas parties he was the special feature, singing and leading the singing.

His wife wrote about his heart for evangelism, his longing to share the love of God in music and words. He continued to reach into the lonely places singing the songs of faith and hope, bringing God's amazing grace that went beyond wheelchairs and prison bars.

Then one day God took Jimmy Home. The music was stilled and the world became a lonelier place without him. "My sweetheart is gone. How I miss him!" wrote Margaret.

I reminded her of how God had used her to put the song of salvation into Jimmy's heart. She was there to prop up his leanin' side. Because of her faith, Jimmy's faith had become a new boldness to share God's love in words and music. Because of Jimmy's music, some who were lonely now have hope, some who were prisoners now have a new freedom, some who were discouraged now have new faith—and by faith the song goes on.

He was there to prop up their leanin' sides!

Perhaps God needed an extra tenor in the heavenly choir and sent an angel to bring him Home. If we walk a little slower, a little more soft-like, it may be that we will hear Jimmy's song: "Amazing grace, how sweet the sound. . . ."

"Love is patient, love is kind . . . is not provoked, does not take into account a wrong suffered, does not rejoice in unrighteousness, but rejoices with the truth; bears all things, believes all things, hopes all things, endures all things" (1 Corinthians 13:4–7 NASB).

Ralph

58

Lena

Greensboro College, a Methodist school formerly for women only, sat on a knoll, overlooking spacious lawns, fragrant magnolia trees, and azalea gardens. Towering oaks and pines stood like sentinels, guarding the memories of yesterday.

I guided my car into the "Reserved for Nurse" parking space and reached for the key to unlock the door to the college infirmary.

It was an old building with spacious rooms, high ceilings, and tall windows. My office overlooked the well-worn path to the snack shop.

It was from this window that I would hear the rumblings of the late sixties as students congregated to exchange their views on life in general, and their own ideas in particular. Even on this, my first day, I sensed an undercurrent of uneasiness. It seemed that young people were like boats loosed from their moorings, becoming slaves to the tide of our times.

Even our own son, Ralph.

A gnawing fear for our youngest gripped me. He had just enrolled as a freshman at Gordon College, Wenham, Massachusetts, but might he now be loosening the tacklings on his boat? *Could that relentless tide be pulling him out to sea?* I wondered—then dismissed the idea as absurd. His older sister, Janice, and brother, Dan, were well-adjusted young people. Ralph, too, would find his place.

This would pass, I mused. Gordon was a fine Christian college and my handsome rebel now was far away from his old friends and old haunts. I breathed a sigh of relief and turned to the task at hand—managing a college infirmary.

At 6:30 A.M. it was quiet in the empty building, so I went into the large kitchen, past the steam radiators, and into a pantry where I found an obviously much-used coffee pot. Upstairs, warm September breezes blew through the open windows, airing lumpy mattresses which had been draped over high metal hospital beds. I made a mental note that eighteen students could be admitted, and extra cots put up for emergencies.

The infirmary was clean, even freshly painted.

Walking around the old building, so reminiscent of the past, I sensed the years flowing together. The events moved as though on a screen: assistant director of nurses, teaching in the school of practical nursing, private duty, office nurse, and now I was a college infirmary nurse. First and last I was Harold's wife, and the mother of three children now gone from the nest. Perhaps that is why these students seemed like my own children. I wondered how this river would flow.

My thoughts were brought back to the reality of the present when I heard Dean Locke's booming voice, "Good morning, Florence Nightingale! You should be so lucky as to get the best maid on campus for infirmary housekeeper." With a sweeping bow he announced, "Meet Lena Rogers, the queen of the pound cakes." In a moment he was gone, racing across the campus as he waved to returning students, then disappearing behind the stone walls of the administration building.

I turned to face smiling eyes and clasped two black hands in welcome. Laughingly Lena said, "I best be cooking that dean a pound cake," but her knowing eyes looked deeply into mine. Her face was a velvet darkness, and I found myself thinking, *a symphony in black.*

"Nurse Jensen, looks like me and you got us a job. Lord have mercy, I never had no baby, and now I gets a college full of young'uns. You take care of the pills and I take care of the pots. I best tend to the kitchen, then we can have a cup of tea." Her joyous singing soon filled the empty building.

In my heart I knew that my introduction to Lena in September 1968 at Greensboro College, Greensboro, North Carolina, would lead to a challenging friendship.

The infirmary door banged open and I heard a frantic, "Where's Lena?"

"Lord have mercy, child, in the kitchen. Where else? Don't go bangin' no doors in my house, boy." Lena's laughing eyes and bear hug countered her law-and-order command.

"Lena, I'm starved. I overslept and can't make the dining room. Got any toast and coffee?"

Jim eased his six-foot frame into a chair, and between bites and gulps he confessed his fears about girls, exams—and life.

"While you're swallowing your food whole I'll sing you a song and then come back when me and you can talk. Every day, son, I stands by this window and looks to that tree, and I says, 'Big tree, you been there in years long gone. You been in the winter and the storm, the spring and the summer. You changes colors, but you still stand. You done watched my children coming and going. You're there when the children go home for the summer and you still standing when they comes back.'

"You know something, Jim? Me and that tree is the same. We both gets life from God. The Bible says that this black Lena is like a tree planted by the rivers of water and the leaf shall not wither and what Lena does shall prosper. My roots are in Jesus—that's my roots—and I drink of the river of life, and when that tree is gone, this Lena still stands forever with the Lord. All that learning you getting, boy, who is telling you that?"

Lost in her own thoughts, Lena sang softly, "Without Him I would be nothing. . . ."

"You best go to your class, and I'll be here watching and calling out your name."

From my window I heard Jim's whistle as he raced across the campus to get to his first class. From the kitchen came Lena's plaintive cry, "Oh, Lord, hear Your child. I'm calling out

Jim's name. Bless him, Lord, and all my children. Bless this here infirmary and all those folks with so much learning from books, but let them get learning from You, Lord. This is Lena, Lord, I come most all the time, so You knows Your black child real good. I knows You too and You don't never fail Your Lena. Thank You."

Within moments Lena was tapping her feet and patting her hands while she sang "Power in the Blood." She was having her own church time with the Lord.

I stopped my paperwork to open my Bible, where I read, "But his delight is in the law of the LORD; and in his law doth he meditate day and night." Another psalm said, "Day unto day uttereth speech, and night unto night sheweth knowledge." I thought about the days and nights of our lives, the joys and sorrows, the agonies and the ecstacies—all part of that river of life. We learn from God through it all. The day, a time of working for Him, and the night, a time to rest in Him. When we see clearly, we act, when it is dark, we trust. In trusting comes the knowing that God works all things together for good.

My "church time" was interrupted with Lena's call, "Here they comes, Nurse Jensen. The throats, the cramps, the allergies, the bad nerves, the wounded, and the homesick with the vomiting or the diarrhea. Didn't know young folks had so many ailments." She rolled her eyes heavenward with a prayer, "Lord help them when they gets old."

When the doctor arrived for the daily office hour, Lena pulled him aside, "You looks plumb tuckered out like you been drove hard and put up wet. Here, eat this bowl of soup and cheese sandwich. No one out there dying, mostly wants attention, first time away from home."

With a sigh he sat down and the tension eased from his face. It had been a rough morning and he faced his own office of waiting patients.

Lena quietly pointed to her tree, "That tree gonna be here when me and you is plumb gone; but, then again, we will be living when that tree is gone."

Oblivious to anyone around her she sang,

When we've been there ten thousand years,
Bright shining as the sun
We've no less days to sing God's praise,
Than when we first begun.

When sick call was ended, the doctor's orders were given: X-rays for possible fractures, chest films, throat cultures, special prescriptions.

All day the students came—before, between, and after classes. Many stopped by the kitchen for a brief visit. Each one received a pat and a hug, and lingered to hear a song or a Lena lecture.

Lena's eyes followed the students as they walked across the campus. The wind carried her promise, "I'll be calling out your name."

One day later in the fall Lena said to me, "Nurse Jensen, don't forget the medicine man is coming." She went to put the toast in the oven while I retreated to my office to complete the medical supply list before the pharmaceutical salesman arrived.

Students were passing under my window, and before long I overheard one of them say, "Go on in and see the nurse. Maybe she'll help you."

"Why should she help me? I'm not a student any more. Nothing but bad luck for me, and now I'm sick and have no money."

"Go on and see her anyhow. She never turns anyone away. I don't know why, but I just know she loves us."

I continued writing at my desk, but stopped when I heard a step outside the office. Looking up I saw a long-haired young man, with a lean, gaunt look, wearing faded blue jeans and sandals. He complained of nausea, headache, dizziness, and weakness. He was jittery and fumbling in his pockets.

About that time Lena came around the corner and took one look at the hollow eyes.

"Tells you what, boy, while nurse gets you some medicine, you best come in the kitchen where Lena keeps her medicine— oven toast, scrambled eggs, and coffee."

He followed Lena quietly and watched her stir the eggs. "Life do get scrambled around like these eggs—but we comes out pretty good when God gets us out of the frying pan." She laughed and poured him coffee.

He ate without looking up, but finally, when the empty eyes looked into Lena's knowing eyes, the words tumbled out. "I had no place to go. My folks divorced. My wife couldn't find a job, and we got on drugs. I couldn't keep up my classes and now I'm out. My old roommate told me to come here."

"Can't do nothing until you get your stomach straightened out, child. All that smoking, drinking, dope stuff got your insides all twisted around. You needs some good oatmeal in that stomach. You come back in the morning and me and you can talk. Can't talk on a empty stomach nohow—head don't work too good. I tells you what—you best bring your wife today for a grilled cheese for lunch. Some things don't take to waiting. God has a way and man has his way that he thinks is right. Jesus says, 'I am the way.' We all has to choose sometime. But time enough for choosing. Now is time for eating."

When the young man left he promised to return with his wife at noon.

Within a short time the door opened again, and a handsome young man introduced himself as the new pharmaceutical representative. Since I had several students to see first, he accepted Lena's offer of coffee. Within moments I heard conversation flowing between Lena and this "medicine man."

When I finished I joined them with my list and we went over the needed supplies.

Before he left, Lena said quietly, "We needs to pray for this family. God going to give this man a baby."

The story unfolded that he and his wife were in the process of adoption. It seemed they had waited for years for a child, and now it was working out. There would soon be a baby available.

"The Bible says, 'Train up a child in the way he should go,' and I asks you what way you be thinking about training that baby God be giving you?" Lena looked into the face of the expectant father.

"I don't know," he faltered, "never thought much about it."

"Now is a good time," continued Lena, "for you, the papa, to be getting the house in order, before God gives you that baby. Jesus said, 'I am the way.' First, you get in the right way, then the mama, and then you both teach the baby the right way. Sing, 'Jesus loves me,' and that baby will grow up the right way."

Lena sang softly, rocking the imaginary baby in her arms.

Jesus loves me, this I know
For the Bible tells me so.

The kitchen was quiet. Lena added softly, "What is there any greater to know? Jesus right here in my kitchen and wants to take you by the hand and show you the right way." She sang:

Precious Lord, take my hand
Lead me on, let me stand.

With head bowed she prayed, "We just poor little lambs that don't know nothing, so take us by the hand and make us something. Help this papa and mama to know You and give them this baby they been waiting for. Thank You, Jesus."

Then he was gone, with the list of medical supplies in hand. When he waved from the car, Lena waved back from her post at the window, and I heard her calling out his name.

Lena continued her work, gathering up laundry, changing beds. There were food supplies to order, kitchen and bathrooms to clean, floors to mop, and furniture to dust. The phone rang incessantly and the door opened to students, salesmen, laundry men, delivery boys, and friends who stopped by to say hello.

"Faith and works goes together," was Lena's theme. She kept the Bible open on the kitchen table and prayed and sang as she worked.

Before I could finish my morning office work I heard Lena. "Time for lunch, nurse, got some good cottage cheese and pineapple and a crust of bread." The crust of bread was cheese melted on oven toast, with a cup of Lena tea. No one knew exactly what Lena had in her tea, but I was sure she used fruit juice and spices. When the students asked about the delicious tea she answered, "Prayer, children, prayer, I just puts praising and praying in the tea. Cures most everything."

We agreed.

For a few moments it was quiet in the kitchen and we bowed our hearts together in gratitude to God for every provision, especially for the crust of bread. We wondered if the young man from the morning visit would return. He seemed in such despair. "He'll come," Lena said. "The Lord will bring him back."

When our quiet lunch was completed, I returned to my desk to get ready for sick call. The doctor would be arriving soon, and so would the students.

I glanced out the window. Apparently Lena's invitation had worked, for down the driveway came the young man of the early morning with a thin girl clinging to his hand.

With a "Praise the Lord," Lena gathered the wife, dressed in a peasant dress and sandals, into her arms. "Oh, child, you come to the right place—Lena. You needs some meat on them bones, so sit down for a crust of bread." The kitchen was alive with warmth and love, and stories, songs, and laughter made two young people temporarily forget their troubles.

Before the visit came to an end, Lena had practiced her brand of psychology. "Something in the stomach first, and a good laugh to clear the head. Can't have no coonching spirits of doubt and fear clogging up the head. That Satum can't tolerate no joy."

In the meantime, one of my favorite students came in for a brief visit. Dave was a strong, handsome Christian married to a lovely girl who worked as a dental technician to help Dave complete his senior year.

After a bear hug for Lena and me, Dave was introduced to the young couple at the table. During the casual conversation Dave learned that the young wife was also a dental technician— unemployed. Dave perked up and invited the couple to his apartment, assuring the young woman that his own wife could give her some job tips. Turning to the husband he added,

"There's always a way to finish school. Let's discuss it over supper tonight."

I watched the couple leave, hand in hand, clinging to each other against a hostile world. This time they were laughing.

Dave turned to Lena, "You pray, and God will work on the inside. My wife and I will work on the outside. You always say faith and works go together."

With a victory sign, and a "Praise the Lord," Dave was gone. I heard Lena calling out his name, "Bless Dave, Lord. Oh, bless him, Lord."

The day was drawing to a close. The evening nurse would be coming soon. Lena was rattling her pans and I had locked up the pills. It had been quite a day, but then they were all like that—busy, with unexpected interruptions. Yet somehow the hours of the day moved with peace and order.

Lena waved good-bye as she crossed the campus to catch her bus. I heard her singing, "One step at the time, sweet Jesus."

In my heart I heard the words, "In all thy ways acknowledge him, and he shall direct thy paths."

As my car turned around the bend of the lake toward home, I wondered about the young couple, Dave, the "medicine man" . . . and Ralph. I looked in the mailbox. Still no letter.

A week later the phone rang for Lena. "Praise the Lord!" she shouted, "the medicine man done got his baby boy!"

59

Lena's Kitchen

In confidential tones, the girls who sneaked into Lena's kitchen whispered their fears of being ridiculed for being virgins. "I must be the only girl in school who believes in waiting for marriage," one girl cried on Lena's shoulder. "I feel like such an oddball."

"Hush, child. You know, a dozen girls already been here to say the same thing, and I expect dozens more to come when they get enough nerve to tell Lena. You want Lena to tell you what the boys tell me? Well, I won't," she laughed, "but I can say this much, there are lots of boys who want friends to talk to and go out with, but they complains that girls want to try everything—dope, liquor, and hopping into bed.

"Once you give away what God done give you to keep private and special, there's no way to go back. What for you call those parts 'private'? That's cause they do be private.

"The Bible says that we should give and it will be given unto us. You gives love, you gets love; you gives your time, you gets time; you gives friendship, you gets friendship. Same way we are taught to give our tithes, and God blesses back.

"Now, on the other hand," Lena rolled her eyes heavenward. "Help me, Jesus. Now on the other hand, you gives hate, you gets hate. When you plant potatoes you not looking for a big ripe watermelon. No, you looks for more potatoes. You think you can plant corn and get onions? Now child, listen to your Lena. You give that 'possible' to any boy come round when God says that be your private, you gets all the 'possible' you want, cause every boy be looking for the 'possible.' You gets what you done give, but you lose the private.

"You think old Lena don't know nothing about 'possibles'? You think I don't know nothing about melting like hot butter when that certain big black man come to Lena all smilin'-like, and all the grease from the garage washed away? He be standing there on a Saturday night with clean shirt, smelling like Aqua Velva, no whiskers, and hair combed. He say, 'Lena, honey,' and, oh, child, that honey come dripping like golden sunshine.

"I be remembering a hard week, scrubbing floors and cooking for the white folks. All week it was 'Lena do this,' and 'Lena do that.' When I got my piece of money, the rent man was waiting and the insurance man. I had to pay the light bill and the phone. I only had enough for the bus until next week. I cooked steaks for the white folks, but I ate fat meat and hamburger. I watched folks going to town, but I couldn't go.

"Then, right in front of me was town coming to me. I was all clean, smelling like Avon talcum powder, ready to be cooking some greens. There he stands. 'Lena, baby, I smells that salad, and look, honey, what I bring you, a nice big steak. How about a baked potato, a big juicy steak, and salad? Lena baby, you got skin like black velvet and I be needing you real bad.'

"My apartment look so clean and nice, but empty. Lord have mercy, but that steak would taste mighty good. I hear that, 'Lena, honey,' dripping like butter and my knees get plumb weak and I get that feeling of plumb lonesomeness all over me and I be needing him like he be needing me.

"He says, so soft like, 'Lena, baby, when you're hungry, you eat. When you're tired, you sleep. So if you gets this lonesome feeling for someone, and that man come to you, it be just like eating when you be hungry. Lena, honey, I be hungry for you.'

"Oh, child, you think that this Lena don't cry out to the Lord? I stay crying out to the Lord. Come Saturday night, I cry harder.

I said, 'Oh, Jesus, help me.' All of a sudden them weak knees get strong, and that sweet, dripping honey looked like poison. I stood tall-like, and said real quiet-like, 'I be mighty busy tonight, studying my Sunday school lesson. You best be going home.'

"He left slow and sad-like, but when he turned around he said, 'I'll be coming back, Lena, honey.'

"That's when I close the door and lock it. I stretched out before the Lord and I cried long and hard. I be mighty lonesome for a man's loving. I ate my collards alone.

"Nowadays they talks about free love. Child, you know how much love cost? It be like you buying a steak, and somebody come and eat it up. You done paid for it, but somebody else eats it. It be like planting watermelons. You buy the seed, plow, plant, hoe, and then, about the time you ready to eat that big ripe one, somebody come along and take it.

"Now you be special . . . only one like you. God made you in His image, to grow, to love, to live, and love Him first of all. God says it is not good to be alone so he makes a boy special, to grow, to love, to live, and love God first.

"Then God says, now study to be approved, and work, for the night is coming. He knows this growing up business is hard, so He says, 'Put on the whole armor of God so you can fight all them coonching spirits.' There be so many coonching spirits, like doubt and unbelief, unforgiveness, resentment, and hatred.

"Oh, child, there be other coonching spirits we don't hear so much about. It's them coonching spirits of lust. That be different from love. Lust eats the steak he didn't pay for. He steals the watermelon he didn't plant. He takes the 'possible' from one and then another and leaves nothing private. Them coonching spirits makes girls wear dress up to the 'possible' and the boys with pants so tight, like Lena don't know what be inside.

"I watches from my window and I see boys and girls a huggin' and a squirming. I cries out to my Jesus to help them go the right way. Jesus is right way—the only way. That boy thinks he found a fun way and that girl thinks she doing her own way.

329

God says that way of rebellion to God's rules that be sin. Sin is death.

"I hope you listens, child—not just your ears, but your heart.

"Love suffers long. It be patient to wait and be kind so no sweet girl gets in trouble. Love isn't selfish, but gentle and understanding. That kind of love be strong. Come Sunday morning, my knees feel so strong and my soul feels so good I just start singing, 'Precious Lord, take my hand,' and the choir come right along and sing, 'O sweet Jesus, take my hand.'

"You know why the choir can sing right along? That be soul music. We feels the same burdens, the same lonesomeness, the same hunger, the same tired from a long week, but we feels the same Jesus taking our hand and first thing you know we got the whole church singing, 'Precious Lord, take my hand,' then the joy comes and we can sing, 'Every time I feels the Spirit movin' in my heart, I pray.' Then we gets happy.

"The Bible says the joy of the Lord is your strength. Now I ask you, child, how you be strong if you not happy? You gets your joy from the Lord, not from the world.

"You best be going, child. Lena got lots of cleaning up to do, but you come back every day so we can keep the joy. Then you be strong."

The blond head rested on Lena's shoulder while the tears fell from baby-blue eyes. Then, looking into Lena's black face, the girl said quietly, "Lena, I'm still private." With a burst of joy she raced across campus to the next class. I heard Lena calling out her name.

I worked quietly at my desk until Lena called me for lunch—a crust of bread (with cheese) and a cup of tea.

During our lunch I told Lena about our Thanksgiving trip to Michigan, our beautiful new granddaughter she had prayed for, and our visit to Chicago to see my sister Joyce, who was married to Howard, Harold's brother. Their three children, Judy, Paul, and Steve, and our three, Jan, Dan, and Ralph, had been more like brothers and sisters than cousins. The closeness of our families was a constant reminder that God's laws and His ways are a protection from the destructive forces around us. I told her how we missed Ralph. Lena shared the "knowing" that Ralph stood in need of prayer.

Christmas holidays were drawing close and suddenly we had an idea.

"We needs joy on this campus!" Lena declared. "So many fine people working so hard to teach young folks, and these children be studying long hours before exams. We need a Christmas party!"

"That's it, Lena! We'll have an open house and send invitations to the various departments, and the students can help with the decorations."

For days I dragged boxes of ornaments from home and students put up decorations and trimmed a tree. We used cotton balls and made bows out of gauze.

A long table was placed in the hall and we served the cookies and cake we had baked at home. We had only one patient, and she had a ringside seat to all the activity. Julie's injured leg kept her in bed, but never did one patient have so many visitors as on the day of our open house.

The college president, Dr. Jolly, and the infirmary physician, Dr. Gilmore, balanced plates of cookies and punch as they visited with students and faculty. In the relaxed holiday atmosphere, the tensions of last-minute term papers and exams were laid aside. Vacation was nearly a reality.

Foreign students looked forward to spending the holidays with faculty members and students. Several students were coming home with me.

All too soon the happy day came to a close and the decorations were dismantled, only to be taken home and put up for our Christmas. Lena closed the kitchen door, and I locked the office. Students left for their parents' homes.

I watched Lena sing her way across campus to catch her bus, and I took two of the foreign students home with me.

Moa from Singapore and Becky from Indonesia helped Dan put up our tree and joined in the Christmas preparations in the kitchen. Their happy giggles filled the house, and Dan's teasing made the girls feel a part of the family. They were anxious to meet Ralph, who was coming home on the next day's flight.

Once again Harold and I were at the airport. "Seems to me there is always one of the children coming or going, but I must say I enjoy the coming the most."

This time I didn't.

It wasn't just the long hair and beard, but the gaunt, hollow look.

"The thing I feared has come upon me," and what had been hints of rebellion now appeared as open defiance against the values our family held dear. Our fun-loving son had become a stranger.

Moa's and Becky's gentle Asian faces looked at me with tear-filled eyes. One time I saw them kneeling in the guest room, and I knew they were praying not only for Ralph, but also for me.

The joy of the Christmas season—the spice-filled kitchen, the decorations, the fragrant pine trees—brought us all together in the traditional preparations. Even Ralph was drawn into the holiday mood and I was confident that the gathering of family and friends would help bring our son back onto the right road.

The agony and ecstasy of life I pondered long into the night. There was the ecstasy of knowing the true meaning of Christmas, and the unbearable agony of knowing our son had made a detour from the truth, the way, and the life. I finally slept, but fitfully.

60

Unclog the Channel

The frozen lake stretched between the barren trees that glistened with snow in the moonlight, and a chilled, wintry wind cut its biting path down from Canada and over the New England fields. The campus buildings of Gordon College, Wenham, Massachusetts, stood like fortresses against the winter.

Hidden springs kept one part of the lake from freezing solidly, but at the other end, where the students could drive their cars across the ice, they started bonfires for warmth.

Ralph and Rob, Ed and David—four rebel college students—decided to slip away from the others, and they raced across the lake to the far end where they shared a forbidden bottle of brandy. They made their own rules.

In the darkness, not missed by the others, they downed their brandy and felt its warmth burning their throats and stomachs.

Allen, Ralph's college big brother, decided to skate across the lake away from the crowd. A few minutes away would be a welcome reprieve from all the pressures. For Allen, school was soon coming to an end. In a few weeks he would graduate and begin his life's work.

With the abandonment of youth, he moved swiftly into the winter stillness.

Happy voices rang out across the winter wonderland. Boys

tightened the skates of the girls, and they all pulled on warm mittens and fastened brightly knit scarves and toboggan caps. Fleece-lined jackets added color to the winter's whiteness. Songs and laughter floated across the lake and soon there was a symphony of skates in rhythm. Everyone was a part of the skaters' waltz. It was a fairyland night.

It was a night no one would ever forget.

At the far end of the lake, the four rebels, warmed by the brandy, drank in the beauty of a winter moon.

Suddenly Rob saw Allen skating toward the danger zone of the lake. The crackling ice gave way, and a cry broke the stillness. A black hole opened and water flowed over the ice.

With the reflexes of an athlete, Rob was off like a shot, with Ralph, Ed, and Dave in pursuit. Then Rob was on the crackling ice, and he plunged into the inky blackness, too.

"I'll get Rob," screamed Ralph, "and you two get Al." Ralph reached for Rob until he struggled to the safety of a far surface. Ed plunged into the black hole in a desperate effort to get Allen out. "Make a chain," he screamed into the night.

By that time the cries reached the other end of the lake and the skaters moved like the wind, but black water was covering the ice. Panic-stricken, some fled; others yelled, "We're going for help."

The four formed a chain and almost succeeded in pulling Allen onto the hard surface. Ed was still in the hole trying to lift Allen, but the heavy skates, the wet clothing, and the cold water were too much. The fast-moving current snatched Allen from their grip and he was pulled downstream into eternity.

The others screamed for Ed to hang on. Time stood still as they gradually pulled him to the safety of the solid ice.

Numb with cold and shock, tears frozen on their cheeks, the four brushed past the other students and moved their icy legs across the snow to the empty solace of the dormitory. In the warm shower the clothing thawed, but their hearts were gripped by cold despair.

Their housemates' silence seemed to hang over the four rebels with quiet accusation. Later they understood it was their own silent guilt.

Warm and dry, the four found their way to the chapel. There they poured out their anguish in tears of hopelessness.

"My God, at least we tried—we tried. If we hadn't been at that end of the lake no one would have seen him. We tried, oh, God, how we tried—but where were the others? We couldn't save Al, but we tried."

In the quiet of the chapel the four wept out their bitterness and frustration, and a dark night of the soul set in over Al's departure from this life.

Into the black despair came one beam of light. "Allen was a Christian," Ralph commented quietly, "He was my college brother. He really is not dead, but home with the Lord. He was a believer. What if it had been us? Where would we be?"

"Yeah, Ralph, what about us?"

The question hung in the air like a heavy cloud, unanswered, but the seedlings of rebellion kept growing. The memory of Allen's icy hand that had slipped beyond their reach lingered like a nightmare with no waking up.

About 2 A.M. word reached the four rebels: The divers had found Allen's body downstream. Despair engulfed them afresh.

At the memorial service, the light filtered through again, "I am the resurrection, and the life: he that believeth in me . . . shall never die."

Into the black despair came the love and gratitude from Allen's mother: "You risked your lives to save him." They wept together as she held Ed close to her heart.

Her love cushioned the hurt, but the winter of their souls— the darkness of their sin—stayed long in the hearts of the four rebels.

Back in Greensboro, North Carolina, I wondered why there was no mail. It was the silence of a dark winter night in my soul, too.

On a cold January morning, I walked into the college infirmary to turn on the lights and heat before Lena arrived. From the backroads of my memory came the dean's booming voice, "Well, Florence Nightingale, you must be living right. Meet Lena Rogers." That was two years ago. Little had he realized that from the kitchen classroom Lena would be teaching her own brand of philosophy, in addition to preparing trays and making beds. The students loved her, especially her "Lena tea" and cheese sandwiches. I loved her—Lena—a symphony in black.

While the steam radiators clanged and hissed, I reached for the coffee pot. At 6:30 A.M., the world outside was still wrapped in darkness just like me. Outwardly I was the starched infirmary nurse, but inside I was broken from grief over our youngest son who had chosen the rebellion of the sixties instead of an education in a fine Christian college.

I heard Lena coming up the sidewalk, singing into the cold wind,

> *We walk by faith*
> *And not by sight*
> *We move one step at the time.*
> *The Word's a lamp*
> *Thy word's a light*
> *We move one step at the time.*

The door banged open with a, "Praise the Lord, Sister Jensen, we got us a brand new day. The Lord done give it to us and the devil ain't gonna take it away. Glory!" She turned, saw me, and stopped short, "Lord have mercy, child, you look like death!"

"I might as well be dead! No way I can live with this grief. Janice, Daniel, and Ralph were inseparable as children, and now Ralph is wandering in a wilderness of drugs and protests. I can't live without Ralph in the fold."

Lena reached for the broom and hollered, "Out, Satum—out! No devil gonna be in my kitchen. You trying to kill my child, and no way you can win! Out! Out! In the name of Jesus!" She swept with a fury through the open door and announced, "Now that we got rid of the devil, we can hear from God."

She gathered me in her arms and I brushed my face against her black cheek and sobbed, "I might as well be dead." With that, Lena straightened her shoulders and looked into my eyes with those black eyes and said words that turned a light on inside me: "If God had wanted you to die for Ralph, He would have asked you! You standing there telling God Almighty He not done enough for your child? That's what the cross am all about. Jesus died for Ralph. He came that you might have life, that your joy might be full. Now I asks you, where is your joy?"

"But Lena, I want my son saved!"

"Your joy got nothin' to do with what you wants. Your joy am Jesus, child! You got Him, you got peace. You got Him, you got it all! Ralph not your business. He God's business. Now I ask you, did the prodigal son's father call in the FBI or the police? No. He trusted God, and he waited. Now Sister Jensen, you must *unclog the channel.* You get the long hair, bare feet, drugs, and that mess out that channel so you can see God. God's getting tired of hearing how bad the boy looks. He's lookin' in the heart. Now today we get the joy!

"First, I takes authority. Lord, we don't want no phone calls, no sick calls in this here infirmary until we gets the joy business settled. Thank You, Jesus. O Lord, this child don't know how to praise. Forgive her, Lord," She rolled her black eyes heavenward and grabbed me under my arm and started marching me around the infirmary. "We begins to praise the Lord till the joy comes."

I sobbed as we started singing the Doxology and then Lena prodded, "Walk, child, walk! March, keep marching. The devil don't like marching—ever since those Jericho walls came tumbling down. We got some walls to march around. Now sing, 'Power in the Blood,' and pat your hands. Satum hates that clappin'. Keep walking child. Hold your head up. You is a child of the King. Thank God for everything—that your child is in God's hands."

When I finally sat down to rest, she picked up the worn Bible and read back to me the promises I had marked for her. She pulled up a chair beside me and sang, "Oh, how I love Jesus." We harmonized together as the tears rolled and hearts were raised in worship. We sang softly, "Holy, holy, holy, Lord God Almighty—all Thy works shall praise Thy name."

"Take off your shoes. We are standing on holy ground." Quietly we slipped off our shoes and fell to our knees singing,

"His name is Wonderful." "For Thou alone art worthy." We bowed in humble adoration.

"Don't see the problem—just see Jesus," she prodded. "Let the joy of the Lord be your strength. Thank You, Jesus, for searching for our lamb," she sobbed. "He done lost his way, but You can find him." Then, "Up, up, Sister Jensen. We now offer the sacrifice of praise!"

We had started with a sobbing Doxology, and two hours later we ended with a victorious "Praise the Lord." Rejoicing, I wrote in my diary, "I won't be any happier the day Ralph comes home than I am today receiving the answer in my spirit, by faith."

Lena looked out across the busy campus and stretched her arms to heaven. "Thank You, Jesus. We done birthed a child in the Spirit."

Not until the close of Lena's prayer did the phone ring and the doors bang. The coffee pot stayed warm.

61

His Eye Is on the Sparrow

The cracking of the woodcutter's ax mingled with the wind blowing through the Massachusetts winter forest made Ralph's arms ache endlessly. He was alternating between hot and cold, and he shivered in the wind. He knew he was sick, but he forced his arms and legs to move with the ax.

While his body moved in automatic rhythm, his mind was free to remember. Blurred images from the past floated before his burning eyes. He swung at the logs, for it was forgetting he needed, not remembering. But the memory insisted.

He had convinced his childhood friend, Billy Welker, to join him in Massachusetts. Through the years they had made similar choices. They knew their mothers prayed, and secretly they were thankful. Perhaps one day they would come back, but gradually the tide of the times was pulling them out to sea.

Ralph thought ruefully, *Yeah, Billy got to go to East Carolina University, but I had to go to a Christian college. They called me "cornbread and grits" . . . well, I showed them, those Yankees, that's not all a Southern boy is . . . but what I wouldn't give for some country ham and grits right now.*

His stomach was empty. He showed those Yankees—huh—

fell right in with all the protests and antiwar sentiment. He sure was glad nothing had happened to his brother, Dan, in Vietnam. Dan was too good to die. It was different with him, though; he had already died to ambition and self-worth. He was part of that so-called enlightenment his friends talked about. He was "enlightened" all right! His eyes were opened to a world of nightmare and fantasy. The things that were looked unreal. The unreal became the norm.

He had always wanted a girl like his sister, Jan, warm and fun-loving, and a good Christian. But he'd only found her opposite. How was he to know those limpid eyes and that warm mouth in a hazy dream world would lead to mere sensual warmth?

He thought about the TV commercial, "Bet you can't eat just one." That's how it was, one more drink, one high, another hazy dream world of soft nights. He felt as though he had been on skis—faster and faster down the snowy slopes, wild with excitement, biting wind. Faster—faster—and then his clenched fist pounded into the tree. In fury he thrust his ax into another log.

He was finished! Expelled from school, and he couldn't go home in defeat. He needed a job—and then what?

Maybe the cook at the college would give him something to eat and maybe he could sneak into the dorm. At least it would be warm. He was so tired, and his throat hurt. *Strep throat, probably.*

He remembered the night after he'd left school, when the gang had talked about home, and someone had asked, "Ralph, why do you stay here?"

"I don't know. That's just it—I don't know where I belong." Then he remembered why he couldn't go home. He had seen those horrible demons coming at him, and the devil laughing at him. "No hope for you. Too late . . . too late. You can never go home again!" Somehow he believed it. There were no more girls like Jan—they were all treacherous, like quicksand. There would be no more picnics or talks around the table. He didn't know what he wanted to do—maybe wander around the world and take his happiness where he found it.

Wish Mom were here to do something for this throat—a bowl

of chicken noodle soup, cocoa with marshmallows. Sure do miss Jo Jo, the beagle—but they'll get used to being without me.

How he detested those long letters from Mom—endless sermons on challenges, potential, and wasting one's life. She should know—but, then again, he did hate to hurt her. Dad was never there when he needed him—always on the road. Besides, he bragged about Jan and Dan and had everyone "pray for Ralph."

He was remembering the time Billy Walker and he got picked up in Greensboro and the policeman gave a warning, "If I were you, I wouldn't hurt your father, Ralph; he does so much good." *How come he didn't have time for me?* he wondered, but then again he remembered how Dad prayed for him at college and was so proud of him. "We'll make up for lost time, son, and have some great times together."

Jan, married to a good, all-right guy—one terrific sister, that gal. Then Dan—always doing the right thing, yet, he made me feel like a dumb kid. And Mom, good grief, she idolized Dan—and only prayed for me. Heck, who wants to be prayed for? I'd rather be loved. I really didn't want to hurt anyone, but it's too late now. They all will have the farm and all their dreams. Who wants me?

That darn throat! I'm so cold and hungry. Why do I always think of Mom when I'm cold and hungry? Why does she write such long letters? Oh, well—I told her to send the weather report.

I wonder what Dad would say if he knew how Billy and I used to play poker in the balcony during church services.

He chuckled to himself, but then darkness engulfed him. The misty panorama of the past swam into focus and his two years of college played before him like a horror movie.

Deep insecurity and low self-esteem had smoldered into defiance at being pressured into attending a Christian school. The only Southern boy in the northern school, along with being labeled "grits and cornbread," he was also called a "barefooted moonshiner."

So he determined to play out the whole Southern-boy role. Turning on the charm, he sought out and influenced other rebellious students, and they formed the YAC Club—Young

341

Americans for the Confederacy. Eventually these New England "rebels" joined the rebel yell of the Confederates.

There was that day at Gordon when they tore down the American flag and raised the flag of the Confederacy. Another day, Ralph found himself among hundreds of protestors at the Boston Commons, waiting to hear the liberal political platforms of the Boston Moratorium speakers. But disillusionment reigned. Even the rebellious hippies, resenting the attacks against their homeland, booed the speakers. In those days the United States was experiencing a lot of conflict and confusion—both internally and externally.

Ralph was confused, too. He felt rage against deserters fleeing to Canada and Sweden, but at the same time, he resented the war. Groping for reasons for his anger, he experienced the lingering pain of injustices—the Greensboro sit-in, the Kent State tragedy, and the antiwar hysteria.

From the midst of this confusion the drug culture emerged, promising a temporary escape from life's harsh realities. Experimenting with drugs dulled the pain.

Branded a racist and a rebel, Ralph justified his actions by judging certain things. He saw cruelty being expressed by some of the black students through a deliberate blow to the eye of a football player or an unnecessarily cracked skull.

One night he was walking with a girl on the edge of the campus, and they were approached by a group of blacks. One of the blacks made an obscene remark to the girl. She was horrified, and in a burst of fury, Ralph clenched his fists and attacked the leader. Fortunately, the others pulled them apart.

Later, when a black girl angrily railed at the black male students for making advances toward white girls rather than black ones, Ralph loudly applauded on the sidelines.

During this time, concerned school officials were seriously attempting to establish campus unity, and several black students from foreign countries had blended into college life. These students demonstrated a deep dedication to the Lord and a significant purpose for living. Their mutual acceptance was evident.

But when Gordon College opened its doors to inner-city

Spanish and black students, the YAC Club continually tried to disrupt peaceful relationships. Harassment and intimidation became popular weapons.

Ralph had started out by playing his part, but soon his deep, genuine resentment surfaced. On one particular Homecoming Day, one of the parade floats portrayed two huge clasped hands, one black, the other white. The theme was "Unity." The explosive rebellion deep within Ralph screamed, "Never!" And in his rage, he set fire to the float. His action incited other rebels; a riot began and a number of the other floats also were set afire.

The floats were artificial, made of paper—but the anger was alarmingly real. Tensions began mounting over other issues, and it was inevitable that Ralph would be expelled.

Chuckling to himself again, he relived one winter night when the brazen rebels defied even the weather. Dressed only in combat boots and underwear shorts, they marched around the campus, and, encouraged by the cheers from the girls' dormitory, dove into three feet of snow.

Ironically, by the time he reached his last semester, he had a thirst for knowledge and a longing to return to serious study—but it was too late. He had exceeded the school's grace and mercy. Payday had arrived.

Some of the inner-city students who were on cocaine also were expelled from school. (Rebellion knows no color. The heart of every man is deceitful.)

Nothing seemed to erase Ralph's deep loneliness, nor the haunting memories, which kept coming like recurring nightmares. *Maybe it was all wrong*, he thought now, *but everyone told me, "Do your own thing—be free."*

The past continued to parade by him with its aura of bitterness and anger. He felt that every segment of society was to blame—home, church, and school.

But now, he had broken away from society's restraints of discipline. Now he was finally free to sail his own ship. Yes, he was the captain of his own fate.

Nuts. It's getting dark and I can't chop any more wood, and, gosh, I hurt all over. What a rotten world! It's supper time at home, and I'll bet Mom has meatballs and mashed potatoes and maybe my favorite cherry pie. Oh, well, they probably don't think about me, except at that stupid prayer meeting at the Masons'. I can hear Dorothy now, "We must all remember to pray for Ralph." Well, let them pray! It won't do any good. But I sure am hungry—and it's so cold.

The woods seemed dark and lonely as Ralph picked up the ax for the final blow. Suddenly across the trees the wind brought a song. He could hear Ethel Waters singing, "His eye is on the sparrow and I know He watches me." He could remember the whole verse.

That's the record Mom played over and over at home! For a moment he was afraid—the wind, the evening darkness, the cold and hot flashes, and that insistent aching.

He stood still in the shadows and the wind carried the song again:

His eye is on the sparrow
And I know He watches me.

"Okay, okay!" he screamed into the wind, "God, if You really watch over me, then give me a ride to Gordon College—and a job!"

In desperation he picked up his ax and went out to the road to thumb a ride to Wenham.

Half-mocking, half-afraid, he waited.

A black Cadillac pulled up and a woman's voice called out, "Need a ride, young man? I'm going to Wenham." In a daze, Ralph got into the car with a "Thank you, ma'am." (They always laughed at his Southern "sir" and "ma'am.") Well, let them laugh—he *was* a Southerner.

They rode in silence until the driver said, "Young man, I'm in need of a man to work on my estate. Are you interested in a job? I'll have a big breakfast waiting for you. Agreed? 8 A.M. it will be!"

Late that night the phone rang at 103 Bethel Spring Dale in Greensboro. "Hello, Mom, it's Ralph. I have a job tomorrow,

344

but I have a bad sore throat. Would you—?" After a pause, I answered, "Of course, Ralph, I'll pray for you."

Unknown to Ralph, miles away, two hands were clasped in prayer— one was white, the other was black.

62

"Rise Up and Walk!"

My dear Ralph,

Praise the Lord! Praise the Lord! We got the property—sixty-six acres for $2,000 down and the rest paid in ten years at 8 percent interest. We all claimed Philippians 4:19, "My God shall supply all your need," and 2 Chronicles 20:20, "Believe in the LORD your God, so shall ye be established." Every step we took has been by the Word of God—even the description of the land.

God will do the same for you, Ralph. He will instruct and teach you. You can get land. All you have to do is trust Him and obey Him.

Read Isaiah 43:25-26. "I, even I, am he that blotteth out thy transgressions for mine own sake, and will not remember thy sins. Put me in remembrance: let us plead together: declare thou, that thou mayest be justified."

Jan sent Dan a book, *Farming in the Bible*. Evelio Perez, our dear friend from Mexico, says the Bible contains wisdom and knowledge for every vocation. All through the Old Testament, God told them and taught them. God taught Noah how to build the ark and made Abraham the greatest farmer and cattleman. He made Solomon the wisest king, Joshua the greatest soldier, Moses the greatest judge, and on and on!

So we have made a covenant with God to follow His way and go by His Word, and have dedicated that sixty-six acres to God and His purpose.

There is one thing I'd like to share with you, and I have told no one else—just you.

All Dad's life he has longed for a little farm, dreamed about it, and talked about it. He finally got enough for a down payment. Like a dream come true. Well, we have been reading the Bible more and listening to tapes.

God starts with the impossible—not the possible. He starts with zero and makes something. God also has us do something. Remember when Jesus asked the fishermen to "lend Me your boat"? Well, God always asks us to do something—like chess. God moves, we move, step by step. So the disciples gave the boat to Jesus—all they possessed.

Remember when Jesus said, "Launch out into the deep," and the disciples filled two boats? You can't outgive God.

Well, back to Daddy. His biggest dream was a farm. So now he had $2,000. (I had put $100 down to hold the land.) He gave it all to Jesus—*all he had*—and said, "This is a down payment for the farm and it shall be called Shalom Valley Farm (means Valley of Peace). The title shall be in Dan's and our name as a family farm enterprise."

I am going to work double-duty to buy a truck. That's my boat for Jesus' glory.

Now, Ralph, you have a choice to make, a move in this game of chess. Move to obey, and give God your will.

We are going to Wild Life (game preserve) tonight for a picnic to celebrate, and then to the farm to start a garden. We're looking for a tractor.

Uncle Gordon called from Brooklyn, New York, and was thrilled about the farm. He's coming to North Carolina. I'm going shopping with Auntie Do.

Believe and you shall receive!

Love,
Mother

Ralph threw the letter in the air with a whoop and hollered for Rob, Kevin, and Billy to get a load of this news—and the weather report: High, seventy degrees; low, sixty degrees. "That's North Carolina for you," he added gleefully.

"Man, oh, man—a farm! They got the farm! When I was a little kid in kindergarten I drew pictures of horses and farms all the time. I always wanted land. Wow! Sixty-six acres! Wow, you guys, there's room for all of us! This I gotta see! Hey, Billy, why don't we hitch a ride to North Carolina?"

The pull from another direction was too great, though, and the question hung in the air like a cloud. Ralph, Rob, Kevin, and Billy were linked together as a family—all out of school.

At times they got together and discussed theology and mockingly reminded each other how they had Sunday school pins for perfect attendance and Bibles as prizes for memorizing Scripture.

"Maybe we ought to be preachers. We know more about sin, the devil, and hell than most preachers." Then a deep depression engulfed them and the mocking laughter died. They all had been to hell and back. For a moment they seemed to grasp a light—the farm. Then the demonic world of drugs told them they could never go home again. From the cliffs of hope to the valley of despair, their tortured minds wandered in a dry place.

It was cold and rainy the day another letter came from home.

Dear Ralph,

High today, eighty degrees and a low of sixty degrees.

Love,
Mother

The mocking demons laughed, "Even your mother will forget you. You're all alone, so why don't you marry that little Russian girl? At least you'll belong to someone."

Late one night, Ralph confided to Billy, "Well, somebody ought to help Lee. Her family is all split up and her brother is a Communist. She doesn't even believe in God. I bet I could

help her. My mom would take her in. The guys treat her like
dirt, but Mom would help her."

"What makes you think she wants to change? We aren't
changing, are we?"

The darkness came over him again. He had to be alone.

The Atlantic washed up with a constant roar over the rocks
off Magnolia's shoreline. Ralph climbed from rock to rock,
watching the water splash. Boats and fishermen were out to
sea. There was always the pull of the ocean, the dreams that
went beyond the horizon. Then memories came with marching
feet, hammering blows on his head—never-ending memories,
sometimes a blur, sometimes so real that the present was lost
and the past regained. Screaming into the wind, he cried to
forget, and then he was afraid he would forget.

From his back pocket, Ralph drew out another letter, one
he particularly had tried to forget.

My dear Ralph,

Rise up and walk—back to your father's house. Everything you ever longed for is back where you left it. Your
work, God's plan for your life, a girl like your sister, Janice.

[O, Lord, how he longed for a girl like Jan—but where
were they?]

Even a son—the one you always longed for—a son with
your name.

Come back to the road where you made the detour.
Come home to your father's house and begin again.

Ralph, in the name of Jesus, rise up and walk—back to
your father's house.

We love you,
Mother

The haunting began again—*home? Begin again? Work?
What can I do?* One of the verses he had memorized came again,
"I will instruct thee and teach thee in the way which thou shalt
go. I will guide thee with mine eye."

Yeah, but I want to do it my way. But where am I going?

A girl like Jan? He sat down and buried his head in his hands while the spray washed over the rocks. The ocean rolled on and on. Such beautiful girls who gave so freely what his sister and others like her guarded jealously for the one man they married. How could he ever deserve a girl like Jan? Besides, he had never met one like her. Jan and Jud were happy and secure. *That's it! That's what I want in a girl, that feeling of a secure love, one to trust and respect. If I could just know she would love me . . . Wow! I've sure been looking in the wrong places—yet some of these girls came from strict Christian homes. Something's wrong someplace!*

Memories washed over his weary mind with haunting scenes of home.

He could see the scrub pine and the trail that he and Dan had cleared at Easter. They hadn't even owned the land, but Lena had said, "Go out there and claim it, in Jesus' name." They did!

Everyone was there—even Jan and baby Heather. Dan cleared a path with the machete and yelled, "Go out there, Moses, and lead the children across the Red Sea." Ralph remembered the big stick he found, and how with baby Heather pulling his beard, he led the way down the path. Mom and Doris and the rest followed singing Lena's song:

> *Go out there, Dan*
> *Possess the land*
> *You move one step at the time*
> *We walk by faith*
> *And not by sight*
> *We move one step at the time.*

Lena called the trail "the Glory Road" and Highway 220 "the Hallelujah Boulevard." It was April and Easter and he felt like he belonged—and then he decided to go back to Massachusetts to tell his friends. The dream soon became hazy and he was drifting again with his friends in a never-never land.

Then May had come and he had decided to hitch a ride to North Carolina to surprise Mom on Mother's Day. He did! He

350

could see them all around the table—Aunt Doris, Uncle Dave, and the cousins—all dressed from church. Mom was serving dinner and when she turned around, there he was!

He remembered telling Billy later, "Wow, you should have seen her face. I guess I looked bad—Ralph, the hippie—with all my dressed-up cousins. Mom hugged me when I gave her the Mother's Day card, and I said, 'You didn't think I'd forget you on Mother's Day?' She just cried and hugged me and sat me down in her place at the table . . . and what a dinner! I wanted to see the farm one more time."

> *Go out there, Dan*
> *Possess the land*
> *You move one step at the time*
> *We walk by faith*
> *And not by sight*
> *We move one step at the time.*

It was getting dark and time to get back to the gang. He looked out again across the ocean, then rose and moved slowly across the rocks while the spray still blew in the wind. He touched the letter in his pocket. For a moment the wind swept the fog from his mind and he saw home, the farm, and his street, Bethel Spring Dale. From across the miles he heard her—that voice kept coming closer. "Ralph Jensen, in the name of Jesus, rise up and walk, rise up and walk. Come back to your father's house. Rise up and walk. Rise up and walk."

He looked around. He was all alone—alone with the wind and the roll of the ocean. But he heard her, he knew he heard her! The voice followed him. "Rise up and walk, back to the Father's house."

63

Time to Choose

My dear Ralph,

Uncle Jack is coming August the first and Auntie Do rented a place at the beach August 8 to 16—so we can all take turns. Uncle Jack loves the ocean. We go to Atlantic Beach at Morehead City August 23 to 31.

Dan and Dad posted the land, checked state roads, and put up signs. The order is in at Duke Power for a big light pole. Today they swing a blade clearing around the apple tree so Doris and I can pick apples.

Sunday, we visited the neighbors and sat on their porch and looked clear across Hanging Rock—absolutely terrific!

The old man looked like Grandpa Jensen and talked about his wife, who died in 1967.

"We had forty-nine years," he told us. "Started out in the holler in a log cabin. Law, but she was purty, and smart, too! I grieved. Then one night the Lord let me see her—right thar, laying in the bed beside me—so purty and smiling. I just reached over to kiss her and she looked at me, and she was done gone! But, oh Lord, she looked so happy and purty. Guess the Lord let me see her so I wouldn't grieve no more."

He wiped his eyes and said, "Gonna be nice to have folks in the valley. Used to have a path for a horse to ride. The last folks were evil, drinkin' folks—got killed in that holler. I'd check that well, no telling who or what be in that well. Mighty good to have Christian folks. Gits so lonesome, just the birds, the pines in the wind. But I don't mind, cause I know she's happy. The Lord done showed me, cause I grieved so much. So purty!"

By that time I was grieving and just wanted to hug the grandpa. I said, "First chance we get, we'll have you come for supper." Boy, he lit up then.

Then we got scared, thinking of all the demons of violence down in our beautiful valley.

Duane [my nephew] said, "We'll just go down there and shout, 'Praise the Lord' and chase all the haunting spirits out. Then the whole community will see the change when Jesus moves in and the devil's crowd moves out." He is terrific, that kid!

Dan met another terrific neighbor—coming over to offer advice. There's another hundred acres joining Dan's side and Auntie Do is heading out to see the man today. We are also checking on some adjoining the other side.

Whew! There is so much to do, but gradually we'll get at it. I guess we'll end up with a prayer meeting in the valley.

God bless you—but *write*, you stinker!

>   We love you,
>   Mom

Ralph took the letter and decided to go for a hike. There were eleven boys living in a mansion surrounded by stone fences, rolling fields, and gardens, but he needed to be alone. Why couldn't he just pull out and leave? No, he had bills to pay and these were his friends. At least he had work now and maybe he could make it and then go home—just to visit. He had to prove he could do it on his own. He had wrecked the car Dad had given him and now he was fixing up an old van. He pulled out another letter. *Wonder why I save all Mom's letters? Oh, well!*

353

Dear Ralph,

Please drop your grandparents a note. They just re-turned from Norway. Grandpa is eighty-two. I called them last night and they are so happy. They had walked to the shopping center and had ice cream. They said they love it there, but want to come to North Carolina. "Count us in," said mother.

Uncle Jack and Dan left for Morehead and then will go to Wrightsville Beach in Wilmington on Sunday. Jan and Heather come Saturday, Jud comes August 15. Jud's parents come the 23rd of August.

Hope you can make it then.

Love you! Rite!!
Mom

Man, oh, man, I sure would like to see Heather, such a cute baby! Wish I had some money so the guys could have a big fish supper tonight. Everyone was broke. The little money they made seemed to go for gas and repairs on old cars. He had bills up to his ears. What he wouldn't give to be free—really free—to go home and be on that farm and build a house and ride a horse. *Wouldn't you know, Dad bought Dan a horse. Dan gets every-thing! He even bought him a car.*

He kept walking and talking to the wind and the haunting reminder came: how Dad had bought him a car and how Mom had been furious! Dad had even given him a heavy leather, fur-lined jacket. Mom hadn't been too happy about that either—thought he should work for some things. Well, he always did work, but the money went faster than he could make it. It really was a rotten world.

How come Jan and Dan were so good and he had to be the black sheep of the family? He felt as though chains held him in a world he didn't want to stay in. Was there no way out? *A bunch of guys in a big house! So what? That's not really a family. I want my own place, a wife, and kids. If only I could break free and do what I know is right.*

354

He stuffed the letters in his pocket. Those letters! Everyone read them—no secrets in this place! It was late and time to get supper—beans, maybe.

"Hey, Ralph," Billy yelled. "Just got back from the post office. Another sermon from your mom. Come on, you guys, Ralph's mom just sent another letter. Let's see what she says this time!"

Dear Ralph,

I had a strong impression to send you $25. Get some good fish for all the gang. Just thought you might be hungry.

I love you,
Mother

"Wow, let's go! No beans tonight! Hey, Ralph, what's the other letter?"

"She sent a letter inside and said not to open it until I'm alone—so I guess we eat first!"

Within minutes frying pans were ready and the vegetables were peeled, and the boys waited for Ralph to return with the fish for supper. There was enough money for ice cream and cookies later. The coffee pot was perking on the stove. "Wonder what Ralph's mom wrote in that letter?" Billy mused. He, too, was haunted by letters from his mom.

It was late! Everyone had eaten and some had drifted off to their old habits that seemed unbreakable. Ralph sat alone in his room. He didn't want to read another letter, yet Mom had sent the money for them. He knew she didn't have it. Reluctantly he opened the sealed envelope.

My dear Ralph,

Something strange happened to me while driving my car to work. I heard (not audibly) a silky voice—subtle and

355

silky—say, "Give Ralph up. Let him go. Let him go. Let him go."

You don't know how many times I have become so weary and sick, watching you throw your life away in sin, that I have almost said, "I'm through. Ralph can go." No one had such love, prayer, and concern from the entire family and still refused to obey God.

I could see the devil laughing, "Give Ralph up—let him go. I want him because he can lead many my way."

Suddenly I could feel the Holy Spirit inside me making intercession with groaning that cannot be uttered or understood. I could feel the prayer go up through me to God.

Then I could sense an interpretation to what I was praying and I cried out, "In the name of Jesus, Ralph, rise up and walk. Walk in obedience to God's way and God will do His mighty acts." That is the same prayer I wrote before. God *is* speaking to you.

This morning the Lord showed me many things again when I determined to obey. This time I will fast and pray until you come through.

My fasting for you can only do certain things. Prayer releases power to fight the enemy in this spiritual warfare, and to break the bonds of wickedness (Satan's hold on your affairs and thinking).

Isaiah 58: Fasting 1. breaks the bonds of wickedness; 2. looses the bands of the yoke (undoes the ties that keep the yoke on you).

Ralph, follow me closely. *You must break* the enslaving yoke. I can't do that. God can't do it. That enslaving yoke is *your will.* It hooks you to the world, that identity with the world. That is the shackle Satan uses to keep you yoked to him—*your will!* Jesus says, "Take My yoke and learn of Me." Jesus asks you—does not force you. Satan forces.

The key is "learn of Me." The reason you are in such conflict is that you have not broken the yoke that still enslaves you to Satan's identification.

I, too, am learning. I am learning, "Not by might, nor

by power, but by My Spirit!" I am learning to die to desires (for creative writing??? for doing the things most women do—out to lunch and shopping and fun things). Every spare moment I'm in the Word—to keep an open heart to listen, to fast, pray, and walk alone that I might move in the Spirit, to lift you up before the throne, and to open my heart to you, to write (Mom's epistles), and share.

I get weary, Ralph, and sometimes feel the time is wasted. Lena keeps reminding me, "You done birthed him in the Spirit, and he be coming out of that dark world into glorious light, and he'll be naked, hungry, and yelling!"

That was last January and now it is August. Ralph, you are so loved. I love you so much, Ralph, and miss you. You have that certain something no one else in the family has.

Duane got a beautiful puppy and came to show us and he was so excited he could scarcely talk. Everyone was too busy to pay attention and later someone said, "If Ralph had been here, he'd know how it feels to get something you've always wanted."

I turned to Doris and said, "Ralph has a feel for life. He responds to living things—a certain reverence for beauty. Oh, Do, I miss him."

Your aunt Doris is my prayer partner, with Lena. The Bible says, two or three. . . . We aren't taking any chances. We are three!

Love,
Mother

P.S. I hope you all had a good dinner. I love all the boys in your house, and pray for them.

Mom

Ralph took off to his place of retreat—the rocky coast, where the ocean's roar mingles with the sound of the sea gulls. Night was coming on, but he sat, high on the rocks, looking out over the dark waters. Tormented by regret, filled with fear, haunted by a demonic world of fantasy, he longed for home and righteousness. He wanted the best of both worlds; sooner or later he would have to choose. That yoke! He was strangled, chained, and held in torment. *How did Mom know? Does she really hear from God?* His thoughts ran together. He wanted to run, but where?

Then it came again, across the wind, "Rise up and walk, back to your father's house. Everything you ever longed for is right back where you left it. Rise up and walk! Rise up and walk!"

Later, much later, he reached for the telephone. This time he dialed 299-2784. He heard it ringing.

Back in Greensboro, I missed Lena during the summer months when the college infirmary was closed. I missed the cup of coffee and the crust of bread, but most of all I missed her singing and constant reminder, "Don't you be letting no coonching spirits of doubt and unbelief come in this kitchen."

With my open Bible before me I sat in my own kitchen watching the ducks and geese glide in formation across the quiet lake. Coffee cup in hand, I nibbled on my crust of bread and remembered the phone call to Lena the night before.

"Oh, Lena, it's been so long, but I know the answer is coming. I sense a great spiritual warfare. Besides, I miss you."

"You talks about a battle, child. I be in one where I work this summer. I'm in a house with sickness and rebellious children, and I just pray and sing all day. I know Jesus is right with me to help that family.

"Sister Jensen, it seems to be that God's children be the ones to take care of the devil's crowd."

"It's been a long, hard summer, Lena, and after weeks of nursing my friend Lydia, she died quietly in my arms. I kept my promise to her, that I would take care of her at home. I stayed and helped the family with all the arrangements.

"Janice and Heather are coming and we are all making plans to go to Morehead City for a good vacation of fishing and swimming. And we've been very busy on the farm. It seems that all the pressures come at once. During all this, we were fasting and praying and still no answer!

"Don't worry, I'm not giving up. 'Unclog the channel! Keep believing and you'll be seeing.' I'm getting to sound more like you every day, Lena. Okay, we agree together: In the name of Jesus, Ralph, rise up and walk."

I poured another cup of coffee and thanked God for a new day. And decided that, as Lena would say, "No devil gonna take it from me." I turned to face the day the Lord had made.

Dan and Harold had gone to the airport to meet Janice and Heather.

Before I knew it, the car pulled into the driveway and the sounds of a home filled the house. Heather, ten months old, held us all her willing captives. Dan and Jan talked about the beach and Harold dragged out old suitcases.

The round kitchen table found us all talking about Ralph. Heather banged her spoon on the new high chair and laughed her approval. *How Ralph used to love this*, I thought. *Everyone around the table, laughing and talking.*

"Enough talk, Dan, let's get this fishing gear together. You and Jan can talk all the way to the beach." Harold urged us on and the packing began in earnest. The hours flew. Before we knew it we were ready to leave. Harold was heading out to the car.

That's when the phone rang! I answered, and a familiar voice from across the miles said, "Mama, I want to come home!"

64

The Purple Van

Harold sat on the porch, waiting. Jan wrapped her arms around her father, "I'm sorry, Daddy. He should have been here by now. Maybe the pull was too great once he got the money you sent him."

"He'll come!"

"Dad, why don't you come fishing with us? Help pass the time."

"Thanks, Dan, but I'll wait right here. I can watch the cars come over the bridge."

"But Dad, you've been sitting there for three days."

"He'll come! I know he'll come!"

The spacious summer home looked over the ocean. Dan, Jud, and his father, Robert Carlberg, headed for the boat, fishing gear in hand. Jan was getting ready for a swim. Helen Carlberg, Jud's mother, was in the kitchen serving French toast for breakfast. It was a beautiful day!

In my mind, I could hear Lena's voice, "God give us a brand new day, and no devil going to take it away. Don't let those coonching spirits of doubt and unbelief come sneaking in."

Ralph's room was ready, new sheets were on the bed, and a gentle breeze was blowing through the soft curtains.

I felt the agony and ecstasy raging within me—a battle between doubt and hope.

Harold sat on the porch remembering the phone call of a few days ago: "Mama, I want to come home." He had been packing the car when I called to him, "It's Ralph." Then Harold heard the same words I had heard: "Daddy, I want to come home!"

"Ralph, I want you home more than anything else. We are leaving for Morehead, with all the fishing gear, so meet us at Charlie's place. You'll probably catch all the big ones."

"Dad, I can't come home. I'm broke."

"How much do you need? I'll send money special delivery. Just take care of your bills and head for Morehead."

"I'll pay you back, Dad—and thanks."

"Don't even think of any payback! God bless you, Ralph, and have a safe trip. Remember, we love you."

At Morehead, Harold decided not to go fishing. Instead he sat on the porch. "He'll come, I know he'll come, and I'll be right here, waiting."

The cars moved slowly over the bridge and with them relentlessly rolled the memories of the irreparable past. I had read somewhere that God is the God of our yesterdays. He allows us the memory of them so we can turn the past into a ministry for the future.

How often we had wondered what we could or should have done differently. Who was to blame? The family? The church? Society?

We shared the past: the struggle to obtain an education; the call to the pastoral ministry; the idealistic devotion to evangelical causes; the love for home and family; and, above all, our dedication to Christ.

Our children had always been a part of our lives, in work or recreation. They had always been with us—trips, picnics, mountains, beaches. Why would one stray so far from us?

I wondered how much effect one nightmarish experience could have on a young child. Was Harold remembering also? It was a long time ago.

Ralph was two years old when Harold had gone into a rural

area with passionate abandon to obey God and pastor the rich and poor, black and white.

But cultural misunderstanding, ignorance, and fear of change brought battle-line hostilities. The way of tradition seemed to war against the grace of God to change people's hearts. Harold chose to leave quietly rather than allow the ministry to be a battlefield. Four-year-old Ralph chose to smash his tiny clenched fist into the face of a man who had cursed his father.

"That's not the way we do it, Ralph," Harold had said. Jan and Dan were older and understood. *Could the seed of rebellion have found fertile soil in this one so young?* I wondered.

Harold later chose to travel in church promotional work, so he was on the road much of the time during Ralph's teen years. Jan married and Dan went away to school. I was working as a nurse. The unique closeness we enjoyed with our young children was now divided into special times, like holidays and vacations. Perhaps the youngest felt the changing times more than the rest of us did. I wondered. Yet, I also knew that into each heart is given the measure of faith to believe—and the free will to choose. We all learn from the past, and no situation is perfect. We have a sovereign God who is able to do more than we can ask or think. Lena would say, "This be a trusting time."

Somehow I knew that rejection, bitterness, and unforgiveness had to be dealt with—even in the very young. My prayer was that our family would allow God's love to flow through us in the days to come.

I read in my journal, "One of the greatest strains in life is waiting for God." I also wondered how often we break the heart of God while He waits for us. Finally, I knew Ralph would come. And Harold would be waiting, watching the cars move over the bridge.

Then he saw it!

A purple van moved slowly in the traffic and pulled into the driveway of the beach house. Within seconds, Harold gathered his youngest son in his arms, and then we were all hugging him at once.

The haunted eyes looked through us. Immediately, I recognized the unhealthy yellow pallor of his skin. Like a tortured prisoner, he had managed to escape. I knew the real journey home had just begun. Fleeting words ran across my mind—*I have miles to go before I sleep.* "Oh, Lena, Lena," I cried to myself, "I thought the battle was over, but it is just beginning. God help us!"

Outwardly I talked about swimming and fishing and suggested that we all have breakfast first. After a good sleep, he could tell us about his trip.

"Helen, here we are, and here is Ralph." Turning from the stove, Jud's mother covered the horror in her eyes with her quiet dignity. The tall young man was not the Ralph she remembered, but she said gently, "Ralph, how nice to see you. Please sit down, and here is some French toast."

Ralph ate hungrily. Heather climbed on his lap to pull his beard and then settled herself there. She had a friend.

After a warm shower, he fell exhausted into a clean bed. I pulled the sheet to tuck him in, and I kissed my youngest son good night. He was asleep.

We cleaned the van and took the soiled clothes to the laundry. When he awoke from several hours of refreshing sleep, he had clean clothes—and an appointment at the barber shop.

The following days were filled with sunshine, swimming, fishing, and eating. Refreshing sleep, good food, and relaxing hours with the family brought a measure of healing to his weary mind and body.

Too soon it was time for us to leave the beach house. Lena and I had to open the infirmary for a new school year. Jan and Jud had to return to Michigan State University. Dr. and Mrs. Carlberg were returning to their ministry, Brooklyn Baptist Temple. Everyone was leaving at a different time. Ralph was to follow us home in his van.

A few days later Lena and I were back in the kitchen to dedicate another school year to the Lord. Ralph, too, came to sit at the table for a cup of coffee and a crust of bread.

"Lord have mercy, child, Lena need to be cooking you some pinto beans and cornbread. I just stomps on them coonching spirits that want to send you back to that 'Chusetts place. What those folks know about feeding a Southern boy? What they know about big fat biscuits with country ham, red-eye gravy, and grits? They never heard tell of pot licker and chittling bread. You right where you belong—where we be putting some meat on your bones. That Satum don't give up easy, but I told that devil to go."

"Lena, you won't believe what happened to me when I left the guys in Massachusetts. My friend, Billy Walker, came home to Greensboro, and I guess I'll be seeing him. We've been friends since second grade. My friends in Massachusetts couldn't believe I was leaving, and neither could I. I still don't know how I got here. Anyhow, Dad sent the money and I paid up my bills—school and car repairs—and then gave a guy a ride to Virginia Beach. That was okay, because I had someone to talk to. When I was alone though, it was like an army of demons in my van, telling me to go back. Sometimes I thought I would lose my mind, and I forgot where I was. My van wanted to turn around, almost like someone else driving it. It was hell, Lena, really hell. I had to scream out loud to shut out the voices telling me to turn around."

"Oh, child, that be when your mama and I be praying, 'Lord Jesus, send the angels to bring that boy home.'"

"When I got to Morehead, Lena, you'll never guess what happened! Two guys in front of my van, right on the street, were flipped out on drugs and having a bad trip. I got out of my van to help them and talk them down. By that time I couldn't even remember where Charlie's big house was. I fell asleep in the van, and when the police woke me up I was right across the highway from Charlie's . . . where Dad told me to come. It was all so weird. When I pulled up in the driveway, there was Dad. He had been sitting on the porch three days—and wouldn't leave. All the time the devil was telling me he didn't care."

"He did more than wait, child. He prayed. That be how that van couldn't turn around. The angels be having a big war with the devil's crowd. God won! Glory to Jesus! Hallelujah! Praise the Lord!"

"Lena, you should have seen me in that barber shop in Morehead. I had an audience, inside and outside. The barber was so mad he cussed me the whole time he cut my hair. He even broke his clippers!

"I figured I had hurt Mom enough and decided to get that long hair off. But I wouldn't let that barber touch my beard. I still belong to my family in Massachusetts—I think."

"God be looking on the heart, child, and one day you be set free. It's the heart needs changing, not the hair—but I must say you looks good with the long hair off."

Ralph came and went, quietly battling a tortured warfare alone.

"Victory coming, Sister Jensen. Just don't be organizing ways for God to do His work. This be our waiting time. God sending out those angels behind the bushes to confuse the enemy that try to send our boy back to that Chusetts place."

The days flew by, filled with the activity of a new school year—reports, physicals, sick call, returning students, and students who stopped by to say hello. New students came, timidly asking, "We've heard about Lena. Is she here?" She was!

Ralph enjoyed his days at the farm, swinging an ax, clearing land, or taking long hikes through the woods.

Life goes on, somehow. Dan was busy teaching school in the mountains, and Jan and Jud were busy in Michigan. Harold was traveling. Lena and I clung to the "believing is seeing." She wouldn't let me doubt.

The purple van stayed!

65

"I Got a Knowing"

"Lena, I've always been restless. I resented the people who had been so cruel to my father. I never wanted to be like them, and they were good Christians! I resented Christians—not my folks—but I thought all the rest were hypocrites and I was out to get even.

"That's why I didn't get along at Gordon. Now I realize how hard Dean Gross and others, even the cook, tried to help me. There are some things I won't forget. Dan and Jan aren't like me. They can forgive and forget, but I just think about the injustice done by some Christians."

"Now Ralph boy, I know something about not being treated fair. Some folks say they be Christians, but not act like Christians. Aren't you forgetting about all the Christians you know? Them good ones? You see so much bad you be blind to the good. When I was very young I had a knowing about folks not fair to Jesus, so I said, 'Lena, you not better than Jesus. If He be your friend, for what you worry about other folks, black or white?' Some day my Jesus makes everything fair and right. I can wait! I be used to waiting! Good things coming, Ralph. You best be learning about waiting. That's why you be home now. Pretty strong rope holding you here. You done got the promise in that letter your mama wrote, that letter about 'Rise up and walk.' Your mama learned to wait.

"By the way child, how did you break that toe? It looks bad—all big and purple. You best get some ice on that foot and put it up on a big pillow. You stay home and don't go driving none. Keep that foot up, hear?"

"Oh, Lena, you won't believe how that happened! I went to Charlotte Saturday, just to get away from that meeting. You know something? It's hard to be around a crowd of happy people when you are so miserable. I figured the best thing for me was either to join them or get far away. You can't stay in the middle with that crowd. Same thing at the Masons' prayer meeting next Tuesday night. Boy oh boy, Lena, you better believe I'll be long gone during that Tuesday night meeting. Wow!

"Anyhow, back to Charlotte . . . and this girl! Boy—the messes I get into!

"Then Mom's letter. That blew me away. Here I was searching and searching and Mom writes, 'Everything you longed for is here where you left it.' Lena, I couldn't get away from it. So, naturally, when I met this girl in Charlotte, I figured she might be the one.

"We were sitting in the van, and I was really thinking about marrying her. My head was a muddle! I thought if I got married and someone really belonged to me I wouldn't be so restless. You know, Lena, I actually felt the chains pulling me back to Massachusetts. Another strange thing though, I also felt a rope tying me to home. What a crazy world!"

"Oh, child, you are feeling the rope of love. That rope be there when you a little iddy baby. God somehow had it figured out that we be tied to our mama so we never be forgetting where we gets our life. Sometimes the papas don't be at the birthings, but there be no birthing without the mama. There be no life without God. Life comes from God and whatever come from God, well, that be good."

"It was like this, Lena. This girl and I were in the van, and I wanted to talk to her about getting married, but she said, 'I don't know what's wrong, but I feel a wall between us.' And

367

there was. Every time I tried to get close to her there was this wall. I turned on the radio, and it blared, 'This is Scott Ross coming to you in the name of the Lord Jesus Christ.' Just like that, I knew! We were definitely not for each other! But when I took her back to her dorm, Lena, my mind was so preoccupied I didn't watch where I was going, and I stepped off the sidewalk crooked—and broke my toe!"

"Well, child, maybe that one time you gave Satum one big kick, and he gave you a stomping on the toe. He getting mad, cause his time with you be getting short. Glory! Hallelujah to Jesus! It be working for good!

"Now you best get that toe tended to, and do what Lena say: no driving that van, and put that toe up!"

With a hug she sent him on his way. Lena watched the van pull out of the driveway. Standing by the window she quietly called out his name.

The sun had not yet risen when I opened the infirmary door, and then I saw Lena coming across the campus carrying a heavily loaded shopping bag. Her song rang out in the early morning, "Praise God, from whom all blessings flow; Praise Him, all creatures here below.

"Glory hallelujah, my child been birthed!"

"But Lena, how did you know? You weren't there and it was so late. I couldn't call you at 4 A.M.!"

"The Lord woke me up and said, 'Lena, your child been birthed.' I just got out of bed and started praising my Jesus. He told me some other things, but first you tell me everything."

"What's in that bag, Lena?"

"That bag come later—now I hear about my boy."

"Oh, Lena, you should have seen Ralph—if his toe hadn't been so sore he probably would have sneaked out the back door to his van. But there he was, in the Masons' prayer meeting in a corner with his long legs stretched out.

"The guitars were playing, and you could hear the music a block away—organ, piano, clarinet, violin, and guitars. Oh, it was wonderful! You could tell the boys—and Ralph—were really impressed with such a crowd, sitting on the floor, stairs, kitchen, and hall, filling every corner! Dan was there, my sister Doris, Frances Dalton from High Point, and lots of friends who had been praying for years. I was squeezed into a corner.

"All of a sudden the door opened and in walked Steve Bezuidenhaut, a young evangelist from South Africa and friend of our family. His blonde curly hair framed a determined face, and his clear blue eyes looked right through the crowd. With his crisp British accent, he called out, 'Hallelujah! Praise the Lord!' With the clear voice of authority he announced, 'I have a message from the Lord! Ye must be born again!'

"Oh, no, I groaned to myself. *That's all these kids have ever heard from preachers.* I expected Steve to come like Elijah, with fire from heaven—dramatic and earthshaking."

Lena rolled her eyes in mock dismay and shook her finger. I continued about Steve.

"'Tonight I'll tell you what happened to me when God touched me.'

"For the next thirty minutes he held those hundred people spellbound. He recounted his youthful life of rebellion—wine, women, and song. He described his last desperate night, sitting in an empty night club saying, 'I've done it all. Now what?'

"'God came to me with the words I had heard all my life from my preacher father, "You must be born again." That night I surrendered my will, and gave my life to Jesus. He delivered me from darkness into His glorious light. Someone here needs a touch from God.'

"Oh, Lena, you should have been there! At that moment Steve saw Ralph's big toe sticking out, and with his wonderful sense of humor he smiled, 'Looks like this somebody needs a touch from God. Come up here!'

"Ralph stood there, Lena, all six feet, five inches of him.

"Steve said, 'Buddy, what's your name?'

"Lena, those hollow eyes looked into Steve's bright eyes and in such a plaintive voice Ralph said, 'Oh, Steve, don't you even know me?'

"I cried, Lena.

"Steve's blue eyes pierced through Ralph and Steve cried, 'My God—it's Ralph!'

"That room full of people called out, 'It's Ralph. It's the Jensen boy! The one we've been praying for.' Some were weeping, others rejoicing. No one had recognized him.

"Steve continued in that commanding voice, 'Ralph Jensen, you have been running long enough. You need more than your toe healed. You need deliverance from the enemy. You need to be born again. Do you want to be free?'

"Ralph reached for the piano to steady himself. Looking into Steve's face he said, 'Yes sir, it's about time!'

"Oh, Lena, that *yes* must have soared to the courts of heaven. In my heart I heard the music of a thousand angels singing, 'Rejoice, rejoice, for the Lord brings back his own.'"

Lena's black face, wet with tears, looked out the kitchen window. "I thanks You, Jesus. I done birthed my child in the Spirit. We carried him nine months and now he is birthed!"

There was a camp meeting in the kitchen. "Our child done come crying out to God, and now he come naked to be clothed in His righteousness. And soon we be seeing shoes on his feet and a ring on his finger. There be feasting in the land! Hallelujah!"

"Lena, that meeting didn't end until midnight. Then Steve said, 'I'm coming home with you, Ralph. We'll study the Word together and reach out to others like you. No more running away!'

"Well, Lena, guess who else was there? Billy Welker! You should have seen those two rascals rejoicing together. The rejoicing continued until 4 A.M. at home and I made cocoa and grilled cheese sandwiches and we finally went to bed. That's why I didn't call you, but I might have known the Lord would tell you.

"The last thing Ralph and Billy said to each other was that they were rounding up their old friends from Hamburger Hill and inviting them for supper so Steve can talk to them and they can tell what happened to them. On my way to work this morning I asked the Lord—like you do, Lena—'I wonder how many there will be!'"

"I can tell you," Lena interrupted, "because I got the knowing that you be having twenty-three young'uns."

370

"Lena! That's the number I got!"

"Why you so surprised?"

"That's not all, Lena. I said out loud in the car, 'I wonder what I can prepare?'"

"I can tell you that, too!"

"Oh, oh, Lena—don't tell me the Lord gave you a knowing menu!"

"Tell me what knowing you got, then I tell you my knowing."

"I got this menu—hamburgers, baked beans, applesauce, and pound cake. But, I said to myself, *That's an easy menu, but no way I can bake a pound cake.* The strangest thing happened, Lena, I got a real knowing—*pound cake!*"

Lena's laughter filled the kitchen. "What you think I be toting in that bag? Look, here be the mixer, the sugar, the butter, and the pound-cake tin—everything we need for the pound cake. The Lord woke me up and said, 'Lena, you get your tote bag. Today you bake a pound cake in the infirmary. Sister Jensen be needing a big pound cake to go with hamburgers, baked beans, and applesauce.'"

"That old stove? The only thing that stove bakes is oven toast!" I laughed and cried at the same time.

Lena scrubbed out the stove and took authority over the coonching spirits that make a pound cake fall. There was no way to regulate the temperature correctly, but Lena prayed, sang, and mixed the cake. It turned out perfect!

"Lena, did I ever tell you how much I love you?"

"Oh, child, at least a hundred times! Now I ask you, why you so surprised when God tells Lena to bake a cake? Didn't Elijah tell that woman in the Bible to bake a cake? God don't change!"

With pound cake in my car I headed for home at the close of the day.

Before going home I had to stop at the store for applesauce. Standing in line I saw a beautiful girl whom I had met previously. Impulsively I called out, 'Come over for hamburgers. Having a gang of young people. And bring friends along! See you later.' Then I was off to get the grill out for Dan and put the beans in the oven.

They came in vans and motorcycles—barefooted, long-haired, and hungry. The warm September air made outdoor serving easy. The girls from school helped pour gallons of tea and Dan kept grilling hamburgers. Platters of baked beans, applesauce, and hamburgers made the rounds. The final touch was a piece of pound cake served on a napkin. When the count was complete, we had served twenty-three people. There was one hamburger left over. Jo Jo, the beagle, came around the corner and caught that one.

I watched the young people sitting on the lawn. Steve was talking earnestly. Later he prayed with three notorious drug pushers.

Monday morning I heard Lena excitedly say, "Here comes my child with the preacher man! I best be putting on another pot of coffee."

The door opened with a "Hallelujah! Praise the Lord, Sister Lena!" and she was ready with a "Thank You, Jesus." Looking at Ralph, she laughed, "And who might that one be?"

With a bear hug she wrapped her arms around Ralph's lean frame and rested her head against him. "Oh, Lord Jesus done found our child and now he gets shoes on his feet to go with good news."

I came out of the office to join the others.

"Lena, you should have seen Steve yesterday morning. He was pacing the floor and yelling for Ralph to get out of the bathroom—with that *beard off!*

"What a Sunday morning!"

Steve and Ralph were laughing, but Steve managed to continue. "Ralph had been asked to give his testimony in High Point, so Saturday I bought a ten-dollar tie to go with his new clothes. 'Nothing but the best,' I told him. Oh, Lena, that beard. What a hassle! There's nothing wrong with a beard. I told Ralph, 'Grow ten beards later, but this beard is an identification with the old drug crowd, and now all things are new.' It was the same hassle with Billy's hair. He jumped out of the barber's chair three times—said chains were pulling him away from obedience."

Ralph joined in, "Billy said the pull was so great that he had to hold onto the barber chair, and he yelled, 'Cut it fast!' The barber thought he was crazy. When he finished, Billy said he felt free, like the chains were off for good. That's how it was with me. Lena, I had to hold onto the piano Tuesday night. I actually felt a demonic power leave my body and I was floating and felt free at last. Few people can understand the power of Satan. It's a miracle I ever got away from my old friends."

Lena poured coffee and passed the oven toast. "What I want to know, child, did you get to the meeting in time? What happened to your toe?"

Ralph laughed. "My poor toe, well, Steve prayed for it. After all, the prodigal had to have shoes on his feet. When I put the shoe on, the pain was gone."

"Glory to Jesus! The prodigal done got birthed like I said and come crying out to the Lord, naked, and he got new clothes, and now got shoes on his feet. Next thing, this child get a ring on his finger—and we been feasting right now on oven toast and jam."

Steve continued, "When that crowd saw Ralph walk in with his face shining like glory, dressed in that sport coat and ten-dollar tie, they burst into applause. Ralph just smiled and said, 'Oh, how I love Jesus.' There was nothing to add, Lena, he said it all."

I had a knowing that this was only the beginning.

66

Christine

It was Monday morning again, and Lena was rattling pots and pans in the kitchen. I could hear the coffee pot getting into the act and smell the oven toast. After a busy morning it would be a welcome break to sit down to a Lena lunch.

"I recall hearing someone say that if you want to be young, stay with young people, but if you want to die young, keep up with them." We laughed together while Lena poured coffee and served her cottage cheese and pineapple and grilled cheese.

"Whoever said that didn't count on the joy of the Lord to be their strength," Lena added with a chuckle. "We can do without sleep when so much joy going on."

"You should have seen Steve Bezuidenhaut, Lena! All weekend he was enjoying the young people, answering questions, or praying with someone. No one wants to go home these days, and the young people just come, sit on the floor, sing choruses, and share their experiences.

"There were some beautiful young people from Guilford College. Billy Welker was having a great time talking to all those lovely girls. Steve gave Ralph a nudge and said, 'Hey, good buddy, if I were a young man, and not married to my beautiful Wendy, I'd marry that girl.'

"Ralph answered, 'I've been thinking about it, but I ought to get introduced first.'

"Those two are impossible!

"There were several beautiful girls, Lynn Marshall, Erras Davis, Georgianne Higgins, a darling redhead, Jane Craven, also Pat and Harold Small, newlyweds; and then there was Christine Fisher."

"That Ralph boy do have an eye for beautiful girls. Now which one he be looking at?"

"Believe it or not, Lena, I saw this girl at a meeting and I thought she had that Grace Kelly look, so poised and dignified, and there was also a warm friendliness about her. I fell in love with her myself and when I saw her at the grocery store, I called out to her to come over to the house and bring her friends.

"She was so friendly and said she'd probably come with her roommate, Jane Craven. There were a lot of young people at the house, but I couldn't help but notice that lovely, tall blonde girl—Christine Fisher. She's a senior at Guilford College, and her hometown is Elizabeth City."

"Wait a minute, child, does she know Jesus? That Ralph boy needs time to grow up in the Lord."

"Oh, Lena, they just met. I do know this, that she was invited to a Campus Crusade retreat and there she learned that Jesus loved her and had a plan for her life. She accepted Jesus as her Savior, and I heard her say that she knew that God would lead her step by step. She has a beautiful, quiet trust in God.

"I am amazed at the spiritual insight these new Christians have. That's not all, Lena, these beautiful young people went to Hyannis, Massachusetts, to witness under Campus Crusade. That's the secret, get into Bible study, learn to pray, and then go out and share your faith. Well, Lena, looks like we see so many young people who live for the things of the world that we forget how many wonderful Christians there are on the school campuses. I can't wait for you to meet all these lovely girls.

"Uncle Howard is visiting from Chicago, and when he saw Christine Fisher, he said to Ralph, 'Now, Ralph, if I were a young man—that's the girl I'd marry.'

"Then Ralph says, 'Uncle Howie, I'm thinking about it!'"

Lena was about to have church in the kitchen. "Thank You, Jesus! You never fail! You said for that child to rise up and walk and everything he longed for would be where he left it—right back at his father's house.

"Now, don't you go organizing just cause you love that girl!" Lena laughed while she shook her finger at me. "You best leave it to Jesus. That Ralph be getting himself in more trouble; now this time the Lord be showing my child the right way. Jesus first, then all the good things follow. If God make the world in six days, and give Eve to Adam, well, I guess He can make a new Ralph and give him the girl he always dreamed of. God sure can get a lot done in six days."

The days ran together like a river of joy. One night Ralph came home. "Mama and Daddy, I have something to tell you!

"Chris and I drove out to the airport and I was thinking of how I had always longed for a girl like Chris—so much like Jan in so many ways. Then I also realized I had nothing to offer, and how could I ever expect to deserve a girl like Chris? Before I realized it, I was saying out loud all the thoughts of my heart. It was as though the things I couldn't say, the Holy Spirit was saying for me. For the first time in my life, I knew what real love was. She was everything I longed for—a beautiful Christian girl, and so easy to talk to. Mom and Dad, it just had to be the Lord, because that beautiful girl said she would marry me. Just like you said, Mom, everything I longed for, right back at Father's house. I still can't believe it! All these years I'm running away from God, and He just waited for me to turn around."

Harold was shouting, "Praise the Lord, Ralph! 'He is able to do abundantly above all we can ask or think.' Now, young man, you and I are going right out to pick out a ring for that girl God gave to you."

I couldn't wait to tell Lena, and when we got together we had church in the kitchen.

"Look at that Mr. Jensen, so happy, you'd think he be the one getting married, and Dan boy, too. He's remembering how he sat in the chair and prayed for his brother. There's joy in the camp today."

Lena got her beat, and while the coffee pot perked she clapped her hands and started singing "I've got peace like a river in my soul."

"Lena, Chris just fits into the family like she was born into it. Jan will love her like a sister. You won't believe what we all did last night, but then by now you can believe anything." Lena laughed.

I continued, "Ralph took Chris into the other room, and when they came out, they had been crying for joy. Chris just held up that finger with a diamond ring on it. She was so happy. Harold said, 'Okay, now we'll go out to eat and go to the State Fair in Raleigh.' I got so excited I wanted them to pick out their china at Belks. You never saw such a family—everyone wanting to do something.

"Chris and Ralph walked all over the fair. What a way to celebrate! Every once in a while she'd hold up that hand and show the ring."

Looking out the window, Lena saw them coming up the driveway. "They even look alike," Lena laughed.

Within a few minutes Ralph was saying, "Lena, meet the girl God gave me, Christine Fisher."

The organ and the harp sounded out the wedding march.

The Reverend Roy Putnam stood quietly looking out over the full sanctuary.

Dan and Ralph waited. How handsome they looked. Ralph turned to smile at me. He was reading my thoughts. The beautiful girls in green velvet dresses walked slowly down the aisle. Jane's red hair was shining in the candlelight. *How could that handsome Billy ever have been such a rascal?* I thought to myself. Then the organ poured forth the majestic chords that brought everyone to his feet.

Ralph's face wore an expression of awe and wonder while he watched God's precious gift walking toward him.

Christine Fisher, in white velvet, came down the aisle on the arm of her father, "Bo Bo" Fisher, retired Coast Guard Commander, who reluctantly relinquished his youngest daughter.

Before the wedding I had whispered to him, "Someday, Bo

Bo, you will understand God's miracle of grace." He stood proud and handsome.

Chris looked like a Christmas angel, her face a picture of transparent joy. Facing each other, Ralph and Chris spoke their vows. They seemed to be enveloped in the sight and sound of Christmas love and joy. They knelt together while the heavens watched. The unseen Guest seemed to whisper, "I love you all with an everlasting love. Continue in My love for each other."

The beautiful service ended. Pastor Putnam pronounced Ralph and Chris man and wife, in the presence of God and in this assembly.

The music burst forth in joyous celebration, "A mighty fortress is our God, a bulwark never failing."

During the reception Lena held court. Everyone wanted to meet her. When friends asked, "How long have you known Ralph?" she answered: "All my life. All my life. I birthed him."

I managed to sit beside her for a moment. "How did you keep from shouting, Lena?"

"Same way you did," she laughed. "I just shouted on the inside, but now I can say, 'Hallelujah, praise the Lord, and thank You, Jesus!' Now tell me, where they be going?"

"Lena, you won't believe what these cousins and friends have been up to. They think Ralph and Chris are going to Morehead and those rascals have a car ready to follow loaded with fishing gear. Well, Harold reserved the honeymoon suite at the Holiday Inn at Wrightsville Beach. Uncle Ralph, a close friend, is going to drive them in his car to their hidden car. They are changing their clothes now and everyone is getting ready to throw rice. Lena, just think, all my family will be together for Christmas."

Under a shower of rice we watched the newlyweds as they were whisked away to their honeymoon at the North Carolina beach. "What God hath joined together, let no man put asunder."

Lena waved until they were out of sight, then raised her eyes to heaven. She was calling out their names.

67

The Master's Touch

The following days were filled with joyous expectation—except for one problem: Ralph needed permanent work. He could always find temporary jobs, but he was searching for work with a purpose.

"The Lord not bring that boy home to leave him flitting around with no roots. God promised work, so he get work." Lena was talking to herself in the kitchen, and that was my signal to stop for my coffee break.

"God never goes halfway. You wrote in that letter to our boy, and God will do what He said—and that be a work, not just a job, but a work God will give him. There be jobs, and then there be a work. The jobs come along to give that piece of money to pay the rent. Sometimes that be a waiting time, until God says, 'Now I give you a work to do.' That be a knowing that your work is unto the Lord, even if it be on the job. Some folks never learn that the cooking, cleaning, sweeping, and yard work, mopping, and carrying out garbage cans, is a work, an offering to God— well pleasing in His sight.

"Now we stand still and see. Can't see, running. While Ralph talking to all the boss men about a job, we best be stretching out before the Lord. The Word says to knock and the right door will open. You just keep knocking till the knowing comes. You keep seeking; can't stop till you find. Nothing in this world be easy. You keep asking until the answer comes. That Satum—oh how I hates that Satum—he come slinking around to close doors God be opening, and to make you stop before the finding. He just come slipping around to kill, steal, or to destroy. That Satum so mad he got beat out of this child he try most anything. We know one thing—Jesus in our child be greater. Hallelujah! We just calls out the army of the Lord, that's what we do. Every good and perfect gift comes from above. All the bad come from that Satum.

"Out, Satum, out!" Lena grabbed the broom with a fury. "Satum, your kingdom must come down! I know your tricks! Jesus defeated you on the cross. That's why you hate the cross so much. Jesus just moved into Ralph boy and no way you win over Jesus. Jesus saved him from your hell—that's what my Jesus did. You lost your power. Out, Satum! Out!

"No use talking soft-like to that rascal!" she told me. "The Bible says, resist, and I reckon resist means what it say—you push harder than he do, and you cry out louder than that debbil can roar. In the name of Jesus our child will do the work God has for him. God never promises halfway. Time we be learning not to give up until the victory all won! Too many folks falling by the wayside. Too many turning around, Sister Jensen. Too many not following all the way. I feels a beat coming in my feet, and a tune coming in my head, and the words coming from the heart. MMMMM—O Lord—MMMMM—O Lord—HUMMMMM—O Lord—it's coming—"

So many falling by the wayside;
O Lord, help me to stand.
So many turning around, Lord;
Please help me to stand.
Oh, my Jesus—help me to stand.
I'm standing on Your Word, Lord;
Help me to stand.
I'm standing in Your name, Lord;
Help me to stand.
Oh, my Jesus, help me to stand.

The duties of the day demanded our attention, and the hours passed quickly. Before we realized it, it was time to head homeward. I heard Lena singing as she crossed the campus to the bus. "So many falling by the wayside. Help me to stand."

I knew she was going home to stretch out before the Lord. It was Tuesday, and tonight I would attend the Masons' prayer meeting.

When I arrived the place was filled, and the music was pouring forth the sound of joy. This time Ralph and Dan were a part of it. Later I eased over to my friend, Frances Dalton, and spoke with her about work for Ralph.

"What do you think he'd like to do?" she asked.

"Since his conversion, Frances, there is such a transformation that even his desires have changed. He says he wants to learn woodworking from the ground floor up. Now really, Frances, I never thought he could hammer a nail. Doesn't seem the type. His teachers predicted he'd be a lawyer. But he says that he feels a call to woodworking, just like a call to medicine or the ministry. No one in our family is known for craftsmanship."

"We'll just pray together, Margaret, and I'll talk to Hunter, Jr. God will open the right door."

And so it came to pass that Ralph went to work for the Snow Lumber Company in High Point. The owner was Hunter Dalton, Jr.

I learned later that Hunter didn't receive the suggestion with too much enthusiasm, but his mama had persuasive powers Hunter could not resist. He never regretted that decision, for Ralph learned well—from the bottom up!

One day, while holding a piece of rough wood in his hand, he remembered a poem his beloved Bestemör (grandmother) used to give at family gatherings.

Ralph had a knowing in his heart that the same creative, redemptive power of God that changed his life would also release the creative power within him to bring beauty out of a piece of rough wood. This gift from God was within him and like the Bible said, he would stir up that gift within him by hard

381

work and study, and learning God's principles for successful living.

Lena's answer to all the blessings was that God never goes halfway. "God gave Ralph his work unto the Lord—while on the job in the lumber yard."

Later, much later, Ralph named his own furniture manufacturing company "The Master's Touch." His beautiful eighteenth-century reproductions stand in spacious homes as a silent witness to the creative, redemptive power of God. When people ask about the name at furniture showings, he quietly tells the story of the Master's touch.

One day Ralph told of his attempt to hide his stained hands while sitting in church. The presence of the Lord drew near during that worship service and he had a knowing in his heart, "Your hands are beautiful to Me." With a heart of thanksgiving he raised his heart and hands in praise and worship.

Upon hearing that incident, I sat down, and for his birthday I wrote the following poem:

Hands

His hand was soft upon my breast,
Tiny fingers curled in sleep.
I offered to God, and him, my best,
A promise, within our love to keep.

His hands grew firm and strong
To hold a bat, or pitch a ball.
Oh, God, keep him from wrong;
Let him grow good, as well as tall.

Then one day he walked away
And waved his hand farewell.
I wept tears like ocean spray.
How far, oh, God, who can tell?

Then one day the Master came—
"Come, take My hand, My son,

For you alone, My life I gave
That we could be as one."
There stands my son, the Master's touch
Upon his heart and hands;
God so loved, He gave so much.
Now, in His power he stands.

The Master Carpenter of Galilee
Made a table out of wood,
Shaped it from His created tree,
Took it from His forest, where it stood.

He took man, made by God
And melted his heart of stone;
This bit of clay, from earth's sod,
He chose to be His own.

Within my son's firm hand
He holds a rough-hewn tree,
And carves an altar to stand
A gift—in God's sanctuary.

He lifts his heart and hands in praise,
His God of all creation,
In song of triumph, hallelujahs raise—
How great is Thy salvation!

When Craig Hyman, a Greensboro artist, read the poem and heard the story, he drew Ralph's hands. The poem, in Craig's script writing, and his life-like drawing now hang in our guest room, which is furnished with Ralph's creative masterpieces.

P.S. One Sunday recently, in our 1,000-member, dyed-in-the-wool Southern congregation in Wilmington, North Carolina, we sat behind a young black family—Carol and James Forte and their two daughters—and suddenly we were struck with wonder at how far we had come. With the highest number of votes ever recorded, James had just been elected the first black deacon of Myrtle Grove Presbyterian Church, and Ralph had been one of his strongest supporters. Ralph and James have developed a steadfast friendship and are now deacons together.

Because of the Master's touch, the racist rebel of fourteen years ago has been transformed.

Other lives have been changed, too. Across the miles . . . in New England, Florida, Mexico . . . other former rebels are now missionaries, ministers, Bible teachers, and successful businessmen.

Old things are passed away.

All things are new.

Harold

68

The Winter of the Soul

Around us tall pines stood like sentinels in the surrounding woods, and the sun pierced the white clouds floating across the blue skies of Wilmington, North Carolina.

The long line of cars followed slowly behind the white hearse. Jan and I rode in silence, the first car in line. It was grey.

"I'm glad the hearse carrying my Daddy is white; I never did like black. Remember going to Orlando to the Bookseller's Convention this last summer and how I followed Daddy's car?"

I remembered. Jan and thirteen-year-old Sarah had sat in the front seat of my blue Pontiac while Chris, Sarah's mother, curled up in the back seat to get some needed sleep. Harold, my husband of fifty-three years, sat in the front seat of his grey Oldsmobile, and Kathryn, ten, watched from the rear to be sure our blue car continued following. Such a short time ago.

Now our daughter Jan and I were in the grey car, and Ralph, our son, was following with his family—his wife Chris, and their children Sarah, Kathryn, Eric, and Shawn.

Jan's husband, Jud Carlberg, came next with their children, Heather and Chad, and their friends, Kris and Jeremy.

Harold was "Papa" to his adoring grandchildren, as well as to all the others he had adopted along the way.

The magnificent live oaks bent their branches over the meandering road.

Tall trees in sorrow bend . . .
You can't go home again.

This quote filtered through the back roads of my mind.

Jan broke the silence. "I never dreamed I would ever follow Daddy like this."

The cars eased along the road while the dogwoods shed their tears into the wind, and the pines mourned as the wind turned cold on that beautiful autumn day, November 4, 1991.

Harold again was in the lead, this time to be buried in the Oleander Gardens of Wilmington, and I wondered for a moment how long a person could live with grief that tears the heart apart.

I knew the beauty of fall would never be the same. Grief like a cold wind would blow the leaves from the oak trees, and my tears would fall like the red leaves of the dogwoods.

The winter of the soul had come, too soon, and without warning.

I wondered how many times I would relive the morning Harold died in my arms.

Night after night I would hear his call, "Margaret, help me!"

Like a shot I was out of bed, running into the bathroom where Harold was leaning over the sink.

"My back!"

I knew he had pulled a lawn mower out of the shed so I thought it was a strained muscle.

"No, this is different. I can't breathe."

"Let me get you on the bed."

Oh, Jesus, touch him! Relieve this pain. Oh, Jesus, touch him!

I eased him onto the bed, praying while I held him. Then he was quiet.

"Oh, Harold, has the pain gone?"

He didn't answer. He was gone! He looked so peaceful.

Then I cried, "Jesus, help me!"

It was 5 A.M., October 31, 1991.

Chris answered the phone. "Tell Ralph to come," I sobbed, and hung up.

Ralph held me in his arms as they took Harold away. Inside, my entire being screamed, "Don't leave me; I can't make it alone. I don't even know how to wind the grandfather clock."

Ralph sobbed, "Daddy, Daddy." We clung together like frightened children, alone in the grey dawn.

Then abruptly Ralph said, "Mama, let us thank God for what we know, not what we see. We know God is sovereign and Daddy is Home with Him. He died so peacefully, right in your arms. We know God's purposes are right."

"I know. I know. And I'll always be so thankful that I was right here."

I put the coffee pot on; then we began reading Psalm 27. "The LORD is my light and my salvation . . . " and I won't be afraid.

But I was afraid!

"Don't talk to Jan, Ralph. Talk to Jud first."

Oh, how I wanted to spare her the news, but grief comes to us all and we can only comfort each other as God gives comfort.

Comfort did come! When Chris came, she plunged into the practical: beds to make, bathrooms to clean, endless telephone calls.

The first ones at our door were the Hiltons, God's faithful servants. They were always there when anyone needed them. They came with their love and prayers, and their tears, and God's peace enveloped us like a security blanket.

"Like a mighty army moves the church of God."

This amazing universal family that the world will never understand, the Church, the people of God, came with their hearts and hands, and with compassionate arms they enfolded us in a love that is beyond human reasoning.

I am glad I'm a member of the family of God. That day we needed our extended family.

The pink hue of morning slipped into the dawn and dispersed its greyness. Throughout that tear-filled day the grandfather clock sounded its clear message that some things never change.

I would learn how to wind the clock, and each Saturday morning I would do it, just like Harold did.

With the familiar sound of the clock I was reminded once again that our times are in God's hands, and He winds life's clock.

I would trust His hand to wind my clock.

69

The Protective Wall

"Paulie pushed the button! Paulie pushed the button! The casket's going down!"

"He didn't mean to. It was an accident. Aunt Jan was explaining about the big hole and how the casket would be lowered."

The wide-eyed cousins stood frozen in their tracks until an attendant stopped the casket's premature descent into the gaping hole.

"We were all looking in the hole wondering how Papa would rise from the grave when Paulie accidentally pushed the button." Kathryn (Katie) usually had an explanation for everything. "The Bible says the dead in Christ shall rise first and we wondered how Papa would get out of that hole."

The young cousins gazed into the hole and discussed the obvious theology: "God will have to figure that out."

They were all there—the aunts, the uncles, the older and the younger cousins.

An S.O.S. always brought the five Tweten sisters together. When news of joy hit the telephone wires we all rejoiced together. The last time we had a fun reunion Harold printed a sign and hung it on the clothesline: "THE SISTERS ARE COMING—HELP!"

When sorrow invaded the happy households, we wept together.

So they came! Jeanelle, the youngest, from Washington, Joyce, the songbird, from Arkansas, Doris from Stoneville, and Grace from Greensboro. They were there like oaks of righteousness.

Harold's brothers Howard and Jack were there, along with a new brother who had joined them, Peter Stam.

The church family, all our adopted children, our friends and neighbors, all came like a protective wall.

"I found Papa's Aqua-Velva in his car, Aunt Margaret. Don't you want it?"

"It's okay, Benjamin, just put it back in the car."

"But Aunt Margaret, Papa always smelled like Aqua-Velva."

"I know!" (I bought expensive Copenhagen cologne for my big Dane, and he still used Aqua-Velva.)

Benjamin trotted back to the car to put the cologne back in Papa's container, along with the mouthwash and a comb. (He always had that meticulously dressed look, even when going to the grocery store.)

One of Ralph's employees was sobbing—hard, choking sobs.

I put my arms around him. "It's okay to cry, but remember how he always said how smart you were, and that you could do anything."

He remembered! All his life he had been told how worthless he was, then Harold came and convinced him he could do anything he wanted to. And he did!

He kept crying. "Oh, I hurt; I really hurt. I loved that man."

"My dad built dreams for others," Ralph said at the memorial service, "even if his own dreams were unfulfilled. He always came along to build dreams for others."

Slowly the crowd retreated to their cars and then it was our turn. Leaving the lonely grave with the yellow lilies reminded us that spring and resurrection follow the winter of the soul.

I could hear our beloved Pastor Emeritus, Horace Hilton: "When we look at the ocean it seems to end at the sky, but if we took a boat and kept going, we'd touch another shore—that's a picture of death."

Our young pastor, Jim Glasgow, read: "Let not your heart be troubled: ye believe in God, believe also in me" (John 14:1). Life-giving words!

"I feel like I've been to a great concert," a friend commented. "Homer McKeithen's powerful baritone voice sang the great hymns of faith into the hearts of the people."

It was a time to weep over their own broken dreams and draw comfort into the wounded places.

When the cars pulled into our driveway, the women of the church were there to serve the crowd with beautifully set up buffets.

"Grammy, your neighbor, Miss Clara, pulled up in her golf cart with a crock of homemade soup." Leave it to Miss Clara, the original.

Later, the cousins, the grandchildren, and all their friends found places on the floor to join the other relatives and friends. Homer led the singing, the language of the soul: the great hymns of faith, a reminder that God is changeless. Then the choruses followed—hand-clapping, foot-stomping, camp-meeting songs.

We laughed and cried but the songs filled the empty places and brought joy that brings strength—then hope.

It was midnight when the cars turned homeward and all became quiet. The lonely grey car stood beside the blue one. I remembered a long time ago when nine-year-old Ralph had burst into the kitchen. "I know what it means to die, Mama. The driver goes to heaven—that's the soul. And the car, the body, can't go any more."

The body was buried in a lonely grave, but the driver was Home—safe!

"Mom," Jan remembered later, "do you realize we sang, laughed, and shared wonderful memories until midnight? If someone passed by our house that person would probably have said, 'I wonder what wonderful thing happened in that home?'"

The wonderful thing?

"Amazing grace! How sweet the sound."

70

The Paint Shoes

"Where is my sister?" Joyce hunted through the house, and Jan suggested I might be in the garage.

I was. Holding a pair of old paint shoes, I stood in the garage crying my heart out.

Joyce cried with me; then Jan came and we all cried over Harold's old paint shoes.

"He worked so hard to paint everything just right." Harold's painting left no room for splash. My talent had more splash than smooth. When I needed cabinets painted I'd use my old trick. I'd say, "I think I'll get some paint and start on the inside."

"Oh, no, Margaret, promise me you won't paint. It takes more work to clean up after you. Just tell me what you want and I'll get to it."

And I'd promise! Of course, I had no intention of painting anything. My trick always worked.

So it came to pass that Harold painted—and painted—and since he was the perfectionist, it was done right.

Now I stood holding his paint shoes and crying. Joyce, with her sensitive wisdom, said, "Put the paint shoes on the shelf and let's go out and dig a memorial garden."

We put the paint shoes on the shelf and took a shovel, hoe, and rake, and began a memorial garden.

My friend Anna brought a bag of bulbs. "Plant these, and think of Harold, spring, and resurrection."

We did. "Look at all the mums friends have sent. Let's sort the colors and plant them like a work of art."

They did other little things, too, to help. Doris saw my old dishdrainer looking a little "gross," so she bought a new one.

When sadness slipped through the door, Jeanelle sat down at the piano and Grace sang, "It matters to Him about you." Joyce is really the soloist, but Grace knew this was the time to sing.

So she sang.

We hung together like clothes on a line. No one wanted to leave.

Eventually, though, everyone had to return home. The college grandchildren had been excused from exams and now had to return to their classes. They had seen their fun-loving family rejoice at our fiftieth wedding anniversary celebration. Then, three years later, their beloved Papa was gone. But they saw the family as one, and they heard the songs in the night.

Chad, the eldest grandson, said it well. "We loved our Papa and laughed at his jokes, his Aqua Velva, and powder on the toilet seat. He was there for all of us."

Now they were going back to the classroom, but what they learned about life and death was not in a textbook. They heard us sing!

Jan and I were alone now—our wonderful daughter of joy, Daddy's special girl.

We had to go through papers, pay bills, change names, check legal documents. And then the insurance! Robert Bale spent hours going over papers. Most of the insurance had expired when Harold turned sixty-nine—Harold was seventy-nine on his last birthday.

I was glad I had memorized Philippians 4:19. Here's my special paraphrase: My God shall supply all your needs, not according to Harold's insurance, but according to God's riches in Christ Jesus.

I felt panic, but then peace.

The bank, the lockbox, the Social Security changes—they overwhelmed me. Harold always paid the bills while I just wrote!

One day I had to get more copies of the death notice. Jan parked outside the courthouse while I ran up the steps and met a woman who recognized me as the author of *Lena* (now titled *Then Comes the Joy*).

"Oh, I'm so glad to see you. Your book helped me through a difficult time. What are you doing here?"

I couldn't say it. I just handed her the death notice.

"Oh, no, your husband?"

I nodded.

"Oh, I am going through a most painful divorce."

Suddenly I was alert. "Oh, no, my dear, that's worse than a death."

We clung to each other on the courthouse steps and prayed. I didn't even know her name.

When I went inside, I found that the clerks also had read my books. Cheerfully they asked, "What can we do for you?"

I couldn't answer, so I handed them the death notice. "I need copies," I choked.

"Your husband?"

I nodded.

They jumped up. "Oh—we'll pray for you."

In a new way I found God's face in the most unexpected places.

When I went to the neighborhood service station I said, "I am Margaret Jensen and I have never pumped gas. I know nothing about cars."

"Ah, yes, we know who you are because your son explained how your husband took care of the car so you could write. 'Take good care of my mama,' he said."

Within moments I was introduced to the crew and given a card with phone numbers. "Call us any time and we will help you, night or day. Don't worry about the car. You just stick to writing."

I autographed a book for each one and left with a tank of

gas, oil checked, and windows washed, on my way to complete a long list of errands: printer's, cleaners, photo service, office supplies, pharmacy, and grocery store.

This was the list Harold checked off, and now I wondered how I would ever have time to write again. The lists seemed endless—bank, post office, UPS, etc.

After endless hours of papers, forms, and figures, Jan had to return home, then taxes stared me in the face. Taxes? I could never even balance my checkbook. My dislike for math made me do all the figures in round numbers! I had visions of going to jail. But maybe then I could write!

The poor tax expert shook her head and wearily asked that I just leave it with her, then suggested a simple setup for my future records.

Evening finally came, and I was alone. Shadows fell across the peaceful neighborhood and lights came on down the street. I turned the outside light on and locked the doors.

I had never been alone before! The noisy Tweten family, with three in a bed, left no time for loneliness. Then it was Harold, the children, visiting missionaries, college kids needing a place to stay—they all kept the household full of activity.

It was when the shadows of evening closed around me that I turned on all the lights.

I couldn't read; I couldn't pray; I didn't care about world news—my world had crumbled!

The hymnbook on the piano drew me to sit down and play some old hymns.

All the way my Saviour leads me;
What have I to ask beside?
Can I doubt His tender mercy,
Who through life has been my Guide?

The grandfather clock struck midnight when I crawled into the king-sized bed, alone!

The teddy bear I had given to Harold last Christmas with a note, "Just hug him until I get home," sat on our bed. I reached over, pulled the bear to me, and held him—and fell asleep.

The early beams of the morning streamed through the window and I recalled: "Weeping may endure for a night, but joy cometh in the morning" (Psalm 30:5).

Joy hadn't come this morning, but hope had slipped in the door.

71

No Voice!

In March 1992 I flew to the West Coast for two retreats, one in Irvine, California, at the Marriott, and the other the next weekend in La Jolla.

Between those weekends I visited my lifelong friend, Rose, and saw my Here's Life publishing family. On Wednesday I enjoyed a great day with Scott and Ann Hilborn and their church family at Canoga Park. God has His nails in sure places (see Isaiah 22:23) all across the land.

On Thursday I had a startling experience—no voice! In a beautiful pink setting for tea, five hundred women were expecting their guest speaker—me—and I couldn't talk!

Just in case of such an emergency I had brought a tape with me and tried to give it to the leaders. "We won't need it," they said. I tried again to give it to them and they wouldn't take it. Instead they prayed! And so did I!

While the happy crowd sang songs of faith and joy, I put my head in my hands. (They thought I was praying, but I was crying.) *If only Harold were here, this wouldn't be happening.* I wanted him to pick me up in his arms and carry me home. Self-pity engulfed me while everyone else was singing. I had never felt so helpless and alone.

"Why, God? Isn't it enough to travel without Harold? Now

am I to be humiliated before this audience? If only I could run away and hide. The guest speaker—and no voice!"

Was God really in charge? Had He allowed this humiliation for a purpose? Why was I here?

I wanted to go home—home, where I was safe and loved and cared for. Chris would be there to fix spice-tea. Ralph would pray peace into my troubled spirit. I wanted my own pillow.

Spiritual warfare was made a reality to me that night, and while everyone else sang I was caught in a battle. This was not a desperate football team; this was a desperate spiritual battle.

Would I go down in self-pity? Or could I rise to acknowledge the sovereignty of God and His promise to work good out of this—no voice?

I yielded to Him. "Lord, forgive my self-pity, and I surrender to Your will." As I prayed, I began to realize in a new way that God doesn't need my voice to speak to His people. (He even used a donkey once.)

I heard God's still voice: "Trust Me."

It was then I heard the leader announce the *speaker* of the evening, Margaret Jensen. Hers was the voice of faith.

When I walked up to the platform I whispered to Jesus, "Okay, it's just You and me. Do it Your way."

I whispered into a turned-up microphone, "I feel like Moses at the Red Sea and I'm not sure the waters will part. This will be a meeting no one will ever forget, and when we all get to heaven someone will say, 'Oh, I know you—the speaker without a voice.'"

Laughter rippled through the audience. Then it was quiet.

"God must have something very important to say to each of us tonight. If you are very quiet, you will hear the Holy Spirit speak to you—and you alone. God doesn't need me or my voice, but when He speaks, we must listen."

Steadily my voice increased and I was beginning to sound like Jimmy Durante. The hushed audience listened to me. I listened to Him, the still, small voice that said, "Trust Me." A gentle presence covered me with peace and I continued two full sessions. When it was over I couldn't even whisper.

Weeks later I was still receiving letters and calls telling me how many guests had been invited who were involved in the occult or the New Age, or who were without any church affiliation.

They listened to this strange speaker and somehow heard.

Someone said to me, "You can't imagine how many tapes were sold—to hear the Jimmy Durante voice."

Perhaps many came with skeptical and cynical minds, but they saw faith in action and knew it was real. God has His own way to speak to His children—and to me.

On Friday I arrived at the La Jolla retreat where I was met by a group of subdued leaders and speakers. They had voices like mine!

With a sense of awe, Patsy, Marilyn, and I filed into the prayer room with Marita and the other leaders, the room where intercessory prayer was made for this retreat.

This was no game! It was real, a strange kind of warfare.

Songs of praise filled the ballroom, and when the musicians led the audience in "There Is Power in the Blood," we knew victory before we saw it. There were tears and laughter and a sense of God's presence as individual hearts heard God speak.

"Not by might, nor by power, but by my spirit" (Zechariah 4:6) became a reality to speakers who were not used to feeling so helpless.

Long after I returned home, messages kept coming across the miles.

"We sensed God's presence in a new way."

"I've never been to a retreat like this one."

"My life was changed."

Out of apparent defeat, God had His ultimate victory.

Hurrah for the team!

72

Borrowed Time

"Grammy, remember when Papa got all upset because we were playing cards? They were just fun cards."

"'Don't you ever play cards for money!'" Katie could imitate her Papa.

"When we asked him why he was so upset, he told us this."

It's a long story. I was only nineteen years old and it was during the Depression. I had a good job at the Bunte Candy Company in Chicago, but I had to quit school and go to work to help support my family.

I got in with some gamblers and learned to be good at cards. I was lucky, and I usually managed to have money when no one else did.

One night, on a big winning streak, I was looking at the great cards in my hand and my pile of winnings in front of me. Then the strangest thing happened—I could hear my mother whisper in my ear, "The devil will take a finger, then a hand, and then he'll get you."

Suddenly I felt a battle raging within me. Money—money—win money! A gambling fever raged!

Then again, through the noise in the smoke-filled room, I heard a voice, "Get out! Leave now, or the devil will get you."

I jumped up, terrified of that burning lust for money and gam-

bling I had just discovered within me. Shouting "Take it!" I pushed the winnings across the table, threw down the cards, and ran—ran from something controling and evil.

Later I learned that a gang had come in and shot the men I sat with. Those were the infamous days of Al Capone. I never picked up another deck of cards because I knew how close I had come to becoming a compulsive gambler. I also realized how close I had come to being shot!

A little while after that, I went to the Humbolt Park Gospel Tabernacle, and there the message of God's love gripped my heart. I walked down the aisle to surrender my life to Jesus Christ.

How frightening to think that I could have been killed at that gambling table and never would have known the forgiveness of sin and God's amazing love.

"Just think, Grammy, we might never have known our Papa. That is some story!"

"That's not all," I added. "Papa was so happy to be a Christian that he spent hours reading the Bible and memorizing large portions of Scripture. He was only nineteen, yet he was asked to teach a large Sunday school class. Also, every night after work he went door to door telling people about Jesus.

"Your Papa's Grandfather Mogenson was a Danish sea captain, and when he heard D. L. Moody preach, he opened his heart to receive Jesus Christ as his Savior. In return, he established a mission in Denmark so seamen could hear the gospel.

"Papa's mother was listening to Dr. DeHaan on the radio when she knelt down by the radio to ask Jesus to be her Savior and Lord.

"When Papa became a Christian he attended evening classes at Moody Bible Institute. Years later I was able to tell stories on 'Prime Time America,' on the Moody Station, with the host, Jim Warren, one of the most talented, creative radio personalities around. It was an honor for me to be on his show.

"Who knows? Katie, maybe you will be next with all your creative stories. Jim and you could do a show and never miss a beat.

"With such a rich heritage, God expects much from all you children. Each of you has to make your own choice to receive

God's gift of salvation. God's amazing grace is offered, but it is not inherited. To obey God is a personal choice. Papa made a choice many years ago, and because of that choice we are blessed. Just so, the generations to come will be blessed by the good choices you make."

"These days should be remembered and kept throughout every generation" (Esther 9:28).

Ralph and Chris went with me to visit the grave. The cemetery was alive with flowers from Easter.

Harold's grave was bare.

A bronze marker had just been placed there and the soil was still waiting for the spring grass to grow.

I couldn't believe his body was there—tie and all!

HAROLD EDWARD JENSEN

1912–1991

Then I saw

MARGARET TWETEN

1916–

I wondered why my last name wasn't there, then forgot about that as I began to wonder how much time I had.

I recalled a day, long ago, when I had felt the pressures of writing and travel smothering me. I kept thinking, *Time is so short, and I have "miles to go before I sleep."*

Panic set in. *Borrowed time—I'm on borrowed time!*

Quietly a woman of God had reached out to me. "You will have all the time you need for God to accomplish His purpose through you, and there is much He has given you to do." Peace settled in like a gentle stream.

God had His marker for me before I was ever born, not in bronze but in the nail prints in His hands. I was safe!

Many years ago in a Youth for Christ rally I sang with all the fervor of youth about being safe and sheltered in the hand of the Lord.

Sixty years later I knew the meaning: "My times are in thy hand" (Psalm 31:15). God winds the clock.

I'm looking now out of a plane window and I see billows of clouds lined up in a row over a sea of glass. Where is heaven? I keep looking into the clouds and wishing I could somehow see the city filled with loved ones, and maybe see Harold waving to me. Sometimes I even say, "Good morning, heaven, wherever you are."

I wish God would open the gates and let me peek, but I'm not sure I would want to stay here then. Maybe I wouldn't be willing to get up at 5 A.M. to catch the 7 A.M. flight. Maybe the stories I had to tell to the nations would not seem so urgent.

So I just tell the clouds, "Go ahead and hide your city. I happen to know it's there because Jesus said He went to prepare a place, and when the time is right He will send for me."

When the grandchildren were young I would tell them that when we got to heaven we'd slide down the white clouds as though they were slippery marshmallows, and we'd play tag.

When Katie was very young she used to say, "I know what Bestemör [my mother] is doing. She's sitting in a rocking chair telling stories to the children in heaven. I will be so happy to go there."

Heaven is real! Beautiful! Happy! A child's faith! We all need it.

When ten-year-old Timothy Tepper died in a car accident, Katie grieved for her "forever friend." When her beloved Papa died, the tears fell when she grieved alone in the rest room at school.

"Grammy, I miss Papa so much, but then the peace of God comes all over me. Now Timothy knows someone in heaven and Papa is holding his hand and taking him all over the place. You know Papa—he had to shake hands with everyone. Now he takes Timothy with him."

That settled it! Faith sees what the eye can never see. Eye hasn't seen nor has ear heard what God has prepared for His people. Children come the closest to seeing and hearing.

Why is it so difficult for us to become like little children? Why do we need all the answers? Somehow the ego in us thinks we have a right to know God's ways. But God tells us that His ways and thoughts are not our ways and thoughts (see Isaiah 55:8).

The awesome silence of God thunders louder than all our screaming questions. Across the corridors of time comes the answer: "Be still, and know that I am God" (Psalm 46:10).

Then the tears come and wash into the deep, hardened crevices of the stony place in my heart. Gently, ever so gently, the Spirit of God plants flowers of faith: "I've come this far by faith" and "I've come too far to turn back now."

I saw the jostling crowds with a new compassion, and I wondered how many broken hearts would harden because they didn't know the God of comfort. I had a story to tell.

P.S. The flowers are on the grave now—beautiful yellow daffodils that remind us of spring and resurrection. The grass is coming through the sandy soil. We know our Papa is not there, and it is a reminder to us. Our days soon fade, like grass and flowers, but we shall live forever in the presence of the King.

We are engraved in the palm of His hand.

73

No Tuna Fish Tonight

The sun slowly sank and the woods in the back of the house looked dark and mysterious.

Number-three grandson, Eric, had manicured the lawn to look like a park. In the yard, azaleas in full bloom dominated the scene and brilliant red, soft pink, and lavender vied for attention. Around the edges, red salvia and yellow marigolds stood at attention.

Two doves, sitting on the edge of the patio roof, decided to take a dip in the birdbath. They are always together—kind of like Harold and me in the yesterdays.

"Come on, Margaret," he would say, "let's take a look at the garden."

We'd tour the fairyland together, pluck a weed here and there, watch for new buds, check the palm trees and pampas grass. We admired the desert gold iris from Grandma Jensen's garden, fifty years ago. I could almost hear her chuckle. "I paid seventeen dollars for these bulbs."

Fifty years later those bulbs had been transplanted from garden to garden. Memories of loved ones never die.

Now I could almost hear Harold say, "Remember when we came to this house fourteen years ago?" I remembered how I

406

had cried when we left our lovely Greensboro home with its roses and azaleas to come to this barren place.

The yard here was a disaster—no grass, only weeds and prickly sandburs. There were no flowers, just some scraggly bushes, and we dug them up.

I recalled crying in the rain while I planted forty yucca bushes beside the college road. Together Harold and I rolled wheelbarrows of sand to fill the sunken hollow by the dead-end road, and then we planted holly bushes, azaleas, and monkey grass.

We found rocks from deserted lots and filled the sliding banks with them. Orange lilies thrived between the rocks.

One day a truck pulled up with ten palm trees.

"Oh, no," I cried, "you must have the wrong house."

"Nope! Got the right house. That's exactly what your husband told us you would say."

Throughout the years, when others played golf, Harold planted gardens. He tilled the ground and planted vegetables, and then he planted flowers and fruit trees. His motto was, "Always leave a place more beautiful than when you found it."

He did!

It was getting dark outside now and I had to close the blinds on the bay window and turn on the lights. That's the hardest part of the day. I don't like to close the blinds because it seems that Harold is out in the yard, watering the flowers around the corner, and I'm shutting him out.

I forgot to water the window box again. Poor Uncle Jack, Harold's eighty-five-year-old brother, shakes his head as only a sorrowful gardener can do. "Margaret, the window box doesn't get rain and those expensive plants will die."

So . . . I watered the window box before I closed the blinds.

That's not all I forgot. The garbage can! Harold never forgot the window box or the garbage can.

One thing I did know. I was not eating tuna fish tonight. No way!

I did that last night when I sat in the breakfast nook and watched the rain splash against my bay window. Harold and I used to enjoy sitting in the shadows of the evening, watching the rain. We loved it when we saw the garden soak up the water of life.

"No need to cook tonight, Margaret, let's just have a tuna fish sandwich and a cup of hot tea and watch the rain."

It was raining last night so I fixed a tuna fish sandwich and watched the rain, alone. I choked on the bread. The potato chips were stale; the tea was cold. Only my tears were hot. I closed the blinds and turned on all the lights. The winter of the soul had set in and the rain cried with me.

That was last night. Tonight I said, "No tuna fish."

The soon-to-be baked potato found a home in the microwave while I prepared a small steak and salad, tea, and a cookie.

Katie's ball game kept me cheering earlier; then grocery shopping occupied my time because the next day was Mother's Day.

I wanted Chris, my angel daughter-in-law, to have a break—she always prepares the traditional Sunday dinner when I travel. But now I was home and it was my turn to cook Sunday dinner.

After my supper, I checked my list.

While the angel food cake rose majestically in the oven, I set the table for Sunday dinner.

Fresh strawberries and real whipped cream, Sarah's favorite dessert. I checked corn on the cob, Katie's favorite, to go with the family's choice of roast beef, mashed potatoes, green beans, and applesauce.

I made one big decision: no more watching the rain alone, and no tuna fish. It was much better to plan a meal for a family of hungry, happy people.

I'll miss Harold's cards and hanging baskets for Mother's Day. I could certainly remember to buy hanging baskets, but it's not the same.

Oh well, I'll do that next week; the patio does look lonely without the flowers. But I can't remember everything! One thing I will remember—no more tuna fish on a rainy night. I'll call the "gang" for pizza!

Somehow I'd make it through another holiday. I checked my

list again, and it was time to go to bed. I turned out the lights while the grandfather clock said good night eleven times.

When the clock announced a new day with six chimes, I knew it was time to put the roast in the oven. I stripped the corn, snapped the beans, cut up the strawberries, and peeled the potatoes. I was off to a running start. But it was another holiday without Harold, and the lonesome song began coming on, so I determined to do the day up right.

I dressed in a white suit and purple blouse and slipped into my wild purple and cranberry shoes. After I checked the roast and turned off the oven I headed for the door, dangling my keys and swinging my purple straw bag. Just as I locked the door, there stood my handsome men, Ralph and Eric.

"No way my gorgeous mother is going to church alone."

Bowing, Eric opened the car door with a flourish, and we were off to church.

Poor Chris, mother of four, would have to make it in the weather-beaten jeep. God is surely mounting jewels for her crown.

I was greeted with, "Wow! Travel agrees with you." I chuckled to myself. Harold would like that. Sharp clothes suited him.

The grandchildren gave me that "you are cool" look and I knew the tears on the inside didn't show. Hurrah for this team!

Chris turned to me and whispered, "Well, Grammy, you did it again—purple and white!"

I whispered back, "I didn't want to look like a grieving widow."

"Well, you don't have to look like such a happy widow."

That's when we laughed out loud.

When Sunday dinner was a treasured memory, I read the beautiful cards again. "You are loved; you are loved; you are loved," appeared over and over.

A Lizzie Hill doll from Jan and Jud sat on the buffet. From a long-ago past, the wooden Miss Hattie, with her basket of ironing, stood beside an ironing board holding an old iron. It was a reminder of when Mama said in her soft Norwegian accent, "While you are dying, iron!"

Today the story said to me, "Don't cry in the rain and eat tuna fish. Call the gang for pizza."

I looked out the breakfast window. There on the patio Ralph had hung three beautiful flowering baskets.

I think I hear Harold cheering.

74

Table for One

I was back in a "lonesome town" one night during the Christmas season of 1992. The wind whipped the rain against the glass doors of my hotel room in Toronto, Canada. That delightful city, teeming with multicultural people, shouldn't ever be called "lonesome town," except for that night, and only by me.

In a dining room filled with couples, I had to ask for a table for one. At home, surrounded by family and friends, I seldom ate alone. This night, though, I sat alone—with Harold across from me in memory.

A plaintive song floated across the room while the rain beat a steady accompaniment against the windows. While I sipped my hot tea, I wondered about other lonely people who sip tea in a silent world of memory. I thought about the brave single mother, rushing home from work to prepare a quick supper for hungry, demanding children. In the silence of memory she saw a happier time when Daddy was home. Then he closed the door and walked away.

At the same time there could be a lonely father somewhere trying to explain why Mommy won't be home.

I could imagine a widow across town rocking in an old chair, with a picture album on her lap and a tear in her eye.

I remembered an elderly man shuffling into the cafeteria to watch the world in motion. He also took a table for one.

There were so many things I wanted to tell Harold, but you can't talk at a table for one. The year before, he had been with me, and I wanted to tell him about the wonderful people I had met this time where I had been a guest earlier that day.

On the talk show we laughed and told Christmas stories, stories of faith and courage, and stories full of humor that bring hope for the future.

I wanted to tell Harold about those people reaching out to the world to feed the hungry, to build camps for children, and to provide shelter for the homeless. But the greatest reach of all was to bring the good news of hope: "God loves you."

Oh, how I wanted to talk about God, who led us through shady green pastures as well as the storms of life. So many things I wanted to tell him, but then he already knew. And, you can't talk at a table for one.

I had to tell myself that the God who never failed me in my youth won't fail me now when I'm alone and my steps are slower and my eyes grow dim with tears.

The day came to an end and I left the table for one, secure in God's love. When morning came I checked the shuttle bus schedule, then headed for the coffee shop—and another table for one.

I was going home! What a wonderful word, home!

Hot coffee, the aroma of bacon sizzling, and English muffins with marmalade seemed a good way to begin the day.

About my third cup of coffee, an old song came back to me that reminded me of that day when no one will sit at a table for one.

The One who fed the multitudes will call us to sit at His table, a table not for one but for all.

The Light of Home! Grandma can put away her album and open her Bible. "Let not your heart be troubled; I have a place for you."

Grandpa can leave the cafeteria and shuffle back to his lonely room, but when he opens the Bible he will read: "Lo, I am with you; you are not alone." In the silence of memory he can see the faces of his loved ones in the Light of Home.

The single parents, with broken dreams, can find comfort and encouragement within the pages of the Book: "Even if you walk through the shadows of death [death of dreams or of loved ones], don't be afraid. I'll walk with you."

Across the world, tears stain the pages of the Book while God speaks through His words to broken lives and broken hearts.

We can't see or even imagine the glories God has prepared for those who love Him, but we can see through eyes of faith and stand tall as we face another day.

The heroes of everyday living don't often make the headlines except in the news column of heaven, a book of remembrance where even tears are recorded. There is coming a day when tears will be wiped away, losses will be gain, wrongs will be made right, and the stretches and reaches of God's faithful people will see the harvest, where the homeless, the hopeless, and the lonely will come marching in, part of the parade of saints.

Rich or poor, famous or unknown, from every tribe and nation—all coming Home because they found the Way, the Truth, and the Life, Jesus Christ, the path to the Father's house. No more table for one; the Light of Home sets the table for all.

It was time to leave and I'm sure my thoughts were heard by Harold, even at my table for one.

Then came baggage, shuttle, customs, and the boarding call, and I was flying toward home.

It was night when I saw the lights of Wilmington; Ralph and Chris would be there, and we'd have a cup of tea before I unpacked.

P.S. Next time I go to "lonesome town," I'll take Kathryn Elise, my eleven-year-old granddaughter, with me. I can see Katie now, walking with confidence into the coffee shop. "Table for two, nonsmoking. Thank you."

75

A Look Back

"When did you meet Papa?"

As a family we often linger after a meal, and sometimes questions regarding the past come from the children. They are encouraged to express their thoughts. And, believe me, that is not a problem for Sarah and Katie.

To me it is sad that some families don't allow the freedom of expression. Not true in our family! Jud encourages the young people to discuss even their radical views—without getting into an argument. That takes God's grace for me!

But Jud is right. It is wisdom to allow the young to beat their words against the rock of our faith; just so we know in whom we have believed, and having made all the arguments, we still stand on the firm foundation, God's biblical perspective.

"Come on, Grammy, when did you meet Papa? Was it love at first sight?"

"Once upon a time, many years ago, Harold visited my father's church in Chicago and he heard me sing a solo, 'Why Should He Love Me So?' He told everyone I was singing for him. I was sixteen years old.

"No, it wasn't love at first sight, but a deep friendship formed out of our mutual love for the Lord and our desire to know God's will for our lives. This quiet friendship continued through nursing and seminary years. During my training years at Norwegian American Hospital in Chicago, Harold brought candy and apples to my dormitory, probably to win help from my classmates.

"Since I had grown up with an explosive father, Harold's quiet thoughtfulness won me over. One year after graduation we were married. Believe it or not, he was shy and quiet."

"Oh, no! Not Papa."

"Oh, yes, your Papa!"

"Well, you'd never know it. He shook hands with everyone, and no one was a stranger to him."

"On 'romantic' Saturday nights we would attend rescue missions, dish out soup and sandwiches, sing duets, and pray with people. Not too 'cool,' huh?"

Katie chimed in. "I wish I had a tape of your duets."

"I've often thought of that. One of my regrets is that I didn't tape Harold reading the Scriptures. Your Aunt Jan is the only one I know who makes Scripture come alive like Papa Harold did, so full of drama."

"I miss Papa's reading the Christmas story." Eric used to complain because we couldn't open presents until Papa read the Christmas story. Now he misses the reading!

"We don't realize how traditions are missed until they are gone. So I hope you remember to continue those special times when you have your families, just like your parents do, and Aunt Jan and Uncle Jud."

Ralph continued. "I remember when right after supper Jan, Dan, and I would groan, 'Oh, no! Here comes Mother with the Bible and the *Reader's Digest.*'"

"Guess what they missed when they went away to college."

"Chocolate cake!" This from Eric.

"Probably that too! But they also missed the stories."

Someone groaned! Eric?

"Before TV or even radio, your great-grandmother entertained us with long, memorized story poems. Whenever a crisis hit our family (a regular occurrence), my Norwegian Mama said, 'Oh, *ja*, it will be interesting to see how God works this one out.' Then she would pray and ideas would come.

415

"In order to enter nurse's training I had to have three hundred dollars, a fortune back then, but Mama cashed an insurance policy that gave me the money. When I went to work at Lutheran Deaconess Hospital after graduation, I paid her back, all three hundred dollars.

"Before Papa and I were married he saved enough money by walking miles to work and school so he could buy a car and pay for our honeymoon to Niagara Falls. That was 1938.

"We lived during the difficult Depression years and Papa's high school education was interrupted so he could help support his family. He went to work at the Bunte Candy Company in Chicago, but he continued his education through correspondence courses. Later he entered Northern Baptist Seminary in Chicago.

"When Mr. Bunte found out that Harold had decided to enter seminary, he tried to get Harold to change his mind by offering him a lucrative position in the company. However, when he understood Harold's determination, he offered his respect and gave Harold a part-time job at full salary.

"Aunt Jan was born in 1940 and I stayed home to care for her. Our food budget was seven dollars a week. Believe me, I learned well from my Norwegian Mama—and we made it!"

"Wow, seven dollars a week! Grammy, Eric spends that at Swensens' on one meal!"

"No wonder Papa liked to take us out to eat. Didn't you ever go to a restaurant?"

"I remember one time. Before Jan was born I just couldn't eat. One night Harold came home from work and classes (sixteen hours, a full load) and suggested we go for a walk. 'Maybe you'll feel better,' he said.

"We passed a Danish restaurant on North Avenue and the menu in the window read 'roast duck.' We stood there for a long time while Harold counted his money. Finally, he said, 'Come on, Margaret. Let's do it!' We ordered the duck dinner and I relished every bite, the first enjoyable meal I'd had in weeks.

"When we would look back over the years, Papa and I would realize we had made some mistakes, financially some big ones!"

"But Mom, how can you be sure they were mistakes? God still works all things together for His good."

"I know, Ralph, that is the grace of God, and He also judges the heart. David in the Bible made some blunders, but he was a man after God's own heart. In spite of his sin he never lost his love for the one true God. Out of all that tragedy came the Psalms, which comfort and encourage people to this day."

Ralph said, "Man's concept of God can be distorted by our own ideas. I remember the night I led a young man who had been addicted to drugs to the Lord. He actually believed that God would make him marry the ugliest girl in town and ask him to do work he despised.

"I laughed with him about that because I had those same weird ideas before I became a Christian. And look who God gave me—Chris, the most beautiful girl in town. He's blessed us with four children, and I'm doing the work I love, creating furniture in wood."

"By God's Spirit within us," I said, "we enhance the talent He gave us, but when we get too involved in 'ministry,' as defined by others, we don't see the whole picture, only the urgency of the immediate. Now, Harold would see the end from the beginning, but the mistakes loom larger for me when I look back.

"But the Bible warns us not to dwell on the past. Instead, it urges us to run the race and not look back. We always hope that the next generation will profit from the mistakes we made.

"When Harold was working at Bunte and attending classes, I felt like a queen in our tiny bungalow apartment, enjoying the most beautiful baby in the world, our Janice Dawn. But one day Harold came home with the announcement that the pastorate of a small suburban church had been offered to him. He was elated!

"In those early years wise counseling was scarce. It was considered 'spiritual' to launch out by faith, when full-time service meant the mission field or the pastorate. So 'by faith' we left the security of our little world to move into the more 'spiritual' zone of ministry.

"The inadequate salary forced me to work the night shift in

417

nursing while I continued the role of wife, mother, hostess, teacher, church pianist, and pastor's wife.

"After Harold graduated from seminary, he continued his education at Loyola University in Chicago. Because of his evangelistic zeal, he also visited people door to door, on top of his schoolwork. Needless to say, his schedule was quite frantic. I played my part well, but in the lonely watches of the night I wondered how this could be God's will for my life. Bitterness and resentment slipped quietly into the cracks of doubt while the 'dedicated ministry' stayed on course.

"Then a well-meaning Christian urged Harold to give up his Standard Oil stock and insurance. 'It must be a walk of faith,' this man said. In his commitment to walk by faith, Harold allowed wisdom to take a back-road detour.

"Your Papa was an excellent student and several scholarships were offered to him that would have helped him fulfill his dream of a doctor's degree for teaching, or his secret dream, medicine. But in the urgency of the moment, to win the world for Christ, he couldn't see the broader scope of opportunity, and he closed the door.

"God says 'Be still and know,' but we heard, 'Be strong and go'! Down the corridors of time, we learned that all work is 'full-time ministry': the mechanic under a car, a pilot above the clouds, a captain sailing the seas—all of humanity, with a heart for God, making God visible in the marketplace.

"Along the way, Harold often was offered lucrative business opportunities, but once again he was warned against 'pride and riches.' In our day it was considered 'spiritual' to be poor and struggling. How often we keep running with a 'work, for the night is coming' mentality when God's loving hand is reaching out to bless us.

"No one wants to remember the mistakes of the past, but perhaps you precious grandchildren can learn to wait on the Lord, trust God's goodness, and not be driven by the demands of the present. God is our Father and He loves us, but we often see Him as a judge demanding performance rather than as a Father longing for our love and trust."

It was getting late.

Shawn, tall and serious with an intense kind of dedication, wrapped his arms around me. "I don't want to miss God's purpose, Grammy, I don't want to miss it. But I don't think Papa missed anything. He never lost his love for God, and look how we all love him! But I don't want to miss God's purpose for me."

Our children remembered that we never went to Swensens' for hamburgers when they were young. That was a tragedy!

Chris and Ralph, with tears in their eyes, remembered what could have been, but with a deep understanding knew what was—the latter years were greater than the former. God's grace!

The time came for everyone to go home, as it always does. The children were ushered out the door. Eric squealed his way out of the driveway and the house was quiet. The grandfather clock said good night twelve times, but I walked into Harold's library and sat in his leather chair.

The treasured volumes looked down at me, and through the tears I realized that the world had missed a great teacher. He was at home in a classroom or in the business world. But zeal without wisdom had brought us to struggling churches during changing times.

> *There is a tide in the affairs of men,*
> *Which taken at the flood, leads on to fortune;*
> *Omitted, all the voyage of their life*
> *Is bound in shallows and in miseries.*
> (Shakespeare, *Julius Caesar*)

On the shelf was the last book Harold read before God took him Home, *The Second Coming*, by C. H. Spurgeon.

I turned out the light and crawled into the empty bed with the teddy bear in the corner. God covered me with His blanket of peace; I was secure in His love.

Harold was Home! Safe! Nothing could hurt him again, and I was thankful that commitment to God and to each other was a fact, not an option. In my childhood I learned to trust the Lord; by God's grace we stayed on course and didn't turn around.

The grandfather clock tried one more time to say good night. One chime told me a new day was on the way, and I fell asleep.

419

76

The Deep South

"How in the world did you two ever get into the deep South, all the way from Chicago?"

We were asked that question repeatedly, and sometimes even we wondered how it happened.

In the early 1950s, Harold was called to be the pastor of a rural church, deep in the heart of Dixie. Though we would later call this community "Heartbreak Town," we loved the people, the beautiful fairyland setting with flowering magnolia trees, banks of colorful azaleas, and a wonderland of pink and white dogwoods and crepe myrtle trees.

A spacious old farmhouse sat by the side of the road, and that's where we stayed until our small house, which was in the building stage, was completed.

The genuine love of a gentle yet colorful people lives deep in my memory. The elderly were respected, and we watched them rock on their porches while shelling peas or telling stories. Children played while chickens scratched for corn and dogs chased cats.

Church homecomings and family reunions were a way of life where young and old belonged together. No one has really lived until he has experienced a Southern "dinner on the grounds" or an all-day "camp meeting singing."

When I was introduced to country ham, sweet potato pie, and black-eyed peas, I became an instant Southerner. You would have loved it, Eric, tables of Southern cooking, especially Southern fried chicken, biscuits, and corn bread. Your Papa ate three helpings of Miss Lottie's strawberry pudding. I stopped him before his fourth.

The country church began to grow and soon was filled with young and old. Within a short time I organized a youth choir of thirty-five members. One lady made robes, and how the youth loved to march in singing, "Everybody ought to know who Jesus is."

A boy with Down's syndrome longed to join the choir, and when he received his robe, he marched in with the others—one proud, happy teenager. During the Sunday evening services the young people in the choir often quoted Scripture and gave a personal witness of their faith in Jesus Christ. One evening, our "special boy" began to speak. Slowly, and with difficulty, he said, "Jesus loves me; I love Jesus, and I know it in my heart." There wasn't a dry eye in the crowd.

Since industry from the North was moving into the South, our country church had visitors from the city who enjoyed Harold's fine Bible teaching and the sound of joyful music.

But from the sidelines we heard grumblings. "Change coming. Yes, sir, change coming. Before long we can't wear overalls to church, with city slickers coming in coats and ties. Yes, sir, change coming."

In spite of these misgivings, a spirit of revival filled the air; the church was full on Wednesday night as well as on Sunday.

One Easter Sunday Harold baptized fifteen young people— the future leaders who would make God visible in the marketplace.

One lady took notes all the time but would never let me see them. "I can't spell, but I can tell you this—the only education we get is from our preacher. We're learning about people and history, and he makes the folks in the Bible real folks. I had to quit school to help on the farm, but I'm sure going to school now."

One day I was asked, "Could we have a party on Saturday nights?"

"Of course—but why?"

"Well, the kids at school have parties on weekends, and they make fun of us, so we thought if we had a party at your house, we could tell our friends that we are invited to a party, too."

Party we did! We made candy, had taffy pulls, popped corn, told stories, played games—and sang. How they loved to sing, especially the Youth for Christ choruses that we taught them. "Every day with Jesus is sweeter than the day before" was a favorite.

Papa loved these "kids," and he was always surrounded by them. He opened to them a world of books and music and gave them new challenges toward higher education.

But changes were coming.

"Fool ideas in young'uns heads. What was good enough for my Pappy is good enough for my young'uns. Heard tell toilets in the church. Well, I never!"

The old-timers rocked on the porch and spat tobacco juice while pulling their overall straps. "Yes, sir, fool women want to run the country. That's what's wrong with the world. Now look at my woman. Says this shack not good enough. Good enough for my Pappy—good enough for us. But she's building a house with cinder blocks. Even made a small room for a bathroom and wants running water in the house. Never heard of such fool notions.

"That preacher puttin' ideas into their heads; yes sir, change coming."

One day we were invited to dinner and we forgot to ask about the time, so we decided 12:30 would be about right.

We got to the farmhouse, went in, and there was the head of the family, sitting in his underwear and overalls. Flies buzzed around the screen door as he pulled his overall straps and said, "Dinner in these parts—12 noon. We done et." He spat tobacco juice into the fireplace. "Help yourself."

After a profuse apology we sat down to cold gravy on mashed potatoes. I pinched the children. "Eat and be quiet." Poor Ralph ate—then went outside to throw up. The cold gravy had done its work.

I recall a happy time when we all gathered in the big yard to enjoy homemade ice cream, and a cold wind suddenly came up. The women put on the coffee pots and we laughed together, with a dish of ice cream in one hand and a cup of hot coffee in the other.

Just as quickly came the cold wind of cultural change and the pot boiled—but it wasn't coffee!

The story began to come out.

Harold and I traveled the country roads together. We visited shut-ins, sat in kitchens, ate ham biscuits, and listened to stories of a long-ago time.

Harold seemed to be motivated twenty-four hours a day, seven days a week—remodeling and painting the church, visiting people scattered in a rural community, spending time with alcoholics and troubled people. His greatest joy was to encourage young people to dream dreams.

If these young people could create beauty out of their hearts of love, there was no limit to what they could do—at home or elsewhere in the world.

He never stopped. He worked tirelessly to build a strong rural church that would send young people into the marketplace to reveal God's love.

When Harold was on one of his treks through the surrounding hill country, he came upon a group of trees that seemed to have shotguns for arms.

Scraggly children hid in the bushes.

Harold called out, "I'm looking for Uncle Zeb."

"Ain't no one here; and you—who you be? A 'revenuer'?"

"No, I'm a preacher, not a revenue officer. How about coming to church sometime?"

The guns were put away, the moonshiners gave clear passage, and Harold made his exit. Later someone said, "Why, preacher, you could have been shot. Those hill folks don't take kindly to strangers. They'd shoot a man over a dog."

The church continued to grow, but when we returned from a visit with Harold's parents, one of the deacons said, "Preacher, all hell broke loose while you were gone. A rumor was started that you were a Communist and a nigger-lover. Folks are saying you should be tending to preaching and not to all that social gospel of bringing food and clothes to the no-good white trash in the hills.

"Some folks said that the Salvation Army and Youth for Christ were Communist fronts. And some folks go so far as to say Billy Graham is no account—him a Baptist and letting all them other folks, no telling what they are, sit on the platform.

"We know that's not true, but when a lie gets rolling in these hills, no telling if it's gonna collect a mob. I remember how you stood up for Billy Graham at the preachers' meeting when they were criticizing him. You said, 'Until we do what Billy is doing to win the lost, we have nothing to do but pray and support him.'

"The preachers have turned against you. I heard about it, so I'm warnin' you, some angry people around."

"Well, I guess people are afraid of change," Harold responded, "but all I want is to see a thriving church reaching into all the area, including the town."

We couldn't believe those things were true, and we continued the work.

Harold found a family of seven sick in a shack and took them to the emergency room. Hepatitis! The dedicated doctor who worked the emergency room must have bemoaned Harold's coming.

Another time Harold found a mother and her children huddled under threadbare quilts in a frigid shack. Pneumonia! Harold went to a town merchant and got a stove. When he brought it to the husband he said, "Now put this stove up so it will be warm for your family. Don't forget to chop enough wood. I have to leave, but I'll be back in the morning."

When Harold returned the next morning he found the stove right where he had left it.

"Well, preacher, just didn't get around to it."

Harold was furious, so he put the stove together himself and started a fire. "Now, you chop wood or I'll get the authorities out here!"

"Ain't no preacher business, you comin' out here to tell me what to do."

One day Harold marched seven children into a shoe store, and all seven came out with new shoes. The merchants admired him! "That preacher's doing more than all the churches put together."

Then they heard the rumors and warned Harold to leave. "This community needs you, Preacher, but you don't need them. Get your family out. Rumors have a way of building up to real trouble around here."

"It's all so ridiculous! I hate communism with a passion—a godless, controlling government that stifles all creativity and motivation. Jesus said, 'If I be lifted up . . . I will draw all men unto me.' So if I continue to preach the truth, men's hearts will turn to God."

One day during this uproar, Jan asked, "Mother, I was walking down the street and a woman spat on me—someone I knew. Why would she do that?"

"See, Eric? I didn't make it up," Katie broke in. "Someone did spit on Aunt Jan. She told me. But she didn't spit back; she just kept walking. I'm not sure I could do that."

"Well, what would you do, spit back? Pretty soon everyone would run out of spit. Ha! She did the right thing—keep on walking and scrub the spit off."

"Well, Grammy, what else happened?"

Papa and I often followed the school bus and waved to our young people on the bus. Then when they got off the bus, we would spend a few minutes chatting with them.

One day we followed the bus and no one waved back. When they got off the bus they turned their backs to us. We sat in the car and cried! This was our youth group! What had happened?

One brave girl whispered to Jan, "It's not us—our Pappy made us. Tell the preacher not to come near our house. Pappy has a gun."

The phone started to ring around the clock and disguised voices called us vulgar names and threatened to get me fired from the hospital. In fact, a delegation went to the hospital board. I heard about it later.

Our Doberman kept constant watch around our home, alert for impending danger. I'm sure this beautiful dog protected us from harm more times than we will ever know. Later, when she was poisoned, we grieved her loss.

Now it was Ralph's turn. "I was so young and that was my special dog. She stood watch over me when I was two and had a broken leg. Our Vickie would growl when anyone touched my cast to sign it.

"One day I saw a man being mean to my dog, and hate began to build up inside of me. Everyone thought I was too young to know what was going on, but I wasn't.

"Now, forty years later, I see it for what it really was—spiritual warfare. It was not men, but unseen powers and principalities working through men's fears and hate to destroy God's work. For years ignorance and prejudice ruled me, but now the light of God's truth and understanding comes filtering through the darkness. Darkness hates light."

"You are so right, Ralph, but at that time we did not understand spiritual warfare like we do today, and we were so convinced that truth and right would win.

"We learned many years later that our weapons of logic and reason were not enough. The Scriptures we had memorized took on new meaning in the battle of experience. We must put on the whole armor of God so we can stand against the wiles of the devil (see Ephesians 6). We don't wrestle against people but against rulers of darkness.

"I want to remind you precious children that the battle is lost or won in the secret places of the will before God.

"There may come a time when you have to make a sudden choice, and the choices we make will affect everyone around us. If we settled our relationship with God in our youth and purposed to do His will, then the choices we make later will be determined in light of His Word. Unless we walk in the light of God's Word we can be slaves to a point of view that is alien to Christ.

"The day came when your Papa had to make a choice."

77

A "Regular Midweek Service"

It was Wednesday night and we hurriedly ate supper to get to church on time for our weekly Bible study and prayer.

As we wound our way through town toward the country road that led to our country church, we noticed heavy traffic and police cars. Drawing closer to the church, we saw a mob outside, with police cars surrounding the church yard. When we pulled into the side road we were met by a giant of a man, a former security guard, who whispered, "Get inside! I'll park the car. There's a rockin' planned."

"A rockin'? What is that?" Katie wanted to know.

We found out.

"Remember when a mob stoned Stephen? Well, that's a rockin'." This came from Ralph. "No one thought I heard things, but I guess I was like Katie. I didn't miss much that older people said. There were moonshiners who had come down from the hills, prisoners who had been released from jail, prostitutes, and others who hadn't darkened the doors of the church for decades—all had shown up for that midweek service.

"A menacing crowd stood facing the road—the rockin' crowd—ready to throw rocks at us and our car. Suddenly we were all gripped with fear, all but Dad. His face was white, but it was more from anger than fear.

"Mother kept whispering, 'God will take care of us,' but we weren't too sure!

"Jan, Dan, and I sat on the front pew, on the side where Mama played the piano. Jan had her arms around us. I was four, Dan was nine, Jan was thirteen. We were too frightened to cry, and we just sat huddled together. Mama was shaking, but she went to the piano.

"I remember how Daddy looked, like a giant, so tall and straight, when he announced the opening hymn. Mama played, and we sang 'Trust and Obey'—loud! We were so scared.

"A woman jumped up on a pew and screamed, 'I move we have the conference!'

"Daddy told her to sit down and be quiet. 'This is not conference night, but the regular midweek service.'

"I looked around and saw people sitting in the open windows, standing everywhere, inside and outside. Police cars were all over the place. Later I learned some of the people even had guns.

"A man ran down the aisle threatening to kill Daddy, but the big security guard sat him down."

"I can't believe you remember so much, Ralph. I thought you were too young. I can still see Jan with her protective arms around you boys. I was shaking at the piano, but Harold was quiet and calm. He had made his choice to stand true to the purpose God had called him to.

"I will never forget how Harold stood up. 'This is our regular midweek service, and there will be order while we turn to Hebrews 12:27: "Removing of those things that are shaken, as of things that are made, that those things which cannot be shaken may remain." The topic tonight is The Unshakable in a Changing World.'"

A quiet came over the crowd that night, and all of a sudden I stopped shaking. This was the unshakable Word of God.

Harold's voice continued:

1. The throne of God is unshakable in a changing world.

2. Psalm 119—The Word of God is unshakable in a changing world. The Word is forever settled in heaven. The Word is true from the beginning; it endureth forever.
3. The church of God—Matthew 16:18: "Upon this rock [thou art the Christ, the son of the living God] I will build my church; and the gates of hell shall not prevail against it." The church of God is unshakable in a changing world.
4. The child of God—John 3:16. . . .

Harold closed with the story of a great preacher who had been told he had a short time to live. While this preacher watched the splendor of the sunset over his beloved mountains he said, "When the sun has set for the last time, and the mountains melt away, I, the child of God, shall live on."

Harold pronounced the benediction and with quiet dignity left the platform, leaving a dazed mob.

I remember telling the children later, "You will always remember this night—your father's finest hour."

Our big friend grabbed the children and hurried us to the car, and he urged us, "Leave town. Go to Florida for a week and perhaps this mob will quiet down."

We took a back road home, and then we packed and left town, quiet and confused.

Jan cried, "Daddy, fight them in court. Get a lawyer."

Dan answered quietly, "Jan, someday we'll all stand before the Lord, and if they talked about us, so what? But the ones who did the talking—oh, brother!"

Ralph said nothing. We thought he was too young. How wrong we were!

When we returned, the church was locked and the wonderful people whom we loved wept with us. The young people especially cried, "Now who will love us?"

"Mother, you forgot something!" Ralph spoke up. "When the security guard pushed us into the car, a man ran up to the window beside Dad and yelled some terrible things. I reached from the back seat and punched him in the nose. 'You don't talk to my Daddy like that.'

"Then Dad did something that I misunderstood. He put me down in the backseat and said, 'That's not the way we do things.'

"Many years later I realized it was that incident that triggered such a big rebellion in me. A smoldering hate began in me and I lumped all Christians together, including my own Dad—they were all wimps!

"Dad didn't even stand up for me. To me he was defending the wrong people. A deep resentment grew out of that misunderstanding. From that day when I was four years old until I was born again at twenty-one, I was in one fight after another. My fists were the way for me to conquer.

"Do you remember, Shawn, when you mistook something I said and went to bed crying? Then I climbed up in the bunk bed and held you in my arms and said, 'Now, you tell me what I said.' When you told me, it was not what I had said at all. You had heard the wrong voice.

"In that instant I began to weep. God's Spirit showed me how I had heard the wrong voice so many years ago. Then I was angry—angry at the devil for cheating me out of years that could have been filled with love and peace instead of fear and fists.

"Now, Shawn and Eric, don't you listen to the wrong messages and get confused. You must hear God's still, small voice. I guess that's one reason to return to the past, so we can learn from it and deal with the future better."

In *My Utmost for His Highest*, Oswald Chambers said, "Leave the Irreparable Past in His hands, and step out into the Irresistible Future with Him."

Forty years ago the future looked dark. That "storm" had ravaged our hearts and the debris gathered dust. Unforgiveness made a crack in the door, and bitterness slithered in.

78

The Wilderness Journey

"Tell about the time someone wanted you fired, Grammy." Katie was determined to hear the whole story.

"Well, Katie, that too happened in Heartbreak Town."

There had been a serious automobile accident and I was helping in the emergency room at the hospital. We quickly determined the most desperate cases that needed immediate attention.

A black woman, dazed and in pain, sat in a corner. I called over to the doctor, "This lady needs attention." Within moments a doctor checked her and admitted her to the hospital.

But a passing visitor heard me say "this lady" and reported me for calling a black woman a lady. "I want her fired!"

The administrator stood up in righteous indignation and replied, "Never! She'll be the last to leave." Tensions were building.

Forty years ago the hospital overlooked a fast-growing city. The Basement, or B section, was reserved for black patients, but the facilities and care were the same throughout the hospital.

A respected black doctor had been educated by a white doctor's family. When invited to eat lunch with the other doctors, he declined and chose to eat with the black janitors. Old ways resist change.

Harold and I had been educated in Chicago with various races and ethnic groups and had little understanding of Southern culture. In hindsight I see that we had bolted in where angels feared to tread.

As assistant director of nurses I often checked the different wards, and my favorite place was the B section. There I heard singing, laughter, tears, stories—and prayers.

But times were changing. Angry marchers with long-suppressed hostilities were demonstrating with a frenzy. When blacks were railing against the injustices of the whites, I wondered if three black men somewhere would be less angry when they remembered Uncle Joe and his white nurse (see chapter 54).

Change comes when hearts are integraı ̇d by love—not by laws alone. Hearts segregated by hate can never change; only God's love can melt the barriers and bring lasting understanding.

I loved them, and I still hold their memory in my heart. I can hear their songs while they worked, their stories and laughter at lunch time. I shared their tears and knew of their dreams for their children. When opportunities came later for those children, I only hope that their parents with their mops and brooms aren't forgotten.

It was true when angry whites called me a "nigger-lover."

"Grammy, tell us how you came to North Carolina." Katie made sure we kept the story going.

"While we were in Florida Harold was offered a position in a school, but during that period of frustration and confusion it was difficult to make a wise decision.

"Looking back, I see it probably would have been a good move, but it is always easier to see what might have been when you look back.

"Harold made another choice. 'I'm not going back into the pastorate,' he declared. Instead, he chose to form his own company, being a consultant in church building programs and financing church buildings through bonds.

"We wept like frightened children when Harold got in the car to venture into unknown territory. He chose to locate in Greensboro, the center of North Carolina."

Ralph shook his head. "It took me years to realize how frightening it must have been for him to go 'cold' into a new field. I only know how fear gripped me when I moved from Greensboro to Wilmington to begin my own business.

"Dad didn't say much; he just acted confident. But years later he told me how fear had dogged his journey. Only the Word of God kept him going. For me, I had to keep saying that God didn't give me the spirit of fear, but of love, of power, and of a sound mind.

"Dad told me something else, too. 'I learned to go to the top official in business dealings,' he said, 'and not to settle for an assistant. When I came cold to Greensboro, High Point, and Winston-Salem, I met with the presidents of the largest banks and introduced church-bond financing. I was at home with legal experts in Raleigh and bankers across the state. God gave me "favor with men" and a new door opened in North Carolina.'"

I continued the tale. "Lexington Avenue Baptist Church in High Point was the first church built by bonds. Harold and the pastor remained friends for years. There is something special about a person's first success story.

"We didn't know too much about what Harold did because the churches were scattered throughout the state. But when I went through Harold's papers after he died, I found letters from pastors all over the state. One of them said: 'Not only did we have fund-raising success, but there also was a spirit of revival and people came to the altar. Not only was there a giving of money but also a giving of self to serve the Lord.'

"I saw through those letters how the pastors of both black and white churches respected Harold and called him 'the pastor's friend.' I remember how he bought evangelical books for the pastors' libraries and enjoyed visiting in the homes of the black pastors where he ate 'chitlins' and swapped stories. One pastor was having a difficult time in his marriage, so Harold gave him money to take his wife on a vacation.

"It was difficult for me to adjust my thinking from the

433

pastorate, of which I had been a part since childhood, to financing buildings. All my life I had been involved in building people. But God, through His Holy Spirit, opened my eyes and made me realize that all of us are in 'full-time service,' making God visible in the marketplace.

"Harold never forgot one special incident from Heartbreak Town. You see, Katie, God uses many different people to show His love. After your Papa drove out of town with us all huddled together, he stopped at a run-down gas station.

"An elderly man, stooped from the burden of bygone years, was unshaven and in oil-splattered overalls. He shook his head. 'Preacher, they done you wrong. Yes, sir, Preacher, they done you wrong. I don't cotton to church-goin', but I know what goes on. Yes, sir, I know what goes on. What you done was good—but they done you wrong.'

"Harold said, 'His weather-beaten face showed such compassion that I wanted to cry. When I reached into my pocket to pay for the gas, he shook his head, reached into his greasy overalls pocket, and pulled out a one-hundred-dollar bill.'

"'Preacher, wherever you're goin', God bless you, and yes, sir, they done you wrong.'

"Harold said later, 'That man never knew how much I needed that hundred-dollar bill, but God knew.'"

"When did you go to North Carolina?"

"Very soon after that, Katie. Your Papa found us a house. After he painted it he came for us.

"We enrolled Janice in a Christian academy for two years; then she went to Wheaton to college. That's where she met Uncle Jud. I worked at Cone Hospital and Harold traveled all over the state."

My world had changed, and I knew it would not be easy to be "in charge" while Harold traveled and lived in motels.

One day Dan and Ralph found me crying. "What's wrong, Mom?"

"I miss Janice," I whispered. "She always set the table and made a fancy centerpiece."

The next day I came home from the store and Dan and Ralph

had set the table with my best china and silverware. In the center sat a bowl of weeds. "See, you have us."

"Of course I have you—and what a beautiful table!"

In the meantime, the suppressed pain from having to leave Heartbreak Town began surfacing in each of us.

A kindergarten teacher confided in Harold that Ralph drew only animals. "He doesn't like people," she said. And we had thought he was too young to understand.

Jan was popular at school but began keeping her friends at a distance. Trust wouldn't come easily—but then she met Jud and trust returned.

Dan was quiet, ever the obedient son—maybe too good?

Ralph used his fists.

I felt a gnawing apprehension that all was not well in our family, which impelled me to work harder to keep order in the home, supply finances for school, and keep acquaintances at a distance. After all, I had my sisters and my parents. They didn't know the details, but they knew how to pray, and I counted on that.

In our own way, each of us had determined never to be vulnerable again.

Harold drove the endless miles, removed from family affairs, convinced that "Margaret can handle it." I used to think maybe I should have given in to my heart's desire and demanded help.

Our wilderness journey had begun, but we didn't know it.

"I remember the time Dad took us to the dedication of a country church way up in the mountains."

"That's right, Jan."

Jan was home from school and we took coffee and cinnamon rolls in the car, since we had to leave about 5 A.M. We wore old clothes and brought our Sunday clothes along.

"Guess we had better stop and change clothes," Dad said. He didn't have to change—he was always dressed up.

We stopped at a deserted gas station and I was pulling on a girdle (those were the days of tight girdles) when I saw someone move in the gas station. Two bearded faces, grinning from ear to ear, were watching my battle with the girdle. You can be sure I beat a hasty retreat!

We arrived at the beautiful new church surrounded by tall pines, with mountains in the background. Trucks and cars filled the parking lot.

We walked in together and sat down. The service began.

"Oh, I see Brother Jensen and his family are here. Please stand up so we can greet you. (Applause!) Now, Brother Jensen, we want you up on this platform."

With tears in his eyes the preacher began. "I never thought we'd see the day when we would have such a beautiful church. Brother Jensen came along and showed some simple plans for a building, then said we could do it. He had such faith, and praise God, we did it!"

The church applauded again and the preacher hugged Harold. We watched in awe. We really didn't know much about his work or how his faith inspired others.

The choir leader got excited and announced, "Now we are going to dedicate the choir numbers to the Jensens."

They sang "I'll Fly Away" and "Amazing Grace" and my favorite, "I'm Standing on the Solid Rock." I think the choir leader saw my face and said, "We'll just do that one more time." And they did!

The singing continued, and then came the preaching. The service was followed by dinner on the grounds.

On the way home Harold recounted some humorous stories. "That preacher and I went to see an old tobacco farmer about buying a church bond. He lived in an old run-down shack, and we thought he'd perhaps buy a hundred-dollar bond for a grandchild.

"He listened, chewed his tobacco, and then said, 'Ma, git the pot from under the bed.' Ma came out carrying a foul-smelling pot and he said, 'Not that one, Ma, the other one.'

"The foul-smelling pot was put back under the bed, and Ma returned carrying the other pot. When she passed it to Pa, I saw it was full of money. Pa counted ten thousand dollars in cash and bought ten one-thousand-dollar bonds.

"'Why don't you put that money in the bank?'" I asked.

"'Nope, preacher; don't trust no banks.' And Ma put that pot back under the bed."

On our way home we looked for a gas station so we could use the rest rooms. We were desperate but we still couldn't find a station. The road was dark, and there were no other cars, so Harold hollered, 'Sorry, no rest rooms; everyone find a tree.' We did!

About that time a stream of cars came around the bend. Their headlights formed instant spotlights and horns honked. We had been caught in the act.

Later we found out an accident had caused those cars to detour down our "deserted road."

No one ever forgot the dedication service of that country church.

One day the president of a bank said, "Margaret, you should be so proud of Harold. He brought millions of dollars into the banks of North Carolina and has earned respect from the entire banking community for his integrity. Because of his wise counsel, no church has ever defaulted."

It was then I realized how many churches had been built in North Carolina because of Harold.

Harold enjoyed the freedom of his work, but I felt imprisoned by responsibilities. I was in my own wilderness.

79

Silent Screams

Days, months, years seem to roll into one when urgency-of-the-moment living turns the calendar pages. There was no stopping place.

I was on a train and never could get off at my station. There was no one to talk to. The children demanded attention, the bills mounted. The days became a blur of white uniforms, household chores all hours of the night, then collapse into bed with the alarm clock ready to sound my 5:30 A.M. wake-up call. One night my sewing machine purred until 2 A.M. as I finished a banquet dress for Janice at Wheaton.

Birthday parties, school functions, and church became routine. It was a case of survival, one foot in front of the other. Years later I learned that even survival is victory.

Harold stayed on the road. Oh, how I wished I could hit the open road—but my feet were in the quagmire of duty.

In desperation I cried out, "Harold, you are going to lose Ralph. He cries for you to take him to a game—or do something with him. The day will come when you will cry for him and he will be gone."

That day came. "Harold, we need to talk!"

"I don't have time—I'm due at a meeting."

His car backed out of the driveway and I screamed, "Come back!"

He didn't hear me; no one heard me—it was a silent scream.

"Mother, what's wrong with Daddy? He won't take time to talk about my wedding plans."

"Jan, he won't talk to me, either. He is locked in a prison of his own."

"Let's face it, Mom, he doesn't care about us anymore."

"That's how it seems, Ralph, but it is not true. I believe he is holding unforgiveness in his heart, and bitterness is silently destroying him."

He wouldn't listen so I wrote letters—no response.

He was there for weddings and graduations, and he wept when Dan went to Vietnam, but still he remained in his captive world. He was there—but not there.

When Ralph went to college Harold gave him—over my objection—a car to make up for time not given. It didn't work. It never does. Ralph rebelled by being a part of the sixties hippie movement.

Harold kept traveling, a desperate man looking for peace, but subtle bitterness kept closing the door.

To find our peace, we all have to go back to the fork in the road where relationships were broken. We all have to return to the "hurting place," to our own Heartbreak Town where only unconditional love and forgiveness can open the door to peace and restoration.

Jan was happily married to Judson Carlberg.

Dan was in Vietnam.

Ralph was in the "far country."

Harold stayed on the road.

In the lonely night watches I kept my journal, a journal of tears.

Heartbreak Town must have affected quiet, disciplined Dan in ways we did not understand. One of his college letters revealed a bitterness I never knew existed in this "too obedient" son.

"Christians aren't real," he wrote. "Just Christmas trees with ornaments, cut off from the stump, dying because of lack of connection between themselves and the stump. Don't write your letters about living 'close to the Lord.' Get off the throne and get down to help people, like Jesus did."

I cringed! Wasn't that what we had been doing in Heartbreak Town? Had he forgotten? And now does he lump us all together like Christmas trees? Oh, God, what's happening to our children?

Harold—come home! The scream was never heard.

Letters came from Jan, the one bright spot in this darkness. "Don't forget to pray for us—you are the most wonderful family in the world. I love you."

Harold wouldn't talk so I wrote notes and put them in his suitcase, pinned to his underwear, socks, and pajamas. In a lonely motel room he would read:

Harold darling,

Your verse has always been Jeremiah 33:3: "Call unto Me—and I will show you mighty things."

You are dealing with God, Creator of heaven and earth. The same power that raised Jesus from the dead is given to you—for life.

The days are short and God wants you all the way. You are traveling in your own strength. Take time with God and get your direction from Him—saves time and money.

You are toiling all night and catching nothing. God will fill your net when you are obedient to His commands. Let's call our family to prayer. We all need God's power these days.

We still have to choose whom we will serve. I'm not asking for material things—just for our family to be one.

I love you,
Twinklex [my nickname]

P.S. Please listen to God.

(Years later I found my letters tied together in his dresser.)

440

Darling Harold,

Life is like a dye that won't come out with washing. Events make a pattern and we can't always shuffle time and events like checkers.

You have so much to give—please don't wait for "someday."

The children have seen enough battles—now is the time for victory.

I love you, and want only the best for you—not a shadow of what could be.

Love,
Twinklex

The grandchildren didn't know this Papa in the dark night of his soul. His children did come to understanding with the years, and they never gave up loving and praying.

I long for the young generation to know that in the storms of life we don't abandon ship—the Captain is at the helm.

God winds the clock.

80

The Camelia Bush

Our new pastor, Dr. Robert Bayley, in his flowing robes, towered in the pulpit. His "thus saith the Lord" found an audience with open hearts to hear. His message today was from Habakkuk. "Oh Lord, I cried, and you didn't answer" (see 1:2). At the conclusion a hushed crowd listened to the benediction as the words echoed in my heart: "The silence of God doesn't mean God is not there."

The congregation from Myrtle Grove Presbyterian Church in Wilmington, North Carolina, streamed into the parking lots, bound for home.

Our pastor emeritus Horace Hilton used to say, "Don't lose your Christianity in the parking lot. Be patient!"

I usually tried to slip out first, but it seemed I always managed to be one of the last. "If Chris and Mother wouldn't talk to a hundred people we could get home faster," Ralph would say.

I headed for the car, mentally checking my list: Put ice in the glasses, make gravy, mash the potatoes. Everyone had a task.

Into my heart crept the silent tread of memories from a long-ago time when both Harold and God seemed silent, when I cried in the night. Now, Harold was Home—safe. God was silent, but I didn't cry. Why? I had learned to trust Him through the wilderness.

While the potatoes took a good beating, the gravy simmered, and the rolls were browning, Ralph came to me with some papers in his hand. "Mother, when dinner is over, I have something to show you."

"What?" My curiosity wouldn't wait.

"I found part of your journal in the wastebasket."

"What part?"

"Look, these papers were mixed in with some college papers I had discarded, but then I recognized your handwriting. Mother, I never knew how hard it was. I read some of this, and I just cried."

"Oh, no, these were supposed to be hidden, only for me to read. I can't believe they got mixed in with other papers."

"I think they should be published, Mother."

"Oh, no, I never intended to expose my heart in public."

"Mother, I can see hundreds of pastors, wives, single parents, and lonely people who think they are all alone in a wilderness. They need to know someone has been there and that God brought us through the valley; not only through the wilderness, but into a land of God's promises and joy. Put it in a book. Our children need to know that God is faithful, that even in the silence, He is there."

So it came to pass that I read again the journal from the wastebasket. This time I wept—not from grief, but from joy.

God had brought us through the wilderness and there is the sound of music coming from our home.

Harold had marked Psalm 89:15: "Blessed is the people that know the joyful sound: they shall walk, O LORD, in the light of thy countenance."

I read someplace that sorrow makes places in the heart for joy. No wonder I could sing now—even though there was a time to cry.

From my journal:

Tonight is Easter night. The lights from the friendly shopping center in Greensboro look like candles in the dark. The halls are quiet as nurses turn off lights and make bed-check rounds. The day has ended!

It began with a splash of light across the grey sky; then the morning sun filled the resurrection day with glory.

I had planned a pleasant morning—warm pecan rolls and coffee, and the table set for dinner. The turkey was ready by 7 A.M. The kitchen was spotless; curtains were hung at 2 A.M. Sleep came like the welcome of a warm blanket on a cold night.

I was engulfed in its luxury when the phone rang with clanging insistence. Emergency call, and I found myself heading into the morning sun with all the gloom of futility, caught in circumstances beyond my control.

I was angry! Tears of resentment blinded my eyes. I had asked for so little, just to be home and have breakfast with my family, and for us to attend Easter service together.

Other mothers would be dressed up in flowered hats and corsages, escorted by proud husbands, adoring sons and daughters. I walked alone into the presence of death—cold, clammy, icy death.

The sun mocked me through dusty windows while Easter music heralded the Resurrection morning. I fought the enemy—death—and he gained, inch by inch.

Visitors filled the halls, and children with Easter baskets visited grandparents. Inside I felt cold and grey. Such a small wish, to sit in church with my own.

It's been a long day. Sixteen hours with death—cold, clammy, chilling death. This is Resurrection day?

I am weary like the watchers at the tomb. The sun has long retreated behind darkened skies. The lights on the highway measure the darkness. Every nerve in me clamors for rest—long, sweet sleep. Yet the tomorrows are filled with more needs, more strain, more battles against fear and death.

Before I go to sleep I'll read the Easter story again. He who conquered death can conquer the tomorrows, with their fears and uncertainties.

This has been a long, lonely, disappointing day. Can this

444

be God's will for me? Is this my Gethsemane, and how long will it last? Am I not to be loved and protected from the battle? Why is so much asked from me? Love, prayer, understanding, patience, the strength of a mule? Why?

Is the power of the resurrection not for us in our twentieth-century living? What hinders the answers to endless prayers to heaven? Do I work until I drop from exhaustion? Is there no other way?

Forgive me, Lord, for the luxury of self-pity. I'm so very human and so much a woman. I need to be loved and cherished and cared for. I need the warmth of the sun to make me blossom into fruition and creativity. But then, You made me. You know what I need.

Must I be watered by tears and the soil powdered by crushing defeats? Perhaps I couldn't stand too much sun and warmth—but please, Lord, just a little!

I love the moonlight and roses, music and candlelight, a little silk and softness. I'm tired of starched uniforms and white shoes. I long to be needed and loved for who I am, not what I can do.

I lean my weary head against the rough-hewn cross. My heart sees the darkness of men's wrongs. You didn't deserve it but You took my place. Take me out of self-pity and to the open tomb. Roll away my stone of doubt and let me look into the tomb and see the empty place. Sometimes in the darkness I search for You, and I cry, "They have taken away my Lord"—but just for the moment.

You promised never to leave me or forsake me. You are the Victor and the Peace, and You live in me. You are with me in darkness for You are the Light, so there can be no dark places.

My eyes are blind, but help me to see again the truths I know so well.

The cross is rough but I press my tear-stained cheek against its roughness. My eyes are dim but I see the empty tomb.

You sent the Comforter to dwell in us and all power is given to us. The long day is done, and the night wraps a blanket over the city.

Resurrection Morning is in my heart.

Thank You, Lord Jesus, for being obedient to the cross, for triumphing over the grave, for giving us the Holy Spirit to indwell us with power. Help me to be obedient to walk in faith, in newness of life. Thank you, Father, Son, and Holy Spirit.

P.S. I'll be glad to come Home where the enemy can't enter. I want to see You, Jesus, to thank You, and I'm ashamed of self-pity. I just needed a little talk with You.

Please come soon!

The waiting is long and I am homesick for heaven.

Easter night, 1964
Wesley Long Hospital

(Another P.S. Twenty-seven years later I received a note thanking me for caring for someone's grandmother and "bringing hope and comfort to the family when God took her Home on Easter, in 1964.")

The camelia bush had outgrown the space beside the front porch.

"Harold, please trim that bush—it's just too big."

The bush was an anniversary gift from Harold's parents, now Home with the Lord, and for years the bush of crimson flowers had beautified our yard.

One day, after hearing my urging once too often, Harold impatiently hacked away at the bush—then drove off to a meeting.

I stood in silence with unshed tears. My favorite bush was dead. Only brown twigs stuck out, ugly and bare. Now it needed to be dug up, but I waited for spring—and then another spring.

The winter came, and the snowflakes couldn't cover the brown twigs. The wind whipped against the ugly bush, but I couldn't take it out.

I felt like that bush—ugly, alone, and bare, with the wind

446

whipping against my wounded spirit. For me, spring would never come.

A godly man, the patriarch of my day, gently urged me to confront Harold. But I was a peacemaker, a "fixer," and confronting was not part of my nature.

"Sometimes God asks us to do difficult things, to stand against a continuous wrong. Harold needs his family, and he loves his family. And I suggest an emotional shock treatment. Threaten him with the loss of his family unless he seeks help."

I did.

"You must make a choice." I was quiet, but firm. "Perhaps you have heard me so much you can't hear God. Please go to some place quiet and alone and listen to God's still voice. You must make a decision—for us to be one and serve God as a family."

I watched Harold drive away with his suitcase and Bible. I stood, still quiet and firm, with a confidence not my own, as the car faded into the distance.

I closed the bedroom door and collapsed. What had I done? I fell on the floor and soaked the carpet with tears until there were no more tears. Clutching Harold's coat I cried, "My God, my God, don't forsake him. Speak, Lord, speak."

There was no more strength in me. It was then that God spoke to me through His Word. "I have loved you with an everlasting love and I will carry you between My shoulders."

Love lifted me! I was the wounded sheep in the arms of the Good Shepherd. I fell asleep.

Nights and days blurred into a misty fog, but the Good Shepherd continued to hold me between His shoulders. One night when I couldn't sleep, I sang to myself, "He hideth my soul in the cleft of the rock . . . and covers me there with His hand." Someone gently wrapped a soft blanket around me—then it was morning. Was it an angel?

The days continued to march in a disciplined routine, while my heart kept crying to God. Even in the silence He was there.

Another spring came and with shovel in hand I determined to remove that ugly bush.

My eyes blinked in the sunlight—I saw white tips on the twigs! "My bush is alive!"

I gazed in wonder.

I heard a step behind me. "Yes, the bush is alive and will bloom again. And so will we!"

Harold was home!

81

Back to the Fork in the Road

"Grammy, you never finished the story. Did Papa ever go back to Heartbreak Town?" Katie was asking. "And that's not all. How did you get to Wilmington? Shawn, Eric, and Sarah were born in Greensboro. Why wasn't I born in Greensboro?"

"I guess you will write a book someday since you know how to keep asking questions.

"One day your Papa talked to your Daddy and Mother about moving to Wilmington to start your Dad's own business. Sarah was a tiny baby when we all moved to Wilmington in 1978. You were born later, a very special Wilmington girl."

Katie remembered. "We lived in a blue house and I could ride my tricycle to Grammy's house. I told my friends how Daddy used to be a hippie but he gave his heart to Jesus."

Ralph grew wistful. "I've often wondered what happened to Dad after Heartbreak Town. Sometimes I think it was like an emotional stroke that paralyzed him from communicating his feelings.

"I'll never forget how he waited for me to come home when I was having such a bad time. He sat on the porch for three days and nights. Everyone else thought I wouldn't come, but he said, 'He'll come!' And I did.

"I promised I would never give up on Dad; he never gave up on me. What really happened to make Dad come home?"

Harold went to a motel and stayed, alone and quiet. He spent time in the Word and really called for God's help. He was terrified of losing his family.

One night he fell asleep and had a dream. His entire life played before him like a video, and all through the years he saw God's love protecting him from danger. Then it was like he came out of a dark tunnel of failure, defeat, and bitterness into the light of God's love and the love of his family.

"I was home again," he said.

Just as God poured out His love to Harold even in the difficult times when he thought God was silent, so Harold poured out his love and joy to everyone he met. That is the man his grandchildren knew—a Papa who was always there for them, full of stories, a good listener, and an encourager to all he met. He was never too busy for his children or grandchildren after that experience.

We had been thrust into the arena of social change and we were almost destroyed as a family. The scars were not evident to the outside world but the wounds were deep.

Years passed before we realized how deep the wounds were in Harold's soul, a gentle, sensitive man. Perhaps that was why our beloved Papa held his grandchildren so close. "Let the world go away," and he held his children's children under his protective arm, closer to his heart.

Harold encouraged me to write, and he told the publisher, "Margaret was my supporter for forty years; now it is my turn to do everything in my power to help her."

He did! He typed, edited, handled travel and schedules, and relieved me from details so I could write.

"But did Papa ever go back to Heartbreak Town?"

One day we received an invitation to a reunion, or homecoming, in Heartbreak Town.

"Daddy, you have to go—you just have to go." Jan rolled her pleading brown eyes and he melted before her gaze. "We'll drive together and you'll see how great it will be. We have to go back. Love and forgiveness are acts of the will, and we can be free."

We drove through the hills and valleys together and stopped at a beautiful home nestled in a forest. It looked like a picture from *Better Homes and Gardens*. Inside the house, beautiful antiques, paintings, and polished floors revealed the creative, artistic taste of one of my "little choir girls" from thirty years ago.

The table was spread with colorful dishes, fancy casseroles, and salads. The "youth choir" was there and sang the songs of long ago. One was "Every Day With Jesus Is Sweeter Than the Day Before."

Now they were parents and grandparents. One was a doctor and two were serving as missionaries. They were all making God visible, through their creative vocations, in the marketplace.

We laughed and cried and sang the old songs, and Harold was surrounded by his "church."

"See, Preacher, we didn't go anyplace. Look at us, still standing on the Solid Rock. We love the Lord, Preacher, and didn't forget what you taught us."

One mother whispered, "My daughter is an accomplished musician because of Janice."

"You said we could do anything! We did!"

Janice remembered when one of our best friends came to see us and asked Dad to read.

"No one reads Scripture like you do, Preacher."

Reverence filled the room as Harold read the Scripture. We all agreed no one could read the Word out loud like Daddy.

Unconditional love and forgiveness, the precious gold, tried by fire, weathered the storms and sailed over to the other side.

"What happened to the bad guys, Grammy?"

"Actually the 'bad guys' were few in number, but they did make a lot of noise. Most of them are dead now.

"Now the shell that Harold had retreated into crumbled completely, and bitterness and unforgiveness slithered away in defeat. Love had washed his heart clean!

"God had restored the years the locusts had eaten, and now Harold—and all of us—were really home.

"'Amazing grace! how sweet the sound,' echoed across the woods and over the lights of the city.

"There is a fountain where healing waters flow. It is called Calvary.

"Yes, Katie, we went back to Heartbreak Town, and someday I want to take you and your daddy, in fact all of you, back to the fork in the road.

"You, too, will hear the music."

God covered our family, even with all our trials and errors, with the blanket of His love, grace, and mercy. He will also cover our children.

The world won't go away; it keeps tapping on my shoulder, but faith hears the sound of God's approaching footsteps of salvation.

"I'll walk with you. I won't leave you. I'm with you. I will wind the clock as you put your times into My hands" (see Psalm 31:15).

Heart's Cry

Forgive me, Lord,
But I can't see
Beyond the cloud
That hides Your face
From me.

Yesterday, I soared
With eagle's wings.
Faith topped mountains
Where the valley
Sings.

Forgive me, Lord;
I plummeted to earth,
Passed by the clefts,
The hiding place—rest
And girth.

Forgive me, Lord,
But I can't hear
Your voice calling
Through this pounding
Fear.

Yesterday, I was warm
With plans and dreams,
A song of praise,
Melody of sunbeams,
Mountain streams.

Forgive me, Lord;
I don't understand
How faith can mount,
But doubt can hide
Your Hand.

I only know,
Although I cannot see,
I will believe
Your everlasting love
Holds me.

M.J.

Book Sources for Chapters

First We Have Coffee
Chapters 2, 4, 5, 6, 7, 9, 11, 12, 13, 14, 15, 17, and 18.

Papa's Place
Chapters 19, 21, 22, 23, 25, 26, 27, and 28.

Lena (now titled *Then Comes the Joy*)
Chapters 58, 59, 60, 61, 62, 63, 64, 65, 66, and 67.

A Nail in a Sure Place
Chapters 3, 48, 53, 55, and 56.

Violets for Mr. B.
Chapters 29, 30, 31, 32, 33, 34, 35, 36, 37, 38, 39, 46, 49, and 54.

Prop Up the Leanin' Side
Chapters 10, 50, 51, 52, and 57.

Stories by the Sea
Chapters 40, 41, 42, 43, 44, 45, and 47.

Who Will Wind the Clock?
Chapters 68, 69, 70, 71, 72, 73, 74, 75, 76, 77, 78, 79, 80, 81, and closing poem.

Chapters 8, 16, 20, and 24 each contain material that has been adapted from both *First We Have Coffee* and *Papa's Place*.